Kentucky's Orphan Brigade

Kentucky's Orphan Brigade
The Soldiers Who Fought for the Confederacy During the American Civil War

ILLUSTRATED

Reminiscences of the Orphan Brigade
L. D. Young

General History of the Orphan Brigade
Ed Porter Thompson

Kentucky's Orphan Brigade
The Soldiers Who Fought for the Confederacy During the American Civil War
Reminiscences of the Orphan Brigade
by L. D. Young
and
General History of the Orphan Brigade
by Ed Porter Thompson

ILLUSTRATED

FIRST EDITION

Leonaur is an imprint of Oakpast Ltd
Copyright in this form © 2021 Oakpast Ltd

ISBN: 978-1-78282-932-4 (hardcover)
ISBN: 978-1-78282-933-1 (softcover)

http://www.leonaur.com

Publisher's Notes
The views expressed in this book are not necessarily those of the publisher.

Contents

Reminiscences of the Orphan Brigade   7

General History of the Orphan Brigade   103

A Soldier of the Orphan Brigade

Reminiscences of the Orphan Brigade

Contents

Introduction	13
June 26, 1916	18
Recollections of the Battle of Shiloh	28
The Bombardment of Vicksburg	42
Murfreesboro (Stone River)	44
Battle of Chickamauga—1863	63
Missionary Ridge	73
Dalton	78
Visit to Resaca—1912	85
Dallas	89
Atlanta—May, 1912	92
Jonesboro	98

To Those Who Wore the Gray and to Their Children and Children's Children, This Booklet is Dedicated.

CHAPTER 1

Introduction

It is for the amusement and entertainment of the thousands of young Kentuckians now enlisted beneath the Stars and Stripes in the world cataclysm of war for the cause of humanity and righteousness that these recollections and reminiscences are published. The author believing they will enable the "boys" to pass what might otherwise be at times lonesome and monotonous hours.

And while refused by the Secretary of War (by reason of age) the opportunity to participate in the great struggle now raging, it is his province now only to watch their career, to pray for them and their success, for their successful and triumphant return.

And by reason of his experience as a soldier he can enter into fully their aspirations and ambitions and share their hopes, rejoice in their victories and their triumphs. He understands the dread suspense of the impending conflict, the thrill and shock of battle, the victorious shout, the gloom and chagrin of defeat, the pangs of hunger and suffering from wounds and disease—for he has seen war in all its horrors.

And he knows that when the supreme moment comes that Kentucky blood will assert itself; that her traditional honour will be upheld, her renown glorified anew.

He knows that these inspirations will insure steadiness of step, strength of arm and force of stroke.

He rejoices that the ever-assertive blood of the Anglo-Saxon flows through the veins of these young Kentuckians, ready at all times and under all circumstances to be dedicated to the cause of humanity and righteousness.

As will be readily seen, at the time of the writing of these chapters, there was no thought of the great war in which the world is now engulfed and it was mainly a work of pastime and personal satisfaction that they were then written and published. But the suggestion has been made that if published in suitable form for distribution and donated by friends to the Kentucky boys now in service that it might be appreciated by the boys "over there," some of whom are doubtless the sons or grandsons of those who composed this little band of "immortals" and who contributed so much to Kentucky's history in the unfortunate fratricidal conflict of almost sixty years ago.

Thank God that the animosities of that unhappy period have long since been banished, and there is now, (1912), but one thought, one aim, animating the hearts and minds of these sons and grandsons, *viz.*, the overthrow of autocracy and the avenging of the outrages of the Huns—and a readjustment and regeneration of the relationship and affairs of men.

In the changed conditions that confront us today we see the history of the Commonwealth being absorbed by the Nation and almost imperceptibly blended into a Nationalised, Americanised whole.

And whatever of history the sons of the Commonwealth achieve in the great war will be accredited to the nation America, and not Kentucky. And recognising this unification as a fixed policy of our government, the writer takes advantage of the opportunity in this little booklet (lest we forget) to individualize and compliment the magnificent record of that little band of Kentuckians, known in history as the "Orphan Brigade" and whose achievements form one of the most brilliant chapters in the history of the State and Nation.

Hence the publication of this booklet. The writer does not for a moment stop to criticise the wisdom of this change (from the volunteer to the conscript system) and he hopes he may be pardoned for expressing pride in Kentucky's unexcelled past history. Henceforth it will not be what Kentucky or Ohio accomplished—in war, but what the Nation, unified America, accomplished. It will now be "liberty enlightening" and leading the world.

> *Then let the battle rage and onward move,*
> *Count not the cost nor falter in the breach,*
> *God, the Great Commander, wields the righteous wand,*
> *And bids you His Love the tyrant teach.*

When that shall have been accomplished (should the author be living) he will be tempted to exclaim in the language of old Moses when from Mt. Nebo he beheld the land of Canaan and exclaimed "Now Lord, I am ready."

In writing these recollections and reminiscences he has aimed as much as possible to avoid aspersions, reflections and criticisms and confine himself to a personal knowledge, which, of course, was more or less limited, because of the restricted sphere of his activities and operations. But he assures the "boys" that his stories, while not classic, are substantially true. He could not afford to, at his advanced age, attempt to misrepresent or deceive, and he hopes the reader will excuse any irregularities in the order of publication in book form for, as previously stated, that was not originally contemplated.

In comparing conditions and surroundings of that day with those of the soldier of today, (1912), we find them so radically different as to be incomparable. And for this the soldier of today should be truly thankful, since in the case of these isolated Kentuckians—none of whom could communicate with friends and receive a message or word of cheer from the dear ones at home, circumstances today are so very, very different.

And while you are called upon to meet and face many and more trying dangers, because of the new and more modern instruments of war, you are in many ways much better provided for than were your sires and grandsires. Now when sick or wounded you have every attention that modern skill and science can command. You have also the angelic help and ministrations of that greatest of all help and comfort, the Red Cross, and many other sources of help and aid that the soldiers of the past did not have.

So that while the dangers may be greater, the casualties more numerous, relief has multiplied proportionately. And you are today soldiers engaged in war which has the same meaning it has always had. Because of the gloom and sorrow that now enshrouds the world, it would be well if we could forget the past—for the events of today are but a portrayal of the past, a renewal of man's "inhumanity to man." But it has been so decreed by Him who *"moves in a mysterious way His wonders to perform, Who plants His footsteps in the sea and rides upon the storm."*

And let us hope—as many believe—that out of "Much tribulation cometh great joy." If it were not for a great and wise purpose, how could it be? It is God's will and submission to His will is man's only choice.

So, let your spirits as they rise and fall,
Ever cling to the Faith that Eight will prevail,

That God will be with you to the end and is all in all,
And no foeman, freedom's banner shall assail.

It is at the instance of the Richard Hawes Chapter of the U. D. C. chiefly that the writer of these recollections and reminiscences has collected and published them.

If in contributing this history of experiences and recollections he shall give in any degree pleasure and furnish entertainment to the "dear Kentucky boys" over the seas he shall feel happy to have had that privilege and opportunity.

He assures them that none more sincerely, more prayerfully hopes for their safe and triumphant return. He knows that this triumph will be the grandest chapter in the world's history and that America will have played her part gloriously in the grand tragedy.

Oh! that he could be one of the actors!

Then will the dark and gloomy days of your absence hallowed by the blood of your lost comrades be made glorious by a triumphant return, the like of which the world has never before seen nor never will see again.

Then will every hilltop and mountain peak blaze with the bonfires of a glorious greeting.

Then will the dear old mother's heart thrill with joy and happiness, then will the old father say "Welcome! Welcome! my dear boy, I knew you would come." Then too will she who promised, watched, hoped and prayed be found seeking the opportunity to say "I am now ready to redeem my promise."

Then will the old soldier (God permitting him to live) who dedicates these lines extend the glad hand of greeting to the noble boys of his acquaintance and say:

> Well done ye noble sons! I rejoice in your achievements, your victories, your triumphs.
> Welcome, thrice welcome, and again welcome, God smiles and the land is yours. Let justice and righteousness prevail now, henceforth and forever.

It is conceivable that forty or fifty years hence some of these soldier boys now participating in the great war will find themselves wandering over these fields upon which the greatest tragedies in the world's history are now being enacted, and it is in full comprehension (because of similar experiences) that the writer can extend the imaginations of the mind to that time.

It will be for him, who may be so fortunate, a glorious day, a thrilling and inspiring reminiscence. To be one of the actors in this stupendous tragedy in the history and affairs of the world; to see, to participate in and realise these grand events is to see things that have heretofore seemed impossible, or inconceivable.

But the times are full of wonders and amazements, and things are happening faster and faster day by day.

If the early history of the writer, read before the U. D. C.'s, contains matter that would seem more appropriate for a novel, because of its romantic character he justifies himself by saying that "youth is full of romance" and he believes, yea he knows, that many a brave boy today feels the impulse and touch of these thoughts and suggestions—and not alone the soldier boy, but the modest, timid, retiring maiden whose heart quavered when she said goodbye.

CHAPTER 2

June 26, 1916

Madame President, Ladies, Daughters of the Confederacy:

I have several times promised your ex-president, Mrs. Leer, that I would furnish her with a brief history of my observations and experiences as a soldier, and have so far failed; but will now, ere it is too late, try to comply with this promise.

But for the life of me I cannot see how I shall comply with this request without (seemingly at least) appearing in the role of one given to self-praise or eulogy, and, modest man that I am, I hesitate; this will explain why I have been so long complying with your request, and shall constitute my apology.

The history of Kentucky Confederates was in most instances very similar and their duties likewise similar. All were imbued with the spirit of patriotism and love for the cause in which they had engaged, each determined to do whatever he could to promote and advance the cause in which he was enlisted. In this I claim to have done no more than other Kentucky soldiers who fought under the "Stars and Bars."

And yet there may be some incidents, some experiences in my history so different from others as to make them somewhat interesting by contrast, and as others have kindly furnished you with a history of their experience, you may be somewhat interested in making comparisons.

Now, so far as relates to my history as a real soldier, the beginning of that career was on the 8th of September, 1861. On the 22d of January following I was twenty years old—quite a youth you are ready to say. But I had been a soldier almost two years, being a charter member of that little band of "Sunday" soldiers—the "Flat Rock Grays"—and which constituted an integral part of what was known at that time as the Kentucky "State Guard." This little company of citizen soldiers were in their conceit and imagination very important and consequential fellows. Invited to all the noted gatherings and public affairs of the day, dressed in gaudy and flashy uniforms and flying plumes, filled with pride and conceit, they did not know they were nursing their pride against the day of wrath. One only of two now living, I look back upon those days and scenes of youthful pride and ambition, with a feeling of awe and reminiscence, and wonder why and wherefore have I been spared through the labyrinth of time elapsed and for what, alas! I am wondering.

The most of the "Grays" left home for the scenes of the war in August, but I had not completed my arrangements and did not reach "Camp Burnett," Tennessee, until September 7. Now the most trying and impressing circumstances of these preparations was the last "goodbye" to my dear old mother and sweetheart, both of whom survived the war; the dear old mother greeting me on my return in a manner I shall leave to the imagination of you ladies to describe. I was her "baby" and had been mourned as lost more than once.

But the sweetheart in the meantime had become the wife of another and gone to a distant state to make her home. Oh! the fickleness of woman and the *uncertainties of war*. Pardon me, ladies, I mean no reflection, but it hurts to this day; yet God in His wisdom and goodness knows I forgave her. Perhaps schoolday love is remembered and still lingers in the heart of some of those I am addressing, then she, at least, can appreciate this sentiment.

The 6th of September found me in this town (Paris, Ky.), where I began preparations for the life of a soldier, by substituting my "pumps" for "Brogans," which I knew would be more suitable, really indispensable for a soldier on the march over rough and rugged roads. I sent back home my pumps and horse, the latter afterward confiscated and appropriated by the Yanks. Now I am sure my brogans presented a striking and ludicrous contrast to my "clawhammer" blue broadcloth and gold buttons, and to which I shall have occasion to refer again. But I was going to the war and why should I care for comment or criticism? That night found me in Louisville, a shy, cringing guest of the old Louisville Hotel, my brogans giving me more concern than anything else, being in such striking contrast to my clawhammer broadcloth and gold buttons.

I recall the scenes of that night and next morning with a distinctness that makes me almost shudder to this day. If it were possible for you ladies to imagine the excitement of those days, filled with the thousands of exciting rumours that were heard every hour in the day, turn in whatever direction you might, and the clangour and preparation for war, you might have some idea of, and appreciate, my predicament. A solitary country boy, who had seen but little of the world, on his road South in quest of Southern rights on the field of battle. Were it not fraught with fearful recollections it would now seem ridiculous. But the night was spent, not in sleep, but in wild imaginings as to the outcome on the morrow and what the morning would develop.

Morning came and with reddened eyes and unsteady step, I came down the winding stairs of the old hotel, my mind filled with fearful misgivings. Going up to the office shyly I began instinctively to turn the leaves of the register; imagine my surprise when I read the names of Generals W. T. Sherman, L. J. Rousseau, Major Anderson of Fort Sumter fame and other Federal officers, *aides* and orderlies, who were stopping there; that humbug Kentucky "neutrality" no longer being observed, I was now almost ready to call on the Lord to save me. But my fears were intensified when a gentleman of middle age, whom I had noticed eyeing me closely, walked across the room, putting his hand on my shoulder and asked me to a corner of the room. "Angels and ministers of grace defend me"—in the hands of a detective. I'm gone now!

Noticing my look of fear and trepidation, he said, "Compose yourself young man, I *am* your friend—the shoes you wear (Oh, the tell-tale shoes! Why didn't I keep my pumps) lead me to believe you meditate joining the army, and if I am not mistaken you are aiming to go South to join the Confederates." I was now halting between two opinions; was he aiming to have me commit myself, or was he really a friend? But proceeding, he said, "It is but natural you should suspect me, but I am your friend nevertheless, and am here to advise and assist young men like you in getting through the lines (a somewhat calmer feeling came over me now) and you will have to be very cautious, for I fear your brogans are a tell-tale—(I had already realised *that*). You see," said, he, "excitement is running high and almost everybody is under suspicion, myself with others." I ventured to ask his name, which he readily gave me as Captain Coffee of Tennessee, to me a very singular name.

Feeling sure of his man and continuing, he said, "The train that leaves here this morning will likely be the last for the state line (and sure enough it was) and you will find excitement running high at the station; they have guards to examine all passengers and their baggage, and when you reach the station go straight to the ticket office, secure your ticket and go to the rear of the train. Go in and take the first vacant seat and for Heaven's sake, if possible, hide your brogans, for I fear they may tell on you." I had by this time become thoroughly convinced that he was really my friend and decided to take his advice.

But now the climax to the situation was, as I thought, about to be reached. Looking toward the winding stairs I saw coming down them (Coffee told me who they were) dressed in their gaudy regimentals (the regulation blue and gold lace), Generals W. T. Sherman and L. J. Rousseau, side by side, arm in arm, behind them the short, chubby figure of Major Anderson of Fort Sumter fame and some other prominent officers whose names I have forgotten, accompanied by their staff officers and orderlies. A "pretty kettle of fish" for me to be caught with—I thought. They passed into the dining room immediately. I shall never forget the hook-nose, lank, lean and hungry look of General Sherman, reminding me of Julius Caesar's description of Cassius.

Later on, I was often reminded of this incident, when Sherman was pushing us through Georgia, toward the sea in the celebrated campaign of '64. I was then almost wicked enough to wish that I had at this time and there ended his career. But, exchanging a few more words with Capt. Coffee, I called for my satchel and took the "bus" for the station; arriving there I acted upon the advice of my new made friend and adviser. Quickly procuring my ticket and entering the car, I secured the rear seat and with fear and trembling attempted to hide my brogans by setting my satchel on them. (We had no suitcases then.) This was a morning of wonderful excitement in the station for it was the last train to leave Louisville for the State line and Memphis.

There were thousands of people there crowding every available foot of space—excitement ran high. The train guards or inspectors—fully armed—were busy examining passengers and their baggage. My heart almost leaped from my bosom as they came down the aisle. But just before they reached the rear of the car the bell rang and the train started.

The guards rushed for the door, leaving me and one or two others unquestioned and unmolested. Like "Paul, when he reached the three taverns," I thanked God and took courage. I doubt if the old station ever before or since saw such excitement and heard such a shout as went up from the people therein assembled as the train pulled out for Dixie. Many of these people were Southern sympathizers and wished us God-speed and a safe journey.

That evening I joined my schoolboy friends and soldier comrades, the "Flat Rock Grays," in Camp Burnett, Tennessee, the Grays dropping their name and acquiring the letter "H" in the regimental formation of that celebrated regiment commanded by Col. Robert P. Trabue and known as the Fourth Kentucky, C. S. A. That night I slept in camp for the first time—as to what I dreamed I am unable to say—it might have been of the sweetheart. The next day was spent in getting acquainted with the dear fellows whose comradeship I was to have and share for the next four years. Here began the experiences of the real soldier, that was to include some of the most momentous events in American history.

Only one day, however, was spent in Burnett, for that night orders came for those companies that had been supplied with arms to break camp early next morning and take the train for Bowling Green—to "invade Kentucky." The companies without arms, among which was Company H, was to repair to Nashville where we procured arms, joining the rest of the regiment a few weeks later at Bowling Green.

I have told you of the beginning, now it is proper and altogether pertinent that I should refer to some of the closing scenes of my career as a soldier. But I am here leaving a gap in my history, the most important part of it, which will be found in other parts of this little book.

Having received my furlough at Jonesboro, where I was wounded on August 31, 1864, the following six months were spent in hospitals; first at Barnesville, later at Macon and then Cuthbert, Ga., and later still at Eufaula, Ala. I had as companions in hospital experiences three other Kentuckians, Captain E. F. Spears of this city, Paris, whom you all know to have been a gentleman of the highest honour and noblest emotions—a gentleman—Oh, how I loved him; and Lieutenants Hanks and Eales, noble fellows and companionable comrades. Here were formed ties of friendship—that death alone could sever.

But having sufficiently recovered from my wound, I decided the last of March that I would make an effort to reach my command (the Orphan Brigade) now engaged in a desperate effort to stay the progress of Sherman's devastating columns now operating in South Carolina. The "Orphans" in the meantime and during my absence had been converted into cavalry. I was still on crutches and bidding Eufaula friends goodbye (with regret) I started once more for the front.

The times were now fraught with gloomy forebodings and misgivings, excitement running high. The South was in tears, terror stricken—the Confederacy surely and rapidly was reeling to her doom. General Wilson's cavalry was raiding through Alabama and Georgia with but little opposition, destroying the railroads and almost everything else of value as they moved across the country.

On the train I had very distinguished company in the person of General "Bob" Toombs, who commanded the Georgia militia, a mythical organisation of the times, and Mrs. L. Q. C. Lamar of Mississippi, whose husband was afterward a member of Cleveland's Cabinet, I was very much impressed with the remarkable personality of this lady and felt sorry for her and her family of seven children, fleeing terror stricken from the raiders. Pandemonium seemed to reign supreme among these fleeing refugees, the air being literally alive with all sorts of rumours about the depredations and atrocities of the raiders. Numerous delays occurred to the train, everybody on board fearing the raiders and anxious to move on.

General Toombs, excited and worried at these delays, determined to take charge of the situation and see that the train moved on. With a navy revolver in each hand he leaped from the train and with an oath that meant business said *he* would see that the train moved on—which it did rather promptly, the general taking due credit to himself for its moving, which the passengers willingly accorded him.

Inquiring who this moving spirit was, I was told that it was General "Bob" Toombs (by this name, *"Bob" Toombs*, he was known throughout the United States). Instantly there flashed into my mind the celebrated speech he made in the United States Senate, in which he said that "ere long he expected to call the roll of his slaves beneath the shadow of Bunker Hill Monument"—and which speech did more to fire the hearts of the North than almost anything said or done prior to the war.

But finally, we reached Macon—where I had been in the hospital—and on the afternoon of the second day after our arrival, Wilson's cavalry took possession of the city. That night some of the fiends, that are to be found in every army, applied the torch to the home of Senator Howell Cobb, the Lanier Hotel and a number of other prominent buildings. I could realise the excitement from the Confederate hospital on College Hill, which overlooks the city, and which was terrifying and appalling beyond anything I had ever before seen. The shrieks and cries of the women and children almost unnerved me. Woe of woes! Horror of horrors! I thought.

But I must do General Wilson the honour to say that he did not order or approve of this fiendish piece of work, for he did all in his power to prevent and stop it; and but for his efforts the city would no doubt have been completely destroyed.

Of course, I abandoned my attempt to join the old boys of the "Orphan Brigade." I was now a prisoner, everything lost (save honour), gloom and chaos were everywhere. Obtaining a parole from the Federal officer in command (something new), I decided to join my comrades Knox and Harp, each of whom, like myself, had been put out of business by wounds received sometime before and who were sojourning with a friend in the country near Forsythe, intending to counsel with them as to the best course to be pursued next.

Having enjoyed the hospitality of our host and his good wife for several days, Knox and myself decided to go down to Augusta for a last and final parting with the remnant of these dear "old boys" of the "Orphan Brigade" whom we learned were to be paroled in that city. We soon learned upon our arrival in the city that General Lewis and staff would arrive next morning.

Next morning the general and staff rode through the city, the most sorrowful and forlorn looking men my eyes ever looked upon; it was enough to make a savage weep. The cause for which we had so long fought, sacrificed and suffered, lost, everything lost, God and the world apparently against us, without country, without home or hope, the old family being broken up and separated forever, our very souls sinking within us, gloom and sorrow overhanging the world; what would we do; what could we do? Learning from General Lewis that the remnant of the little band of immortals who had contributed so much to the history and renown of Kentucky in the great conflict would be paroled at Washington, some twenty miles from Augusta, Knox and myself proceeded to that place for a last and final farewell.

The associations of almost four years of the bloodiest war in modern times up to that day were here, to be forever broken up. The eyes that gleamed defiance in the battles' rage were now filled with tears of sorrow at parting. The hand that knew no trembling in the bloody onslaught now wavered and trembled—the hour for the last parting had arrived, the long struggle ended forever—goodbye, John; farewell, Henry; it is all over and all is lost, ended at last; goodbye, boys; goodbye.

Are their deeds worth recording, worth remembering? It is for you, dear ladies, rather than men, to say whether it shall be done or not, and in what way. *I* am content to leave it to you, knowing that it will be well and faithfully done.

Resuming the closing scenes of my experiences at Washington and the final sad leave-taking of these dear old "Orphans," I must revert to my friend and well-wisher (as he proved to be), General Toombs.

The Confederate Government had saved from the ruin that befell and overtook it several thousand dollars in coin and which was being transported across the country, whither, no one seemed to know—in charge of a certain major.

Now Washington was the home of my hero of the train incident. The powers that were left decided to distribute a part of this coin among the faithful veterans who were being paroled at this point. The cavalry, who did not enlist until later in '62, receiving $26, in some instances more, while the Orphans received as their share only $3.50, a very unfair and inequitable distribution, character of service and time being considered. The cavalry in this, as in some other instances, receiving the lion's share and getting the most of the good things that fell to the lot of the "pooh" soldier. This money consisted mainly of "double eagles," three of which fell to the remnant of my company.

The perplexing question now was how could we divide this money. The matter was finally settled by the boys commissioning me to go down into the town (a mile or more away) to see if I could exchange it for smaller coins. Still on crutches, I finally consented, but it was a task. Going into town and from home to home—all business houses long since closed—I at last staggered on the home of General Toombs—not knowing he lived there. I recognised at once the moving spirit of the train incident. He and another gentleman were seated on the veranda engaged in earnest and animated conversation. Saluting in military style, I at once made known my business.

The general protested that *he* had no change, but referring me to his guest, Major ——, who, he said, was in charge of some funds in the house belonging to the government. The major remarked if I would wait awhile he would furnish me with the required change, at the same time retiring to a back room of the house where I soon heard the sound of a hammer or hatchet, presumably in the hand of the major, who was engaged in opening a box or chest.

In the meantime, the general invited me to a seat on the veranda and began plying me with numerous and pertinent questions—not giving me a chance to refer to the train incident—asking to what command I belonged, when and where I was wounded and how I expected to get home and many other questions, not forgetting in his vigorous and vehement way (for which he was noted) to deplore the fate of the Confederacy and denouncing the Yankee in unmeasured and vigorous terms.

Finally, after so long a time the major returned with the required change—all in silver and while not much, it gave me (already tired out) great worry before I reached camp on my crutches. Of course, I thanked the major and apologised for having put him to so much trouble, and saluting him good day, I started for the gate, the general preceding me and still asking questions. Opening the gate, for which I thanked him, I tipped a military salute and started up the sidewalk.

But the general seemed very much interested in me and walking alongside the yard fence he suddenly thrust his hand into his vest pocket, pulling out a twenty-dollar coin and quickly reaching across the fence, he said, "Here, lieutenant, take this from me. You will doubtless need it."

Dumfounded at this sudden change of affairs, I politely declined it, but the general, in a spirit of earnest command, forcefully said, "Here, take it, sir; you are a d—n long way from home and you will need it before you get there." Comprehending the spirit which prompted it, I accepted it and thanked him, extending him my hand, which he grasped with a warmth that thrilled my soul to its very depths.

Thus, the diamond in the rough that I had seen on the train at once became the glittering jewel that sparkled and shed its brilliance to the depths of my then thankful and weary soul. I love to think of this incident and this great man (for he was truly a great man of his time) and transpiring at the time it did and under—to me—such distressing and discouraging circumstances, it is one of the happy and cheering oases of my soldier life.

Going from Washington back to Augusta I met and spent the following night in company with Hon. E. M. Bruce, one of the best friends I ever had, whose friendship, magnanimity and generosity toward myself and other Kentuckians was, as in my case, made practical, he presenting me with three double eagles, which I was *compelled* to receive as a recompense for acts of friendship and assistance rendered him during the trying times of the preceding four years. I have never known a grander character than E. M. Bruce, a truer friend, a nobler man.

But now, with more than $80 of *real* money, I was quite well equipped for the return to dear "Old Kentucky," which I was glad to see after an absence of almost four years, spent under the most dangerous and trying circumstances to which it was possible for man to be exposed.

There were doubts in my mind as to what our status as citizens would be and just how we would be received and regarded by some; returning as we did, overcome, discomfited, defeated. But we well knew how we would be received by those who loved us and whose sympathies were manifested in a thousand ways not to be mistaken or misunderstood. Here in these manifestations was recompense for the long years of absence amid dangers, trials and suffering.

And now after a lapse of more than half a century, with its wonderful history, we are still remembered by some of the kind and gentle spirits that greeted us on our return, and other charming and lovely spirits of the U. D. C. descendants of the noblest ancestry that ever lived and inhabited this, the fairest land that God ever made.

These circumstances, these surroundings and inspiring scenes make hallowed the lives of these few surviving old veterans, rendering it a panacea for all that we as soldiers of the "lost cause" encountered and suffered.

From the fulness of my heart I thank you, noble ladies, for your kindness and patient attention. This opportunity to appear before you today is more than a pleasure and I feel honoured to find myself in your presence and appreciate your happy greeting.

CHAPTER 3

Recollections of the Battle of Shiloh

(From an address delivered at the meeting of the Morgan's Men Association at Olympian Springs, September 2, 1916.)

Mr. President, Old Comrades, Ladies and Gentlemen:

I must confess that this is somewhat embarrassing attempting to talk in public at the age of seventy-two, never having attempted such a thing before. But the subject upon which I am expected to talk is certainly, to myself, at least, interesting, and the occasion I am sure is happy and inspiring, had I only the ability to do them justice. However, by reason of my inexperience in matters of this kind, I believe I can safely appeal to the charity of my audience to overlook any failure I may make to properly interest them in what I shall have to say.

You ask sir, that I shall relate some of my observations and experiences of the great Battle of Shiloh. Well fifty-two years and more is a long time and takes us back to that important event in American History that transpired on the banks of the Tennessee on April 6 and 7, 1862. Some of these old veterans now seated before me can doubtless remember many of the exciting and intensely interesting scenes of these two eventful days. It is more deeply impressed upon my mind, because of the fact that it was our initial battle and early impressions are said to be always most lasting.

This was the first of a series of grand and important events in the history of that renowned little band of Kentuckians, known in history as the "Orphan Brigade," but which for the present occasion I shall designate as the Kentucky Brigade, it not receiving its baptismal or historic name until the celebrated charge of Breckinridge at Murfreesboro. But what a grand and thrilling opening chapter in the lives of these Kentucky boys, as soldiers, for we were only boys, as we now look back at things, a majority of us being under twenty-one.

Now, if I were called upon to say which in my judgment was the best planned, most thoroughly and systematically, fought battle of the war in which I took part, I would unhesitatingly say Shiloh. As time rolled on and with subsequent observations and experiences on other important fields, such as Murfreesboro, Chickamauga, Resaca, Atlanta, Jonesboro and a number of others, I am still constrained to say that Shiloh was the typical battle. I mean, of course, battles fought in the West and in which Kentucky troops took a prominent part.

If in relating my story I shall seem somewhat partial to Kentuckians, I hope I may be excused for it is of them I shall talk mainly, besides, you know I love them dearly. And in the exercise of this partiality I claim to be justified from the fact that a number of the leading characters in this grand tragedy of war were Kentuckians. First among whom was the great general and peerless leader; others were Breckinridge, Preston, Tighlman, Trabue, Helm, Morgan, Monroe, Lewis, Hunt, Hodges, Wickliffe, Anderson, Burns, Cobb and last but by no means least, Governor George W. Johnson whose patriotic example was unsurpassed and whose tragic death was one of the most pathetic incidents of the great battle.

A conspicuous figure indeed was he, so much so that when found on the field mortally wounded by the enemy, they believed him to be General Breckinridge. Private John Vaughn, of my old Company H of the Fourth Regiment, relates this story in regard to this sad and lamentable incident. Vaughn was severely wounded and was lying on the field near where Governor Johnston fell and from which he had just been removed by the enemy, when General Grant rode up and inquired to what command he belonged. When told by Vaughn to what command he belonged, Grant said:

> And it is Kentuckians, is it, that have been fighting my men so desperately at this point?

Here is where the four desperate charges and counter-charges were made on the Seventh and noted by Colonel Trabue as commander of the Kentucky Brigade in his official report of the great battle, the bloodiest part of the field where Kentucky gave up many of her noblest and best. This is the field to which General Grant refers in his *Memoirs*, when in writing of the desperate fighting of the Confederates, he says:

> I saw an open field on the second day's battle over which the

Battle of Shiloh

Confederates had made repeated charges, so thickly covered with their dead that it might have been possible to have walked across the clearing in any direction stepping on dead bodies without touching a foot to the ground.

Here were enacted scenes of sublime courage and heroism that elicited the admiration and comment of the civilized world; here the soil of Tennessee drank freely the blood of her elder sister, Kentucky.

But Grant, when told by Vaughn that he belonged to the Kentucky Brigade, turned to one of his *aides* and ordered a litter to be brought and had Vaughn placed upon it saying, "We have killed your General Breckinridge and have him down yonder," pointing in the direction of their field hospital. He then had him taken down to where the supposed General Breckinridge lay. It seems that they were doubtful of and wished to establish his identity. Pointing to the body of the dying governor he asked Vaughn if he was not his general. When Vaughn told him that it was Governor Johnson and not General Breckinridge, Grant turned away quickly with a look of disappointment upon discovering his mistake and learning who he was.

Vaughn used to relate this incident with considerable feeling and pride as connecting him with General Grant at this particular time and under such peculiar and painful circumstances. I mention it because it contains more than ordinary interest to some of us Kentuckians, who had the opportunity of witnessing the heroic conduct and sublime courage of this noble citizen of Kentucky.

But let us notice while passing some of the sacrifices Kentucky made in this first great battle of the war in the West and the compliment incidentally and unintentionally paid us (as Kentuckians), by the greatest general that ever commanded the Federal Army.

First among whom was the great general and peerless leader, Albert Sidney Johnston, whose name I always mention with feelings of profound pride and admiration, I would liked to have said veneration. George W. Johnson, the noble beloved citizen and patriotic governor, whose voluntary example of sublime courage and heroism was without a parallel in the great battle. Thomas B. Monroe, the youthful and distinguished journalist, statesman and accomplished soldier, a man with scarce a peer at his age in either civil or military life. Charles N. Wickliffe, the gallant and dashing colonel of the Seventh Kentucky, and a thousand other Kentuckians many less distinguished but equally brave—the flower of Kentucky youth and manhood. Is it any wonder

I am partial to Kentuckians and proud of their record in this great and memorable battle?

Oh, how well I remember the morning of that eventful Easter Sabbath, April 6, 1862. So beautiful and lovely that all nature seemed proud and happy. Trees budding, flowers blooming, birds singing, everything seemingly joyful and happy in the bright sunshine of early spring, save man alone. But with what awfulness the scene changes when we contemplate man's actions at this hour and time bent upon the overthrow and destruction of his fellowman and how ominously significant the preparation.

Just at early dawn we were quietly awakened by our officers—many a noble and brave boy from his last sleep on earth; the bugle not sounding the reveille, for fear of attracting the attention of the enemy, it being part of the great general's plan to take him by surprise, which succeeded admirably, notwithstanding the oft repeated denials of General Grant to the contrary. Quickly arranging our toilets and having hastily despatched breakfast from our haversacks we formed in double column by company, the band in front leading, playing "Dixie," which sounded upon the early morning stillness in this deep wildwood, as it never before sounded, soul-stirring and inspiring. What patriotic soldier could fail to be moved by its charm and pathos?

The veil of caution and silence now removed by the band, down through the woods of massive oaks we moved at quick-step, every man doubtless believing himself the equal of half a dozen Yankees. A very erroneous notion indeed, soon dispelled by hard and stubborn facts to the contrary. But on we moved stopping but once to unsling knapsacks, which with our Sunday clothes and precious jewels we never saw again. Ah, some of those precious jewels! Still on we moved. Now the roll of the skirmishers' rifles away out in front told that the issue of battle was being joined, not Greek against Greek, but American against American in one of the most desperate and sanguinary conflicts of the great war. Led by two of the greatest military chieftains of the age; here the high spirited and chivalrous youth from the Southern plantations and the daring, hardy Western boy from the prairies of the West, had met in battle array.

Here was to be a display of courage and chivalry unsurpassed in the annals of war. Now an occasional *boom, boom,* of the big guns, began to echo up and down the valley of the Tennessee as Hardee's batteries seemingly in chorus with those of the enemy in reply, began to open on Grant's battalions now hurriedly forming, having recovered from their surprise caused by the sudden and unexpected attack of Hardee's advanced lines. Stirred by the highest ambition of our youthful hearts on toward the front rapidly and steadily, now in column of fours, moved the Kentucky Brigade.

Passing down a little narrow valley just to the left and on the higher ground, we passed that gallant little band of Kentuckians known as Morgan's Squadron at the head of which, seated on "Black Bess" the real (not the mythical "Black Bess" that some of you fellows sometimes talk so loudly about and never saw), but the real Black Bess—was that grandest specimen of a Kentucky soldier, save one—the immortal Breckinridge—Captain John H. Morgan.

The Kentucky Brigade was proud to find itself in such noble, such royal company, though for a passing moment only. Oh, how it thrilled our hearts as these Kentucky boys, Morgan's men, greeted us by waving their hats, cheering and singing their famous battle song;

> *Cheer, boys, cheer; we'll march away to battle;*
> *Cheer, boys, cheer, for our sweethearts and our wives;*
> *Cheer, boys, cheer; we'll nobly do our duty,*
> *And give to Kentucky our arms, our hearts, our lives.*

General Duke, you remember this incident. Do you not, sir? More than happy am I with such a noble witness to attest the correctness of this part of my story. It was the second line of this famous *stanza* that touched my soul most and sunk deepest into my youthful heart, for I had left back in old Nicholas a little, black-eyed, curly-haired maiden whose image at that very moment seemed fairer than all the angels in heaven. My old heart still beats quick when I think of this thrilling incident and those charming eyes.

Now there are doubtless some of you old veterans who are listening to me that left home under similar circumstances as myself kissing farewell, as you thought, perhaps for the last time, the dear little girl you were leaving behind and who felt on the battle's verge as I did and was tempted to exclaim with me in the anguish of your heart, "Oh cruel, cruel relentless war, what sad havoc you have wrought with lovers and lovers' lives." Verily, old comrades, I believe I am growing sentimental as well as very childish, but these thoughts crowd my memory and must have vent. Still to the battle's breach I must go where the "pride, pomp and circumstances of glorious war" invite.

Pressing rapidly forward we quickly passed through the enemy's outer encampments from which they had fled when attacked and sur-

General John C. Breckinridge

prised by Hardee's skirmishers, leaving behind them untouched, their breakfasts of steaming hot coffee, fried ham and other good things with which their improvised tables seemed to be heavily ladened, and which under other and more favourable circumstances, we would have quickly appropriated. But the scenes of greatest moment and absorbing interest were on the front toward which we were rapidly hurrying where the clash of steel, shot and shell was resounding with the fury of desperation.

How well I remember the first victim of war—a Confederate—I saw on this eventful morning. How well, too, I remember the hiss and scream of the first shells of the enemy's guns that passed closely above our heads, and how quickly and ungracefully we bowed in acknowledgment. How well, also, I remember the first volley fired at us by Colonel Worthington's Forty-Sixth, Ohio, our neighbours from just across the river. We had hardly completed the formation of changing "front to rear" on our first company in order to confront them squarely by bringing our line parallel with theirs, when they opened fire on us, getting the drop on us, if you please.

Now I need not say much about this experience, for I am sure that every old veteran remembers well the first fire to which he was exposed, but I do believe that my hair must have stood on end and fairly lifted my cap for I felt as they levelled their rifles, that every man of us would surely be killed. Not many however, were killed or seriously hurt, for the enemy in their eagerness and great excitement fired wildly over our heads. The next was ours, and as we had been previously cautioned by Major Monroe to fire low, we made it count. Quickly reloading our rifles, we had hardly fired the second volley when the sharp shrill voice of Major Monroe rang out amid the roar and din of battle, "Fix bayonet" and was quickly repeated by the company commanders.

My, my; oh Lord; but the cold chills darted up and down my spinal column as I contemplated the use of the bayonet. Now if there is any scene upon the battlefield more exciting and more terrifying than the glimmer and glitter of a fixed bayonet in the hands of a desperate and determined enemy, pointed directly at your throat or your stomach, I have never seen it. Terrified at the gleam and clatter of our bayonets Worthington's men broke and fled through the woods rallying on their reserves, stationed some distance in rear of their original position. It was well perhaps for them that they did, for thoroughly drilled as we were in the bayonet exercise, they would doubtless have found themselves at a great disadvantage in the use of this weapon, had they stood to make the test.

But with fixed bayonets, accelerated by the Rebel yell, we followed at a double-quick, passing over their dead and wounded halting just beyond. What a ghastly sight; what a terrible scene! Here was pictured for the first time in our experience the horrors of the battlefield in all of its hideousness. How well the new Enfield rifles, with which we had been armed just before leaving Burnsville for the battlefield two days before, following the reading of General Johnston's famous battle order, were used upon this occasion, the dead and severely wounded of more than three hundred of the enemy grimly told. Colonel Trabue in his official report says more than four hundred but I hardly think there were so many. There were enough at least to attest the efficiency of our new Enfields and the correctness of our aim.

Many of these poor fellows begged us piteously not to kill them as though we were a band of savages without pity or compassion, knowing nothing of the usages and customs of civilized warfare. It was an insult to our sense of honour and chivalry. But we soon convinced them by every act of kindness possible under the circumstances that we were both civilized and chivalrous, notwithstanding the teachings of the Northern press to the contrary. How false, absurd and ridiculous these charges by some of these stayed-at-home sycophants of the Northern press accusing us with brutal and inhuman treatment of their wounded that fell into our hands.

But, just before the encounter of the Fourth Kentucky, which occupied the extreme left of the Confederate battle line, with the Forty-Sixth Ohio, the roll of musketry and the roar of artillery came down the battle line from right to left (a distance of more than three miles), like the successive waves of the ocean as Grant hurled his battalions in echelon against the extended lines of Johnston, opening fire in rapid succession as they deployed and struck our lines, to which, the Confederates in like successive manner instantly replied.

Oh, I tell you this was sublimely grand beyond the power of man to describe. As Grant's battalions were successfully met and hurled back, that terrible and ominous sound, the "Rebel yell" heard by us for the first time on the battlefield told that the day was surely and steadily becoming ours. The enemy made another desperate and determined stand and from their advantageous position occupied by their reserves on which their broken columns had rallied, they poured a deadly and destructive fire into our ranks killing and wounding many of our men.

We had been pushed forward under the enemy's fire and halted to await the movement of our reinforcements moving in our rear and to our left, and while awaiting the execution of this movement we learned quickly for the first time the importance of lying flat on our faces as a means of protection from this deadly fire of the enemy.

This was trying indeed under orders not to fire; compelled to remain passive and see your comrades being killed all around you, momentarily expecting the same fate yourself. At last co-operating with the flanking column on our left, with fixed bayonets we made a desperate direct attack and drove the enemy from this very formidable position which they had been holding for some time, not however until we had lost in killed and wounded more than two score of our brave and gallant boys. I am now speaking of the operations of my own regiment—matters were too absorbing to pay much attention to what others were doing.

Again, pushing forward we quickly encountered the enemy's reinforcements, which they had thrown forward to resist our advance and were again exposed to another scathing and deadly fire. Again, resorting to our former tactics of lying flat on our faces, we returned their fire, turning upon our backs to reload our rifles, then again upon our faces to deliver fire, here the battle raged furiously, for some time and here again we lost a number more of our gallant boys. I shall never forget the anguish of the boy immediately to my left, as he expired from the effects of a ball that passed through his body. In the meantime and while the battle was raging at this point, Burns's and Cobb's Kentucky batteries of fourteen pieces, which were stationed upon the extreme right of the Kentucky Brigade, were hurling shot and shell, grape and canister, with terrific and deadly force into the enemy's moving columns, as they shifted from right to left of the battle line.

Grant seemed anxious to turn our left, but was anticipated and promptly met by counter-movements of the Confederates, he having a most worthy rival in the art and skill of manoeuvring troops upon the battlefield. Finally the terrible and desperate assault of the Tennesseans away to our right, led by the gallant Breckinridge and the peerless Johnston against the enemy's centre and his stronghold, known as the "Hornet's Nest," compelled Grant to yield every position he had taken and seek shelter and protection under the banks of the Tennessee. This was the sad and fatal moment, for here in this desperate charge the great general fell.

Co-operating with the troops on our left the Kentucky Brigade hinged upon Burns's battery, the whole left wing of the army swinging like a massive gate to the right, joined in this last desperate charge and had the proud satisfaction of participating in the capture and impounding of Prentiss's division of more than three thousand men, including the celebrated Watterhouse battery of Chicago with its magnificent equipment of new guns and fine horses. This magnificent battery had been equipped by this great millionaire for whom it was named, we wondered how he felt when he learned the fate of his pets.

I never in my entire experience as a soldier saw such a humiliated and crestfallen body of soldiers as these men were; prisoners driving their own magnificent battery from the field. It looked really cruel to thus humiliate them. But then you know it is said, that all's fair in love and war. To the first of which saying I am compelled to demur for I know that all is not fair in love, however, it may be in war. But in striking contrast what a jubilant and overjoyed set of fellows we Confederates were, what a time for rejoicing!

This was one of the proudest moments of my soldier life, exciting and thrilling almost beyond description. Their artillery being driven from the field by their own gunners; their infantry formed in a hollow square stacking arms and lowering their colours; their officers dismounting and turning over their horses and side arms; Confederate officers and orderlies galloping to and fro in every direction; excitement unbounded and uncontrolled everywhere. Imagine these transcendent and rapidly transpiring scenes and think for a moment if you can, how these "boys" unused to such tragedies must have felt amid such stupendous and overwhelming surroundings. Why we made the very Heaven and earth tremble with our triumphant shouts. And I doubt not, I know they did, for General Grant intimates they did, the enemy routed and hurrying to the banks of the Tennessee for protection, trembled also.

Now the scene changes somewhat, reforming our lines and filing to the right and left around this enclosed square in which these prisoners were held, we again moved forward to the front expecting to deliver the last and final blow. Four o'clock three-quarters of an hour later, with more than two hours of sunshine in which to deliver the last and final blow, found us drawn up in the most magnificent line of battle I ever beheld, extending up and down the river bottom to the right and left as far as we could see, straight as an arrow; every man in place standing at "attention" exuberant with joy, flushed with victory, all understanding the situation, eager for the signal to be given that they knew would finish the glorious day's work.

Grant's army cowering beneath the banks of the Tennessee awaiting the final summons to surrender. What a moment of grand anticipation and oh, how quick the heart beat! But at what fearful cost to the Confederate cause, the apparent great victory! The voice of the great commander, now silent with a successor unwilling to finish the day's work so gloriously begun and so successfully executed up to the hour of his fall. And oh, how important the hour to the new born nation! How portentous the signs! Here and in this hour was sacrificed the opportunity of the Southland's cause, here was thrown away, so to speak—the grandest opportunity ever offered to any general in modern times. Here the "green-eyed monster," jealousy, must have whispered into the ear of Beauregard. Here I must draw the black curtain of disappointment and despair to which I never can be reconciled. But let it rest as lost opportunity and bury it in the oblivion of forgetfulness. Paradoxically speaking here was lost the opportunity of the "Lost Cause." But what followed, many, yes all of us know too well.

It is strange what momentous events sometimes turn upon seemingly trifling and insignificant circumstances. With the prevailing tenseness of the moment, if one man had leaped to the front of that battle line and shouted "forward," Grant's army as a consequence would have been overrun and captured. Grant known no more in history; the "Stars and Bars" would have been planted upon the banks of the Ohio; Kentucky redeemed and history differently written. Had Johnston the great captain, lived, this would have been accomplished. But it seems that Providence decreed it otherwise by removing the master mind.

From this magnificent battle line which I have attempted to describe and this moment of proud hope and expectancy we were by order of Beauregard, withdrawn to the camps of the enemy from which we had driven them during the day—*not worn out and exhausted*—which Beauregard gave as his excuse for failing to carry out the plans of the great commander to crush Grant before Buell could come to his rescue.

Passing the night in the camps of the enemy; recounting the exciting incidents of the day; indulging in the rich and bountiful supplies of a plethoric commissary, and no less rich and bountiful supply of sutlers stores in great variety, just received from the North, we enjoyed a "Belshazzar" feast not knowing, and little thinking of the "handwriting on the wall" in the form of 30,000 reinforcements then crossing the Tennessee to be met and reckoned with on the morrow.

Why, oh why, did Beauregard not allow us to finish the day's work so gloriously begun by Johnston? Every man must answer this question for himself. Beauregard did not answer it satisfactorily to the soldiers who were engaged, whatever the opinion of the world. What, but the spirit of envy and jealousy and an overweening ambition to divide the honours of victory with Johnston, which he hoped and expected to win on the morrow could have controlled his course? That and that alone, answers the sad question in the mind of your humble friend and comrade. I am aware that this will be considered presumption in me, but it is history in part and as observer and participant, I have the right to criticize.

The morning of the fateful 7th came and with it the direful results that followed. The arrival of Buell, the Blücher of the day, turned the tide and sealed the fate of the cause—the golden opportunity lost, lost forever! The history of that day is well known to all students of the great war and to none better than the few survivors of that little band of Kentuckians afterward known in history, as the Orphan Brigade, and whose part in the grand tragedy was such an important factor. It needs no studied eulogium or lofty peroration to tell the story of the part played by this little band. A loss of forty *per cent* in killed and wounded tells the story, and is the panegyric offered by Kentucky on this memorable and bloody field.

I might speak more in detail of this last day's bloody work and describe more at length many of the horrible sights witnessed and the terrible suffering of our wounded in their transfer to Corinth during the next three days over almost impassable roads—the most horrible the mind could possibly picture, exposed to the almost continuous downpour of rain and the awful, awful sadness that filled our hearts in the loss of so many of our comrades, kinsmen and school-fellow friends and the further deep humiliation of final defeat, but the story would be too horrible and sad to elaborate.

I have already taken too much of your time in relating a little of personal romance in connection with something of history and in conclusion will say I am here in part for what may be, though I hope not, a last farewell handclasp with these dear "Old Boys," Morgan's men, the equals of whom as soldiers and citizens, Kentucky and the world will never again see. I thank you for your attention and the courtesy you have shown me.

It seems altogether natural and opportune now that a large part of the world is engaged in war that our minds should revert to the past and the historic battle scenes in which we engaged should be renewed in reminiscence.

CHAPTER 4

The Bombardment of Vicksburg

Because of the similarity of scenes now transpiring on the Western front in France I am tempted to describe a scene that occurred and that I witnessed during the siege of Vicksburg in July, 1862. My regiment (4th Ky.) had been detailed and sent on detached service down to Warrenton, some miles below Vicksburg, leaving in camp a number of sick that were unable to go, among whom was Capt. Bramblett and myself.

On the morning of the 15th of July just at sunrise, suddenly, unexpectedly, as if the infernal regions had suffered an eruption, the earth rocked and trembled, the Heavens seemed pierced and rent with the roar and thunder of cannon of all sizes, mortars from gunboats, siege guns, land batteries and everything of a terrifying and destructive character, that man was capable of inventing appeared to be turned loose, an explanation of which no one would venture to make.

Directly however, news came that the Confederate ram *Arkansas* had run the blockade of the upper fleet of federal gunboats and transports, and was lying at the wharf in Vicksburg. The news was magical on some of us sick fellows, and myself and Sergeant Knox started immediately, without breakfast, to see the wonder and learn the news of the exciting episode. Arriving at the wharf we soon saw the cause of the terrible outburst of excitement and terror.

The *Arkansas* had been constructed at Yazoo City. Whisperings of its existence and probable descent upon the blockading fleet in the Mississippi had been heard for some time, and now we could see the monster (so to speak) in her grim and battered condition with numerous holes in her smoke stack, made by shots from the enemy's guns, and a large piece torn out of her cast prow. Her crew was composed of the most daring despicable smoke-begrimed, looking set I ever beheld, but who were elated at their successful victory. It was both interesting and amusing to hear them discussing their recent experiences.

That night the world went wild and pandemonium reigned supreme in and around Vicksburg; for every gun and mortar in both the upper and lower fleets turned loose every element of hell and terror they possessed, with the seeming determination to destroy everything in and around the devoted old city. The Confederate siege-guns with "Whistling Dick" for leader joining in the grand Orchestral chorus of ruin and chaos.

The scene was the most spectacular and pyrotechnical event of the war and has never been equalled unless it has occurred in the awful experiences on the Western front or at the Dardanelles. It was sublimely grand and tests the wildest imagination of the mind to describe it.

The air was literally burdened, with ascending and descending shells which were easily traced in their course upward and downward, shells from the upper and lower fleets, crossing each other in their flight Heavenward, before they reached their zenith, others in their downward course and a few at the apex and still others, that failed to explode reached the ground destroying everything with which they came in contact. The flashes from these guns illumined the surroundings for miles, and reminded you of a terrific thunderstorm with continuous flashes of lightning.

Every colour of the rainbow could be seen in this terrible and grand display. Balloon shaped clouds of smoke from exploding shells could be seen, floating slowly, softly, through the air, adding amazement and wonder to the grand aerial tragedy taking place in the Heavens.

In reading of the terrific bombardments in the great war now raging, and comprehending these descriptions and pictures, I count myself no stranger, and this scene I have attempted to describe I am sure will compare favourably with anything in the great world-war of today, (1912). Not all the wonders and terrors of war are yours, boys! Some of us older warriors have seen something of war too. But it's all grand and glorious, isn't it boys?

CHAPTER 5

Murfreesboro (Stone River)

It is to the great and interesting Battle of Murfreesboro and some of the incidents and circumstances preceding it, that I shall devote this article. History will someday accord it but one name, whereas it now has two—Murfreesboro and Stone River—but I shall use the former.

Here a mile or so Southeast of the city, on a beautiful little plain or suburban scope of country, was encamped for a period of three months, the Orphan Brigade. The weather was beautiful and we enjoyed both it and the many good things we had to eat and the hospitable greetings of the good people of the town and surrounding country. But while we were enjoying these good things, we were undergoing a strict military training, being drilled in the school of the company, battalion and the more comprehensive and enlarged movements of the brigade and division manoeuvres, some of which we had seen employed at Shiloh and elsewhere by exigencies in actual battle. It was a matter of general pride in which as a member, I still glory that the Orphan Brigade was the most thoroughly drilled and best disciplined body of men in the Confederate Army.

In substantiation of this claim, I refer to the compliment paid us a little later on by General Hardee, in a trial drill with the First Louisiana Brigade, held at Beech Grove in the Spring following, and at which trial drill General Hardee was one of the judges, and was heard to say that to excel our drilling would require the construction of a different and better code than was laid down in the system of tactics bearing his name. The truth was we were determined to allow no body of troops to excel us in anything pertaining to these accomplishments or history of the soldier. This was accomplished in a great measure by the requirements and training of that military martinet, "Old" Roger Hanson. I use the appellation with the most profound respect. The facts as to these accomplishments can be attested by numbers of men still living and who often refer to General Hanson's rigid discipline and requirements with feelings of respect and pride. I must instance one circumstance, in support of this assertion.

Sometime after he took command, he issued an order that all officers and privates alike should be in full dress and in proper places at roll call in the morning after the sounding of the reveille. This did not suit many of the officers who wanted to take a morning snooze, but "Roger's" orders were inexorable to officers and soldiers alike and it was for a few mornings laughable to see these officers hustling on their clothes and into line. There was nothing that pertained to discipline and order that escaped his notice. It was sometimes amusing to hear some fellow relate his experience in attempting to outwit and fool him, and the fellow that attempted it was always caught. It just could not be done.

But the whirligig of time was rapidly turning and bringing with it lively and exciting times; big with importance to the country and the Confederate cause and especially and particularly to these dear Orphans of mine.

While in Mississippi and preceding his disastrous Kentucky campaign and in which his malevolent nature was displayed, Bragg refused us the great joy we so earnestly and hopefully prayed for *viz*, the return to Kentucky with his army, where we might see the dear ones at home, and incidentally aid the cause by inducing enlistments.

But the fact that quite a number of our fellow Kentuckians were coming out with the newly enlisted cavalry commands and bringing with them the news from home and friends—the first of consequence for a year or more—gave us some comfort and consolation. In the meantime, some interesting matters of thrilling moment were transpiring down here, "Where the oak, the ash and red elm tree, all grow green in old Tennessee."

Rosecrans, not satisfied with results at Perryville, was cutting across the country for another opportunity to test his military skill and prowess, and to punish these unrepentant rebels for daring to offer resistance to the "old flag" and trying to "break up the best government the world ever saw," and over which government some of these same people are now fussing among themselves.

Excuse me, please. I see I am again off my base. Back to my beloved Orphans I must go. Oh, how I do love them!

The change from the ordinary routine of drill manoeuvre and

review was brought about by the plan of General Morgan to attack the enemy's advance post at Hartsville, North of the Cumberland and about thirty miles or more from Murfreesboro. This movement included in its plan the co-operation of the Orphan Brigade and making it a distinctly Kentucky command, planned, led and fought by Kentuckians, and which was one of the most complete and brilliant affairs of the war. Some of us to this day feel the sting of disappointment of not being privileged to share in this "*coupe de grace*" as the Fourth and Sixth Regiments were left at Baird's mill to guard against the possibility of an intercepting column from Nashville.

My heart went out in sympathy (practically) to these boys on their return to our encampment, worn out with fatigue, exhausted and hungry and almost frozen, the weather being bitter cold and the ground covered with snow to a depth of several inches. I confess also to a feeling of sorrow for the poor blanketless prisoners who passed a night of suffering, though we did the best we could for them by furnishing them with fires.

But here again the Orphans engaged in this fight paid dearly for their honours, especially the Second Regiment, which lost heavily in both officers and men, the Ninth Regiment also losing considerable. But this seemed but the prelude to the grand Christmas entertainment staged to come off later and when Breckinridge's Kentuckians received the soubriquet Orphan Brigade by which they have ever since been known and which will pass into the annals of history, alongside that of the "Tenth Legion," the "Old Guard" and "Light Brigade."

With a sense of feeling that impresses me with my utter inability to at all do justice to the subject of Murfreesboro (or Stone River), I fear to undertake the task.

To the writer this was in some respects one of the most interesting, exciting and captivating battles of the war in which he took part. Captivating, because the great battle of the 31st was witnessed from my vantage point of view—the left of our entrenchments on Swain's Hill—overlooking the stretch of country on which the battle was fought, extending as it did from the Nashville turnpike and railroad, which at this point are parallel, and at which point also stood the famous "Cowans' burnt house," referred to by historians and which I saw burn, the afternoon before. From this knoll I could see the principal part of the field.

Before attempting to describe the battle on this part of the field, I must look up my Orphans and see what they are now, and have been

GENERAL ROGER WEIGHTMAN HANSON

doing these last few hours. On the afternoon of Monday, the 29th they took possession of this hill, which was the acknowledged key to Bragg's position of defence. And herein lies a kind of mystery, why he would trust to these men, in the judgment of whose officers he showed later on he had so little confidence, this the most important point in his whole line, and why should it be entrusted to them—the Kentucky Brigade. Some were wicked enough to say, and his course toward us later, as that of Friday, strengthens this belief that he wanted us all killed, hence placing us in the most perilous position.

Now mind you, gentle reader, I am not giving this as my opinion, but others have given it as theirs. While "bivouacking" a little behind this hill the enemy's skirmishers a little after dark made quite a determined onset on our skirmishers in front of the hill, but were driven back finally with considerable loss to both parties. It was a daring and courageous move and created no little excitement and concern and looked for a time like a night attack was pending. The 30th was spent in getting ready by both parties to the battle.

And early on the morrow we took our position on Swain's Hill in support of Cobb's and the Washington artillery. From my vantage position I could see more plainly the Confederate lines than the Federal, because the Confederates were on a direct line extending Southward, while the Federals were obliquely to the front and partially obscured by an intervening cedar glade and in the afternoon the Confederates swung like a great gate on their pivotal position, while just behind and to the left of this was the enemy's strong point of resistance, to which he had finally been driven.

The smoke from the guns of the long lines of infantry, as they moved forward to the attack and the counter stroke from the enemy's resisting columns, the dashing to and fro, up and down the lines and over the field by officers, orderlies, *aides* and couriers, carrying orders and dispatches, with here and there a battery belching forth shot and shell was a sight wonderful to behold and never to be forgotten. The most thrilling incident to that view was early in the day when a body of cavalry, supposed to be "dragoons," swung into line from behind the cedar glade with drawn sabres, gleaming and waving in the crisp chill sunlit air, dashed down over the open fields in a grand charge upon the Confederate infantry, whose movements a few moments before convinced me of this approaching cavalry charge.

We had been instructed by Buckner, Monroe and others on the drill field in the formation of the "hollow square" to resist the charge of cavalry and when I saw these regiments doubling column at half distance, I knew what was coming. To see the field officers on horseback rushing within the squares as they closed and the front-rank kneeling, all with fixed bayonets glittering in the frosty sunlight, and these oncoming charges with waving sabres and glittering helmets was a sight unsurpassed by anything I witnessed during the war.

The nearest approaching it was by Sherman's charge at Resaca. As soon as the squares were formed the artillery in the rear opened fire through these intervening spaces made by the formation of the square, whereupon artillery and infantry combined swept the field and the charging column turned in confusion and route, scurrying helter-skelter back over the field, leaving numbers of men horseless.

Soon the "Rebel yell" down the line told us that things were going our way and looking we could see our friends moving forward like a mighty serpent drawing his coils.

While this was transpiring on the left a battery in our front on the opposite side of the river was industriously employed in shelling Cobb's and Slocum's batteries stationed on Swain's Hill, and whose business for the time it was the Orphans to support. When I saw this cavalry charge, to which I have referred, the thought instantly and involuntarily came to my mind of the repeated attacks of Napoleon's cavalry on the squares of Wellington's infantry at Waterloo. The sight was so thrilling that I hoped they would repeat it. But how foolish, I thought this was, in this body of cavalry attempting to ride down regiments of veteran infantry. Their officers must surely have thought that they could reach the Confederate line before they could complete this formation. If so, they paid dearly for their mistake.

The battle progressed steadily and satisfactorily to the Confederates until about four o'clock, when they, in the language of the "bum," "run against a snag." Woods' and Sheridan's divisions, with other of Rosecrans' forces had concentrated upon his extreme left, which was his strongest position for a final and last stand. The conflict here was desperate and bloody, neither party seeming to have much the advantage.

The National cemetery now occupies this identical ground and in which there are more than 6,000 Federal soldiers buried. A beautiful and fit place for the remains of these brave Western soldiers to rest, for here upon this field was displayed a courage that all men must admire.

Both armies slept that night upon the field with the greater part of the field in possession of the Confederates and the advantages and

General Braxton Bragg

results of the day almost wholly in their favour.

The Orphans spent the night in the rear of and among the artillery they had been supporting. When morning came, we found that the enemy was still in our front instead of on the road to Nashville as Bragg believed. Both parties seemed willing that a truce should prevail for the day and scarcely a shot was heard. Bragg believed that Rosecrans' army was "demolished" and would surely retreat to his base (Nashville), and so informed President Davis.

But old "Rosy" had something else in his mind. He was planning and scheming and matured a plan for a trap and Bragg walked right into it with the innocence of a lamb and the ignorance of a man that had never known anything of the art of war, and the butchery of the next day followed as a result of his obstinacy and the lack of military skill. Had he listened to the protestations of General Breckinridge and his officers he might have saved for the time being his military reputation and the lives of several hundred brave and noble men.

The recounting of the steps that led up to this ill-conceived and fatal denouement and the efforts by General Breckinridge to prevent its consummation, by one while not high in rank, but who claims to know something of the facts in the case, may not go amiss even at this late day.

Early on the morning of January 2, Captain Bramblett, commanding Company H, Fourth Kentucky, and who had served with General Breckinridge in Mexico, received orders from him (Breckinridge), to make a thorough reconnaissance of the enemy's position, Company H being at that time on the skirmish line. Captain Bramblett with two of his lieutenants, myself one of them, crawled through the weeds a distance of several hundred yards to a prominent point of observation from which through his field glass and even the naked eye we could see the enemy's concentrated forces near and above the lower ford on the opposite side of the river, his artillery being thrown forward and nearest to the river. His artillery appeared to be close together and covering quite a space of ground; we could not tell how many guns, but there was quite a number.

The infantry was seemingly in large force and extended farther down toward the ford. Captain Bramblett was a man of no mean order of military genius and information, and after looking at, and studying the situation in silence for some minutes, he said to us boys, "that he believed Rosecrans was setting a trap for Bragg." Continuing, he said:

If he means to attack us on this side, why does he not reinforce on this side? Why concentrate so much artillery on the bluff yonder? He must be expecting us to attack that force yonder, pointing to Beatty's position on the hill North of us, and if we do, he will use that artillery on us as we move to the attack.

At another time during the afternoon I heard him while discussing the situation with other officers of the regiment use substantially the same argument. I accompanied Captain Bramblett to General Breckinridge's headquarters and heard him make substantially in detail a report containing the facts above recited. Captain Tom Steele was ordered (his company having relieved ours) on the skirmish line to make a reconnaissance also, and made a similar report, and lastly General Breckinridge, to thoroughly and unmistakably understand the situation and satisfy himself, in company with one or two of his staff examined the situation as best he could and I presume reached the same conclusion, and when he (Breckinridge) repaired to Bragg's headquarters and vouchsafed this information and suggested the presumptive plan of the enemy, Bragg said:

> Sir, my information is different. I have given the order to attack the enemy in your front and expect it to be obeyed.

What was General Breckinridge to do but attempt to carry out his orders, though in carrying out this unwise and ill-conceived order it should cost in one hour and ten minutes 1,700 of as brave and chivalrous soldiers as the world ever saw. What a terrible blunder, what a bloody and useless sacrifice! And all because General Breckinridge had resented the imputation that the cause of the failure of Bragg's Kentucky campaign was the "disloyalty of her people to the Confederate cause."

Could anyone of the thousands of Kentuckians that espoused the cause of the South, complacently acquiesce in this erroneous charge and endorse the spirit that prompted this order and led to the slaughter of so many of her noble boys? This was the view that many of us took of Bragg's course.

How was this wicked and useless sacrifice brought about? "That subordinate must always obey his superior"—is the military law. In furtherance of Bragg's order, we were assembled about three o'clock on the afternoon of January 2, 1863 (Friday, a day of ill luck) in a line North of and to the right of Swain's Hill, confronting Beatty's and Growes' brigades, with a battery or two of artillery as support. They

The Orphan Brigade at Stone River

being intended for the bait that had been thrown across the river at the lower ford, and now occupied an eminence some three-quarters of a mile to the right-front of the Orphan's position on Swain's Hill.

This was the force, small as it was that Bragg was so anxious to dislodge. Between the attacking line and federal position was a considerable scope of open ground, fields and pastures, with here and there a clump of bushes or briars, but the entire space was in full view of and covered by the enemy's batteries to the left of the line on the opposite side of the river previously referred to. If the reader will only carry these positions in his eye, he can readily discover the jaws of the trap in this murderous scheme.

A more imposing and thoroughly disciplined line of soldiers never moved to the attack of an enemy than responded to the signal gun stationed immediately in our rear, which was fired exactly at four o'clock. Every man vying with his fellowman, in steadiness of step and correct alignment, with the officers giving low and cautionary commands, many knowing that it was their last hour on earth, but without hesitating moved forward to their inevitable doom and defeat. We had gotten only fairly started, when the great jaws of the trap on the bluff from the opposite side of the river were sprung, and bursting shells that completely drowned the voice of man were plunging and tearing through our columns, ploughing up the earth at our feet in front and behind, everywhere.

But with steadiness of step we moved on. Two companies of the Fourth regiment, my own and adjoining company, encountered a pond, and with a dexterous movement known to the skilled officer and soldier was cleared in a manner that was perfectly charming, obliquing to the right and left into line as soon as passed.

By reason of the shorter line held by the enemy, our line, which was much longer and the colours of each of our battalions being directed against this shorter line, caused our lines to interlap, making it necessary, in order to prevent confusion and crowding, that some of the regiments halt, until the others had passed forward out of the way. When thus halted they would lie down in order to shield themselves from the enemy infantry fire in front, who had by this time opened a lively fusillade from behind their temporary works.

While lying on the ground momentarily a very shocking and disastrous occurrence took place in Company E, immediately on my left and within a few feet of where I lay, A shell exploded right in the middle of the company, almost literally tearing it to pieces. When I recovered from the shock the sight I witnessed was appalling. Some eighteen or twenty men hurled in every direction, including my dear friend, Lieut. George Burnley of Frankfort. But these circumstances were occurring every minute now while the battle was raging all around and about us. Men moved intuitively—the voice being silenced by the whizzing and bursting shells.

On we moved, Beatty's and Growes' lines giving way seemingly to allow the jaws of the trap to press with more and ever increasing vigour upon its unfortunate and discomfited victims. But, on we moved, until the survivors of the decoy had passed the river and over the lines stationed on the other side of the river, when their new line of infantry opened on our confused and disordered columns another destructive and ruinous fire.

Coupled with this condition and correlative to it, a battery of Growes and a part of their infantry had been cut off from the ford and seeing our confused condition, rallied, reformed and opened fire on our advanced right now along the river bank. Confronted in front by their infantry, with the river intervening; swept by their artillery from the left and now attacked by both infantry and artillery by an oblique fire from the right, we found ourselves in a helpless condition, from which it looked like an impossibility to escape; and but for the fact that two or three batteries had been ordered into position to check the threatened advance of the enemy and thereby distract their attention, we doubtless would have fared still worse.

We rallied some distance to the right of where we started and found that many, very many, of our noblest, truest and best had fallen. Some of them were left on the field, among whom was my military preceptor, advisor and dear friend, Captain Bramblett, who fell into the hands of the enemy and who died a few days after in Nashville.

I shall never forget our parting, a moment or two before, he received his wound—never forget the last quick glance and the circumstances that called it forth. He was a splendid soldier and his loss grieved me very much.

Many another gallant Kentuckian, some of our finest line and field officers, were left on the field, a sacrifice to stupidity and revenge. Thirty-seven *per cent* in one hour and ten minutes—some say one hour—was the frightful summary. Among the first of these was the gallant and illustrious Hanson, whose coolness and bearing was unsurpassed and whose loss was irreparable. He with Breckinridge, understood and was fully sensible of—as indicated by the very seriousness of his countenance—the unwisdom of this move and as shown in their protest to Bragg. What a pity that a strict observance of military rule compelled it to be obeyed against his mature military mind and judgment, causing the loss of such a magnificent soldier and gentleman—uselessly and foolishly.

Contemplating this awful sacrifice, as he rode by the dead and dying in the rear of our lines, General Breckinridge, with tears falling from his eyes, was heard to say in tones of anguish, "My poor Orphans! My poor Orphans!" little thinking that he was dedicating to them a name that will live throughout the annals of time and crown the history of that dear little band with everlasting immortality.

I have tried to give you above a description from memory's tablet—of the Battle of Murfreesboro, and I shall now relate some of my observations made on my recent visit together with further references, to the events that transpired on that eventful field—the study of which is of almost overwhelming interest.

A Visit to Murfreesboro in 1912

Here, as elsewhere and on other fields, the view is especially and particularly interesting, because of the country being more level and more open with the view much less obstructed. It was worth a half dozen years to live over, in reminiscence, this week of intense excitement, interest and danger. And here too, as at Chickamauga, memory refused to be satisfied, and I find myself wishing I could see it again. I feel that I could never tire looking at the different aspects of the view and studying the tragic scenes as they transpired on this eventful closing of this eventful year of 1862, and the no less eventful opening of the year 1863. To those who lived in this historic decade and participated in these events of bygone years are of intense and ever thrilling interest, but few realise that these things happened a half century ago.

Here as elsewhere events came back to me and I had but little or no difficulty in locating the leading and many of the minor places of interest.

The immediate vicinity of our long encampment is changed considerably by houses being erected nearby and, on the ground, where our camps stood, but the big spring house, however, still does duty as of yore. The place on the Shelbyville turnpike where we held guard mount and review is much changed. So also, are the grounds on the East side of the city where we held brigade and division drill, it now being "built up." But one of the leading landmarks of the town and of special interest to the Orphans and other Kentuckians is still intact and but little changed in appearance but now used for a different purpose.

I refer to the Judge Ready residence where General Morgan captured his grand prize. There is not an old Orphan now living, that does not remember how he used to primp for the march by this house, and how proudly he stepped and with what perfect mien he marched to Billy McQuown's best pieces, all to have the privilege of "showing off," and having the opportunity for a sly glance at the beautiful Queen sisters standing on the upper veranda. You know, old boys, just how this was, don't you?

But my mind is taking me back to the battlefield where the things of real excitement were transpiring, where "the pride, pomp and circumstances of glorious war are to be found."

Starting out in company with Rev. Everett Smith, we took the Nashville pike crossing the river at the same place we crossed when on the retreat from Bowling Green to Shiloh in February, 1862, and where I had crossed several times while encamped later, near the town and over and beyond which I saw the celebrated cavalry charge and the victorious columns of the Confederates move on December 31. My mind was so completely occupied and crowded that I scarcely knew what to do or say. I know I must have been a study, to my young friend for a time at least.

I could see again in imagination the smoke and red fire and could hear the crackling flames as they leaped high in air of the famous "Cowan" house as we rode by. I imagined as we rode on that I could hear the yells and shouts of the contending lines as they surged forward and across the turnpike to the famous cut in the railroad, where Wood and Sheridan saved the day to the Federals against the last grand charge of Cleburne, Preston and Pillow of the Confederates.

As before stated here is a fitting place for the six thousand Federals who rest here. Here at the cemetery, I was introduced to Captain Thomas, the officer in charge, who was exceedingly polite and courteous and whom I found by conversing with, that I had faced at Shiloh and who had the most perfect recollection of many of the chief points and incidents of that battle. I regretted very much that I could not spend more time with him, as he impressed me as being a man after my own heart. But my young friend and myself had promised to be back at the dinner hour and I was therefore, compelled to close my interview.

I spent the afternoon in glancing over town and meeting and conversing with old soldiers and others whom I found interested in my mission, and willing and anxious to give me any information I desired.

I met and arranged with Captain Mitchell, who now owns a part of the field over which the celebrated charge of Breckinridge was made, to go out with me next morning and in company with him and a young friend, W. H. Hargett, of Pittsburgh, Pa. We started early, going over the same road, crossing the same bridge, as the day before to a point near the cemetery where the road to McFadden's ford leaves the turnpike and runs North by the bluff, the famous bluff where Rosecrans' fifty-eight pieces of artillery were stationed that wrought such dreadful havoc upon Breckinridge's men as they moved across the fields to attack Beatty and Growes (the decoy) on the other side of the river, here we crossed the river at the lower ford, so famous in history but which is properly known as McFadden's. Here we "tied up" and in company with my companions we took to the fields and woods, which latter exist now in fancy only.

Up the gradual slope we go to the crest of the ridge (now a cotton patch) to where Beatty and Growe were stationed, swinging around as we go to the point overlooking the river on which stood the massive oaks where the Sixth Kentucky, led by that incarnate demon of war, "Old Joe" Lewis, with flashing sword and blazing eyes, more terrible than the eyes of a raging lion and who impressed me as I was never impressed before or since, with the devil in human form.

He presented a picture at that time I shall never forget. It is as grimly and immovably fixed in my mind as the sun and the stars and I become enthusiastic whenever I think of him and the incident. Now we move along the crest Northward to the point where the Fourth Kentucky struck Beatty's line. Looking East and South towards the Lebanon pike, we can see the vicinity where we started in the charge about midway between the crest and the pike.

Turning around we can look down the North slope of the ridge and over which we pressed Beatty and the right of Growes' brigade to McFadden's ford, dropping into, as we move down the narrow sag or depression that leads from the top of the hill straight to the ford and which furnished the only protection from the murderous fire of the fifty-eight guns massed on the bluff. Out of this depression, going or coming, we were exposed to this dreadful and incessant fire. Opposite to and some forty yards from this ford is the picket fence where we were compelled to halt and which is so well remembered by many of the Orphans.

The Federals passed around the end of this fence, they being acquainted with the situation, but we struck it square and were compelled to halt. Just outside and along this picketing were piled the enemy's drums and upon which the minnie balls from their new and supporting line on the opposite side of the river were beating a funeral dirge for many of our dear boys who were here compelled to halt and die to no purpose whatever. I walked along this picket fence, which looks just as it did then, but of course has been rebuilt, and over the very ground on which my dear Captain Bramblett fell and with whom I exchanged glances a moment before.

To give expression to my feelings as I contemplated this last glance, this look in life at my dear friend and leader is impossible and I turn away with sickened heart from the fatal spot and retrace my steps over the field to the rallying point, every step of the way marked by exploding shells and flying shot from the enemy's battery of fifty-eight guns which seemed determined to show no mercy at all.

Lest someone may say I am magnifying this story of the "battery on the bluff" I will quote here *verbatim* from the tablet on the twenty-foot granite monument which marks the place occupied by these guns to mark the place from which the death-dealing shot and shell were hurled that resulted in the death of so many of Kentucky's noble and brave boys.

I understand this monument was erected by the president of one of the great railway systems, the N. C. & St. L., who had participated in the famous charge. It is the most interesting and historic point of all the very interesting points of this eventful field. It was with awe and overpowering wonder and feeling that I indulged the scenes of fifty years ago, (as at 1912), enacted on this spot. Here the very earth trembled beneath the thunderings of these fifty-eight cannon, sending death and destruction into the ranks of us poor unfortunate Confederates.

The tablet upon this monument reads as follows:

On January 2, 1863, at three p.m., there were stationed on this hill, fifty-eight cannon commanding the field across the river and as the Confederates advanced over this field the shot and shell from these guns resulted in a loss of 1,800 killed and wounded in less than one hour.

What a harvest of death in so short a time was wrought by shot and shell! The most of whose victims were mutilated and lacerated beyond recognition or description. Had the earth been torn by an earthquake the scene would not have been more terrible and hideously appalling.

On a board marker, nearby, in faded letters is this indefinite inscription:

> Col. S. Mat——, Third Division 14th A. C. Fed——, Col. S. W. Price commanding. Holding Lower Ford, Dec. 31, 1862.

This evidently refers to the battery that played upon Cobb and Slocum on Swain's Hill.

It would seem from these last words of this poster that the Federals were afraid on the first day's fight that the Confederates would attempt to turn their left by crossing at this ford, hence the placing of this battery here. Bragg, it seems, had no such thought, and, however, it was stationed in our immediate front, West from Swain's Hill and as the battle progressed on the plain South of the railroad and turnpike it played upon Cobb and Slocum with increasing vigour and spirit. As before stated, the Orphans were stationed at this time in support to these batteries, and it was from this point that I witnessed the thrilling sights on the West side of the river.

In company with my new-made genial and accommodating friend, W. G. Beatty, whose father owned the land on which the battle of the 2nd was fought, I visited Swain's Hill, which is evidently a mistaken name for the place, no one with whom I conversed, old or young, knew it by that name. I found on the hill, which I very readily recognised from the distance, the old entrenchments intact, save from the levelling effects of time, and on which an occasional locust sapling is growing with quite a thicket of the same in the immediate front.

But from the left of this line of works and where I was stationed on the 31st, the view overlooking the railroad, turnpike and plain is perfectly clear. From here I looked, studied and wondered. Why should I not linger and contemplate? Never until the great day of judgment do I ever expect to witness such a thrilling and awe-inspiring scene as I here witnessed on that eventful day of December 31, 1862.

Beatty contemplated me with interest, if not astonishment. So intensely interesting were these scenes and recollections I was almost tempted to spend another day contemplating and reviewing them. But we returned to the city at night to attend a church affair at the instance and invitation of my young friend from Bourbon, Rev. Everett Smith, whose guest I had been while here.

I tried hard to forget and partially succeeded in forgetting the thoughts and reminiscences the day had suggested—in the presence of so many charming ladies and gallant gentlemen of Brother Smith's congregation and the additional enjoyment of the ice cream, cakes and strawberries, my appetite of fifty years ago suddenly returning to remind me of the difference twixt now and then.

Next morning my friend Beatty was on hand early with his automobile and speeded me over the city which I am frank to say is one of the most beautiful little cities I ever saw. I was charmed by the old time warmth and hospitality of its people and the greeting given me and I shall remember them as among the happiest of my life. And if I were young once more, I would be almost tempted to cast my lot with these good people in this good country, both of which are the next best to Kentucky.

I must not forget to remind the old Orphans and others who may read this paper that after considerable inquiry I was able to find the old Haynes home, in which General Hanson died, and which is now occupied by Hon. Jesse C. Beasley, the present Democratic nominee for Congress in this district. I was shown through the house by his good little wife who although taken somewhat by surprise at my sudden and unexpected visit, but who courteously invited me to examine and inspect until fully satisfied. I stood in the room in which he died almost dumfounded with emotion. Here, in the presence of his heart-broken wife, and sorrowing friends his life gradually ebbed away and took its flight to the realms above.

I was reminded to tread lightly and speak softly on this solemn occasion, for here, passed away into the Great Beyond one of Kentucky's grandest and greatest noblemen.

I attended that afternoon, in company with Captain Baird, Beatty and others, the anniversary decoration of the Confederate graves and listened to a fine oration and the delightful rendering of several appropriate songs by the Murfreesboro quartet. When they sang "My Old Kentucky Home," I hugged tightly, the tree against which I leaned and fear I betrayed a weakness for which I am not altogether ashamed, for what Kentuckian that lives, especially when away from home, whose soul is not moved, when he hears the sweet strains of this touching and soul inspiring song. How can he, when thus reminded of his old Kentucky home, keep from exclaiming (in mind at least) in the language of the poet:

Lives there a man (Kentuckian) with soul so dead,

Who to himself hath not said, this is my own, my native land.

Before closing this chapter, I must not fail to say that I found on this trip a manifestation of the same liberal hospitable and magnanimous spirit, that has ever characterized this noble and self-sacrificing people. To the good women of the South I owe my life; to them I bow and acknowledge obeisance as the truest, purest, sweetest and best of all God's creatures.

No sacrifice, that mortal man could make is, too great a recompense for the love and devotion of these dear women who sacrificed, wept and suffered during the four long years of midnight darkness. They are the angels of the earth today; to them, as such I uncover my head and I hail them.

Finally, I wish to acknowledge my thanks to Mr. and Mrs. C. D. Ivie, at whose home I was the guest of my friend, Rev. Smith and his charming little wife. To Editor Williams, W. G. Beatty, Captains Baird and Mitchell, Dr. Campbell and others, I am indebted for many courtesies and favours.

CHAPTER 6

Battle of Chickamauga—1863

I am now attempting to write from this Lookout Mountain, one of the most picturesque as well as interesting places on the American continent. Nearby and round about here some of the greatest episodes in the world's history transpired near the close of that eventful year, 1863.

Chickamauga, Lookout Mountain, Missionary Ridge, where the lives of sixty-five thousand Americans were either destroyed or more or less wrecked.

A feeling of philosophy and awe prompts me to ask why all this great sacrifice of human life, misery and suffering?

Was the Great God that made man now looking on this awful scene of carnage and woe again repenting that He had made wicked, rebellious and murderous man; or was it a part of His omnipotent plan for man's inherent folly and wickedness driving him to destroy his fellowman?

Whatever it was it seems to have been accomplished here amid these towering mountains.

But so, it was and I, one insignificant actor in the grand drama, am still permitted to live and recount some of the thrilling scenes as they were enacted. It is beyond my power to describe minutely and correctly all the thrilling sights that I witnessed on this eventful occasion (Battle of Chickamauga) and I shall refer to those only that concern myself and my Kentucky comrades, unless incidentally it shall appear necessary to my story.

I will, therefore, not attempt to note the manoeuvring, the marching and counter-marching, back and forth, up and down the Chickamauga Valley, in and about Rossville and Crawfish Springs and their vicinity; all of which, at that time, seemed to me was but the waving of the red flag in the face of Rosecrans in "*I dare you to come out*" spirit on the part of Bragg.

Whatever motives, schemes and strategy it contained we all knew, rank and file, field and staff, that we were on the eve of momentous events. We all knew that here the question of "Greek meeting Greek" would soon again be tested and two of the mightiest armies of modern times would be locked in mortal combat. We had not long to wait for on the morning of the nineteenth (September 1863) an occasional *boom, boom,* away to the right and front told us of the coming storm that was about to break over and sweep Chickamauga Valley with a mighty avalanche of thunder and horror that shook the very earth itself. Slowly but steadily the roar of artillery increased and by the middle of the afternoon became almost incessant.

Longstreet's Virginians had come out to show the Western army how to fight and they were now learning that Rosecrans' Western veterans could give instructions in the art of war as well as they and that they were not facing the aliens and wage soldiers that constituted a large part of the Army of the Potomac. They also found, as the battle progressed, that the Western Army of the South knew as well and were as willing to "stand up Johnnie" and give and take blow for blow as they. The evening wore on and occasional reports from the front brought news that the Confederates were holding their own and a little better.

Meantime the "Orphans" were on the move toward the front and facing the enemy's moving column on the Chattanooga road, which led to Rossville and near Glass Mill, at which place the artillery of Breckinridge's division, commanded by the gallant Major Graves, engaged the enemies in one of the fiercest artillery duels it was my pleasure to witness during the war. I say pleasure advisedly, for it was a magnificent sight to see from where I was stationed Graves moving among his men and directing their every action, which was done with an admirable celerity and precision that was perfectly charming. I must here do Graves the honour to say that he was the most perfect military man I ever saw. But this was but the prelude to the play of the morrow; both parties seeming (after a half hour's engagement) to say we will settle tomorrow. "Sunday is a better day."

Shifting our position to Lee and Gordon's Mill, further down the Chickamauga, in the afternoon, we here awaited developments and that night made a long detour and crossed at Alexander's Bridge, several miles down the river. Next morning, we found ourselves on the extreme right of the dividing line of the stage of action marked out by the respective commanders for the grand tragedy that day to be enacted upon the stage of war. Early, very early the Fourth Kentucky Skirmishers (and I here glory in the fact) had the honour of firing the first shots in the opening that day of the greatest battle ever fought on the American continent, if not the greatest in modern times. This assertion may be called in question by critics, but if I mistake not there were more men killed and wounded at Chickamauga than in any other engagement of the war.

Here the old and somewhat sacrilegious saying of "Hell broke loose in Georgia" was fully and forcefully emphasised by the almost continuous thundering of 200 cannons that made the very earth tremble, besides the constant rattle of musketry and the shouts of more than a hundred thousand struggling combatants determined on each other's destruction. Americans all, and all for what? That a God-made inferior race might occupy the same plane with the superior was the object of one, while that right was disputed by the other. But I fear I may be digressing somewhat from the original purpose in these chapters.

Still these thoughts are hard to suppress. Reviewing the incidents of the great battle and the part played by Kentucky Confederates I return to the skirmish line of the Fourth Kentucky, which covered the front of the Orphan Brigade and which was commanded by Col. Joe Nuckols, who was wounded at the very outset of the engagement and compelled to leave the field.

The writer was the subject at this particular time and place of the most ridiculous and practical joke of his entire war experience, but which (thanks to the Bill of Rights) he is not here compelled to relate. This was the beginning of that chapter in the history of the Orphan Brigade, which took the lives and blood of so many noble Kentuckians to write. In the first and desperate onset, led by the noble and intrepid Helm, whose name is a household word with almost all Kentuckians, fell here, together with Graves, Hewitt, Dedman, Daniel, Maderia and other officers of the line, and many splendid men of the Second and Ninth Regiment's, who paid with their lives tribute to Mars and added to Kentucky's old traditional glory and renown.

Three regiments on the right, Fourth, Sixth and Forty-First Alabama, swept everything before them—the enemy being in the open field. But the Second and Ninth encountered the enemies' breastworks and were repulsed with terrible slaughter. Here was where the officers just mentioned fell in one of the most desperate struggles of

BATTLE OF CHICKAMAUGA

the day. Here "Pap Thomas'" veterans took advantage of their works and exacted deep and merciless toll. More than once during the day was this position assailed by other bodies of Confederates with similar results.

About the middle of the afternoon the assembling of Cheatham's and Walker's division in conjunction with Breckinridge warned us that the fatal moment had arrived and the hour of desperation was at hand.

The old veteran needs no one to tell him when a crisis is approaching, he instinctively and otherwise comprehends the meaning of these movements and nerves himself for the desperate work before him. His countenance would convince the stoic of what his mind contained, in modern parlance he "understands the game." When the signal gun was fired, we knew its meaning, so also did the enemy. Then three lines in solid phalanx, desperate and determined men, moved forward on the Federal stronghold to be met by a withering and blighting fire from the enemy behind their works.

But so furious and desperate was the onslaught that Thomas' veterans, who had withstood all previous attempts to dislodge them, could no longer face the line of gleaming bayonets of the Confederates as they leaped over the breastworks the Federals had so successfully defended up to that hour.

Some surrendered, others made their escape and still others met their doom—many, not hearing the shouts of the victorious Confederates as they rushed over and among them.

This was the culmination of the struggle. Similar movements with similar results were taking place simultaneously all along the line, closing the most stupendous struggle of the war. But at this particular point and at Snodgrass Hill, where the Fifth Kentucky contributed additional and unsurpassed glory to Kentucky's part in the great battle, were the keys to Rosecrans' position, and here the fighting was the hardest and the losses heaviest.

In the first charge in the morning where the right of the brigade was so successful, we captured a section of the enemy's artillery. The writer seized the trunnion of one of the guns and with assistance turned it on them while the other was turned by others of our men; but we could find no ammunition to fire them and were deprived of the anticipated glory of firing on the enemy as they fled from the field. I wish here, and in my feeble way, to lift my hat to do honour to the gallantry of the captain commanding that battery (who I learned was from Indiana) as doing the most daring and chivalrous act I ever saw performed by an enemy during my entire war experience.

Both his lieutenants and a number of his men having been killed before he abandoned his guns, which were in a battery just on the West side of the Chickamauga road and in the face of us Confederates, who had reached the East side of the road, he dashed into the road and past us, lifting his hat and waving us a salute that would have put to shame a Chesterfield or a Prince Rupert. The act was almost paralyzing and not a man of the fifty or more who fired at him point blank touched him or his horse. If there is such a thing as a charmed life, this captain must have possessed it on that occasion. If living I would gladly travel miles to shake his hand.

Our next move was to unite our separated line which we did by retiring later on to the point from where we started.

During the occasional lulls in the musketry firing the artillery from left to right and especially on the left about Snodgrass Hill, was thundering defiance and sending death into each other's ranks that seemingly made old earth shake from centre to circumference, set the birds to flight, caused reptiles, lizards and all manner of wild animals to flee from the wrath of murderous man, among which was a cottontail deer that was seen by some of the men running in a bewildered and dazed manner in the rear of the contending lines, not knowing which way to flee or what it all meant.

The enemy routed, the conflict ceased—about dark—with the Orphans (those left) on the West side of the Chickamauga road, some of the men playfully astride the enemy's guns—several in number—that had been abandoned at this point, others prostrate on the ground resting and recounting incidents of the day, all glad enough that it was over.

Here General Buckner rode up, he having come over from the left where his artillery and division of infantry had done such splendid work and who was greeted with a cheer from the surviving Orphans that must have done his soul good and which he acknowledged with a smile, lifting his hat gracefully in acknowledgment of the greeting.

What next! We all expected that we would follow immediately without an hour's delay on the heels of the retreating and discomfited Federals and overtake and completely route and possibly capture them before they could get settled behind their fortifications around Chattanooga. But here the fatal mistake of Beauregard at Shiloh (and for which Bragg censured him) was duplicated by Bragg himself.

Back to the field among the boys where we spent the night among the dead and wounded; and awaiting orders from Bragg, who was spending his time in sending congratulations to President Davis while Rosecrans was busy preparing to receive and entertain him from his fortifications around Chattanooga.

The writer having learned that we would likely spend the day on the field resting—"*resting*" (I toss my head in derision of the thought), obtained permission to visit and inspect the field of battle, and in company with one or two comrades started early next morning from the extreme right, where we opened the battle, and traversed the entire length of the field, a distance of seven miles or more. This was the first time such an enviable opportunity had ever presented itself and I seized it gladly, notwithstanding the many horrible and ghastly sights I knew I would see. On every hand, in every direction, were evidences of the desperate conflict of the preceding day. The forest trees splintered and torn by the plunging shot and shell from the cannon's deadly throat, dismantled caissons and artillery wheels, dead horses, guns, cartridge boxes, bayonets and almost every kind of war paraphernalia imaginable were strewn promiscuously over the field. Trees and saplings, not larger than a man's body to a height of six or eight feet, contained from a dozen to as high as sixty rifle balls.

But worst of all with upturned faces and glaring eyes, torn and mangled bodies of not less than four thousand dead men on the field and at the hospitals. At the latter, especially at the Snodgrass place, there were acres covered with wounded and many dead. Here I witnessed the most appalling sight my eyes ever beheld, a description from which I shudder and shrink at this distant day, and which is too terrible for delicate and sensitive natures to ponder; and which involuntarily reminds me of Sherman's saying again.

The citizens of today (1912) will doubtless wonder how any man could escape such a rain of shot and shell, but by the old soldier it is readily understood. While ninety *per cent* of these shots were being fired the men were lying flat on their faces and were overshooting each other when suddenly one or the other would spring to his feet and with a bound and a yell rush at a double-quick upon their foe, giving him time to fire one or at most two rounds when his ranks would be broken and compelled to retire.

After seeing these appalling sights, I retraced my steps and reached the starting point about twilight to find that my command had been ordered forward toward Chattanooga and the vicinity of Missionary

Ridge, which we reached next day to find Rosecrans occupying his fortifications and redoubts ready to receive and entertain us. We were formed in line of battle at or near the foot of Missionary Ridge and expected when the formation was completed to be hurled against the forts and redoubts to certain and inevitable destruction.

Many expressions of evil and forebodings of disaster were indulged in and anathemas were hurled at the commander without stint for holding us back for this, the hour of our doom. Many farewells were being exchanged, mingled with jeers and sarcasm, all knowing and understanding fully the gravity of the situation. It was an hour of intense, of dreadful suspense, which could only be felt and not described.

But thanks to an all-wise and merciful Providence which at the last moment withheld the hand and changed the mind that commanded. But for this change of mind he who writes this story would doubtless now be *"sleeping the sleep that knows no waking on fame's eternal camping ground."* When we were ordered to retire to Missionary Ridge many were the long-drawn sighs of relief that we had escaped from this threatened and, as we felt, certain doom.

The Writer's Visit to Chickamauga—In May, 1912

I have visited scenes of the great conflict twice, traversed the very ground from the point where we formed line of battle and moved to the charge against "Pap" Thomas' veterans and am still unsatisfied. Not that the points of greatest interest have been lost to memory, but because memory will not be satisfied. I can see in my mind the anxious look in the faces of those brave Kentucky boys, as they stepped into line and touched elbows in obedience to the commands "dress to the right; dress to the left; steady, steady, men; quick step, forward, march!"

Tell me I shall ever forget these commands or this hour! Never, while "memory lasts and reason holds sway."

From this very starting point I traced the ground over which we moved (in 1863) taking the monument erected to the memory of General Helm as a guide and allowing for the space of the two regiments to occupy the right, coursing Westward, the exact direction we moved, crossing the LaFayette road at or near the very point where the two pieces of artillery were captured and previously referred to. The tablet here tells me who my gallant captain of Indiana (Bridges) was and recites the facts of the capture correctly. There, too, is the open field through which the broken regiments of infantry were fleeing that I was so anxious to assist with shots from their own battery.

Here I must criticise a little at the risk of censure. I will do so by quoting from memory, not literally, from Gen. Breckinridge's official report saying that:

> A strong supporting line at this moment, thrown on Thomas' flank and rear, would have resulted in dislodging and overthrowing Thomas early in the day.

This was plain to line and field officer alike. The opportunity was presented but not availed of; why, I know not.

The tablets here with their historic record briefly stamped in metal are substantially correct. My version of the battle previously stated to the guides while going out (I. P. Thoeford, an old Confederate) and S. P. Black were so nearly identical that these men threw up their hands in amazement when I read from the tablet. It was no trouble to convince them that I had been there and knew something about the battle and the positions of the troops on that part of the line. Here stands nearby the Glenn House, some old log houses.

Not far away is the Kentucky monument, a fitting memorial to Kentuckians of both sides crowned with the Goddess of Love and Peace. Northeast is the monument to that gallant, lovable character, Ben Hardin Helm—my hand trembles as I write his name, for I really believe he was one of the kindest hearted and best men I ever knew. Near this spot was where so many of the Second and Ninth fell, some of whose names are already mentioned in this chapter on Chickamauga. I could write much, very much, more of this very interesting and historic field, but will not trespass further on your time and space.

BRIGADIER-GENERAL BENJAMIN HARDIN HELM

Chapter 7

Missionary Ridge

From here (Missionary Ridge) about the last of September the Orphans were sent to Tyner Station as a base from which to guard the commissary stores at Chickamauga Station, that place being the depot of supplies for the army investing Chattanooga.

But when it was seen that Grant, who had arrived and assumed command of the Federal Army, was planning to move on our lines on Lookout and Missionary Ridge, we were ordered back to our original position on the Ridge, not far from Bragg's headquarters. From this point we could see on the night of the 24th of November the flashes from the rifles of the contending lines on Lookout, like so many fireflies on a hot July evening.

The extravagant talk about Hooker's "battle above the clouds" is a misnomer, that has found its way into print, and for a long time filled the papers and magazines and is nothing but a magnified myth (unsupported by facts) that is absolutely incredible. At no time were the contending forces more than half way up the mountain, and all the glory arrogated by the Federals was achieved over a light line deployed as skirmishers, composed of Alabamans. For a long time, this twaddle was absolutely and positively sickening.

But I must return to my beloved Orphans. Next morning (25th) before daylight we were ordered to the extreme right (Northern point of the Ridge) as support to Cleburne's division, a man who was never known to ask for support. This move was a complete waste of that important element of strength at this critical and all-important time, for we, the Orphans, rendered practically no service at all on that eventful day.

But here I conjecture and philosophise again. May be and perhaps it was providential, for had we kept our place in the line between and among Cobb's guns, "Lady Breckinridge," "Lady Buckner" and "Lady Helm," and his other guns to which the Orphans were lovingly endeared, they would never have been surrendered while a man was on his feet. Lucky indeed for Sheridan and Wood that day that the Orphans were away from home, and perhaps equally lucky for some, if not all, of us, for we had sworn never to abandon this position while a man of us lived.

This, in my mind, was the strongest natural position with one exception (Rockyface Gap) ever held by the Confederate forces in the West, and its abandonment was a disgrace to Confederate arms. Imagine our mortification and deep chagrin when we learned that our battery—Cobb's—with the endearing names inscribed thereon, had been cowardly abandoned after we had successfully defended them at Shiloh, Vicksburg, Baton Rouge, Murfreesboro, Jackson, Chickamauga and other places. It was enough to make an angel weep and justified the anathemas hurled at the commander and the cowardly troops that were left to defend them. The circumstance left a sting that never can be forgotten while an Orphan survives.

We never knew what had happened until about dark, when we were ordered from our position toward Chickamauga Station. Then the truth took first the form of conjecture, then misgiving and lastly the sad news that we were to cover the retreat of the army. Then all was explained.

The retreat that night was one of intense hardship and excitement, and it was entrusted to the Orphan Brigade, with the help of Cleburne's division, to protect the retreating army. We were in their grasp had they only known it. Passing so near one of their pursuing columns we could actually hear them talking and see them moving around the camp fires they were kindling. To prevent being ambushed we threw out a string of guards on both sides of the road, who moved along parallel with the road and near it. Every moment we expected an attack.

The feeling was one of intenseness and we were greatly relieved when at last we became assured of our escape.

Had the Federals only known it, they had our retreating column cut in two and could have made a finish of the day's work and probably the Confederacy as well.

But they, too, as well as the Confederates, failed sometimes to grasp their opportunities. One of the pleasant and enjoyable features of this night's experience was the wading of Chickamauga River, waist deep, which had a tendency to further exasperate us and cause the men to express themselves in anything but Sunday school phrase and song.

Next day was but little less exciting. The Federal advance was pressing us with unusual vigour and compelled us to turn time and again from the line of march and check their advance. It was fight and run until Cleburne determined to, and did, put an end to it, ambushing them at Ringgold Gap, where they paid for their persistence with the lives of several hundred men.

After this costly warning from Cleburne we were permitted to continue our retreat unmolested and reached, the next day, that haven of rest, Dalton, about which I have written in a subsequent chapter.

I am making my chapter on Mission Ridge short because there is nothing pertaining to it that is to the credit of the Confederate soldier as a whole. Yet there were some commands of the army that did their duty well and creditably.

In looking at the tablets of many—in fact most of the Federal regiments and brigades which contain a summary of their losses—I was struck with amazement at the very light loss sustained in this memorable engagement, so disgraceful to the Confederates. Some regiments losing only one man killed and ten or twelve wounded, and no brigade, so far as I noticed, lost more than thirteen men, which was an average of three to the regiment. We had a single company, Company I, of the Fourth Kentucky, that lost more men at Shiloh than a whole brigade here.

When considering the great advantage of position held by them and the insignificant losses inflicted upon the Federals, the losses but emphasise the fact that the Confederates must have been badly rattled on this summit and would no doubt have made a better fight from their entrenchments at the base of the mountain bordering the valley, over which the columns of Grant moved to the attack.

But let us think and reason for the moment, and if possible, find some excuse for this miserable failure. It is well known to the expert marksman and sportsman as well, that in shooting on a steep decline you are much more apt to overshoot than when directing a shot horizontally or upward. This was the case there on these steep mountain sides, which furnishes the one excuse only for such bad marksmanship and the low *per cent* of casualties just noticed.

But notwithstanding this fact a much more creditable record could have been made by rolling the huge boulders that were abundant down upon the Federals, whose progress was, of course, necessarily slow; and, lastly, when the enemy reached the summit exhausted, what were their bayonets for and why did they not use them? These are questions that suggest themselves to the mind of the writer at this distant day, while looking at this natural and seeming impregnable position.

As stated before, the history on one part of the field would have been differently written had not the Orphans been taken away from their pets—"Lady Buckner," "Lady Breckinridge," "Lady Helm," "Lady Hanson," "Lady Lyon" and others of their companions in war. A feeling of chagrin creeps over me when I think of the surrender of these guns with their endearing names and hitherto immortal history.

But General Bragg, in his wisdom—no, his unwisdom—thought it best to send us away from our idols and hazard them in the keeping of those who betrayed their trust, and left us, like Rachael, weeping, because they were lost and we "also refused to be comforted."

I find almost innumerable tablets, markers and monuments placed here to commemorate the deeds of valour here performed by the Federals; but I find very few (which is well) to mark the Confederates and their deeds. But could I have my way every one of these would be removed and in their stead, I would place the Goddess of Liberty, weeping for shame that her children had so dishonoured their heritage.

I have said that I would be brief, and choking back the feeling of remorse and disgrace that this one incident in the history of the Confederate soldier has fixed upon their otherwise brilliant and incomparable record, I close by referring the reader to Murfreesboro.

Battle of Missionary Ridge

CHAPTER 8

Dalton

Who that spent the winter of '63-'64, at Dalton does not recall some circumstance or incident to remind him of the dreary "winter of discontent" spent in this mountain fastness of Northern Georgia? To many of us it seemed like an age, but withal it was a season of much needed rest and recuperation. Here in and around this little city flanked by majestic mountains, pondering over the disasters of Lookout and Missionary Ridge, we spent the time in comparative comfort and ease, some planning in mind the future campaign and its outcome, others indifferent as to the future and caring but little, willing to entrust all to those at the helm, and making the most of circumstances and the ever present, little thinking or caring for the great dangers and hardships that awaited us.

There was from the time we turned our faces Southward from Bowling Green to the very close of the war an air of indifference, a "devil may care," happy-go-lucky spirit, about these young Kentuckians that made them ready to cheerfully undertake any enterprise, no matter how dangerous or exacting the duty or perilous the undertaking. They had become so accustomed to all these things, and so thoroughly inured to hardships, that they felt themselves prepared for and rather coveted them, no matter how great or trying. While here we enjoyed more liberty and recreation than any time during or since the war began. Some of the men were furloughed and enjoyed a few days of rest with relatives and friends (if perchance they had any) in the South. The writer spent his in gay old Richmond on the James, in company with General Lewis, Captain McKendrie and other Kentuckians there assembled. All amused themselves as best they could in camp and town.

Drilling had been dispensed with—no need now for that, for in this we were perfect. Dress parade, guard mount and review were about the only exercises now required. A great sham battle broke the monotony once, and a snowball battle at another time was a diversion indulged for one day. A very pertinent question was often asked toward the close of the winter—"Who would command in the next campaign?" When at last it was given out that General Johnson would command, the spirits of the men revived and hope was again renewed.

While contemplating the future, news came that the enemy were now moving Daltonward. We indulged the hope and wondered whether Sherman would undertake to force the pass in Rockyface Mountain through which the railroad and wagon road both ran. We thought of Leonidas and his Spartans and hoped for an opportunity to imitate and if possible, to eclipse that immortal event at Thermopylae. But not so the wily Sherman. That "old fox" was too cunning to be caught in that or any other trap.

We were ordered out to meet him and took position in the gap and on the mountain, from which we could see extending for miles his grand encampment of infantry and artillery, the stars and stripes floating from every regimental brigade, division and corps headquarters and presenting the greatest panorama I ever beheld. Softly and sweetly the music from their bands as they played the national airs were wafted up and over the summit of the mountain.

Somehow, some way, in some inexplicable and unseen manner, "Hail Columbia," "America" and "The Star Spangled Banner" sounded sweeter than I had ever before heard them, and filled my soul with feelings that I could not describe or forget. It haunted me for days, but never shook my loyalty to the Stars and Bars or relaxed my efforts in behalf of our cause.

While thus arrayed in his grand encampment, his banners flying and bands playing, a part of his force (McPherson's Corps), like a gladiator, was rapidly and stealthily gliding over the plain West of the mountains to seize Snake Creek and Dug Gaps and strike Johnson in the rear at Resaca. But you know *"the best laid schemes of mice and men gang aft agley."* We arrived there first and gave him a hearty welcome, as described in my chapter on Resaca.

Dalton, like other towns and cities, has changed wonderfully in the days since the war. From a quaint old mountain town of a half century ago to the modern and thrifty little city of today, putting on airs like many other towns. To me no landmarks are visible save the old stone springhouse, near where General Lewis had his headquarters

The Mountain Campaigns in Georgia etc.

and Captain Phillips, A. Q. M. of the Fourth, had his quartermaster store and where his lovely little wife graced his "marquee" with the air and dignity of the queen that she was.

I walked over the ground on which the Fourth was encamped and stood upon the very spot where Captain Hugh Henry's tent was pitched, and in which we were often entertained by the Kentucky Glee Club, which was composed of some of the finest talent in the army. While it may not be altogether relevant to the purpose of these chapters, I cannot refrain from referring to and mentioning the fact that the Fourth Kentucky was admitted to have the finest band in the Western Army, led by that accomplished and expert musician who (after the war) became a teacher in the Boston Conservatory of Music—Billy McQuown.

Many, many times were we regaled by the music of our band and carried back to the bosom of friends by the sweet strains of "My Old Kentucky Home" and other familiar and inspiring airs played by this band. It is no stranger, than it is true, that music exercises a wonderful and inspiring influence over the soldier, making him forget the hardships, trials and dangers to which he is almost constantly exposed, and troops are never happier than when being entertained in this way, unless it be at a full mess table.

I have been reluctantly compelled to pass by Kennesaw and Pine Mountains, both of which are places of much interest to surviving Orphans. On the former we left several of our best officers and men. Among the former was Major John Bird Rogers of the Fourth Kentucky Regiment, and Lieutenant Bob Innis of the Second. Than the former there was not a more capable and gallant officer identified with the history of the Orphan Brigade as was also Lieutenant Innis.

Pine Mountain, a lone sentinel of nature, was made sacredly historic by the blood of the great preacher, General Bishop Polk. I saw the "grand old man" as he, Generals Johnston and Bates and others rode by the Orphans' position to the summit of the mountain to view and examine the enemy's position in front, and could not but admire the graceful and dignified bearing of the grand old man as he saluted in true military style as he passed. I saw the smoke from and heard the thunder of Simonson's guns as they sent the fatal shot that tore his body and ended his earthly career.

Sad and awful moment for the Confederacy! But we have here presented one of the most noted and conspicuous characters in America history. I stood on the very spot on which he fell not twenty minutes after the sad occurrence—Burton's sharpshooters with their Kerr rifles having driven Simonson and his gunners to cover. I believe the sacred spot should have erected on it a monument commemorative of this tragic incident and the life and character of this great man. It is certainly a picturesque and interesting spot.

But before I go, I must tell of my visit to Rockyface Gap. Here is one of the grand sentinels of nature—a lofty and stone-crowned mountain towering above and looking contemplatively down upon his neighbours and the low-bending valleys upon whose bosom Sherman pitched his grand and imposing encampment in the make-believe that he was going South through this impregnable pass held by Johnson.

Next to Lookout it is the grandest mountain in the Appalachian chain, and one well worthy of a visit by the tourist lover of nature. I climbed to the top of it this morning, going over the same identical path travelled by us while doing picket and observation duty. Here we had the only human telegraph line I ever saw, which was made by placing the operator (an officer) on the summit to report the operations and movements of the enemy to the first man in the line, he repeating it to the next in line and so on down the mountain to its base where the general had his staff officers and couriers to receive the message and report to him at his headquarters. The scheme worked like a charm, notwithstanding its uniqueness.

I was impelled to make this trip—although I felt when I reached the summit I was about to collapse—to see the resting place of a noble and brave old Orphan who was killed while on duty here—George Disney of Company K, Fourth Kentucky—an account of whose singular death is noted by Virginius Hutchings in the history of the Orphan Brigade. I learned before going on this trip that the Boy Scouts of Dalton, under Captain Sapp, county clerk, had only two days before gone up and placed a marble headstone to the grave to take the place of the board that had so long marked his resting place—a place that a monarch or king might envy, hundreds of feet above common man.

I wished while there, so high upward toward Heaven, that I could wield the pen of a Gray or a Kipling, that I might do this subject of my thoughts justice. The subject, the inspiration, was here, but language to express it was lacking. Poor George! You have had one friend after these long years to leave a tear of tribute to your memory.

I cannot close without first thanking the good daughters of Dalton for the compliment they paid me by really forcing upon me undeserved attentions in a very fine lunch set before and out of time specially for me just before taking the train at 11:50 a.m., and who I think had a scheme to force me to make them a speech—it being Decoration Day—but I slipped through their fingers and got away.

The Orphan Brigade

Chapter 9

Visit to Resaca—1912

May 14th, found us after a tiresome night's march at Resaca, from which point I again write you.

Here today and on the morrow was fought the first battle of magnitude in the great hundred-and twenty-days' battle of the celebrated Georgia campaign from Dalton to Atlanta. I say hundred-and twenty-days' battle, which may seem a little far-fetched, but which is almost literally true, for there was not a day or night, yes scarcely an hour, that we did not hear the crack of a rifle or roar of a cannon. Their sounds were our lullaby, sleeping or waking—to their music we slept, by their thunderings we were awakened, and to the accompanying call of the bugle we responded on the morning of May 14, to engage in the death grapple with Sherman's well clothed, well fed and thoroughly rested veterans—a matter "*of Greek meeting Greek again.*"

Sherman had pushed down the West side of Rockyface Mountain and through Snake Creek Gap the day and night before in an effort to cut Johnston's communications and take him in the rear. But we had been doing some marching and digging, too, and when Sherman's columns four or five deep debouched from their positions—a long, heavily wooded ridge—into the narrow valley, on the East side of which we had constructed rifle pits, he found us ready to receive his gay and awe-inspiring columns, who moved in perfect step, with banners flying and bands playing, as though he expected to charm us.

The eagerness of our own men could scarcely be restrained until they had reached the point to which our orders had been given, seventy-five to eighty yards, when our lines opened almost simultaneously a deadly and murderous fire from both infantry and double-shotted artillery, that flesh and blood could not withstand. Retiring in disorder to their original position in the woods, they rallied and reformed, while their artillery was busy playing upon our batteries, from which they received no response whatever, a mystery at the time to many of us, but which we understood a little later on when they again moved down to the attack, to be met in the same manner with both infantry and artillery, and with similar results.

Three times during the morning and early afternoon were these attacks made upon our lines, with the same results. It was a veritable picnic for the Confederates and was the second time in the history of the war, up to this time, that we had presented such a glorious opportunity, protected as we were by earthworks, with clear and open ground in front. Had Sherman continued this business during the entire day (as we hoped he would) the campaign would have ended right here, as we had not called into requisition any of our reserve force. The principal part of the afternoon was spent by the artillery—after the infantry had gotten enough of it—on both sides pounding away at each other in a lively and entertaining fashion.

Some daring and courageous deeds were performed by the Federal officers and men on this occasion, the recollection of which is refreshing and exhilarating to the writer, but for want of time I shall be compelled to pass over. However, one instance, I will relate as being somewhat interesting to Kentuckians as showing the home spirit and natural feeling existing between them as Kentuckians, although now engaged in the deadly breach.

That night some of our boys of the Fourth Kentucky learned from inquiry of our "friends" in our front that we were confronting the Federal Fourth Kentucky (Colonel Tom Croxton), whereupon a bantering of epithets and compliments was at once begun and exchanged in a very amusing and interesting way. I listened to the colloquy with great interest and amusement, which was conducted on our side by Lieutenant Horace Watts, who was a noted wit and humourist. But I regret that I have forgotten the name of his interrogator, whom I recall, however, was from Vanceburg, Ky.

That night was spent in strengthening our works and preparing for the work of the morrow, which work we well knew was coming. When morning came the appearance of Old Sol was greeted with a signal from a battery immediately in our front, which had been stationed there during the night and protected by substantial and elaborate earthworks. The shots from this battery were directed against Hotchkiss' battalion of artillery, and which the Fourth Kentucky Infantry was supporting. The enemy's guns from every part of the line kept up a continuous fire throughout the entire day and was the greatest open field bombardment of the war.

We were much amused at the manner of firing of the battery in our front, which was done by bugle signal, the meaning of which our men soon learned, for a moment later our works would be pierced by their shells and when they exploded threw high in the air a cloud of dirt and smoke from the embankment that almost covered us up. At intervals of about every five or ten minutes the bugle's *"whe-whee-deedledee-dee"* told us of the crash that was coming and almost lifted our scalps and rendered some of us deaf for weeks. Had the day been an hour longer we would have been compelled to abandon our works, for the embankments were almost levelled and the trenches filled.

Two of Hotchkiss' guns were cut down and had to be abandoned, and but for the fact that they had been run back beyond the crest, not a splinter of them would have been left.

Our batteries did not fire a gun that day, having been ordered to withhold their fire in anticipation of another attack by the enemy's infantry. This day's work was a very clever ruse of Sherman's and demonstrated the cunning of that wily general, for while he was thus entertaining us with the main part of his army, especially his artillery, like the sly old fox that he was, he was planning our undoing by sending down the river to our rear Dodge's Corps to fall on our rear and cut our communications and intercept our retreat.

Had his plan been expedited by Dodge, as it might have been, it would surely have been "all day" with us poor devils of Confederates. It was certainly a "close shave," for which we were all very thankful. But we here on the 14th, enjoyed the "picnic" for which we Orphans paid most dearly on the 28th, at Dallas, and which I shall describe in another place. War, it seems from my experience and observation, may be described as a dreadful and costly game of "tit-for-tat."

The losses sustained by the Orphans in this engagement at Resaca were insignificant compared with that inflicted upon the enemy in their front. There is not a single recognisable object here save the ground where we fought, from the fact that we arrived here in the night and took our departure in the night. The narrow valley and the long extended ridge in its front and the spur occupied by Hotchkiss and the Fourth Kentucky, is all that I see to remind me of the two days of "pride, pomp and circumstance of glorious war." But how's this, we fighting behind entrenchments and the enemy in the open, four or five lines deep?

Our loss was 2,747, and his (Johnson's) 2,800. I fought offensively and he defensively, aided by earthwork parapets.—(General Sherman's statement.)

There must have been some bad shooting on this occasion—the advantages all on one side, but results so nearly even.

Today, May 16 (1912), marks the forty-eighth anniversary of this important event, and finds me on the ground. Here, as at other places previously mentioned and described, things came back to me and I see them being re-enacted. I was accompanied on this inspection by an old comrade (J. H. Norton), who lost an arm at Chancellorsville, and who has lived here in Resaca almost all his life and who was at home at the time, having been discharged on account of the loss of his arm, and who assisted in burying the dead, and he pooh-poohed Sherman's statement as to relative losses.

Another old comrade, who is a merchant in the town, told me that he had bought over a hundred thousand pounds of minnie balls picked up on the ground where the battle was fought, I saw a three-bushel box full in his store today. How many poor devils were killed by these would be impossible to tell. They have a neat little cemetery near the town, in which there are nine Kentuckians (Confederates) buried, some of whose names I have copied.

CHAPTER 10

Dallas

Here, as at Balaklava, "someone blundered," and while we have not had a Tennyson to immortalise the event, it is of more than ordinary interest to Kentuckians, especially those who participated in the bloody event. More because of the fearful slaughter and the mournful fact that it was the result of a failure to deliver orders at the proper time. The official report showed a loss of 51 *per cent*, a loss, considering the time actually engaged, unparalleled in the history of the war. To my mind it was the most desperate and disastrous of all the many engagements in which the Orphans took part during their four years of experience.

The actual time under fire did not in my judgment exceed thirty minutes. To describe accurately the position of the enemy at this distant day would be a difficult task, but when the reader is told that they occupied two parallel lines of entrenchments, from both of which he delivered simultaneously a destructive and murderous fire, that was so fatal that nothing but the protecting hand of an all-wise and merciful Providence could save. The first of these lines was a few yards below, and in front of the second, which ran along the summit of the ridge and enabled the second line to fire directly overhead without endangering the first.

Besides this double advantage, they were able to enfilade our line with their artillery from both extremes of their line. Smith's brigade, on our left, having received orders (which were also intended for us and which failed of delivery) to withhold the attack, enabled the enemy to deliver an oblique fire upon us from his infantry on the left, as well as from his two lines directly in front. At every step Kentucky was paying double toll with the lives of her noblest and best. To push forward meant certain and complete annihilation; to remain where we were some seventy-five or eighty yards in their front, meant the same, only a little slower death.

The order to "fall back" having been given, we were only too glad to attempt our escape from the death trap into which we had been ordered. Many of our wounded and all of our dead were left on the field or intervening space between the entrenched lines of the opposing forces. Several of the wounded crawled back after nightfall and in this way made their escape. The grounds in the rear of our works presented an appalling sight when I reached them with my burden on my back—Sergeant W. E. Knox, who had a broken leg. Nothing but a miracle saved us both from the murderous fire of the enemy. Here fell the gallant and polished Major Millett within ten paces of our entrenchment, he being the third major of the Fourth Regiment to be killed on the field.

Several incidents of a thrilling and miraculous character occurred on this field, as afterward related. Some of our wounded who approached nearest the enemy's works and fell into their hands were taken to the little town of Dallas, a mile or two distant, where they were found two days later, and left in a shamefully neglected condition. Among them was one of the most noble gentlemen and gallant soldiers it was ever my good fortune to know, Captain D. E. McKendrie of the Sixth Kentucky, and who died a few days later.

There were really only two brigades engaged in this encounter, the Orphan Brigade and Findlay's Florida Brigade. The burden of the encounter fell upon the Orphans, as shown by their greater loss. But here again was displayed that daring, regardless of consequences, which had been so often displayed by this little band of Kentuckians on so many fields from Fort Donaldson to this eventful day. I hope I shall not be accused of egotism for seeming to arrogate to myself and my fellow Kentuckians homers to which we are not entitled and of which all of her people may be justly proud. The loss of 51 *per cent* tells the story more graphically than anything I may say by way of compliment or eulogy.

The reader may wonder why this attack was ordered against a force so strongly and irresistibly posted. The answer is easy to the old veteran who knows the difficulty in ascertaining an enemy's position in a heavily timbered country like this, with trees and bushes in full leaf, and how great the danger from the ever-alert sharpshooter to the man attempting a reconnaissance. The object was to develop his strength at this point, the commander believing Sherman to be only feigning while he was carrying out other and ulterior plans. But so, it was, we paid dearly for the desired information.

I have reviewed every foot of this ground the second time, stopping here and there to pick up a minnie ball lodged in the enemy's works, fired at them by my dear old "Orphan" boys, and while thus engaged the familiar faces of many a noble comrade and in one or two instances school fellows' images passed before my mind in panorama that almost unnerved and dumfounded me. Studying coolly at this time the great advantage the enemy had in position and numbers, I am surprised that any of us escaped at all. I had no difficulty whatever in locating at once the position of both parties and the exact spot on which my regiment and company fought. Most of the Confederate lines have been partly and in some places completely obliterated by the plough, but hills and hollows are still there. The enemy's lines have been little disturbed and are mostly intact even at this distant day.

I must confess that I am wont to linger about this hallowed spot and my heart beats heavily when I think of the comrades and friends who died here and whose bodies I assisted in giving the last rude sepulchre. I turn away from it with tearful eyes and sorrowful heart.

CHAPTER 11

Atlanta—May, 1912

I am writing this from historic Atlanta, the "gateway of the South." How very different to the Atlanta I knew in the days gone by when her streets were filled with the tramp, tramp of marching armies, when her walls were rocked by the thunders of the cannon's mighty roar, when the rockets' "red glare gave proof through the night that our new flag was still there." Oh! what a wonderful change 'twixt now and then.

Lovely city now, quiet and mighty in her peaceful ways, may the God of war never again sound his bugle calls over her peaceful slumbers, and may she know the ways of war no more forever.

How very, very different to the Atlanta I saw in June, 1865, when on my way home from the South, returning disabled, discomfited, defeated. What darker picture could be imagined unless it be *Dante's Inferno,* than a city of destroyed homes with blackened walls and chimneys punctuating the fiendish spirit that prompted the ruin of its people and their homes. When General Sherman first gave expression to his oft-repeated apothegm he must have had in mind the ruin he had accomplished in the destruction of this fair city of the South. Certainly nothing but a fiendish spirit could have prompted it.

But two buildings of prominence were left—the Masonic Temple and a hotel. But her people are now enjoying the blessings of peace and prosperity, having risen, Phoenix-like, from her ashes.

I must now return to some of the incidents and events of the defence of Atlanta in which I was an humble participant. On the 9th of July, General Johnston's army crossed the Chattahoochee River on pontoons and the time until the 22nd, was employed by Johnston and Hood chiefly in marching and counter-marching to checkmate the movements of Sherman. A circumstance happened about this time that gave Sherman great pleasure (he says so) and correspondingly great sorrow and despondency to the Confederates, heretofore so successfully led by General Johnston, *viz*., the removal of Johnston and the substitution of Hood.

While Hood was a Kentuckian as well as we Orphans, and we priding in everything pertaining to the history of Kentucky, we had unbounded confidence in General Johnston. But once before had we felt such sadness and regret—when General Breckinridge was taken from us and sent to Virginia. This feeling was intensified by the belief that Bragg was responsible.

On the 20th, the Battle of Peach Tree Creek was fought and given a prominence in excess of the facts as the writer saw it; a straggling, haphazard kind of hide and seek affair, magnified into a battle. On the 22nd of July, was fought what is known in history as the Battle of Atlanta.

The night march of the 21st, from our place in the line of defence on the left and to the extreme right near Decatur, where this battle was fought, was the most trying, with one exception, the writer remembers to have ever experienced, occupying the entire night in dust ankle deep, without a drop of water or an hour's rest. It is remembered to this day with a distinctness that makes me fairly shudder.

When morning came, we looked like the imaginary Adam "of the earth earthy," so completely were we encased in dust. But for the nerve stimulus that imminent and great danger gives a man on the eve of a great battle, I don't think I could have rendered much service, on this occasion, after such exhaustion and suffering from thirst. In fact were it not an indispensable part of my plan I should have little to say about this whole affair, for it was to me the most ill-conceived and unsatisfactory executed plan of battle of the whole war in which I participated.

There were difficulties to overcome that might easily have been avoided had the proper engineering skill been employed in time and the necessary reconnaissance been made. So far as results accomplished were concerned, it was barren and fruitless. Especially was this the case on the extreme right, where Bates' division fought and where the Orphans took part. Not that any man or body of men proved recreant, but there was a lack of understanding and cooperation of movement, coupled with almost insurmountable obstacles that might have been avoided. For instance, the Kentucky Brigade was compelled to struggle through the mire of a slough and millpond filled with logs, stumps, brush and what-not in water and mire knee-deep, the men in many instances being compelled to extricate their comrades by pulling them onto logs and other footings before we could pass the obstruction.

This so deranged our battle alignment that in the press and excitement of the moment, caused by the enemy firing at this critical moment, we were never able to correct it and present a solid front. Out of dust ankle deep into water and mire knee-deep was too much for the nerves and patience of the strongest man and most patient Christian. And then, to be finally pitched in one disordered and confused mass against a well disciplined and strongly posted line of veterans, behind earthworks, was too much for the best soldiers of the times. And yet with the proper use of artillery at the right time and place, we might have accomplished more decisive results.

This affair was the more lamentable to the Orphans because of the loss of quite a number of our best officers and men without any tangible results. The whole thing was disappointing and to me really disgusting. Hood at Atlanta, like Bragg at Murfreesboro, might profitably have spent more time with his engineers in examining and surveying the ground on which he expected to fight. General Johnson was doubtless better posted. But the final result would have been the same; Atlanta was doomed—by Sherman's force of three to one. After summing up results and exchanging regrets and expressing sorrow for the loss of comrades, we returned to our original places in the lines of defence to await the next scene in the grand drama.

This came on August 6th, at Utoy Creek on the Sandtown road leading Southwest from Atlanta. The Orphan Brigade and Tyler's Tennessee Brigade had been pushed forward on a kind of salient to the left and front of the main line and touching the little stream known as Utoy Creek. Here occurred the battle known by the above name. I here recognise more distinctly than any other place, so far visited, the general appearance of the ground and especially the falls of the little creek at which on the day previous to the battle I enjoyed the only refreshing bath for several days. It is quite an interesting place to the writer.

I here witnessed on the morning of the battle the capture of Lieut. Isham Dudley, in command of the videttes, together with some half dozen men of the Orphan Brigade, they having been completely surprised just at daybreak by a sudden and unexpected rush of the enemy.

The writer had the honour to command the skirmish line covering the Confederate position and had a fine opportunity to witness the charge of the two Federal brigades, which were composed chiefly of East Tennesseans, as they swept past the right of our skirmish line, they doubtless not knowing that they were about to encounter breastworks of a formidable character, receiving at the same time a scathing flank fire from the Fourth Kentucky and the skirmish line above alluded to. But they were plucky fellows and charged to within a few yards of our works, paying dearly for their courage and temerity. In this affair we were attacked by a force somewhat superior in numbers, but the advantage that our breastworks afforded us made the victory easily won. I here quote the order of General S. D. Lee, commanding corps, congratulating them and incidentally complimenting the defenders.

> The lieutenant general commanding takes pleasure in announcing to the officers and men of this corps the splendid conduct of a portion of Bates' Division, particularly Tyler's Brigade and the Second and Fourth Kentucky regiments of Lewis' Brigade, in sustaining and repulsing on yesterday afternoon three assaults of the enemy in which his loss in killed, wounded and prisoners was from eight hundred to a thousand men, with three stands of colours, three or four hundred small arms and all of his entrenching tools. Soldiers who fight with the coolness and determination that these men did will always be victorious over any reasonable number.

In this engagement we lost only about eighteen men all told, while the enemy's loss in killed alone was 160. I walked over the ground ten minutes after it occurred and found the crest of the hill covered with the dead and wounded, swords, guns, cartridge boxes and other paraphernalia of war.

I found here the thing I need and coveted most of all at this time, a fine black *sombrero*, which furnished me ample protection thereafter from the intense rays of the August sun. I "swapped" my spoon-bill cap with the fellow who had worn this hat, to which he, of course, raised no objection. Others provided themselves in like manner, which was entirely legitimate, of course, the original owners having no further use for such things. But a flanking column that night, as usual, compelled us to abandon the position of our recent victory and we retired to our original position in the circle of entrenchments.

I have this day, May 13, 1912, carefully and studiously reviewed the very spot on which those 160 men lay dead, and I feel safe in saying that it is not larger than one-half a city block. They were met square in front and were fired on from both flanks, and had they attempted to remain there as much as one hour there would not have been a man of them left on his feet. It was a death trap similar to the one into which we Orphans fell at Dallas. I could hardly control my emotions when viewing this place, and my mind was almost overwhelmed as I walked along on top of these still distinct and undisturbed parapets, stopping now and then to pick up a "Yankee bullet" lodged in them, or a small stone that had been thrown out by the Confederates. The surroundings here are perfectly familiar to me, notwithstanding opinions of friends at home to the contrary. So interesting is this spot that I have made the second visit to it.

Here the time from August 7 to 29, 1864, was spent in listening to the music of the rifle and the cannon and an occasional sweet, faint and harmonious symphony from the enemy's brass bands as they played, seemingly for our entertainment, "The Star Spangled Banner," "Hail Columbia," "Yankee Doodle" and, to taunt us, "Dixie." At night they would vary the entertainment by sending up innumerable rockets, which some of the men interpreted to mean the arrival of a new command or shift of position, but to most of us it was "Greek and Hebrew."

But this condition was not to last; Sherman's definition of war was in him and must come out. On the 29th we packed our knapsacks and bidding goodbye to the Atlanta of the day, soon to be no more, we again turned Southward to meet the flanking columns of Sherman at Jonesboro, with a description of which I shall close these recollections.

Before leaving this dear old city, I must take one more last look at her steeples, her walls and her streets, shake the hand of friends in the last farewell grasp and say goodbye forever.

I find Atlanta so wonderfully changed, commercially, assuming metropolitan airs and wearing her honours so gracefully that I dare not attempt a description of her present status. Besides, these things are well known now by the whole American people. Still I find myself comparing her (in mind) with what she was "before and during the war."

The fact that I am now looking upon her for the last time, and the further fact that she contains many warm and true friends whom I shall never see again, causes a feeling of sadness I wish I could resist.

But I break camp and take up my line of march for Jonesboro.

But before I leave, I must tender my thanks to my young friend from Bourbon, W. H. Letton (who is now a prosperous business man here), for many favours and courtesies so cheerfully extended me. It were cruel to allow him to spend with me so much of his time from his lovely little Georgia bride, so recently taken to himself. But this is Kentucky, you know, and he inherits it. I am also indebted to my old comrades, J. W. McWilliams of the Forty-Second Georgia; J. M. Mills of the Soldiers' Home, and C. L. Ingram of Fort McPherson; ex-Sheriff Barnes, Major Jones of the Seventeenth Infantry at the fort (McPherson), and last, though not least by any means, Mrs. Jones of the city at whose boarding house I was a guest.

Chapter 12

Jonesboro

I begin here the last inspection and reminiscence, on my return trip from attending the recent Confederate reunion at Macon, May, 1912, and while I distrust my ability to do the theme proper justice, I am tempted to undertake the task through the love of the brave "old boys" who still survive and the memory of several hundred noble young Kentuckians whose life blood consecrates the soil of Georgia on every field from Chattanooga to Jonesboro.

My mind becomes a whirlpool of recollections as I stand here and "view the landscape o'er" and contemplate the horrible scenes enacted here forty-eight years ago, and in which the Confederacy was surely and rapidly expiring in the throes of dissolution.

It is not my purpose or aim to controvert in any instance the descriptions and recitals of the historians, but merely as a pastime to revert to some of my personal experiences and recollections. Nor shall I attempt to enlarge upon or embellish the history of that glorious little band of Kentuckians known as the "Orphan Brigade." That has been done by others, done by such men as Prof. N. S. Shaler, Gens. Joseph E. Johnson, W. J. Hardee, Stephen D. Lee, Ed. Porter Thompson and many others, able and eloquent men, historians and statesmen, and in whose history Kentuckians of all beliefs must ever rejoice as one of the brightest and most interesting pages in her history. And why not, since they represented so many of the noblest and best young men of the state and were led by such men as Breckinridge, Hanson, Helm, Lewis, Monroe and others whose names are a synonym of glory and greatness.

When we arrived here (Jonesboro) in the great campaign there were many absent—not without leave, thank God, but with honour, whose brows had been crowned with everlasting wreaths of honour—in death "on Fame's eternal camping ground." When the roll was

The Battle of Jonesboro, Georgia, Sept. 1st, 1864

called no response came from many. Hanson, Helm, Hewitt, Graves, Rogers, Dedman, Madeira, Daniel, McKendrie, Millett, Williams, Innis, Bramblett, Bell and three thousand others failed to answer. But as the "blood of martyrs is the seed of the church," so the sacrifice of these Kentuckians is a diadem in the wreath that encircles her history.

But now I stand on this historic spot where forty-eight years ago (as at 1912), the unequal, almost suicidal conflict raged with destruction and fury, and see, in my mind's eye, the raging conflict and hear the cannon's mighty roar, the screaming shot and shell and the ping and whistle of the deadly minnie, the shouts and yells of the combatants as they grapple in the deadly conflict. Here I experienced the pangs of a painful wound from a minnie ball, while assisting a dear friend (Lieutenant Neal), being in the throes of death, both he and the man on my left falling simultaneously. How well I remember the look of anguish upon his noble countenance as he held up both hands, imploring my assistance. Brave, noble fellow and Christian gentleman, I trust and believe his soul rests in peace among the angels.

Imagine my grief on reaching the ambulance (assisted by comrades) to find my bosom friend (and by many said to be my double), Ensign Robert H. Lindsay of Scott County, in the ambulance, he having received a mortal wound from which he died that night while lying upon the same blanket with myself. The reader can imagine my feelings when the dawn of morning came and I threw back the blanket that covered us and beheld his noble countenance cold in death, with the fixed glare of the eyes that told me that my beloved comrade and friend had passed to the realms of eternal glory.

Poor Bob! I tried in vain, while on the way to the field hospital, to extort a parting message, a last farewell to mother and family, but the messenger of death held him in his grasp and refused compliance with this last request of his friend who loved him as a brother. A circumstance coincident with his death was the fact that we prepared and ate our dinners together that day, meantime talking over the probable results of the approaching battle and making certain requests of each other in the event that one or the other should fall. Hence my anxiety to hear a last farewell from his dying lips.

Memory takes me back over the intervening years and I am tempted to exclaim:

Sing thou music of the spheres
The song of the weeping pines

As the days and years go by,
But let me, Oh! let me not forget,
The dear friend who 'neath them lies.

I have always thought this a singular circumstance, that the three friends—boon companions—holding the same rank, should be stricken down almost at the same moment—that "two should be taken and the one left," but such are the vicissitudes of war.

I can recognise only two landmarks of this historic spot and its surroundings—the old stone depot and the prominent knoll, occupied by the enemy's skirmishers on the morning of the battle, (August 31st), and which Lieut. Heck Burden, the commander of that gang of army sleuths, that Sherman and his officers admitted they dreaded—known as the Kentucky sharpshooters—and myself, in a spirit of daring, approached within easy rifle range, by means of a deep gully, and which terminated in one less Federal officer reporting to his commander.

I have looked upon this particular spot with no little concern, for it was near this my two dear friends just noted fell, and where I also received my quietus—as a reward, perhaps, for my daring of the morning. This circumstance (my wounding) precludes the mention from personal experience a description of the second day's fight and in which the Orphans sustained the loss of a number of men and officers and resulted in the capture of the greater part of the survivors, Sherman's overwhelming numbers enabling him to outflank and overpower the left of the Confederate line. But they were held as prisoners but a short time and were exchanged and returned to service almost immediately.

Here, as in other instances, the enemy outnumbered us three to one and enabled them to envelop our flanks more readily than in previous engagements, the country being without the natural barriers and obstructions that had previously favoured us in the mountain section of the country through which we had passed. Here at Jonesboro ended my service to the Confederacy and my experience as a soldier in the field.

The next six months, which brought the war to a close, were spent by me in hospitals, which also came near bringing my earthly career to a close. But, thank God, I am still here and now engaged in reviewing our movements of the past. And I shall be happy if what I may have written should fall under the eye of some old comrade or friend and afford him pleasure or food for contemplation.

General History of the Orphan Brigade

Confederate flag

Contents

Introductory Remarks	109
Organisation of the First Kentucky Brigade	120
The Second Kentucky and Graves's Battery	143
Battle of Shiloh	159
Siege of Vicksburgh	196
The Battle of Baton Rouge	211
Return to Murfreesboro'	236
Battle of Stone River	261
Battle of Chickamauga	301
Battle of Mission Ridge	327
The Army in Winter Quarters at Dalton	334
The Dalton-Atlanta Campaign,	343
May 5th to September 8th, 1864	343
The Dalton-Atlanta Campaign, (Continued)	359
The Brigade, As Mounted Infantry, In Georgia and South Carolina	390

To the
Sons and Daughters of the Confederacy
This Book is Dedicated.

Thousands of the men whose names and deeds it records have heard "the soldier's last tattoo," and it cannot be long before their few surviving comrades will have "passed over the river" to rest with them.

It devolves upon their children to see that the motives which identified them with the South in the Great Conflict are not misunderstood, and that their conduct during the four bloody years in which they added a brilliant chapter to others which Kentucky had written in American history shall not pass from the memory of man.

The principles for which they suffered and fought, and so many of them died, were

The Inalienable Right of a People to Choose Their Own Form of Government,

And

The Sacredness of Constitutional Guarantees.

Though the Confederacy failed of establishment these still live and must live if human liberty is to endure on this continent. The children of the Confederate soldier can best illustrate the soldier's virtues by maintaining his principles in peace, and defending them in war if need be, for the great country to which only their allegiance is now due.

Ed Porter Thompson.

MONUMENT TO MAJ.-GEN. JOHN C. BRECKINRIDGE,
Lexington.

CHAPTER 1

Introductory Remarks

Some months prior to the close of the war I conceived the design of preparing, at some future time, a history of the Orphan Brigade. In November, 1864, the plan of the work was set out in writing, with a view to interesting others, and of obtaining such muster-rolls and other papers as could be furnished while the command was still in the field, and at the close. This letter or circular was lost before the end came, but I recall a sentence:

> However this war may terminate, if a man can truthfully claim to have been a worthy member of the Kentucky Brigade, he will have a kind of title of nobility.

I was young and ardent, and of course such an expression was somewhat extravagant, even when received only as it was intended—to convey, by a figure, the simple idea that such a man would be distinguished among the thousands of surviving soldiers and receive honourable recognition from his fellow-citizens. The circumstance is worthy of note as indicating that the fame of this body of Kentucky soldiers did not depend upon factitious circumstances, which assume undue proportions when viewed through the haze of time, nor is it at all attributable to that glamour to which the poet refers when he declares that "*distance lends enchantment to the view.*"

On the contrary they were proof against that insidious depreciation which results from long and familiar association with men of narrow limitations and unfavourable characteriztics, to which reference is made by the trite maxim, "*Familiarity breeds contempt.*" The writer had from the first borne a humble part with those of whom he spoke, having a place with them till after Shiloh, first as a private in the ranks, then as a non-commissioned officer; afterward holding line and staff commissions; had noted their conduct in all the multifarious conditions under which a faithful soldiery, through years of unequal conflict and peculiar trials, find themselves; and after all had not merely a pride in his corps in the abstract, but an admiration for those composing it, which gave birth to the idea that no history of the command would be adequate that did not take cognisance of all the individuals whose conduct helped to make the fame of the organisation, and which is carried out in that department of the present work entitled, *Brief History of Individuals, Field and Staff, Rank and File.*

Coarse, ill-fitting, and ragged clothes, tattered shoes, and battered hats, ugly and cheerless surroundings, could not seriously depress and could not at all disguise the intrepid spirits who were as ready in the almost hopeless days of 1865, to spring to action at a word as they were in the first flush of their martial experience, when they had no thought but that battle meant victory, and victory meant the establishing of a government founded indeed and in truth upon the consent of the governed.

A student of history, he had considered the conduct of famous soldiery, ancient and modern; and with what light he had, he could not see that this body of young Kentuckians suffered at any point by comparison. He was not without a certain warm admiration of the Tenth Legion of the Roman Army and of Bonaparte's Old Guard; but after all, in contemplating them, he saw rather Caesar, the great Imperator, and Bonaparte, the fiery Corsican, who moulded them and made them famous; in contemplating the Orphan Brigade we see the men who made their own fame.

True, they were proud of their commanders, and were influenced by them; were quickly and intelligently responsive to their efforts to develop soldierly qualities and promote efficiency; but it was rather that they regarded these commanders as of them, not over them; rather as gallant and capable fellow-countrymen on whom they could rely, and whom they could proudly follow, than as martinets and masters who held their places only by virtue of commissions from the War Office. If Buckner or Breckinridge or Preston, Hanson or Helm or Lewis, had proved in any sense incapable or craven, they would not have sunk below themselves on that account, but would have driven him from his place by manifest contempt.

It is well to note here the quality of these soldiers as representatives of their people. It is probable that there was never any other organisation of equal number that had so many bright and well-educated men.

They were in the main of old pioneer stock, and they were proud and self-respecting. They had due regard to family honour, and a strong trait was their State pride. To use the words of Dr. Holmes' biographer, they had that "noble clannishness which is one of the safeguards of social morality," and, it may be added, of the fair fame of a commonwealth.

Indeed, it was the name, Kentuckian, which touched them to the quick, and gave them a feeling of responsibility in guarding it from reproach. It made them patient under privation and steady under unusual trial. It gave them fortitude under suffering and fierceness in fight. If this feeling seems to have been somewhat overweening, and to have manifested itself at times in a way to make them appear to "think better of themselves than they should," it must be observed that it partook not in the slightest degree of mere personal vanity. This latter characteriztic is incompatible with a just and manly pride of either family or State.

It should be recorded, too, that they represented Kentucky as a whole and not any particular section of it, not any particular class of its citizens. They came together from eighty-three counties, from homes dotting the State from the Big Sandy to the Mississippi; from the Ohio to the Tennessee line, from the mountains, the bluegrass regions and the western plains; from city and hamlet and country places; from factories and shops, mines and farms; from schools, commercial houses and the offices of professional men.

But the fact that the brigade held a remarkable place in an army of much-enduring and splendid fighting men does not rest upon what might otherwise appear the too partial estimate of an admiring comrade; but the evidence of others, contemporaneous and subsequent, not only justifies his conclusions, but gives them increased significance. Shortly after the battle of Shiloh, Judge Walker, of New Orleans, who was on the field during the engagement, published an account of it, which was circulated in pamphlet form, and in which he mentioned several of the Kentucky officers by name, and spoke of the conduct of the brigade in terms of the highest praise.

In drill and discipline, it was acknowledged to have no peer in the Army of Tennessee, after the trial-drill, May, 1863, with the Louisiana Brigade, which had set up a claim to superior training and skill in manoeuvre.

After a review at Dalton, January 30, 1864, Major-General Hindman, then commanding Hardee's Corps, issued a complimentary order, in which he said:

It is announced with gratification that the commanding general was much pleased with the appearance and bearing of the troops of this corps on review today. Without detracting from the praise due to all, the major-general deems it but just to mention the Kentucky Brigade as especially entitled to commendation for soldierly appearance, steadiness of marching, and an almost perfect accuracy in every detail.

General Joseph E. Johnston once told a prominent Confederate officer that there was "no better infantry in the world than the Kentucky Brigade." In the winter of 1863-64, when General Breckinridge was ordered to Virginia, he applied to General Johnston for permission to carry the brigade with him, under promise from President Davis that a brigade of other troops should be furnished as an equivalent. Johnston replied:

> The President has no equivalent for it. It is the best brigade in the Confederate Army.

It is said that he made substantially the same remark at the Continental Hotel, in Philadelphia, sometime in the winter of 1865-66. While he was United States Railroad Commissioner, Judge William L. Jett, of Frankfort, called to see him in Washington one day, and incidentally referred to having seen the above statements. "Yes," he replied, "the Kentucky Brigade was the finest body of soldiers I ever saw." Judge Emory Speer, the eminent Georgia statesman and jurist, writes recently to Capt. J. T. Gaines, in whose company he served for some time:

> I am glad to testify that our old general, Joseph E. Johnston, told me, when we were Congressmen together, that the Orphan Brigade was the finest body of men and soldiers he ever saw in any army anywhere.

Coming from a trained West Pointer, an officer of the old United States Army, a veteran of two wars, and a citizen of another State, these expressions must be regarded as of extraordinary significance.

When the dismounted detachment moved through Columbia, South Carolina, April, 1865, one of the men inquired of a citizen: "Did the mounted Kentuckians pass through here?"

"Yes," he replied; "and," said another, standing by, "they were the only *gentlemen* who have passed through here since the war began."

A medical officer of White's Battery was asked, in the same city, whether a certain command (naming it), was fighting below Camden. "No—no," he replied, "they never stay at one place long enough to get into a fight."

"Where was Lewis?"

"Oh," said he, "Lewis was there. "It is *his* men who are doing the fighting, and they'll stick to it as long as they can find a foe to shoot at!"

About this time, too, Major-General Young gave free expression to his admiration, and declared that an army of such officers and men, with adequate means, could bid defiance to the world.

And one of the prominent Southern journals, referring to General Hood's defeat at Nashville, had this remark:

> A correspondent of one of our exchanges writes of the unfortunate disaster at Nashville, and incidentally pays the highest compliment to Lewis' brigade, then absent, which was *never known to falter*.

The *Mobile Advertiser and Register*, speaking of a certain point of Hood's defence, on the same occasion, remarks:

> Troops should have been placed at that point of whom not the slightest doubt existed. Had the Kentucky Brigade been there, all would have been safe.

It is well authenticated, also, that the United States Army knew them; and as the veteran soldiers of every civilised nation admire those most who oppose them most manfully, they respected them highly.

When a large part of the brigade was captured at Jonesboro, General Jefferson C. Davis, by whose division they were made prisoners, expressed his admiration of them, and assured them that they should be treated as gentlemen; and no insult was offered by the soldiers, nor was the then common custom of depriving prisoners of watches and other private property resorted to by anyone. On the contrary, while expressing their joy at having captured them, they incidentally extolled them in no measured terms.

The foregoing are a few of the many expressions that were heard from Donelson and Shiloh to Camden. It is unnecessary to swell the number.

Something of the interest which gathered around the command was no doubt due to the singular position they occupied. Almost the sole representatives in the Confederate infantry of a State renowned of old for the gallantry of her sons, displayed on almost every field since the Revolution; completely isolated from home, and for the time in direct antagonism to the authority of their Commonwealth, without the comforts and encouragements that others enjoyed—the soldierly qualities exhibited in battling so manfully, suffering so patiently, bearing themselves so loftily under all, were such as would have attracted the attention of the country under any circumstances, and would seem to deserve special notice at the hands of the historian.

In physical development and powers of endurance their superiority was manifest. Official tables of measurement taken during the war show that among from three to four millions of volunteers from all parts of the Union, natives and foreigners, those born and reared in Kentucky exceeded all others except Tennesseans in average height, weight, size of head, circumference of chest, and ratio of weight to stature. Two peculiar instances of their hardihood are given:

During the first siege of Vicksburg, when they were encamped about the city for five weeks succeeding June 28, 1862, and doing duty along the river under very unusual conditions (to them)—poor rations, bad water, an enervating climate, and miasmatic influence—the mortality among them, as shown by surgeons' reports, was less than that of troops whose homes were in the Southern States. On the march from Jackson to Big Black beginning July 1, 1863, and the return, many men belonging to the Southern and South-eastern States fell out, and some died from the effects of the intense heat and fatigue, while the Kentuckians withstood all and were on hand for duty when operations were resumed at Jackson.

Their indomitable resolution and constancy were well exemplified by their action at Greene's Cut, Ga., February 11, 1865. No one at all conversant with the history of those times needs to be reminded of the long and arduous service which they had performed, the trials to which they had been subjected, the manifold disappointments and discouragements which they had experienced from the beginning, now extending well into the fourth year. Apparently, they had had enough to break the spirits of brave and true men. There was disaffection among the people for whom they were fighting; newspapers were basely advising submission—crying for peace on any terms—and the governor of the great State of Georgia was rated among the most captious of the critics who had long called in question the policy of the Confederate Government, and fomented opposition.

It was a sorry spectacle to Kentuckians; and they denounced the spirit that prompted such exhibitions of disloyalty to a Government which they had helped to create, and which Kentuckians were sacrificing much and risking all in trying to establish.

The officers and men assembled on the day alluded to and passed resolutions condemning in strong terms all that tended to encourage defection, deplete the ranks of the soldiery, withhold from the Government aid and comfort, and encourage the enemy. Every regiment was represented by officers and men on the committee that drafted the resolutions, while field and staff, rank and file composed the meeting that passed them without a dissenting voice. Our services, our sacrifices, they said substantially; give us the right to speak; we accept no excuse for relaxing effort to conquer a peace and establish independence; we are exiles from our homes and those who are nearest and dearest to us, but we are not willing to return upon terms now proposed; we believe the minie-rifle is our best peace commissioner; we suggest that disloyal editors be placed beside true men in the ranks, where they can be taught, with Enfields in their hands, how a government should be supported; we reassert our devotion, and we send this our greeting to General Robert E. Lee, to be read to the noble army of North Virginia, as our assurance that we will stand shoulder to shoulder with them, as it were, in this war of right and justice.

These resolutions were published in the *Atlanta Constitution* and in Virginia, and whether their effect to stay the rising tide of disloyalty and dismay was much or little, Kentuckians were put on record as being ready to stand to their guns as long as a Confederate flag floated over the capitol at Richmond. It was the only time during the war that they stopped to substitute resolutions for rifle-shots, and these were not aimed at the common enemy, but at the dangerous malcontents in the South.

Let us next advert to conclusions reached by a scholarly gentleman and popular writer, who was a Union man, and whose prejudices and affiliations, therefore, did not predispose him to judge too favourably. Professor N. S. Shaler, in the course of his able ethnological studies, in Scribner's (1890), entitled, *Nature and Man in America*, gives the following remarkable estimate of these men, based upon statements and statistics relating to the troops of the two opposing armies:

> Last of all, we have the test afforded by the trials of the struggle between North and South. War has ever been the rudest and the most effective gauge of certain important qualities. The actual advance to which living beings have attained has been

in large part determined by the measure of resistance which creatures have been enabled to make against adverse circumstances, not the passive inertia of inanimate things, but the active and long-continued contest in which all the latent powers are applied in determined action. The military struggles of men are but an advanced and complicated form of the immemorial rivalry of lower creatures, out of which, through infinite pain, infinite good has been won. There is no more searching test of the moral and physical development of a people than that which is afforded by a great and long-continued civil war. That such a strife affords a measure of the physical power which is in the people of maintaining determinations is manifest. The contact of armies in the field gives, moreover, an excellent measure as to the moral state of the people. Nothing so tests the firmness with which the motives of sympathy, of justice, are rooted in men, as the temptations which campaigns expose them to.

It is hard, in our ordinary, well-regulated societies, to ascertain how far men are held to right by the machinery of the law, how far their relations to their fellows are fixed by their own motives. The ratio of compulsion to spontaneous motives becomes evident when the men of the State are marshalled into armies. This test was made thorough-going by the circumstances of our civil war. In the first place the combatants fought for more ideal issues than men commonly do. It was not for the love of chieftains, or for conquest, but for theories of institutions, of plans for States, that they contended. No war was ever so humanely conducted as this. There were grievous things about it; all war is a succession of griefs; but the conduct of the armies in the field was more humane than in any other similar campaigns which the world has known. The interest of women and children was almost invariably considered.

The soldiers born upon the soil generally carried the civic sense, the order of peaceful society, with them in march and battle. Good-nature and sympathy were written on their banners. We have but to compare the struggles of the French and Spaniards in Florida, or the wars between the American colonies of the British and French, to see how humanised our armies were under circumstances, which, in other lands and times, have awakened the devil in men. The issue of the combat, the perfect accord and loving humour which now mark the men who met on battlefields, shows this in the clearest possible manner. I take it to be plain that the rebellion proves our people to have lost nothing in the moral gains which the race won in the Old World. If we compare the issue of the contest with the chronic conditions of dispute between Great Britain and Ireland, I think we may claim that we have gained in the moral qualities which appear in the conduct of public affairs.

The conduct of our armies in the field shows clearly that the combination of physical vigour and moral earnestness which make a good soldier exists in unsurpassed measure in the man whose ancestors dwelt long upon the American soil.

Some years ago, I sought carefully to find a body of troops whose ancestors had been for many generations upon our soil, and whose ranks were essentially unmixed with foreigners, or those whose forefathers had been but a short time upon this continent. It proved difficult to find in the Northern Armies any command which served the needs of the inquiry which I desired to make. It seemed necessary to consider a force of at least five thousand men in order to avoid the risks which would come from imperfect data. In our Federal Army it was the custom to put in the same brigade regiments from different districts, thus commingling commands of pure American blood with those that had a considerable percentage of foreigners, or men of foreign parents.

I found in my limited inquiry but one command that satisfied the needs of this investigation, and this was the First Brigade of Kentucky troops in the rebel army. In the beginning of the war this brigade was recruited mostly in the slave-holding district of Kentucky, its ranks being filled mainly with farmers' sons. It is possible to trace the origin of the men in this command with sufficient exactitude by the inspection of the muster rolls. Almost every name upon them belongs to well-known families of English stock, mainly derived from Virginia. It is possible, in a similar way, to prove that, with few, unimportant exceptions, these soldiers were of ancient American lineage. Speaking generally, we may say that their blood had been traced upon the soil for a century and a half; that is, they were about five generations removed from the parent country.

When first recruited, this brigade contained about five thousand men. From the beginning it proved as trustworthy a body of infantry as ever marched or stood in line of battle. Its military record is too long, too varied, to be even summarized here. I will note only one hundred and twenty days of its history in the closing stages of its service. On May 7, 1864, this brigade, then in the army of General Joseph Johnston, marched out of Dalton 1,140 strong, at the beginning of the great retreat upon Atlanta before the army of Sherman. In the subsequent hundred and twenty days, or until September 3rd, the brigade was almost continuously in action or on the march. In this period the men of the command received 1,860 death or hospital wounds, the dead counted as wounds, and but one wound being counted for each visitation of the hospital. At the end of this time there were less than fifty men who had not been wounded during the hundred and twenty days. There were 240 men left for duty, and less than ten men deserted.

A search into the history of warlike exploits has failed to show me any endurance to the worst trials of war surpassing this. We must remember that the men of this command were at each stage of their retreat going farther from their firesides. It is easy for men to bear great trials under circumstances of victory. Soldiers of ordinary goodness will stand several defeats, but to endure the despair which such adverse conditions bring for more than a hundred days demands a moral and physical patience, which, so far as I have learned, has never been excelled in any army.

From Professor Shaler's unqualified use of the term rebel and rebellion the men whom he otherwise characterizes with such dispassionate judgment must dissent; and they can but wonder that a mind so philosophical and candid accepts a phraseology which the historians of the future (and not distant future) will discard; but his testimony is the manly and striking tribute of an honourable adversary to an organisation of Kentuckians whose fame is now the joint heritage of all her citizens.

In his article in the May (1896) *Century Magazine*, "Are Nervous Diseases Increasing?" Dr. Philip Coombs Knapp says:

Up to the period of the civil war the American was denounced as physically degenerate, inferior in bulk, strength and endurance to his English cousin. This war put an end to such talk. No armies ever endured more than ours in the field; no people endured more than those who stayed behind, waiting and helping. The record of the First Kentucky Brigade (here he recapitulates Shaler's estimate and adds) has never been surpassed. These men were of the purest American stock.

Different accounts have been given as to how the command acquired the designation of Orphan Brigade. Its attitude toward its native State—expatriated by reason of identification with a cause which Kentucky had not formally approved; its complete isolation from its people; its having been time and again deprived of its commander by transfer to other service, or death in battle—these, all and singular, may have suggested the name, which soon fixed itself in the popular mind, and has come to be the real one by which it will be known in history.

That its record should be carefully written for the information of the present generation, and for transmission to posterity, is not a matter of mere personal concern to its survivors and a just tribute to the memory of its dead; it concerns the State. If Gladstone's dictum, that "*no greater calamity can happen to a people than to break utterly with its past,*" is true in general, it is especially true of any episode of that past in which the people acquired enlarged title to distinction, and in which lessons were taught which should enter into its life and mould its future.

CHAPTER 2

Organisation of the First Kentucky Brigade

The eagerness with which the people of Kentucky, in common with other slave States, looked forward to the inauguration of Mr. Lincoln, and a consequent authoritative declaration of his policy, was proportioned to the momentous character of the crisis. As events of a startling nature crowded upon each other, and a thousand rumours were borne to the public ear respecting the evident designs of the President-elect, and the ill-concealed disposition on the part of the Republicans to resort to force, and compel the seceded States into submission to whatever course the government should choose to pursue, the interest deepened into anxiety, at last into a feverish, painful suspense, which, contrary to hopes which had been entertained, was in nowise relieved, but rather intensified by the circumstances immediately connected with the journey of Mr. Lincoln to Washington, and the unusual character of the proceedings on the day of his induction into office.

The Inaugural Address itself, so far from removing the suspense, proved rather a means to increase the doubt and bewilderment of the people, insomuch as it was like the famous shield which drew the contending knights to battle—each party interpreted it from his own point of view, and contention waxed hot, and uncertainty grew almost to madness before the guns of Charleston harbour dispelled the mental haze, and effectually opened the eyes of men to the astounding fact that one of the mighty scourges of heaven had fallen upon the American people—that war, gigantic, unrelenting, had displayed his "wrinkled front" once more upon the hitherto happy continent.

"The mutual animosity of separate countries at war with each other," says the most pleasing of modern historians, "is languid when compared with the animosity of nations which, morally separated, are yet locally intermingled." Though the people of the United States were regarded as one people, they were divided among themselves—they differed in local institutions and prejudices—were "morally separated" to such an extent as to make them as hostile as though they were two nations "intermingled;" and passions, long pent up, now burst forth with a power that threatened to sweep away all political and civil landmarks, and plunge the country into anarchy and consequent destruction.

The different views entertained by the people of Kentucky among themselves, in a time of so great excitement, when moderation was forgotten, and the denunciatory epithets of "abolitionist," "submissionist," and "traitor," were bandied about on all occasions, naturally engendered deadly feuds within her own borders, that derived an additional intensity from the fact already adverted to, that internecine broils are characterized by more than the wonted force of those that exist between people who naturally consider themselves foreign, and therefore not under the same obligations of neighbourhood and kindly office. When hostilities had actually begun, and war was no longer a vaguely looked-for evil, but a present and dreadful certainty, the restraints that had hitherto operated to prevent lawlessness and outrage were measurably removed, and the opposing parties began to assume more perfectly defined and antagonistic shape.

The machinery of civil government, however, went on; and the uncertain position of the State itself had the effect of preventing violent outbreak and frightful intestine hostilities. Both parties clung to the hope that the commonwealth would adopt some authoritative policy in perfect accordance with its own wishes, thus giving one the legal right, as well as the power, to drive the other from the country, until that measure of delay, wearing the face of a compromise, neutrality, was agreed upon. Nothing was now left to them, apparently, but individual action; and while the State authorities were busy with governmental schemes, the determined spirits of both parties began to prepare for legitimate war by ranging themselves under their respective banners, and resorting to camps of instruction and drill. The more aged and thoughtful deplored the unhappy strife, and to such the words of the repentant Otho came home with peculiar force:

Our dispute is with each other; and whatever party prevails, whether we conquer or are conquered, our country must suffer. Under the victor's joy she bleeds.

But by far the greater part were lost to reason, and took counsel of passion alone. Some of the more impetuous of the Southern party organised themselves into companies, and in May left the State and repaired to Virginia, where they were identified with the army of General Johnston, and were finally banded together as the First Regiment Kentucky Volunteer Infantry. Camp "Joe Holt" was established near Jeffersonville, Indiana, and recruiting officers were sent into Kentucky to encourage the enlistment of those who desired to battle for what they were authoritatively told was solely the preservation of the Union.

The rallying cry of the Government party, "the Union, the Constitution, and Enforcement of the Laws," was not only in the mouths of their orators and their officers, but was placarded in the streets, and in bold capitals formed the motto of their political organs, accompanied always by the representation of the "old flag," which had been, they said, wantonly fired upon and ruthlessly insulted at Sumter; and which the administration and its designing friends seized upon as a means of appealing to that singular proneness of the less refined and cultivated among men to embody their ideas.

This "old flag" was not merely the ensign of a government, but it was invested with a kind of sentient existence, and carried in its sacred folds a nation's honour, a nation's weal, almost a nation's being. On the other hand, the Southrons laughed at the singular infatuation, and asked, with mock seriousness, what corporal or spiritual change had come over that emblem since 1854, when, according to their poetasters, sanctioned by their political great high priests it was so far from being sacred that:

Its stripes were bloody scars—
A lie its vaunting hymn:

. . .and they found a superior beauty in their own "Stars and Bars," and an insult offered to their standard would have caused them to rave in turn. Rival bands played "Dixie" and the "Star Spangled Banner," in each other's hearing, with a kind of savage satisfaction that made it seem as though some unwonted spirit had possessed the horns; and blue coats and gray coats rubbed against each other in public places with a smothered energy that told too plainly the conviction of the wearers of each that the other would furnish a most desirable and beautiful target for practice at musket range. But, busied in recruiting and preparing for the two armies, they abstained from seeking occasions for armed collision, and spared the State for a time the disgrace of those atrocities that were perpetrated by cowardly assassins and thieves after the real soldiers were arrayed against each other upon fair fields and according to the usages of war.

Though these preparations began at an early day after the call of the government for troops, there was little disposition, after the first of May, to seek a distant field. It was whispered about, notwithstanding the neutrality declaration, that Kentucky would yet constitute the battle-ground, and men seemed to entertain the conviction that they would be needed nearer home, and that it was unnecessary for even the most sanguinary to hunt for earlier opportunities to shed his blood than would be furnished in due course of time, ready-made to hand.

In June, Colonel Temp Withers, Robert A. Johnson, and James W. Hewitt determined to recruit a regiment for the Southern Army, and they set about the necessary arrangements to carry this into effect. They were aided in the enterprise by some of the most wealthy and influential citizens of Louisville, who spent freely for transportation and supplies, and laboured in every laudable way for the promotion of the scheme. Authority was obtained to establish a recruiting station at some point contiguous to Kentucky, and of easy access, and to organise bodies of troops for the Confederate service.

Accordingly, a spot was chosen in Montgomery county, Tennessee, two miles to the right of the Louisville and Memphis railroad, and seven miles from Clarksville, in a heavily-timbered forest, well supplied with water, while fields furnishing sufficient open space for drilling large commands were convenient; and here, in July, 1861, Camp Boone was laid out, and cleared of undergrowth, and the nucleus of the Second Regiment Kentucky Volunteer Infantry pitched their tents, and entered upon the duties peculiar to the recruit in the earlier stages of his discipline.

Colonels Lloyd Tilghman and R. P. Trabue also obtained authority to raise, each, a regiment, and the first men who enlisted under Colonel Tilghman came out shortly after those under Withers. The Second Regiment was organised on the 17th of July. The Third Regiment was organised a few days afterward, with the following officers composing field and staff: Lloyd Tilghman, Colonel; Albert P. Thompson, Lieutenant Colonel; Ben Anderson, Major; Captain Alfred Boyd, A. Q. M.; Captain J. S. Byers, A. C. S.; Dr. J. W. Thompson, Surgeon, and Dr. J. B. Sanders, Assistant Surgeon. We have not been able to learn who the original Adjutant was. Colonel Tilghman was promoted to Brigadier General in the autumn, and, upon the promotion of Thompson and Anderson to the positions of Colonel and Lieutenant Colonel, Captain A. Johnson became Major.

The Third Regiment, however, did not constitute a part of the command afterward known as the First Kentucky Brigade, though it was connected with it as part of Breckinridge's Division till September, 1862, and fought with the Fourth, Sixth, and Ninth Regiments at Shiloh, Vicksburg, and Baton Rouge, as did also the Seventh Regiment, recruited about the same time in Western Kentucky.

Early in August a battery of light artillery was added to the new force. About the same time, the first companies, or parts of companies, designed for Colonel Trabue's regiment, came out and prepared Camp Burnett, three miles south of Boone. The companies were rapidly filled up, and the Fourth Regiment was organised in September. On the 20th of September, Colonel Joseph H. Lewis established a camp at Cave City, and about the same time, Colonel Thomas H. Hunt began to collect recruits at Green River. Colonel Cofer also had authority to raise a battalion in connection with Major Thomas H. Hays (then Captain of a company of the State Guard).

When Colonel Hanson fell back from Munfordsville (as hereafter noticed) these recruits established their camps also at Bowling Green, and Colonel Hunt effected temporary organisation of his regiment in October. His own commission bore date of October 3, 1861, but no other field officers were appointed until after the battle of Shiloh. (See another part of this book for field and staff.)

In order to avoid confusion and repeated reference to the fact hereafter, it is necessary to anticipate, in some degree, the history of Colonel Hunt's regiment. The temporary organisation having been effected before that of any other one subsequently to the Fourth, it was numbered by the War Department as the *Fifth*, and bore that designation until October, 1862. As the "Fifth Kentucky" it passed through the engagements of Shiloh, Vicksburg, and Baton Rouge, and in all official orders and reports it is so mentioned.

But the regiment of Colonel John S. Williams *perfected* its organisation on the 14th of November, having full complement not only of men, but of field and staff officers, duly commissioned; and the War Department, in consideration of this fact, and perhaps also the commission of Colonel Williams was of some days' earlier date than that of Colonel Hunt, decided that it should be known as the *Fifth* Kentucky, and an order was issued naming Colonel Hunt's as the Ninth, but which was not received, as before stated, till the brigade reached Knoxville, October, 1862. In the reports of battles herein published we have substituted Ninth Kentucky for Fifth Kentucky throughout; but in reading other accounts of the battles referred to, and the various allusions to them by other writers, it should be borne in mind that there were at that time *two* Fifth Kentucky regiments of infantry, one with General Breckinridge, the other with General Marshall.

Colonel Lewis and Colonel Cofer, finding that they could not succeed in recruiting either two full regiments or battalions in time for the active operations which were now being inaugurated, agreed, after consultation with the officers, and through them with the men of the several companies, to unite the two battalions in process of formation, and organise a single regiment. Early in November, then, the tents were pitched together, and on the 19th of that month the organisation of the Sixth Regiment took place. In addition to the ten companies of which the regiment was thus formed, Captain McKinney, of Logan County, had a company, then on duty at Hopkinsville, and on the 25th of November, this was ordered, by General Albert Sidney Johnston, to report to Colonel Lewis, as on detached service, but to be incorporated with the Sixth Regiment.

It was accordingly entered upon the records as Company L. When reinforcements were sent to Donelson, this company was sent forward to report at that point, and fought there with the Eighth Kentucky Infantry. It was surrendered with the other companies of that command; and though Colonel Lewis made an effort, after it was exchanged, to have it report to him. it was never with the Sixth Regiment, and soon ceased to be considered a part of it.

On the 7th of November, Colonel Hanson addressed a note to General Buckner, then commanding Second Division of the Central Army of Kentucky, saying that:

> The artillery known as Spencer's Battery could probably be attached to this brigade, provided we furnish enough men to fill up the company—not exceeding fifteen men from each regiment—the battery to be then under command of Adjutant Rice E. Graves. Such an arrangement would be most acceptable to me, should it meet with your approval. I write this to signify our desire to have another battery, and our willingness to furnish the men.

Arrangements were accordingly set on foot, looking to this end: the guns were procured, and on the 16th of November a call was made for sixty men to man them, apportioned among the five Kentucky regiments. The number specified volunteered for that service promptly, as they were called upon in that manner, instead of by detail, and on the 3rd of December, Company B, of the Fourth Regiment, was temporarily detached for the same duty, with a few additional men from the Second Regiment, and the whole was placed under command of Graves, who was at once recommended for promotion to the rank of captain of artillery.

Lyon's Battery (subsequently Cobb's) had been previously connected with the brigade, the guns being manned partly by men enlisted for that purpose, and partly by the company of Captain Somes, of the Third Regiment. The foregoing constituted the Kentucky infantry and artillery organised on the Tennessee border and at Bowling Green. The First Kentucky Cavalry, under Colonel (afterward General) Ben Hardin Helm, was in the field, and at Murfreesboro', some months subsequently, it was temporarily brigaded with the infantry regiments named, but was not subject to the orders of the same general officer after having reached Burnsville. The squadron of Captain John H. Morgan was mustered into the service by Lieutenant Frank Tryon, of the Second Infantry, on the 5th of November, and was nominally a part of the brigade until the spring of 1862.

Though these commands were some of them yet in process of formation, as the reader will observe, they were regularly brigaded on the 28th of October, the day on which General Johnston assumed immediate command of the Army Corps of Central Kentucky, and, General Breckinridge not having arrived, they were placed under command of the senior colonel, Roger W. Hanson. On the 5th of November, Colonel Thomas H. Hunt was given command of all the unorganised regiments and companies, subordinate to the brigade commander, and reporting to division headquarters through him; and Captain John McGill and a Lieutenant Dudley were assigned to the duty of drillmasters to the new recruits.

Major Alexander Cassidy, who had been serving on the staff of General Buckner as A. A. G., was appointed superintendent of the recruiting of volunteers in Kentucky, (he was succeeded on the staff of General Buckner by Major G. B. Cosby), and Lieutenant Frank Tryon mustering officer, with a view to active and efficient work in augmenting the forces. The organisations already adverted to were filled up, and by the 1st of December regular military routine was established. Even the recently-formed regiments began to acquire rapidly that proficiency in the drill and manual for which they were afterward distinguished. But after that period the work of recruiting went on slowly. The provisional governor (Johnson) issued, on the 7th of December, a stirring proclamation, in hopes to raise two additional regiments, infantry and cavalry, but the golden opportunity had passed.

Two classes of men had, during the past six months, connected themselves with the army; the more impulsive and ambitious, who naturally seize upon an occasion of the kind to "seek the bubble reputation, even at the cannon's mouth," and those more deeply and earnestly enthusiastic characters, who are actuated by a stern sense of duty, that forbids them to maintain any doubtful middle ground.

Of those who entertained Southern feelings there were yet at home two distinct classes—one consisted of politic, cautious characters, having a somewhat overweening regard for personal advantage; the other, of those who are naturally conservative, and who, not from any base motives of fear or love of ease, are yet hardly to be persuaded to see a military enterprise in any other light than as a struggle for mere mastery on the part of governments, and of renown to the individual who engages in it.

The influences at work at and previous to the time to which we have referred, were wholly adverse to the success of the Confederates in swelling their ranks. The one class could be reached only by an appeal to their selfishness; while the other could scarcely have been convinced that their country really needed them and would suffer without their help. Though they gloried in Southern valor, they were not ambitious of that distinction for themselves; and though they would have resisted unto death any attempt to array them against the Southern cause, they deemed themselves perfectly justifiable in standing aloof from both, and the conclusion was strengthened by a rather unconservative opinion that the Confederacy was able to sustain itself with what forces it had already in the field.

On the 16th of November, Brig.-Gen. John C. Breckinridge assumed command, and named the following officers as composing his staff: Capt. George B. Hodge, A. A. G.; Maj. Alfred Boyd, A. Q. M.; Capt. Clint. McClarty, A. C. S.; Lieut. John C. Beech, Ordnance Officer; and Capt. T. T. Hawkins, *aide-de-camp*. (Lieutenant Beech is included, in regular order, in the above list, but the appointment was not made until February 22, 1862.) No assistant-inspector general was appointed, that duty devolving, for the time, upon other officers of the staff. On the 27th of December, Hon. Jilson P. Johnson was announced as volunteer *aide-de-camp*; and in March, 1862, Capt. William L. Brown and Capt. Charles J. Mastin were announced as additional volunteer *aides*.

At every change of the scope of General Breckinridge's command, and every change of troops, corresponding changes and modifications were made in his military family, but no effort is made to record other than those who were appointed to these places while he was brigadier.

The difficulty of arming the Kentucky troops was one which was not entirely surmounted until after the battle of Shiloh. At the time when General Breckinridge assumed command, there was not a sufficient number of small arms to supply each man one of any description, and the want of uniformity was a serious drawback upon efficiency. The Second, Third, and Fourth Regiments had been partially supplied with Belgian rifles, but numbers, even in those regiments, were armed with rifled muskets, and some of them of the old flintlock pattern. And among the new recruits, the display of small arms and ammunition would have moved the mirth of any but a Confederate himself, who looked upon it as too serious a matter to be treated lightly.

There were rifled and smoothbore muskets which had been brought in by State-Guard companies, that would have been excellent weapons if there had been uniformity, or any means of supplying the proper style of cartridge to suit each man's case; but these made up the lesser portion of the strange collection. There were guns of almost every kind known to the troops of the United States since Miles Standish "looked his last upon the sky."

Some of them had been altered from the flint to the percussion lock, but the most of them were flintlocks still, and no few of them in a condition to be fired only by a match or a firebrand. There were squirrel rifles of every age, style, and bore; shot-guns, single-barrelled, double-barrelled, old and new, flintlock, percussion, or no lock at all; carbines of every character, pistols of every patent, and huge knives that were looked upon as too little to be useful if they weighed less than two pounds avoirdupois.

They had, too, various supplies of ammunition, and various means of supplying more. There were some few cartridges, mostly for the smooth-bore and rifled musket; and these were the most destructive species of missile then at command. Troops armed wholly with these muskets, with suitable bayonet, and supplied with the "buck-and-ball" cartridge—consisting of a heavy round bullet, about an ounce in weight, to which was attached on its face opposite the charge of powder, three buckshot—would have every advantage of those bearing Enfield or other improved rifles, except in the matter of comparative range. At the distance of not exceeding three hundred yards, the former would be prepared to do an execution more terrible than any that the Enfield rifle is capable of.

There were various moulds for running bullets in cases of emergency. There were hunters' powder-horns and sportsmen's flasks. Some few cartridge-boxes, cap-boxes and belts; and a limited supply of bayonets, here and there, had found their way to the new camps. Governor Letcher, of Virginia, gave General Breckinridge a number of percussion muskets, and these were divided proportionately among all his regiments, about the 12th of December, and every effort was made to secure uniformity throughout companies, if not regiments, and to procure suitable ammunition; but even so late as the 2nd of January, 1862, complaint was made that the Ninth Regiment had not arms of any kind for half its men, reports showing that there were but two hundred and forty-six really serviceable guns, besides seventy old flintlocks.

Tents, clothing, and commissary stores, however, were at this period abundant. In fact, there was a great superfluity of the former two, since tents were extravagantly plentiful, and almost every man went into camp with a supply of trunks, valises, wearing apparel, books and other adjuncts of traveling gentlemen, that would have absorbed all the transportation space subsequently allowed to a company.

In the latter part of November, when affairs had begun to assume a truly military shape, and it was hoped that the Central Army of Kentucky would soon be brought to a high state of efficiency—when the discipline of regular drill, and instruction by competent officers, was daily going on, the genius of the great Johnston rapidly bringing "order out of confusion," and supplying the chief wants of the department—disease, not hitherto prevailing to any extraordinary extent, began to make alarming inroads, and particularly among the newly-enlisted men, though no single organisation in the corps was exempt. It was induced, not so much by a necessary change in the habits of life, or necessary exposure to inclement weather, nor yet by deficiency of commissaries and clothing, but by a want of knowledge and skill in the preparation of their diet.

It was observed that the hardest marches made during the autumn, even in the most inclement weather, were not productive of what might reasonably have been considered a corresponding amount of sickness. Nor could it be attributed to confinement in quarters and a want of healthful exercise, since the necessary fatigue duty and drill compelled an amount of daily activity as well calculated to preserve health as to form soldierly habits. The vessels furnished for cooking were simply of sheet-iron—a mess-pan, as it was called, and a camp-kettle—wholly unsuited to the proper preparation of food.

The bread was consequently fried, or rather boiled, in grease, the thinness of the mess-pan preventing its being baked, and vessels of cast-iron being but few. This bread, a horrid compound of flour and hog's lard, was eaten by a great majority of them with bacon, and though this was generally varied with much that was wholesome and palatable, it was enough of itself materially to affect the health of the command.

The most common and alarming sickness was a singular type of measles, that, in many instances, baffled the skill of the medical department, and carried off scores of men. The hospitals in Bowling Green were crowded, and the houses of private families in the neighbourhood seemed almost turned into hospitals themselves, as there were many of them, in various localities, where from one to a dozen could be found under treatment.

About the 1st of February, 1862, this crisis had been passed, and those who had survived had generally returned to duty. True, the proportionate number of men always making up the sick list of an army were in the different hospitals at Bowling Green and Nashville, but the general health was restored, and the ranks showed no such signs of marked depletion as were exhibited in December and the first three weeks of January.

By this time, too, the men began not only to become habituated to the new manner of life, but to know by experience that their own comfort and safety depended largely upon themselves, and that they must adopt certain provisions and exercise certain care wholly ignored in the earlier stages of their connection with the army. They began to manifest that disposition and ability to adapt themselves to circumstances and make the best of everything that afterward characterized them, and rendered them cheerful and often comfortable in situations that would have puzzled a philosopher to extract from them any grain of either. They devoted their means to the purchase of whatever was indispensable in preparing their diet, and in all other cases where the resources of the departments failed, they fell back upon their own.

As remarked, there was, then, not only a better state of physical health, but a more thorough preparation for the work in the state of feeling existing. They had learned conformity, in a great degree, to military regulations; and the first feelings of embarrassment and trouble having been measurably overcome, the spirits resumed their elasticity, and the men were ready for their earnest and momentous work. The consciousness of being soldiers rapidly developed the soldiers' pride, and lent a zest to their privations, duties, and dangers.

Not only did cheerfulness reign among them, and hope, coupled with resolution, impart an air of calm determination, but mirth-provoking practices came in vogue, wit and humour found a field for unrestricted display; and the regiments afterward to compose in the main the Orphan Brigade were ready to encounter fate, and do their part in sustaining the old renown of their commonwealth, whatever fortune might have in store for them.

General Johnston assumed command of the Western Department early in September, 1861, when, as has been seen, the Second and Third Regiments, and Byrne's Battery, had already been organised, and the Fourth had nearly completed its complement of men—it being organised on the 13th, only a few days from the time of General Johnston's arrival at Nashville. General Buckner had been named to the command of a brigade, of which these Kentucky troops were to form a part, and repaired to Camp Boone to enter upon his duties. About the middle of September, he received orders from General Johnston to take charge of them and of all the Tennessee troops then available for that purpose, and to move into Kentucky, with a view to occupying Bowling Green, the centre of a line of operations and defence fixed upon by that officer.

The necessary arrangements having been made, the command moved by rail to Bowling Green, with the exception of two hundred men of the Fourth Kentucky, and a number of the Third, also, who were without arms. These were sent to Nashville, for the purpose of being armed and equipped. The Second Regiment, a company of Tennessee cavalry, and Byrne's Battery, augmented by a field-piece captured at Bowling Green, were sent forward to Green River, and encamped near the bridge, with a view to its protection and a probable advance—the Federal forces occupying Elizabethtown.

The remainder of the brigade, though some of them passed up the road as far as Horse Cave, where the cars were thrown from the track by the act of an enemy, were finally all encamped at Bowling Green, and the work of fortifying began. They were joined here early in October, by the detachment sent to Nashville for arms, and, a little later, by the recruits of Hunt, Lewis, and Cofer.

The Second Regiment and other troops remained at Green River Bridge until the first week in October, when they moved back to Bowling Green, followed in a short time by the squadron of Morgan, which had entered upon adventurous outpost duty almost immediately after having joined Colonel Hanson, at the place above alluded to.

Upon the advent of the respective armies of Johnston and Anderson on Bowling Green and Elizabethtown, restraints which had hitherto operated to prevent outrage, were measurably removed, and the conflicting passions of the populace broke out into occasional acts of violence among them. The most quiet and honourable citizens were not safe from molestation, provided they were known to entertain decided sentiments in favour of the South, and possessed, withal, an influential power which was likely to be exerted for the Confederate Government. In many instances, too, the more unprincipled and baser sort took advantage of the unsettled state of affairs to wreak personal vengeance upon those, either Southern or Northern sympathizers, toward whom, justly or unjustly, they bore either secret or avowed enmity, since, under the pretext of serving the Union or the new Confederacy, as the case might be, they could commit acts of revengeful cruelty with perfect impunity from the laws.

The vile practice of exciting the military authorities against private citizens, by spiteful and malicious reports, was productive of much evil and danger to those who were outspoken in favour of the Southern movement.

An affair in which members of the Sixth Regiment were engaged took place in Barren County, and is an instance of the manner in which it was sought to drag private citizens from their homes, on charges trumped up, perhaps, by secret and designing foes. On the morning of the 10th of October, 1861, Colonel Lewis, then encamped at Cave City, learned that an apprehended movement was on foot to arrest Mr. C. B. Hutcherson, living near the intersection of the Munfordsville and Burksville road with that running from Greensburg to Glasgow. His character had never been other than that of the honourable, high-toned gentleman and enterprising citizen. His crime was that he favoured the Southern Government. By request, Colonel Lewis agreed to send ten men, as volunteers, to guard him against what was looked upon as simply lawless violence.

The party consisted of John G. Hudson, Thomas G. Page, Samuel

Anderson, A. G. King, Robert J. Hindman, John B. Spurrier, Gideon B. Rhodes, Joseph L. Tucker, John C. Peden, and a man named Mansfield. The citizens present who engaged in the fight were C. B. Hutcherson, M. H. Dickinson, George Wright, and Samuel Marshall.

The soldiers repaired to Mr. Hutcherson's during the day, but it is supposed that they were either unobserved by citizens friendly to the Federal cause, or that, if any such noticed them, they did not know that a movement was on foot to seize him that night. Having taken the precaution to throw out some pickets, the remainder of the party awaited developments. They had nine or ten muskets, while some of them were armed with nothing but repeaters.

The alarm that a body of horsemen was approaching was given by a picket sometime in the night, and the Confederates arranged themselves in the front yard, in which direction the enemy was reported advancing. An open grave-yard was but a short distance from the house, on a slight eminence, and a little to the left of the front gate. It was but a short time before men were observed coming steadily and as stealthily as possible, and, when well advanced, and occupying the burying-place, with ground, perhaps, on the left and contiguous, someone in the yard called to them to halt.

Instead of answering the challenge in form, however, they fired, and at once the party of Confederates replied, firing as rapidly and as accurately as possible in the darkness, which produced instant confusion, not only in the attacking party, but among the horse-holders, whom they had posted in a hollow in the field some distance back.

There was a noise of men in hurried retreat, mingled with groans from the graveyard and the running of horses evidently stampeded and dashing about the enclosed pasture. The darkness of night and the weakness of the Confederates (there being but fourteen, all told) necessarily prevented their assuming the offensive, but the aggressive force was already completely routed. Their number has been variously estimated at from fifty to a hundred men—supposed to have been a full company of a Federal regiment. The fire of the Confederates was not so destructive as it would have been had there been proper management in taking position and proper concert in action; but, all things considered, the punishment inflicted compares favourably with any of the war, considering the forces engaged.

The Federals were, doubtless, four to one, at least, and well-armed, while, as before remarked, the Confederates had several men armed with nothing but revolvers. One Federal was killed outright; two were brought in next morning very severely wounded; five others are known to have been wounded, some of them badly; others are rumoured to have been wounded; and thirty horses, with equipments, were captured. No Confederate was even touched; and the only damage done was the putting of some balls through the house—one of these having evidently been fired at a lady who looked out of an upper window to see how the storm was raging below, as it struck the right half-shutter while she had the left one open and her head out.

Early next morning a small force of cavalry went out from Horse Cave under command of Col. Jack Allen; and Col. Lewis sent additional volunteers from the Sixth Kentucky Infantry, to reinforce the little party there, as it was apprehended that the enemy might be on the move from Greensburgh; but no further trouble occurred. Among the horsemen were Wallace Herr and James H. Rudy, who afterward became distinguished members of the First Kentucky Cavalry.

Another minor affair took place while Johnston's troops were at Bowling Green, in which some men of the Ninth Kentucky were engaged. This was at Whippoorwill Bridge, on the Louisville and Memphis Railroad, some five or six miles below Russellville. On the 13th of November, Colonel Hunt, who had three companies reporting to him from Russellville, without having ever been to Bowling Green, went down with those collected at the latter place, was joined there by the three companies, and the whole established themselves near town, at what they called Camp Magruder, in pursuance of a custom then much in vogue among the Confederates, of calling encampments after noted officers of their army.

They remained here till about the 1st of December, and returned to Bowling Green, with the exception of thirteen men, under command of Sergeant (afterward First Lieutenant) Peter H. O'Connor, of Co. H. The names of three of this detachment cannot be ascertained; but the others were: George Campbell, Co. A; Joseph Hall, Co. C; H. D. Dougherty, Thomas Lilley, Joseph Wilson, and Hatch Jupin, Co. B; Paul Burgess and John E. Cook, Co. G; Isaac Duckwall and James Johnson, Co. H.

This force had been detailed to guard the bridge aforesaid from destruction by the Federal Home-Guards. It was left on duty when the regiment went back to Bowling Green, except Sergeant O'Connor, who had to go to Bowling Green for a supply of ammunition. On the morning of the 4th of December, the detail was attacked by ninety men, under command of a Captain Netter, who had come out cautiously from Rochester for the purpose of destroying the bridge. The guard stood gallantly to their arms against these overwhelming odds, and fought until they were surrounded (a number of Federals having found the way to their rear as well as front), when the survivors surrendered.

Two of them (George Campbell and Hatch Jupin) were killed; and Joe Wilson, of Co. B, was severely wounded in the hip, but fought on till he had a finger shot off, and the proximity of the enemy rendered further resistance vain. He was left on the ground. The Federals barely took time to fire the bridge, which they did in such a manner that it failed to burn, before they took up their march for Rochester, carrying their own wounded and the prisoners with them.

It was never ascertained what loss they suffered, though citizens stated that a number of them were wounded but none killed. Some of the prisoners escaped before they reached Rochester; the others were sent to prison, and were not exchanged till the autumn of 1862. Surgeon Pendleton, who had been left with sick at Russellville, made up a party for pursuit as soon as possible after the truth was ascertained, but Netter had made good his escape from the neighbourhood.

Apprehensions were entertained about the middle of November that a Federal force would be sent across by way of Rochester, on Mud River, to interfere with the Confederate communications, by striking the Memphis road, either at Russellville or below, and on the 17th of that month an expedition, consisting of the Second Kentucky, the Third Kentucky, and a part of the Fourth, with cavalry and a battery of artillery, was sent out to Mud River, but nothing of particular note occurred, and they returned to Bowling Green about the first of December. A little subsequently, a similar force was sent out in that direction, but with no more important results.

The enemy was now known to be rapidly repairing the bridge over Green River, a pier of which had been destroyed by the troops stationed there in October, and, being in great force on the north bank, disposed between Munfordville and Elizabethtown, an advance upon Nashville, either directly through Bowling Green or by an attempt to turn the right of General Johnston's immediate strategic position, would probably take place as soon as their arrangements for crossing the river and keeping open their communications could be perfected.

Scouts reported that a movement was apparently on foot looking to an advance upon what is known as the "upper pike," or the turnpike road running from Louisville to Nashville by way of Glasgow and Scottville. On the 18th of December a portion of the brigade was sent forward to Oakland Station, ostensibly to support, or act in concert with the brigade of General Hindman, who had been out continually as far advanced toward Green River as prudence would allow. Part of the brigade was then at Bowling Green and part of it at Oakland. On the 20th some of the troops were thrown six miles still further forward to Dripping Springs.

On the 21st, it having been reported that a column of the enemy was actually advancing, so as to threaten Bowling Green on the right, the brigade, including Morgan's cavalry, had orders to march next day, by different roads, to the point where the pike between Glasgow and Scottville crosses Skeggs's Creek, over which stream there is a bridge. Accordingly, early on the morning of the 22nd, the various organisations struck tents, and took up the lines of march designated. The rain, which had begun falling at an early hour, increased, and it was not long till all were thoroughly drenched, and the roads were almost impassable, on account of the mud. But the command struggled bravely on, the officers in many instances setting a noble example of cheerfulness and fortitude, and in the afternoon reached the vicinity of Merry Oaks, by which time the rain had almost entirely ceased, and the wind had set in steadily from the north.

In addition to being wet, the men were now likely to suffer with cold; but they hastily erected the few tents that had been brought forward, kindled fires, and were soon comparatively comfortable. The next morning was bitter cold, the ground was frozen and rough, and thin snow had fallen, and continued to fall in fitful gusts, during the day. Information having now been received that the enemy was quietly encamped north of Green River, they were marched back and encamped, first at Oakland Station, then on the lower pike, thirteen miles above Bowling Green.

Though these marches to Rochester and Merry Oaks were productive of no immediate advantage in either an offensive or defensive point of view, they served as an admirable introduction to the career of hardship and exposure to which the men were so soon to be subjected. On the first march to Mud River, the weather was for some time very inclement—heavy rains pouring down, and the roads in such horrible condition that the artillery and baggage wagons could scarcely be conveyed over, or rather through them; and the supply of cooking utensils was so meagre that the men were obliged to fall back upon their own resources, and devise expedients which afterward served them on many occasions and in more momentous times.

Many of them resorted to the baking of bread on their ramrods, and taking their ration of bacon without any cooking at all. On the march to Merry Oaks, even the "raws" began to feel themselves duly inducted into the mysteries of a soldier's hardships and privations, and the means he adopts to modify the more disagreeable features of his condition, and adapt himself with a stern grace to whatever circumstances may surround him.

General Johnston had, meanwhile, pushed on the fortification of Bowling Green to such an extent that, to eyes unused to formidable preparations, it seemed to render the place almost impregnable to any direct attack. General Hindman was out in the region of Bell's Tavern and Cave City; and Helm, and Morgan, and Biffle were engaged in constant outpost duty—scouting, picketing, and an occasional brush with the enemy.

Meanwhile affairs had assumed different aspects, too, as regarded the fortunes of those fellow-Kentuckians whom they had left above Bowling Green. Early in February, General Johnston had learned the sad tidings of the defeat and death of General Zollicoffer at Fishing Creek; a Federal force was pressing General Crittenden back rapidly from the scene of that disaster, so that the left of the Confederate defensive line was irretrievably broken, and General Johnston's flank uncovered; a large force was concentrated in the vicinity of Munfordville, ready to be precipitated upon Bowling Green at the auspicious moment; Fort Henry had been evacuated; a powerful army under General Grant was menacing Donelson, and the odds were so vastly against it that its successful defence was a matter that scarcely admitted of hope.

Pen-and-ink warriors were clamouring for they knew not what, and the people were impatient of delay. Every adverse influence, every depressing circumstance seemed to be concentrated upon the devoted head of the commander, who wisely kept his own counsel, and acted in accordance with the superior dictates of patriotism and duty, as one who could trust to results to vindicate his course, and who could therefore bide his time. Finding it necessary to abandon Bowling Green, he at once adopted a course as judicious as any which could be conceived, and carried it into execution with an independence and a success as rare as any in the annals of strategy.

To establish a new base and line of operations at such point as would enable him to collect his own scattered forces, even in case of disaster at Donelson, as also to unite his own forces with those of General Beauregard, was the object which now claimed his attention, and the wisdom of his decision and his action has never been questioned since he gave up his life on the field of his choosing. After the defeat of General Crittenden at Fishing Creek, he quietly withdrew the ordnance and army supplies from Bowling Green, by rail, southward, and everything was put in readiness by the evening of February 11th for the withdrawal of the Central Army from that place.

Before treating of this movement, however, let us notice the Battle of Fort Donelson, which occurred while it was in process of execution, and the conduct of the regiment and artillery detached from the brigade a few days before to reinforce the garrison there.

INCIDENTS AND ANECDOTES: WHILE THE BRIGADE WAS TAKING SHAPE.

1. Hard-Hearted Surgeons.—A man was found occasionally who repented of having committed himself to the "lugging of knapsack, box, and gun," and sought by one device or other to get out of his bargain without actually running off. A sort of odd-fish came into one of the regiments, at Bowling Green, with an appetite keenly whetted for Yankees; but he soon lost his zest, and wished himself at home. He conceived a plan to get off, and quickly put it to the test.

One morning at sick-call he put himself under the sergeant's care, marched off to surgeon's quarters, and poked out his tongue in due form; but there was nothing the matter that the tongue could disclose, so he took it in, and was marked for duty. He was bent on being discharged, though, and concluding that starvation would do the work, he declared himself too sick to eat, notwithstanding the surgeon's verdict; and he used afterward to laugh heartily over it himself—how nearly he came starving to death, and yet couldn't make the surgeons think he deserved a discharge! He finally gave up the attempt, and, being too much of a man to desert, made a good soldier.

2. A Deadly Disease.—Few among the volunteers, outside of the medical profession, understood the meaning of that scientific term, "nostalgia," which in the earlier days of the service was so often found opposite names of the sick in surgeons' reports. An orderly sergeant who had puzzled himself over it asked his surgeon one morning, when he found it set time and again against the names of his men, what it meant. "Homesickness," he answered; "that's the plain English of it." The inquirer was astonished to learn that it was not only recognised as a disease, but that it was one which would kill; but subsequent observation convinced him that during the first year, at least many a really noble fellow died of it.

3. Too Short.—Co. I, Fourth Kentucky, enlisted a jolly, good-humoured son of Erin, Tom Conelly, upon whom the officers wasted a good deal of time, trying to fit him for service in the ranks; but teaching proved ineffective and scolding was useless; it was clear that "Tommie," as he came to be familiarly called, could not keep step. He could dress, right, left or centre, with a little nudging from the next file; but when the drill-master cried "step"— "step," or "left"—"left," or even sung out Graves's vigorous though somewhat strident "hup"—"hup," Conelly seemed to lose himself in attending to the sound, and his legs went their own gait. To see him try to catch step by a resort to the crow-hop was almost enough to make a wooden man laugh.

Repeated remonstrance as to his failures elicited only the reply: "Ah, captain, I am not the height for a soldier; I'm not the height." It was finally decided to put Tommie on detail duty, and he was assigned to the medical department, where he proved himself useful. After the command was mounted, he was made orderly on General Lewis's staff.

A member of the Ninth Kentucky says:

> But, whether carrying water or riding his mule, Tommie was ever the same Irish, original, and comic self. He was never known to refuse a drink, and yet he avers that he was never drunk on medical whisky. He had a singular proclivity for gathering up cartridge belts, and always wore about a half dozen, while he kept a score on hand to supply his comrades. A story is told on Tommie relative to his first impressions of a 'Vicksburgh lamppost,' or Yankee shrapnel. One night as he and Joe—another indispensable member of the medical staff (everybody remembers Joe's light-bread and baker's yeast)—with others, were returning from carrying rations to the men on picket in Vicksburgh, they had to pass through a long railroad cut. When about midway, one of those terrible shells came whirring along over their heads. Tommie jumped forward in alarm, exclaiming: 'Be jabers, boys!—faith, and why don't ye get out of the way? Don't you hear the locomotive coming?' At the close of the war Tommie returned to his home in Russellville, covered with honours and with, belts.

4. Conquering a Peace.—The Fourth Regiment, having been organised sometime before the Sixth and Ninth, and very carefully drilled, felt themselves veterans when the latter were still raw, and rallied the "awkward squad," as they called them, unmercifully. At Burnsville, however, the Ninth found an opportunity to pay them back in one species of their own coin, and they made such use of it as to force the "veterans," who also called themselves "Buckner's Pets," to sue for a treaty of amity. The tents of the two regiments were pitched on the same slope and in such close proximity that it was not deemed necessary to keep two separate camp-guards; so they agreed to dispense with that part of the detail, at least, which would be required to watch the two lines near the point of contact, and to have a guard proportioned to the strength of each regiment detailed for duty around the two commands.

They now became better acquainted, and things went on swimmingly till one morning, when a certain valuable cooking utensil was missed from the Ninth. A careful reconnoisance developed the fact that it had found its way to the Fourth, and a plan of retaliation was at once instituted. The night which followed was dark and favourable to the enterprise. After tattoo, and when the men of the offending regiment were fully committed to their slumbers, a party of the Ninth stole quietly among their tents and bore off every cooking vessel upon which they could lay their hands. The astonishment of the veterans next morning knew no bounds, when they found that instead of a single piece of camp furniture's being gone, there were more indications that they had been visited by Ali Baba's "forty thieves."

But the true state of case was soon discovered, and there was a large meeting of plenipotentiaries from the respective regiments, who entered into a solemn league and covenant, providing that, no matter what might be practiced upon outsiders, the strictest forbearance was to be observed toward each other. There was then a restoration of the property, but the Fourth had a late breakfast that morning. From that time a warm friendship sprang up between these two regiments, and the treaty was never. broken. "Buckner's Pets "very naturally concluded that men who, with so little training could avenge their wrongs so promptly, were worthy of esteem and confidence.

5. *Tried for High Treason.*—John H. Dills, who was discharged February 12, 1862, because of disability by disease, had a peculiar experience subsequently—being the only man tried during the war on the charge of high treason. When the Confederate Army was on the point of withdrawing from the State, he had not recovered from the effect of a dangerous attack of typhoid, and applied for a furlough, but the authorities decided that he should be discharged. His friends had him conveyed to the home of Frank Rogan, in Sumner County, Tenn., but before the army had left Murfreesboro, he had ridden horseback and

joined his company intending to enter the service again.

Finding himself too weak to accompany the army southward, he went to Abingdon, Va., where he stayed until his strength was somewhat restored. He then came back to his home, within three miles of Cynthiana, to secure recruits for the Southern Army. The Federal commander at Cynthiana learned of his return, and had him arrested. A formal complaint was filed with the United States Commissioner, charging him with high treason, and he was sent to Frankfort and committed to jail to await the action of the Federal grand jury.

At the June term, 1862, a formal indictment was found, and the case set for trial, to be had before Judge Bland Ballard. James Harlan, the father of Judge John M. Harlan, now of the United States Supreme Court, prosecuted. A. H. Ward, James F. Robinson and Thomas N. Lindsay, were engaged for the defence.

After a careful test of every man of a special venire summoned, a jury was made up of "twelve good men and true;" but the prosecution suspected the "unconditional loyalty" of some of them, and moved the court to take a recess of ten days, on the ground that Congressional action was about to be had to prescribe an additional challenge for the purging of juries in capital cases. The motion was granted, and the defendant remanded to jail. When the case was called again Harlan produced the law for which he had been waiting. It bore date of the day when the court had taken recess, had been rushed through both houses under a suspension of the rules, and was signed by the President, all on the same day.

The jury therefore had again to be made up. The prejudices of the soldiers and the Union people were intense, and it took a brave man to refuse the test of loyalty prescribed by the new law. As it proved, every member of the venire took the required oath, and the old jury was chosen with the exception of one man who was sick.

When the case was called, Judge Ballard excluded newspaper reporters on the ground that the defendant was entitled to fair and impartial trial, and the publication of the proceedings would prejudice his cause. Only a few prosecuting witnesses were called; and as no two of them could testify to the same overt act or indeed to any overt act, a verdict of "not guilty" was returned, July 2, 1862. On his return home from Frankfort, Major Bracht, the Provost Marshal of Lexington, had him brought before him and required a pledge to keep the peace towards the United States during the war, under bond in the sum of $10,000. This bond and pledge saved him from a military prison; but his troubles were not yet over.

A number of swash-bucklers, parading themselves as home guards, held a meeting on the night of his return from Lexington, and passed resolutions condemning the United States Court that had failed to convict, and so had turned loose upon the community such a dangerous man. A formal notice was prepared and served upon him, ordering him to leave the State within ten days, or he "would be shot or otherwise roughly dealt with." Before the expiration of the time, however, General Morgan visited Cynthiana, and the survivors of that indignation meeting afterward preferred to cultivate Dills' favour rather than act as his executioners.

He removed to Texas in 1875, and is now an honoured, citizen of Sherman. He has been twice elected to represent Grayson County in the Legislature; and the circle of his friends is limited only by that of his acquaintance.

CHAPTER 3

The Second Kentucky and Graves's Battery

In trying to follow the fortunes of the Kentucky Brigade, it is no part of the author's plan to discuss either grand or special strategy as employed in connection with the Army of the Tennessee, nor to enter into any elaborate description of each special field and the disposition and manoeuvres of all the troops engaged. In general, these things tend rather to confuse the reader than to give him a clear view of the conduct of a particular organisation. In the present instance, it is sufficient to notice that shortly after the defeat of Gen. George Crittenden, at Fishing Creek, (January 19, 1862), Gen. Sidney Johnston detached from the Central Army of Kentucky the divisions of Pillow and Floyd, and a part of Buckner's, and sent them under command of these officers to reinforce the garrison at Fort Donelson.

The Second Kentucky and Graves's battery, constituting a part of Buckner's division, were at Russellville, when, just after the fall of Fort Henry, they were ordered to proceed by railroad to Clarksville, thence by steamer to Dover, where they arrived after midnight of February 8th. They were quartered in the town until sometime during the 10th, when they were marched out about a mile to the northwest, and assigned to the extreme right of the Confederate line, westward, and across the Eddyville road. This was the right of General Buckner's division, resting on a kind of slough or backwater from Hickman Creek and extending southward in the general direction of the Eddyville road towards its point of intersection with the Charlotte road above Dover. The water batteries, upper and lower, the approaches to which this division was set to cover, were almost immediately east, about twelve hundred yards in rear of the position assigned to the Second Kentucky.

143

The men were set to work to construct rifle-pits, with earthworks and abattis fronting, in the usual manner, along a line about one-eighth of a mile in length, and they worked night and day on these, by relays, until the morning of the 12th, when their tools were surrendered to others; and by the morning of the 13th General Buckner's entire position, a half mile or more in length, was considered to be in a fair state of defence.

Two regiments—the Twenty-Sixth Tennessee and Twenty-Sixth Mississippi, had been detached and placed under Pillow's orders. The troops in hand were disposed as follows: Hanson on the extreme right, with the Eighteenth Tennessee (Colonel Palmer) in position to reinforce him; Porter's battery occupied an advanced salient, near the centre of three Tennessee regiments forming Brown's brigade, and not far from the left of the Second Kentucky, where it could sweep the road which led to the front from the direction in which the Federals had advanced, as well as flank the entrenchments right and left, with the Fourteenth Mississippi in position to support; the Third Tennessee, Thirty-Second Tennessee, and Forty-First Tennessee, (under command of Colonel Brown) extended the line from Hanson's left; and Graves's battery of six guns was placed on a declivity near the extreme left of the division, where it could sweep the valley leading down between General Buckner's left and the right of Heiman's brigade, which occupied Pillow's right, and also by flank-fire protect Heiman's front.

This much of explanation, to enable us to understand, without entering into the details of the battle, the part played by the Kentuckians on that field.

Early on the morning of the 12th, the Federal Army, in two divisions, commanded respectively by Smith and McClernand, was marching by two roads from the vicinity of Fort Henry, from twelve to fourteen miles distant; by sundown they had reached the neighbourhood of Fort Donelson. There was some fighting between pickets in the right front of the Second Kentucky that day. Smith and McClernand were ordered to find position in front of the Confederate line early in the morning of the 13th, Smith to face Buckner on the right, McClernand to face Pillow and close the Charlotte road so as to leave General Floyd no communication southward except the river; but it was found that when they reached the designated lines their combined forces were not sufficient fully to envelop the place, as McClernand could not extend across the Charlotte road and still connect with Smith's right flank, even by dispensing with reserve force and keeping all his troops advanced; but this was remedied next day, as we shall see. The gunboats under Commodore Foote had come up the Cumberland meanwhile, and the Confederate position was now almost completely invested.

On the night of the 12th, four companies of the Second Kentucky occupied their entrenchments; early on the morning of the 13th the six left companies were disposed along the whole line of rifle-pits and the other four companies held in reserve. Shortly after daylight, Federal batteries began to play upon the position, and presently a Federal force in line of battle was seen marching through the woods. This was allowed to advance within a few yards of the abattis which fringed the front of the Kentucky position, where they were halted, reformed, and then ordered forward in plain hearing of the men in the works.

Not until they had approached within a hundred yards was fire delivered from the pits. A volley was poured into them; but they did not break until they had pressed forward, under rapid and almost continuous fire from the Kentuckians, to within sixty yards, when they fled in confusion. Three times that day they attempted to storm these works; but they were driven back, leaving the ground almost literally strewn with their dead and wounded.

Away off to the left Graves and his men were alert, and they made McClernand's efforts to form along Pillow's front uncomfortable—firing up the valley as they crossed it toward the southeast; and when the Federal batteries had gotten into position he engaged them by firing to the left, along Heiman's line of battle. The sharpshooters of both armies got in their deadly work from time to time.

The casualties among the Kentuckians were not great during the day, though the repeated onsets of the enemy had been gallant and their contact close; but they had a realisation of what it meant to fight a foe superior in numbers of unquestioned courage, and led by officers who had seen service—some of them with General Buckner in the old army. As has been explained by General Wallace, the men of the North and Northwest on one side, and of the South and Southwest on the other, had grappled. Greek had met Greek. At the close of this day the men of the South had the best of it; they were on the defensive, and the Federals had sustained much of their loss while fighting for position.

It is worthwhile to study briefly the manifestations of these Kentuckians in this their first great battle—how keenly they were alive to all that was going on, how observant they were of individual conduct, and how the feeling of comradeship asserted itself. It was remarked that a Mr. Garth, of Southern Kentucky, not a member of the regiment, had gotten into one of their pits with a fine Enfield rifle, and brought down an officer far off in the wood before the first charge was made upon them; they noted with admiration how steadily the attacking column had behaved, stopping within fair gunshot to reform, and taking from their officers before moving the order to dress on the colours, and that to march before they dashed at the abattis behind which lay the earth-works, and behind those works their grim foemen, with their deadly, though soon-to-be-discarded buck-and-ball muskets.

It was observed that Neil Hendricks, the orderly sergeant of Co. B, afterwards its captain, was shot in the breast at the first fire, and that Nelson was the first man of the regiment, the first of the brigade, to be killed in a great battle. And he, their first offering to Mars, was buried that night, doubtless with all the honours of war that could be shown in the face of the enemy, though this is not recorded. The muffled drum, the march with reversed arms, the salute fired over the newly-filled grave—all the ceremony which they had learned at Camp Boone—perhaps these had no part in the performance; but a detail of his comrades went back to Dover that night and got boards of which a rude coffin was constructed, and he was carefully laid to rest—it may be as silently as Sir John Moore—by these loyal souls who afterward on many a battlefield were content if they could do only so much for their slain fellow-soldiers as to wrap them in their own blankets, and bury them here and there, where they fell, under the sod they had reddened with their blood.

And again, to one who wrote of the casualties of Saturday it seemed not sufficient to say only that Lieutenant Hill was mortally wounded during the duel, but "a cannon ball was seen to strike the ground and come bounding along like a rabbit. It struck Lieutenant Hill, of Co. F, on the knee; he was removed to the field hospital; and he died that night."

Up to the afternoon of the 13th the weather had been almost springlike, and overcoats were an incumbrance; but now there was a sudden change: the wind blew cold and almost continuously from the north all night long; rain and snow fell, and soon there was a coating of sleet; and both armies, in their unsheltered and inadequately clothed condition, shivered on their lines of bivouacs and their picket posts through the dreary hours. The Second Kentucky occupied the rifle-pits by reliefs, and the men who retired to the rear to rest and sleep found little comfort and only fitful slumber, as they could not kindle fires without betraying their position to the Federal artillerists.

The 14th was a day of comparative inaction, except on the part of Foote's squadron in its attack on the water batteries and the fort, which resulted in the disabling of some of his gunboats and the permanent retirement of all.

In the early afternoon a division composed of General Lew Wallace's brigade and a battery, which arrived from Fort Henry about noon, and of reinforcements which had been conveyed up the river and assigned to Wallace, was placed between McClernand and Smith, enabling the former to push further toward the right and envelop the Charlotte road, while keeping an ample reserve force in support. The work of complete and strong investment of Floyd's position, so well begun on the 13th, was now complete; and though the Confederates had so well maintained themselves on the landside that day, and, on this, Foote's flotilla had been driven off, there were sufficient indications that a desperate struggle was at hand.

The weather continued cold, the ground was covered with ice and snow, and that night the men who slept at all had but a few hours of uneasy sleep. Between 2 and 3 o'clock on the morning of the 15th the Second Kentucky was called up and marched to the left, leaving the Thirtieth Tennessee (Colonel Head), from the fort, in its entrenchments. It was formed as a reserve to Baldwin's troops now attached to Colonel Brown's brigade, and not far from Graves's men and guns.

In the early dawn Pillow began his attack upon the right wing of the Federal Army, in accordance with plans agreed upon at the council of war held at Floyd's headquarters the night before; and Graves opened upon a Federal battery in rear of McClernand's left, which responded promptly, and the two were soon engaged in a duel which was observed with deep interest by General Buckner, who walked composedly up and down near the battery and off to the left front of the Kentucky infantry, setting a noble example to the men in this new feature of the lessons they learned on that field.

About 9 o'clock General Buckner sent Colonel Brown with two regiments, the Third Tennessee and the Fourteenth Mississippi, to silence the battery with which Graves was engaged and strike McClernand's left, his right being now hard pressed and giving way. The troops indicated moved off promptly and attacked in splendid style; but the battery was well handled and the support strong, and Colonel Brown failed to move them. His regiments became partially broken before he reached the top of the declivity, and were presently coming back. General Buckner rallied them as they came and placed them in the entrenchments; then going back to the Kentuckians he said: "The Second Kentucky will have to do that work!" Just then Graves came over the hill in the rear of his position, and behind which the regiment was sheltered from direct shots, and cried out: "Where is the Second Kentucky? Come to the aid of my battery."

This was mistaken by some who were nearest him to be an order which in an emergency he had a right to give; and the impetuous young commanders of Cos. B and G, Higgins and Spears, were more ready to obey than to question, and these companies dashed off with a shout, passing the Kentucky Battery, then down the slope and across the little valley to the foot of the hill from which the Federal guns were still raining shot and shell upon Graves and his support, and flanking which were the riflemen who poured into them a galling fire. They pressed to within fifty yards of the Federal lines, and there, it was estimated, they gave the enemy shot for shot for fifteen minutes, without signs of wavering, when Colonel Hanson brought the remaining eight companies up on their right, advancing quickstep, with fixed bayonets, but without firing a shot, steady as on parade; and now the entire regiment charged with a yell, and the enemy broke and abandoned the battery.

It was at this juncture that Col. John A. Logan, with the Thirty-first Illinois, and Colonel Ransom, with the Eleventh Illinois, were fighting desperately to hold the ground from which the rest of Oglesby's men had been driven, as shown by Gen. Lew Wallace; and Logan fell severely wounded about the time these last regiments were compelled to retire. The Second Kentucky now carried some of the guns of this battery and turned them over to Graves; and after a rest the regiment was ordered back to its entrenchments on the extreme right. It set out in high glee over its successes, though these had not been won without a costly sacrifice in killed and wounded; conscious of the admiration of all who observed them, and hearing the warm comments of some on the "incomparable regiment;" but a disappointment was now in store for them.

While the movement led by Colonel Brown, and afterward concluded by the Second Kentucky, as explained above, was being executed, General Buckner had taken the remainder of his division and a section of Graves's battery up the valley extending out from about the centre of the Confederate line, and was engaged with Wallace's division, with every prospect of success in clearing the Wynne's Ferry Road, had his order to Hanson and Brown to join him not been countermanded by Pillow, who also sent to him to retire and reoccupy his entrenched position on the right.

Before he could fully execute the latter order Gen. Charles F. Smith, with Lauman's brigade and the Fifty-Second Indiana, had begun his gallant, skilful, and, (as it proved to be), successful movement. When Colonel Hanson, on approaching his position, received information that the Federal troops were coming up the hill, he ordered six companies to make a dash for the rifle-pits, while four were held in reserve. A number of these pits, on the right of the line, with intervals of about twenty yards, faced almost directly north, the direction from which Smith was approaching; while the rest extended about parallel with the Eddyville road, almost at right angles to those on the right, and looked west or perhaps slightly west by north.

The companies that made a run for those on the right were met by the enemy, and few of the men got in. Captain McDowell, with thirteen men of Co. F and a few of the Eighteenth Tennessee, succeeded in getting into one of the pits and were rapidly firing at the Federals in the woods before them, and almost upon them, when they suddenly found themselves flanked and covered also in the rear, and received at close range a destructive fire, which killed and wounded more than half of them, McDowell receiving two shots. He was not disabled, however, and he and his men fought their way back obliquely to the right, and rejoined the main body of the regiment as it stubbornly retired, keeping up a rapid fire. It was told of McDowell that when he and his men found the Federals upon them in front, he insisted on standing, feeble as the force was, and giving them the bayonet; but when he found his little band attacked also flank and rear, he saw the impossibility of effecting anything, and they fought out.

The companies that ran to the entrenchments on the left found, on looking westward, that no enemy was directly in their front; but they had hardly observed this fact before they saw the Federal soldiers pouring over the works on the right and swarming through the intervening spaces, while a stand of the enemy's colours was planted on one of the slight ramparts, and these left companies of the Second Kentucky were now subjected to an enfilading fire.

The enemy would have quickly massed in their rear and captured them had they not rapidly retreated. The reserve companies and the support furnished by part of the Eighteenth Tennessee and some of

Head's Tennesseans were not sufficient to check the enemy and enable the broken Confederates to halt and re-form there, and all were driven back in some confusion; but they rallied just over the crest of a ridge in the rear, looking northward.

Before reaching this ridge the men of the two regiments, pressed back over a short length of line, had become intermingled, and their officers were trying to form them on their respective colours, when General Buckner came up and ordered them to fall in without respect to regiments or companies. Aided by the officers, he established the line and stopped the enemy's advance. Graves had heard the heavy firing, and rightly apprehending that his friends were in trouble, ordered two of his sergeants, Bell and Colston, to take their pieces and go with him to their assistance. Under his direction these guns were quickly in position and playing upon the enemy. He was in too great force and too firmly lodged to be moved; but after Graves came up the two regiments effected separate alignment and held the position until nightfall, when they retired behind the ridge and out of range.

Colonel Hanson, here as elsewhere during those days, was with his men, directing, encouraging, sharing their dangers, showing a genuine soldier's appreciation of the conduct displayed by the command of which he had expected so much, and which had not disappointed him. "And Buckner," said one, "stood where men were falling around him as calm as on review." His speech indicated that the Kentuckians could not hide from him how they were smarting under the necessity of falling back before even a superior force, and because their position had fallen into the enemy's hands, and that he wished to reassure and cheer them. "It was not your fault," he said, "my brave boys, it was not your fault."

The rigor of the weather was still unabated, or rather it was even more bitterly cold than previously; and the men, worn out with the marching and fighting, hovered over the little fires which they ventured to kindle under the shelter of the hill, or lay around them, and moodily repined over their lost advantage, and thought of what they did not doubt must be the bloody work of tomorrow. They reasoned that the enemy must be driven from their lines, and rather unreasonably felt that this was necessary to "maintaining untarnished Kentucky's name for undaunted courage." High-spirited young fellows!—they had not yet learned that chiefly in defeat and disaster and long expatriation under divers adverse conditions, was it reserved to them to show how great Kentuckians could be. Those who lay down and fell asleep arose with aching limbs, numbed with cold, and real rest and recuperation had been small when at 3 o'clock on Sunday morning, February 16th, they were formed and marched again to the left.

The rumour had gained currency that the army would attempt to cut its way out and retreat towards Nashville. Halted in a ravine southwest of the fort, they remained an hour or two awaiting developments, when Colonel Hanson gave the order to right about; and then, wrote a member of the command, "said to us in a husky voice: 'Go to your places, boys, and cook something to eat. The war is about over for us!'" This was the first announcement that the battle was lost, and that they were now captives. They were put under guard till next day, when they were marched to the river and embarked for Northern prisons.

In the Brief History of Individuals, mention is made of the killed and wounded of the regiment and its battery as far as it was possible to obtain them when that feature of the work was planned, or as is shown by certain muster and pay-rolls now on file among the captured Confederate archives in Washington. To say that the ranks of the regiment were decimated would be to express far less than the truth. As for their efficiency, that is best attested by the published reports of Federal officers with whose troops they came in direct contact.

These show that they were destructive much in excess of their own losses, though they were without cover except on Thursday, when they repelled the repeated assaults of a strong force of men of approved courage and remarkable steadiness. A participant in every action during the three days wrote from prison to an absent brother: "We fired low and deliberately." Experienced soldiers know the importance of heeding at least that part of battle orders generally given to new troops about to engage: "Aim low," or "Fire at the enemy's knees."

What may be called the echoes from a battlefield are often strikingly indicative of the character of commanders and men. It is frequently difficult to trace the origin and transmission of these; but to a certain extent they are more expressive and more truthful than dispatches and bulletins. The other Kentucky regiments had hardly reached Murfreesboro, on Johnston's retreat from Bowling Green, when a much-discussed topic around the mess-fires was the battle of Donelson and the Kentuckians who participated in it. There were many among them who had acquaintances, friends, or relatives in the Second Kentucky and Graves's battery; and of them and their deeds these echoes of the conflict were filling the camps. They took shape in more or less coherent and credible stories, nearly all of which trumpeted the praise of these absent comrades or signified that this or that one had earned a soubriquet which, in soldiers' mouths, told of a marked character or expressed admiration.

It was told that Hanson had perpetrated a kind of *double entente* on one occasion, grimly connecting his crippled foot and heavy shoe with that strong will of his which would win a battle or a game if it were possible to win, saying: "Boys, clubs are trumps!" And the name "Old Flintlock," which had been bestowed upon him, acquired now a new significance and new importance. Graves, too, a youth of less than twenty-four years, came in for allusions that would have led the unacquainted to suppose that this particular hero of Donelson was as old and as wise as Priam was when Troy fell. And so on of others at that time less known.

In the gloomy days that followed the defeat of Crittenden, the fall of Fort Henry and Fort Donelson, and the retreat southward, the consciousness that their fellow-soldiers of Kentucky had made themselves a name which shone out despite the clouds served to console, to quicken hope, to kindle anew the martial fire in those who claimed them as their own.

Here the Second Kentucky took for the brigade the initiatory in that bitter experience which followed it like a Nemesis to the close.

The blind believer in Fate would say that these gallant sons of Kentucky had fallen under inexorable decree and that it was malevolent. Let the reader, whether prepossessed in favour of the Southern movement or of the coercive measures of the Washington government, consider, with what impartial spirit is now possible to him, the conduct and the characteriztics of these men and their trials, and say whether they were not typical of all that followed. If he sees aright, he can but wonder that as the years went by despairing rage did not move them to cry out against circumstances not of their own making, that seemed to mock their courage, laugh at their constancy, and wanton with their blood. Here was Buckner, a trained and experienced soldier, with the confidence of the army,—but unhappily subordinate to others, and without power except to perform the part assigned by others.

How well he did it, let Federal as well as Confederate writers and archives attest. The sturdy and heroic Hanson, and the knightly Graves, who of himself was an "*oriflamme* of war" and needed not helmet or plume to lead others "amid the ranks of war," but could come "looking," as a soldier said, "like a common gunner," and rouse his fellow-countrymen to dare anything with him,—these and such as these Kentucky had there, and during these terrible days how nobly they maintained the name they bore! No supineness in preparation; no faltering in fight; no tame submission to repulse, but ever a readiness, even an eagerness, to regain lost ground and keep their standard well to the front,—the rank and file, so led, fought their foes by day and withstood the bitter elements by night; and so well did they do what they were set to do that up to the very hour of capitulation, notwithstanding the enemy had gained a lodgement on the part of the line which they had left with the troops from the fort, they believed that victory was theirs.

The temper they had shown justified the conclusion that if at 10 o'clock on the morning of February 15th the Confederate Army had marched out by the Charlotte road, as it could have done, with Buckner as rear-guard, his Kentuckians, (and nothing invidious as to the others of the division is meant by this—they were gallant fellows all), could not have been driven into precipitate flight or thrown into disastrous confusion, but would have fought and fallen step by step, all day, to stay the rush of the victors upon Floyd's retreating columns.

But this privilege was denied them. They stacked arms and marched away captive. It was but natural that they should contemplate with some bitterness their costly sacrifice in blood and in suffering that brought no substantial advantage, but consigned them to prison; yet, they had nothing with which to reproach themselves.

Note the career of the brigade henceforth. Go with it to Shiloh, to Stone River, and to Chickamauga; follow its fortunes on that long and trying campaign in which Sherman pushed it away towards the sea, through Georgia and South Carolina, in its efforts to narrow the track of the destroyer,—and what do we find but a repetition of the fortunes of the Second Regiment and the Kentucky Battery in their main features, with additional and intensified evils?

These men were volunteers, fighting for the establishment of a government in whose principles they believed, rather than for one of their own, as Kentucky, according to their seeing, was now in the gall of bitterness and the bonds of iniquity, from which even the success of the South might not relieve her; yet they fought as though to drive an invader from their own doors or to avenge a wrong that had touched them above other men.

Ever faithful as they were, ever prompt to attack and loth to yield, they nevertheless had one ever-present grief; though they executed their part in all operations that looked to the discomfiture of the enemy and helped to win victories; bore without serious complaint the hardships to which all were subjected (though many in less degree); had their honoured, able and trusted leaders taken from them by orders, or killed leading them in fight, one after another; reddened every battlefield with their blood,—this grief, this always unanswered question, was with them, as doubtless it was with the brave fellows who were floated away captive from Dover wharf. "What does it avail? After we have done all and borne all, where is the strong and cunning hand to seize and keep what we bleed and die for?"

Of the prison life of the regiment and battery, but little need be said. It was similar to that of all others at that period of the war. Gen. Buckner and Col. Hanson were carried to Fort Warren, in Boston Harbor; the line officers at first to Camp Chase, then to Johnson's Island; and the non-commissioned officers and men of two companies to Camp Douglass, the others to Camp Morton. At that time prison life, either North or South, had not assumed the horrible features that afterward characterized it; and the confinement and surveillance were disagreeable chiefly because of monotony; of restlessness away from their comrades in the field; of the sore discomfort that the freeborn feel when watched and guarded and in danger from the shots of murderous sentinels, of whom some were found in almost every prison—cowardly creatures who were strangers to the manliness of those foemen that seek to kill only in honourable battle and respect each other when the battle is done.

To give even the more interesting details of this prison experience would require a volume, and this cannot be attempted. These Kentuckians, though they had been overcome, in connection with others, were not subdued; and to them any enforced confinement was so hateful that it was natural that they should lay plans to escape, either singly or in squads, or by general uprising. Many actually got away; and all would have done so, it is said, had it not been that from some source the authorities got information and were prepared to prevent the execution of their plans.

On one occasion they made a march in force over a weak part of the enclosure, which they had discovered, and which they passed without difficulty; but they were met just outside by a body of Federal troops drawn up in line, who had been made acquainted with the design, and were posted there in readiness, both to prevent escape and punish for the attempt. The prisoners had managed to procure a few arms; but though they resisted, its only effect was to cause the shedding of their own blood. Such of them as had arms returned the fire of the soldiers, hoping to find but a small party, which they could succeed in driving; but they speedily learned their mistake, and were remanded to the prison barracks where they were kept under more rigid control than even before.

INCIDENTS AND ANECDOTES: AT AND AFTER DONELSON.

1. First Men of the Brigade Killed.—When the detail of thirteen men made the gallant little fight at Whippoorwill Bridge, December 4th, 1861, against Netter's detachment, which outnumbered him nearly seven to one, George Campbell, Co. A, and Hatch Jupin, Co. B, (Ninth Kentucky), were killed. These were the first of the brigade to be killed in action; and H. B. Nelson, Co. G, (Second Kentucky), who fell at Donelson, February 13th, 1862, was the first to be killed in a great battle.

2. Carson's Wrath When Semple Fell.— A participant in the battle says: "As the eight companies of our regiment came up on the flank of B and G, after their separate charge, and these were endeavouring to take their proper places, I heard Lieut. Carson, of Co. K, call out in ringing tones, 'Forward, men! Avenge Charlie Semple's death!' Though of another company, I had learned to like Semple, and felt a deep pang of regret that so gallant a soldier had fallen. I never meet him now without thinking of poor Carson (killed at Chickamauga), and the fierce wrath with which he urged on his men to avenge his friend and brother officer. Semple was wounded, but not killed as he supposed; and he lives today, (1898), one of the noblest survivors of that gallant band."

3. Still Full of Fight.—When Lieut. Ed Keene was mortally wounded in the engagement on the left Saturday morning, Lieut. Higgins asked permission after the firing ceased to take his servant and carry him to the boat and see that he had proper attention, little expecting that there would be another fight before he could get back. That afternoon as the regiment was hurried to its rifle-pits, Adj. Stake took charge of Co. B, now without a commissioned office; but when it rallied on the crest of the hill, Hanson put Lieut. Ed F. Spears in command of Co. B, so that he led both B and G. Wounded as Spears was, (carrying one arm in a sling), "he seemed ready, indeed anxious," wrote a member of Co. B, "to lead us in a bayonet charge to drive the enemy out of the works which they had taken from us."

4. Buckner's Shot at Impertinence.—Though Grant treated Gen. Buckner with characteriztic manliness, there were not wanting smart fellows among his officers who could not profit by their chief's example. As Buckner, with his faithful staff, stepped on board the boat that was to convey them northward, one of his regiments raised a thrilling cheer, when a Federal band, apparently in derision, struck up Yankee Doodle. An officer afterward asked Buckner in Grant's presence, and in a very sarcastic tone, whether the national air did not revive in his mind some pleasant associations of the past. "Yes, Colonel," he replied, "but it also reminds me of an incident which occurred a few days ago in our camp. A soldier was being drummed out of one of the regiments for a serious offense. The musicians were playing the Rogue's March. 'Stop,' cried the fellow, 'you have mistaken the tune. Play Yankee Doodle; a half million of rogues march to that every day.'"

5. Escaping from Camp Morton.—From the diary of a prisoner, I copy a few lines referring to escapes, previously noticed: "We had some rare times planning to get away. One fellow was put into a trash box and carried out by some negroes captured with a Mississippi regiment—and these negroes were as true to the Southern cause as the best of us. Once a collection was taken up, and of our scanty funds we contributed enough to bribe a Lieutenant of the Guard to let four of our boys escape. The men had a way, too, of getting out at night; and the sentinels had a very disagreeable way of firing into camp when anything unusual occurred. Those inside would, of course, lie low while this was going on."

6. Dying in Prison.—A hospital is no doubt a fearful place under any circumstances; but when the inmates are prisoners, suffering and dying away from home and friends, it beggars description. The cries of some in their last agony are heartrending. "Where is my mother?" "Oh! tell my wife to come to see me before I die!" "My poor little children! Left without a friend on earth! "These, and such as these, and the attendant scenes—they give us vividly one of the dreadful aspects of war. One captive brought in had been unable to tell his name and his command, and nothing was known of him when he died except that he was No. 13.—From a Camp Morton Diary.

7. A Fratricidal War.—A gallant and keenly observant soldier of Co. B, Second Kentucky, to whom the author is much indebted for valuable information, tells of a singular and affecting circumstance that occurred during the fighting at Donelson: Oliver B. Steele, of Henderson, was one of the members of Co. B, Fourth Kentucky, (afterward a lieutenant), and the company, as hitherto explained, was then part of Graves's Battery. Passing one day over a portion of the field from

which the enemy had been driven, Capt. Graves discovered a young Federal soldier, badly wounded and suffering greatly, and learned from him that he was Ollie Steele's brother. Graves had him removed and placed under shelter of the rifle pits occupied by his brother's company, and everything possible was done to relieve him; but his wound was mortal and he died there.

A somewhat similar case occurred at Shiloh which is recorded as another instance of the singular relations which existed at that time between members of families, while the ties of nature were still strong, though brother's arms were turned against brother in the terrible strife. The writer, wounded at Shiloh, was helped off the field by Assistant-Surgeon Newberry and Ike Martin, and the way to temporary hospital was strewn with dead and dying Federal soldiers. He presently noticed that Newberry was scrutinising with apparent anxiety the countenance of every one who lay near the road, and he was led to ask why he did so.

The reply was: "I am looking for Hiram! Everywhere I have gone with the infirmary corps today I have been looking for Hiram!" This was his brother, whose regiment he believed to be in the fight, and though he did not find him, he learned soon afterward that he was mortally wounded there and died after being carried northward to hospital.

8. "Whar's 'Baze'?"—Captain (afterward Colonel) McDowell and Lieut. Tom Beaseman, of Co. F, Second Kentucky, went to Donelson with a joint interest in a negro cook, George, who was at the time as rank a Southerner as his masters. After the surrender George was talking over the battle with a German in the Federal Army, and indignantly repelling the charge that his Confederate friends had been beaten. "We whipped you," said George, "every time we went after you."

"Yes," rejoined the German, "but we caught you all at last."

"Caught us all, did you?" retorted the loyal George, "Whar's Baze?"

Now, Beaseman had declined to abide by the terms and gotten off with some of Forrest's men (though he was captured before he reached Nashville), and from the lofty tone of the negro the other thought "Baze" was someone in high command and that Grant hadn't at all made a clean sweep of the Kentucky contingent.

9. Wouldn't Take His Own Medicine.—While the reserve companies of the Second Kentucky were under fire at Donelson for the first time, the boys, who had to stand and take it without returning as good as they got, very naturally dodged and ducked their heads as the bullets zipped by. Col. Hanson called attention and told them to be steady—that there was no use in dodging, as when they heard the bullet it was already gone by. Just as he concluded his speech one came near getting him, and he involuntarily ducked his head. This raised a laugh at his expense, which he good-humouredly parried with: "Boys, you may dodge a little if they come too close."

Chapter 4

Battle of Shiloh

It has been noticed in Chapter 2 that after the defeat of Zollicoffer and Crittenden, Gen. Johnston withdrew his ordnance and the bulk of his army supplies southward from Bowling Green, by rail, and was ready by the afternoon of February 11th to leave the place.

On that evening, orders were received in the various regiments of the Kentucky Brigade to march out on the pike at nine next morning, and wait for further instructions. Rumour had already been busy, and it was looked upon among all ranks and classes of soldiers as certain that Bowling Green was to be evacuated; but the uncertainty which must always rest upon the minds of the great body of an army during the execution of a movement was to the Kentucky troops painful in the extreme, for it had been whispered about that Kentucky was to be abandoned.

Those who were in the confidence of the general officers, and knew the facts as regarded the situation, could not for a moment have contemplated an advance on either flank or front; but the wild hope obtained with many that it might be the initiatory to active operations in Kentucky; that the disaster at Fishing Creek would be retrieved; and Kentucky be yet secured to the Confederacy by some bold stroke on the part of the commander.

The troops, whose homes lay in the direction in which the stores had been sent, had great cause to fear the overrunning of their own territory; but still, to soldiers who have but a feeble and indefinite idea as to the value of any single step in a campaign, the thought of turning their faces homeward, and once more revisiting the land of their love, silences question as to its propriety in point of public good; and whether the general blunders or is guided by wisdom, they are sure, in the inception of the movement, to be in accord with him, as, actual knowledge of the real facts being meagre, their reasoning is largely influenced by their feelings.

From a similar cause, the Kentucky Brigade experienced nothing but gloom and apprehension on that morning, when drawn up on the turnpike awaiting anxiously for the order to determine the direction of the march; and though everything seemed to point that way, it was with sinking, sickened hearts that their faces were turned toward Bowling Green, and they realised, in all its force, the sad fact that their homes must be given up to the enemy. A thousand painful fancies thronged their minds, and lent a poignancy to the grief that they would have felt to depart, under any circumstances, for an indefinite period, from all that was dear to them in life. They were not only to be absent, but the foeman was to be there. Throughout the length and breadth of the State, soldiers in actual uniform, or the worse enemy born and reared among them, but opposed to them and their families, would swarm; and legal restraints, and moral restraints as well, were measurably removed. What had they not to fear? What was lacking to complete to their minds a picture of wrong and oppression—of insult, danger, suffering, to those whom they had hoped to protect?

The first day's march, however, did not serve to awaken them fully to all the bitterness of the truth. At Bowling Green, they reasoned, some new developments might take place, and from that point some speedy march upon a body of the enemy might be made that would change the relative position of the armies; and though they went forward in a half-despairing, sullen mood, they were fain to comfort themselves with this one grain of hope, that Kentucky would not be given up without a struggle.

The night of the 12th was passed in the huts built by the Second, Third, and Fourth Regiments at Mill Springs, three miles below Bowling Green, on the left of the Nashville pike. The next morning marching orders were received which dispelled the last ray of hope, as far as continued occupancy of the State was concerned; and the Central Army of Kentucky took up its line of march toward Nashville, the Kentucky Brigade constituting rear-guard of infantry, one company of the Fourth Regiment special rear-guard for brigade, while Morgan and Biffle moved in front, and in call of the infantry. Gen. Hardee, who had commanded that army from early in December, was still in the rear with the remaining cavalry force and some light artillery.

The enemy shelled Bowling Green that day from early morning until they had fired the depot, and the last Confederates had retired—

Gen. Hindman, who was in the rear of Gen. Breckinridge on the march of the 12th to Bowling Green, having destroyed the bridge across Big Barren, just as the head of the Federal column, now in pursuit, had appeared in sight, and thus prevented their immediate passage into the town.

The difficulties attending the retreat were great, but a more orderly and more successful one, under all the circumstances, was perhaps never accomplished. Popular indignation, even rage—blind, but full of confidence and of such force as would have goaded common minds into desperation—was poured out upon the head of the commander. The wintry season, inclement, unpropitious beyond measure for such an undertaking, was calculated both to tax the skill of the general, and destroy the martial ardour, even the ordinary morale, of the troops. Dangers menaced the retreating army as much as hardships marked its course. The surrender of Donelson took place on Sunday morning, the 16th, and Nashville was uncovered twelve or fifteen hours before the rear-guard of his army passed over the bridge.

Demoralisation almost unavoidably consequent upon the state of the public mind and the nature of a retreat threatened to destroy the efficiency of bodies of troops who could not have been spared in case of an attack. And the state of the weather—heavy rains having set in before the command had quitted the vicinity of Nashville—foreboded evil, in retarding, if not arresting, the progress of the army, by swollen streams and impassable mud. But everything went on with a regularity and a degree of order that seemed to have been the result of circumstances working in entire harmony with the plans of the great general, instead of having been adverse at every step; and he reached Corinth with so little loss of men or munitions as to mark him one of the first administrative minds of his age and country.

But to return to the more immediate notice of the command under consideration. They bivouacked on the night of Thursday, the 13th, two miles north of Franklin, the capital of Simpson county. The weather, which had been for the last two days comparatively pleasant, turned cold during the night, and on the morning of the 14th the ground was covered with a slight snow, the wind had set in from the north-west, and it was intensely cold. Preparations were made for an early march, but upon reaching Franklin a halt was ordered for some purpose, and the suffering was so great that it was with difficulty that the men could be induced to keep together.

Stragglers from the ranks filled the town, and many showed themselves already adepts at procuring whiskey, and what the cavalry afterward taught them to call the "square meal." At 10 o'clock the march was resumed, but another halt was ordered when scarcely out of sight of town, and unavoidable depredations upon private property began. The place was an open lane, where no cover from the wind was afforded, and they acknowledged the force of the trite maxim, that "necessity knows no law." Long lines of fires speedily appeared, and physical comfort was secured for the hour at the expense of the consciousness that some man's rail fence had been speedily devoted to destruction. They finally got properly under way, and reached Camp Trousdale that night. This consisted of a lot of frame buildings, at Mitchellsville, Tennessee, just over the Kentucky line, which had been used as quarters for the Tennessee troops recruited in that section of the State during the preceding summer.

The night was one of the most disagreeable that they had ever passed. The cold was bitter, and not only was fuel hard to procure, but fires, built on the ground, inside the houses, were intolerable on account of the smoke, which, having no proper egress, filled them, and drove either the occupant or the fire from the building. After an almost sleepless and a restless night spent here, the march was resumed on the morning of the 15th (Saturday), and, after traveling twenty-seven miles, the brigade went into camp about night-fall. The cold was still severe.

On the afternoon of this day, it was rumoured that a Federal force of some description was in front of the marching column, and hasty preparations were made to meet it. The men, though almost exhausted by exertions necessary to proceed at the rapid rate which they had travelled during the day, were nevertheless prompt to fall in and march to what they deemed the threatened front. It soon transpired that there was no enemy in the neighbourhood, and the march was resumed.

Next afternoon, the brigade passed over the bridge and through Nashville, thence five miles out on the Murfreesboro' pike, and went into camp. Intelligence had already reached the city that Donelson had fallen, and the wild rumours which heralded the approach of the Federal transports had thrown the population into a frenzy of excitement, and a widespread demoralisation, which threatened violence among the people, and even the destruction of the city. The efforts of soldiers, sent in for the purpose of restoring order, availed little, and confusion reigned triumphant throughout that terrible night and the next day. Property, both public and private, was ruthlessly destroyed or appropriated, and a perfect exodus of the people seemed taking place.

At the encampment of the Kentucky brigade, too, everything was dreary enough. The weather had undergone a change during Sunday, and now the rain poured down continuously. Having arrived in the night, the tents were erected in a careless manner, generally without the precaution of ditching, and consequently afforded little protection against the storm. The comfortless appearance of everything next morning—men whose clothes had been flooded in their tents during the night, hovering over the smoking pretence of fire, that could scarcely be coaxed into burning; heaps of blankets as thoroughly drenched as though they had lain out in the open air; the braying of uneasy mules and the swearing of teamsters; pools of water all around, and, in some instances, inside the very tents from which men had emerged; a lowering sky and still drizzling rain—all combined to complete a picture of half-despondent wretchedness that cannot be described.

On the 17th, the command remained in camp, while Gen. Breckinridge was having some additions made to the transportation facilities of his troops, and securing quartermaster's and subsistence stores. On the afternoon of the 18th, the brigade moved five miles farther down the pike and encamped till the 20th, when it was marched to within two miles of La Vergne, and thence, next morning, to Murfreesboro', or rather a mile below Murfreesboro', and encamped in the enclosed woods to the left of the Fayetteville road.

These few details are given to convey some idea of the hardships and exposures in camp and on march in the inclement season of winter, which the brigade encountered almost in the very outset of its career.

At Murfreesboro', Gen. Johnston was joined by Gen. George B. Crittenden, and the army was reorganised on the 23rd of February. It comprised three divisions under Generals Hardee, Crittenden and Pillow. Breckinridge's brigade was designated "Reserve Brigade," and was made to consist now of the Third, Fourth, Sixth and Ninth Regiments Kentucky Infantry; three battalions of other infantry troops under Lieut.-Cols. Clifton, Hale, and Crews; First Regiment Kentucky Cavalry, under Col. B. H. Helm, Morgan's squadron, and the light batteries of Byrne and Cobb. In addition to the officers already mentioned, Gen. Breckinridge attached to his staff Capts. Theodore O'Hara and A. L. Lindsey, as Assistant Inspectors-General, and Dr. B. W. Avent, as medical director.

On the 28th of February the march southward was resumed, and after something near a week's delay at Decatur, where the army crossed the Tennessee, Gen. Breckinridge encamped at Burnsville, Miss., on the 22nd of March.

The march from Murfreesboro' to Burnsville was attended with little less suffering and little more of interest than that previously described.

Nothing of special historic interest, strictly pertaining to the Kentucky troops, occurred during the time which elapsed between the 22nd of March, when tents were pitched at Burnsville, and the battle of Shiloh. The usual routine of drill and camp duty went on, and no means were neglected to improve them in all the habits and general attainments of the soldier.

On the 29th of March, Gen. Johnston announced that still another reorganisation of the forces had been determined upon, and that it would be known as the "Army of the Mississippi." A division was organised and placed under command of Gen. Breckinridge. This was named as the Reserve Corps, and consisted of the Kentucky brigade, Statham's brigade, Bowen's brigade, Forrest's regiment of cavalry, Morgan's squadron, a company of cavalry under Capt. Phil B. Thompson, which had reported to Gen. Breckinridge as a body guard or headquarter scouts, and the light artillery pertaining to each organisation.

On the afternoon of the 3rd of April, an order was received, the purport of which was that the Reserve Corps would march on the morrow, at daylight, prepared "to meet the enemy in twenty-four hours." Some Enfield rifles, with accoutrements and ammunition, just received, were distributed about nightfall, to displace the most inferior guns in the Kentucky Brigade, as well as to supply those who were yet without any whatever. Rations were prepared during the night, and at daylight on Friday morning, April 4th, tents were struck, baggage wagons loaded, and most of them sent immediately to Corinth, while the ordnance and supply train prepared to accompany the troops, and the march began which was to result in one of the most wonderful battles of the age.

They went out by way of Farmington and Monterey—the Reserve Corps numbering, perhaps, seven thousand men, of all arms. After a hard day's march, considering the nature of the ground over which it passed, it went into camp, or rather bivouac (for no tents had been brought out for the troops), and during the night the rain poured down almost incessantly from 11 o'clock till daylight. The artillery, or a portion of it, was late at night reaching its position, as much of the road passed over during the day had been ill adapted to the advance of the heavier pieces and the now well-laden caissons.

Next day, though fair for the most part, was more unpropitious for military movements than the preceding, since the rain had rendered the roads almost impassable; and it was not until near nightfall that the reserve reached the point which it should have occupied the night preceding, according to the original plan of Gen. Johnston, to attack on the morning of the 5th. This was near the junction of the Burnsville and Corinth roads leading to Pittsburg Landing, and about four miles from the river.

The remainder of the army, consisted of three corps, under the respective command of Gens. Bragg, Polk, and Hardee, numbered in the order in which we have named their commanders. The Third Corps, consisting of fifteen thousand five hundred and twenty-four men, was thrown well forward and placed in position for the attack, which was to be brought on by Gen. Hardee next morning. The First Corps, under Gen. Bragg, consisting of nine thousand four hundred and twenty-two men, was formed also in line of battle a quarter of a mile in rear of Hardee. Gen. Polk was formed in column of brigades on the Corinth road, with its junction with that from Burnsville; while Gen. Breckinridge lay in similar column on the Burnsville road, and nearly opposite or on the right flank of Polk. The troops slept on their arms.

The night was clear, calm, and beautiful as such nights always are in the spring-time in such a clime; and the broken slumbers of the previous one, together with the fatigue of the day just closed, had prepared them for sleep. They lay down early, and were soon lost in slumber that was to be the last one of earth to thousands who gave themselves up to its restoring and refreshing embrace, and were awakened next morning by their officers, without the usual reveille.

Gen. Johnston's plan of attack—the failure to reach the ground on the evening of the 4th, as he designed, that he might have ample time to crush Grant before Gen. Buell could arrive with the Army of the Ohio—the position of the Federal troops between Lick and Owl Creeks, the nature of the ground, all things of this kind, in fact, have been so often described, and so dwelt upon as to have become trite, and we feel our inability to add to a proper understanding of the situation.

Sunday morning, April 6th, was one of the most serene and lovely of the season; there seemed, indeed, to be a peculiar stillness pervading everything, even to the birds and beasts, for though the sun rose in unclouded splendour, and the elevated ridge upon which the reserve troops were bivouacked glittered in its dewy robe, everything but man seemed to be drinking in delight, instead of indulging in noisy demonstration, and he moved almost silently about, with thoughts bent upon the coming storm.

The troops of Breckinridge and Polk had scarcely time to take their morning meal before Hardee's artillery began to roar—slowly at first, at a single point; then more rapidly, and from different parts of his line. Gen. Breckinridge had orders to move forward as soon as Gen. Polk should clear the road in front, and hold himself in readiness to strengthen the advance lines, or attack in force should it become necessary. The enemy were at first driven precipitately back, but the nature of the ground, most of which was covered with forest trees, and in many places with a dense undergrowth, which afforded a complete screen from observation, enabled them to recover, in a measure, the advantage lost by the carelessness of their commander in allowing them to be surprised. They hastily reformed, and the conflict began to rage in earnest. Hardee and Bragg intermingled.

In a short time, Polk had sent forward one brigade to support Bragg's right; then one to support his left; then the remaining two were led against the enemy's strongest point, the centre. Meanwhile indications were plain that an attempt was being made to turn the Confederate left, resting on or near Owl Creek, and Beauregard ordered Breckinridge to leave the Kentucky brigade to meet that movement. It thus became, for the day, a virtually independent organisation, under command of Col. Robert P. Trabue, of the Fourth regiment. The following is the careful and exhaustive report of that intrepid and capable officer:

> Headquarters First Kentucky Brigade, Reserve Corps,
> Corinth, Miss., April 15, 1862.

Capt. George B. Hodge, A. A. G.—

Sir: I have the honour to submit the following report of the conduct of this brigade in the actions of the 6th and 7th instant, at Shiloh, and during the few days succeeding:

The brigade was composed of the Third Kentucky Infantry, Lieut. Col. Ben Anderson commanding; Fourth Kentucky, Lieut.-Col. Hynes, (see *Biography* of Maj. Monroe); Sixth Kentucky, Col. Joseph H. Lewis; Ninth Kentucky, Col. Thomas H. Hunt; Fourth Alabama Battalion, Maj. J. M. Clifton; Hale's Thirty-First Alabama Regiment, Lieut.-Col. Galbraith; a battalion of Tennessee infantry, commanded by Lieut.-Col. Crews; battery of light artillery, Capt. Edward P. Byrne; battery of light artillery, Capt. Robert Cobb, and Capt. John H. Morgan's squadron of horse—amounting, in all, to about twenty-four hundred men, exclusive of the squadron, which did not receive orders from me.

The Reserve Corps, commanded by Gen. Breckinridge, having moved on Friday morning, at daylight, from Burnsville, in the rain, bivouacked that night, after a day's march of twenty-three miles, near Monterey. On the next morning, shortly before daylight, after having been exposed to the rain during the night, the corps was moved up to near Mickey's house, where it became necessary to halt until the roads were cleared of the troops in front, which, occurring in the afternoon, enabled Gen. Breckinridge to march, on the neighbourhood road to the right of Mickey's house, to a point within three or four miles of Pittsburg Landing, where, on Saturday night, we again bivouacked.

On Sunday morning, the 6th, having advanced about one mile from place of bivouac, with this brigade leading, the command was again halted at the intersection of the "bark" and interior roads until the front was cleared by the march forward of a portion of the command of Polk (who was to precede the Reserve Corps). When this occurred, I received Gen. Breckinridge's order to move forward in a condition for easy deployment in rear of Polk's line, and almost immediately afterward was commanded to form line of battle and advance in that manner. The line having been instantly formed, the Third Kentucky on the right, and the Fourth Kentucky on the left, with the batteries in the rear and opposite the centre, the brigade was put in motion, following Polk's command.

Having proceeded thus a short distance, Breckinridge communicated to me an order, just then received by him, to move with his two rear brigades on the Hamburg road, which led far to the right of the position first assigned to him. He at the same time directed me to continue moving forward on the line previously indicated (inclining to the left of the principal line of battle), in the rear of Polk, and he then parted from me.

Moving forward as directed, I came under the enemy's fire at half-past 9 o'clock a.m., having reached the verge of a long, crescent-shaped, open field (which was without fencing), about one and a half miles from Pittsburg Landing. The shot and shell from the woods on the opposite side of the field fell thick and fast around us, but caused very few casualties. Governor George W. Johnson and Col. Robert McKee, volunteer aids, here lost their horses, when the governor shouldered a musket, and joined the company of Capt. Ben Monroe,

Fourth Kentucky.

I here halted the command for an instant in a slight depression of the ground, and rode forward on the open field to observe what might lie before and around me, and to place Cobb's Battery in position, which I did, but it was afterward moved under orders from someone, and without my knowledge.

Shortly before this, by order of Beauregard, I had detached the Third Kentucky, Fourth Alabama Battalion, and Crews' Battalion, with Byrne's Battery, to the right, to support Gen. Anderson; and in the engagement, Lieut.-Col. Anderson, commanding Third Kentucky, and Maj. Johnston, of the same, were wounded. Captains Stone, Pierce, and Emerson, Lieut. Bagwell, commanding company, and acting Lieut. White, of that regiment, were killed. Capt. Bowman, Adjt. McGoodwin, and Lieutenants Ross and Ridgeway were wounded—the adjutant severely. My aid, Charleton Morgan, was also wounded here, and my volunteer aid, John Hooe, had his horse killed. Not having been specially informed of the casualties that occurred here in the Alabama and Tennessee battalions and Byrne's Battery, I am unable to speak definitely of them.

The examination which I made from the old field showed it to have been the scene of recent conflict, but at that time our lines there seemed to have been broken, and no troops of ours were in sight. I discovered also to my left and front two camps of the enemy still occupied by his troops, and I saw them also in the woods across the field in front of his camps. I immediately moved by the left flank to the left, and confronted him. I had scarcely taken my new position—in fact, was changing the front of the left wing—when he deployed before me. I opened my fire on him when he was thus employed, and soon received his in return. The combat here was a severe one, and lasted an hour and a quarter. I had only three regiments in line (the Fourth, Sixth, and Ninth Kentucky), the Thirty-First Alabama in reserve, and no battery at command (both of my own having been sent further to the right, at which point we seemed to be pressed).

The enemy appeared to outnumber us greatly. Ignorant of the topography of the country, and not knowing his force, I was for a while reluctant to charge; and as he was in the woods, too, with some advantage of position, I fought him, as I have said, for an hour and a quarter, killing and wounding four or five hundred of the Forty-sixth Ohio Infantry alone, as well as many of another Ohio regiment, a Missouri regiment, and some Iowa troops, from all of whom we eventually took prisoners. It would be impossible to praise too highly the steadiness and valor of my troops in this engagement. I lost here many men and several officers, among whom were Captains Ben Desha and John W. Caldwell, severely, and Adjt. William Bell, mortally wounded, all of the Ninth Kentucky; also, in the same regiment, Capt. James R. Bright, Lieut. J. L. Moore, and Lieut. R. M. Simmons were wounded. In the Fourth Kentucky, Capt. John A. Adair, First Lieut. John Bird Rogers, commanding Co. A, and Lieut. Robert Dunn, were severely wounded, while in the Sixth Kentucky, Capt. W. Lee Harned was wounded mortally.

The Thirty-First Alabama, on the left, lost several officers and men, and elicited general praise for its gallantry. During the engagement the men of no part of the brigade, at any time, faltered or fell back, while the enemy had to reform more than once.

At length, after having extended my line by adding my reserve to the left of it, and obtaining, as a support, Gen. Stewart with a part of his brigade, and a part of Gen. Anderson's command, which I found in my rear in a wooded ravine, I gave the order to fix bayonets, and move forward in double-quick time at a charge, which was executed in the handsomest manner, and with complete success. The enemy, unwilling and unable to stand this charge, ran through their camps into the woods in their rear, whither we followed them. They were, however, too badly routed to make a stand, and for several hundred yards I moved forward without opposition. These woods intervene between the field and camps I have described, and the field and camp in which Gen. Prentiss surrendered, and are about three quarters of a mile in width.

Soon after having entered the woods I found the ground broken and covered with a thick undergrowth, so that I was obliged to move cautiously, and with my front covered by skirmishers. I was likewise delayed and embarrassed by some Louisiana troops, who were off to my left, and dressed in blue colours like the enemy, as also by a battery, which was firing across my front from the right. I sent out an aid to learn the identity of the Louisiana troops, and a detachment to ascertain the character of the battery; and having had the fire of this changed, I moved forward to the verge of the field in which Prentiss surrendered, having encountered and dispersed a regiment, said to be of Missouri, and taken several prisoners, who were sent to the rear.

At this field Gen. Breckinridge and others were hotly pressing the enemy on the right, many of whom attempted to gain the woods through which I had passed, and at one time I was apprehensive they would turn my left, but, by altering my position and delivering several well-directed fires, they were turned back upon their camps, into which also, for some time, I directed my fire with effect. The lines being gradually—after much hard fighting—drawn more and more closely around this camp, forced the surrender of Prentiss, who seemed to be the last of their generals who made a stand. This brigade entered the camp nearly simultaneously with Gen. Breckinridge and others from the right. I was halted here for a moment by order of Gen. Hardee, and directed to send a regiment back in charge of the prisoners, and I assigned to this duty Lieut.-Col. Crews (who had rejoined me) with his battalion.

Finding the troops who had come in from my right halting one or two hundred yards in my front, I allowed the Sixth and Ninth Kentucky Regiments hastily to exchange their guns for Enfield rifles, which the enemy had surrendered, and I then moved up and rejoined Gen. Breckinridge, who, with Statham's and Bowen's brigades, was occupying the front line, being on the crest of the hill (or high land) overlooking the narrow valley of the Tennessee River, on which, and nearby, was Pittsburg Landing. (He here alludes simply to those of the Sixth and Ninth, who had not been supplied when Enfields were distributed at Burnsville, on the evening of the 3rd inst.)

Having been halted here for more than an hour, we endured a most terrific cannonade and shelling from the enemy's gunboats. My command, however, had seen too much hard fighting to be alarmed, and the Fourth Kentucky stood firm while some of our troops to the front fell back through their lines in confusion. In Co. D, of this regiment, I lost at this place eleven men, and Lieut. H. M. Keller, of the Ninth Regiment, was wounded.

From this position, when it was nearly dark, we were ordered to the rear to encamp, which movement was effected in good order. I followed, in the darkness of the night, the Purdy road, after having reunited to my command Byrne's Battery and the others of my troops who had been detached to the right, not including, however, Cobb's Battery. This battery, after having been moved from the position in which I had placed it (as previously stated) maintained itself with extraordinary gallantry, as I am informed, against a large force, which, however, killed, in the contest, nearly all its horses, and killed and wounded thirty-seven of the men. Having been thus disabled, Capt. Cobb moved his battery off the field, with mules, to the rear, under orders to do so, all danger being past.

My command occupied the vacated camps of the Forty-sixth Ohio and Sixth Iowa Regiments, on the Purdy road, near the bridge over Owl Creek; but the tents having been mainly destroyed, my men were again exposed to rain, which fell during the night. The camps, however, were rich in subsistence, as in almost everything else, and, after a bountiful supper, they slept, despite the rain.

After having obtained returns from the whole command, I myself rode till eleven o'clock p.m., to find a general officer to whom to report for orders, and then sent an aid (with a mounted escort) for the same object, who rode all night without success.

Thus, closed Sunday, with a loss to this brigade of about seventy-five killed and three hundred and fifty wounded.

Early Monday morning, having caused the arms to be discharged and cleaned, I prepared to renew the contest. Soon hearing firing to the right, and somewhat to the front, and seeing Gen. Ruggles' division marching to my rear, to form off the right, as I understood, and being also informed that the enemy was to the left, I ordered Byrne's Battery in position at the Owl Creek bridge, and formed in line parallel to the road. In a short time, my volunteer aid, Capt. Samuel Gray, of Kentucky, whom I had dispatched to the front for orders, returned with directions from Beauregard to move forward to whatever point the firing seemed heaviest.

I accordingly moved forward on the road, marching by the flank at double-quick; and, having passed Shiloh Church, leaving it to the right, I advanced about three-quarters of a mile beyond it. At this point I met Bragg, who ordered me to form line perpendicularly to the road and to the left of it, which I did by fronting the brigade, and then changing front forward on first battalion.

While this movement was being made, I rode forward and placed Byrne's Battery in position, on a slight eminence or ridge at the edge of a field, behind which (and at its base) the change of front would bring my line, thus being myself at the same time at a point where I could observe the execution of this movement. In this position, Capt. Byrne served his guns with skill and gallantry, silencing one and greatly damaging another battery of the enemy. The enemy's right wing was in our front; and for four hours, in the presence and under the orders of Bragg, we checked his advance at this quarter.

The battery of Byrne drew the continuous fire of several guns from the enemy, by which I lost several men. It was pleasing to see with what alacrity my men volunteered to aid the battery as its men were wounded or became exhausted.

Meanwhile the firing had been approaching nearer and nearer to us from the right and centre, and I was ordered to move from my position to the support of these points of our line. In advancing to the right, I perceived that our forces were passing from their right toward the left, while the enemy were moving on parallel lines with them, and in a corresponding direction. In proceeding, I became engaged with the enemy in woods to the right, and a little in rear of the position I had just left, and bordering upon an old field, in which was a house that seemed to have been used as a forage depot. In and around this the enemy seemed well posted, in strong force, though much concealed behind logs and bags, apparently of corn, which appeared to have been arranged with that view.

While I was moving to my new position, the Fourth Kentucky Regiment and Fourth Alabama Battalion by Bragg's order, and without my knowledge, were moved out of the line and advanced against overwhelming numbers at the north side of the field, and to the north of the house just spoken of, being advised that they would be supported in the movement by Anderson's brigade.

At this time, I was with the Sixth and Ninth (and a remnant of the Third) Kentucky Regiments, on the west side of this field, and to the west of the house. The enemy was posted in the form of a crescent, the inner side being the front. The Fourth Kentucky Regiment and Fourth Alabama Battalion having approached to within one hundred paces of the enemy's line, opened fire upon him, and received in turn a destructive fire from both the wings and the centre. (See *Biography* of Col. Nuckols.) The contest was here continued for about twenty minutes, when the enemy fell back on their reserve, and the regiment and battalion prepared to charge them with the bayonet; but before this could be done the enemy again advanced, with redoubled forces, and they fell back on Anderson's brigade, four or five hundred yards in rear.

United with this, they again drove back the enemy, and thus, forward and backward, was the ground crossed and recrossed four times. This engagement is represented as having been most terrific, and, judging from the results, could scarcely have been exceeded in the courage and heroism displayed by our troops. Here that matchless officer, Thomas B. Monroe, Jr., after performing prodigies of valor, was killed near the close of the scene. Here, too, Adjt. Forman was killed, as was also Lieut. Dooley. Lieut.-Col. Hines, whose conduct was most cool and courageous, was here slightly wounded. Senior

Capt. Joseph P. Nuckols, who had been mounted, was likewise, after the most decided coolness and gallantry, severely wounded. Here also were wounded Captains Ben J. Monroe, Tho. W. Thompson, and James Fitzhenry. Lieut. Thomas Steele was severely wounded and afterward made prisoner, while Lieutenants John B. Moore and George B. Burnley were seriously, and Lieut. Peyton, slightly wounded.

All these officers were of the Fourth Kentucky, which went into action Sunday morning with 431 men. Many officers also of the Fourth Alabama Battalion, whose conduct was excellent, were among the wounded—for more definite mention of whom reference is made to the report from that command.

And here also fell that noble patriot, Gov. George W. Johnson, after having fought in the ranks of Capt. Ben Monroe's company (E, Fourth Kentucky), with unfaltering bravery from early Sunday morning to this unhappy moment. Eventually, seeing that they must be overpowered, these troops were withdrawn, and ordered a short distance to the rear, where they remained until reunited to the command.

With the Sixth and Ninth Regiments, on the west side of the position I have described, I was hotly engaged for an hour, at and during the time just mentioned above, when I had occasion often to admire the courage and ability of Colonels Joseph H. Lewis and Thomas H. Hunt, as well as the steadiness of their men. Our forces here were insufficient for a charge, and seeing the enemy's masses moving to his right, as also our own troops—being ordered by Gen. Breckinridge, to whom I had reported here, he stating at the same time that he could maintain himself to the right, where he was, but that the enemy's movements required more troops of ours on the left—I followed the movement and soon reached the brow of a hill on the main road to Pittsburg Landing, and about one hundred and fifty yards to the right of Shiloh Church.

At this point, upon my instance, Col. Marmaduke, with his Arkansas regiment, united with my command in support of the two twelve-pound howitzers which I had obtained from Gen. Polk, some three hundred yards in the rear, and had brought up to that position. The fragmentary forces of both armies had concentrated at this time around Shiloh Church, and, worn out as were our troops, the field was here successfully contested for two hours, when, as if by mutual consent, both sides desisted from the struggle. Shortly before the close of the combat, having heard from one of my aids that some troops were in line a few hundred yards in rear, I left Col. Hunt, Ninth Kentucky, in command, and galloped back to urge them to come up (intending with such a re-enforcement to charge the enemy with the bayonet), but I failed to secure their assistance.

Returning, I found that in my absence, Col. Hunt, with his usual gallantry, had ventured upon a charge, but found the enemy too strong for him, when he retired to the west side of Shiloh Church, where the command remained long after all other troops had been withdrawn, except a small force with Col. Tappan, of Arkansas.

In the conflicts of this day, Lieut.-Col. Robert A. Johnson, after exemplary conduct, was wounded; Capt. William Mitchell was killed; and Capt. George A. King, and Lieutenants Gillum, Harding, and Schaub were wounded—all of the Ninth Kentucky. In the Sixth Kentucky, Lieut.-Col. Cofer, a cool, brave, and efficient officer, was wounded; Capt. W. W. Bagby and Lieut. M. E. Aull were mortally wounded; Captains D. E. McKendree and John G. Hudson were likewise wounded, as were also Lieutenants L. M. Tucker and Charles Dawson, the last named of whom was taken prisoner. The Thirty-first Alabama Regiment behaved with praiseworthy gallantry. And here, though out of place, I will mention that of the Ninth Regiment four colour corporals were killed, and three colour corporals and the colour sergeant were wounded.

Late in the evening, my command being reunited, we rejoined Gen. Breckinridge, with Statham's brigade, and halted at the junction of two roads, both apparently leading from Pittsburg Landing, and about one and a half miles west of Shiloh Church, in the direction of Corinth.

******

Col. Hunt, being senior, was left, as stated, in command of the Sixth and Ninth, and had the honour, as chief in command of the two regiments, of firing the farewell shot—his being the last fighting of that eventful day. "Long after all other troops had been withdrawn," as Col. Trabue remarks, he was reunited with the remainder of the brigade.

******

With this force and some cavalry Gen. Breckinridge undertook to check any pursuit of our retiring army, and cover the retreat. This was a hard duty, exposed as the command had been, and wasted as they were by the loss of more than half their numbers; but the general was equal to the great undertaking, and his officers and men shared his devotion to duty.

Here we bivouacked in the mud, and were exposed to the rain which fell during the night. Gen. Breckinridge had in some way provided subsistence for the command, sufficient for the night and morning.

The enemy did not appear that night, and the next morning we slowly moved off three miles, to Mickey's house, taking with us the wounded, whom we found in abandoned wagons and in the houses on the roadside, as well as some captured property, which had been abandoned by other Confederate troops.

Arrived at Mickey's house, (where was a large hospital, with four or five hundred wounded men, a part of whom were Federal prisoners), we remained there three days, laboriously engaged in removing the wounded, burying the dead, and sending forward captured property. All having been accomplished, upon receiving orders from Beauregard, Breckinridge with his command moved into Corinth, arriving there on Friday.

While at Mickey's house, we had been advantageously posted to avoid surprise and repel attack. On Tuesday, Gen. Sherman's brigade of the enemy came to within a mile and a half of us, but, being attacked by our cavalry, which Breckinridge had stationed in the rear, that brigade was routed, losing forty or fifty killed, and about seventy-five prisoners, who were sent to Corinth.

Here I must be permitted to bear testimony to the resolution, ability, and endurance of Gen. Breckinridge, which in these last days were severely taxed, but were not wanting to the demands of the occasion.

Thus, I have given an account of the conduct of this brigade, in the battle of the 6th and 7th instants, and in the three or four days succeeding. I cannot too highly commend the gallantry and steadiness of these brave men.

The courage, coolness, and ability of Col. Hunt, of the Ninth Kentucky, were conspicuous, as were also those of his lieutenant-colonel, Robert A. Johnston, who was wounded on Monday morning, but kept his place. No man could have possessed more gallantry than was shown by Col. Lewis, of the Sixth Kentucky, and his lieutenant-colonel, Cofer. Major Hays, too, of the same regiment, behaved well. I had occasion often to remark the self-possession and ability of Lieut.-Col. Hynes, in command of the Fourth Kentucky (who was wounded, but did not leave the field), as also the conduct of Capt. Joseph P. Nuckols, of this regiment (who had been mounted).

The conduct of the lamented Monroe, Major of this regiment, was unsurpassed, and challenged the admiration of all. The conduct of

Lieut.-Col. Anderson, commanding the Third Kentucky, is reported to me by one of my aids as having been extremely gallant, as was that of Maj. Johnson, both of whom were wounded. Lieut.-Col. Crews, commanding Tennessee Battalion, behaved well.

Maj. Clifton, commanding Alabama Battalion, detached from me early on Sunday, did not again come under my notice, but is said to have done his duty. Lieut.-Col. Galbraith, commanding Thirty-First Alabama Regiment, executed to my satisfaction, several orders I gave him, and in the early fight Sunday, although not drilled, his regiment did excellent service. Capt. Byrne, as I have already said, managed his battery with skill, and fought with great gallantry.

Capt. Cobb, commanding light battery, unfortunately lost most of his horses and two of his pieces, but is represented to me as having fought with great courage and skill. Capt. John H. Morgan, with his squadron, was not under my immediate control, and has only today returned from the scene of conflict. On receiving his report, I will add a supplement to this. His conduct is represented to have been such as all expected of so gallant a commander.

The captains and subalterns of the command who fought with distinguished courage, are too numerous to be mentioned in this report. Regimental reports are referred to for justice to them. It may not be out of place to say, however, that the Third Kentucky came from the battlefield and from Mickey's house, under command of Lieut. C. H. Meshew.

I am under obligations to my adjutant, Joe Linden Robertson, and my volunteer *aides*, Samuel Gray, John Hooe, Tho. B. Darragh, Robert W. McKee, and Charlton Morgan, all of Kentucky (the last of whom was wounded on Sunday morning), and Charles J. Mastin, of Alabama, all of whom exhibited decided gallantry.

But I have to mourn the loss of many who were very dear to the command, among whom Maj. Monroe is very deeply lamented. He fell nobly at his post. No officer of his rank could have been his superior, and no man in the army could have possessed more merit as a gentleman. At the same place fell Governor George W. Johnson, whose death will be mourned by thousands of his countrymen.

The command went into action with something less than 2,400 men, and the table of casualties shows an aggregate loss of 844. The list of missing is ninety-seven, all of whom were probably killed or wounded.

The losses of the different regiments, etc., were as follows:

Third Kentucky Regiment	174
Fourth Kentucky Regiment	213
Sixth Kentucky Regiment	108
Ninth Kentucky Regiment	134
Hale's Thirty-first Alabama	79
Clifton's Alabama Battalion	30
Crews' Tennessee Battalion	55
Cobb's Battery	37
Byrne's Battery	14
Total	844

All the horses of the command belonging to the field and staff engaged in the action, with one or two exceptions, were either killed or wounded. Respectfully, your obedient servant,

R. P. Trabue,
Colonel Fourth Kentucky, Commanding Brigade.

The preceding report, it will be observed, gives a close account of the action taken by all those troops that constituted the brigade proper, but Gen. Breckinridge and his staff, separated from it nearly all day of the 6th, as explained, are necessarily merely referred to as regards the operations of that day; and in order to a just view of their action during that time, we quote the following from Gen. Hodge:

> Two o'clock had arrived, and the whole army was now, or had been, for hours engaged, with the exception of Bowen's and Statham's brigades of the Reserve Corps. The enemy had been driven through and from half of his camps, but refused to give back further. Having given way on his right and left wings, he had massed his force heavily in the centre, and poured an almost unintermitting hail of fire, murderous beyond description, from his covert of trees and bushes, when Gen. Breckinridge was ordered up to break his line. Having been most of the day in observation on the Hamburg road, marching in column of regiments, the reserve was now moved by the left flank, until opposite the point of attack, then deployed rapidly into line of battle, Statham's brigade forming the right and Bowen's the left. The long slope of the ridge was here abruptly broken by a succession of small hills or undulations of about fifty feet in height, dividing the rolling country from the river bottom; and behind the crest of the last of these the enemy was concealed.

Opposite them, at the distance of seventy-five yards, was another long swell or hillock, the summit of which it was necessary to attain in order to open fire, and to this elevation the reserve moved in order of battle at a double-quick. In an instant the opposing height was one sheet of flame. Battle's Tennessee regiment, on the extreme right, gallantly maintained itself, pushing forward under a withering fire, and establishing itself well in advance. Little's Tennessee regiment, next to it, delivered its fire at random and inefficiently, became disordered, and retired in confusion down the slope. Three times it was rallied by its lieutenant-colonel, assisted by Col. T. T. Hawkins, *aide-de-camp* to Gen. Breckinridge, and by the adjutant-general, and carried up the slope, only to be as often repulsed and driven back; the regiment of the enemy opposed to it, in the intervals, directing an oblique fire upon Battle's regiment, now contending against overwhelming odds.

The crisis of the contest had come—there were no more reserves, and Gen. Breckinridge determined to charge. Calling the staff around him, he communicated to them his intentions, and remarked that he, with them, would lead it. They were all Kentuckians, and though it was not their privilege to fight that day with the Kentucky Brigade, they were yet men who knew how to die bravely among strangers, and some, at least, would live to do justice to the rest. The commander-in-chief, Gen. Johnston, rode up at this juncture, and learning the contemplated movement, determined to accompany it. Placing himself on the left of Little's regiment, his commanding figure in full uniform, conspicuous to every eye, he waited the signal. Gen. Breckinridge, disposing his staff along the line, rode to the right of the same regiment; then with a wild shout, which rose high above the din of battle, on swept the line through a storm of fire, over the hill, across the intervening ravine, and up the slope occupied by the enemy.

Nothing could withstand it. The enemy broke, and fled for half a mile, hotly pursued, until he reached the shelter of his batteries. Well did the Kentuckians sustain that day their honour and their fame! Of the little band of officers who started on that forlorn hope but one was unscathed, the gallant Breckinridge himself. Col. Hawkins was wounded in the face; Capt. Allen's leg was torn to pieces by a shell; the horses of the fearless boy,

J. Cabell Breckinridge, and of the adjutant-general were killed under them, and Gen. Johnston was lifted, dying, from his saddle. It may well be doubted whether the success, brilliant as it was, decisive as it was, compensated for the loss of the great captain

The general repulse of the enemy had now thrown the reserve on the extreme right of the Confederate line. Far on the left was heard the musketry of the Kentucky Brigade, and the roar of its artillery, as it pushed its columns forward. It was fighting its way to its gallant general, and the hour was drawing near when they were to meet in the pride of glorious success. Capt. Byrne, of the Kentucky Battery, riding on the flank, observed heavy bodies of the enemy in rear of his line, from which he was constantly drawing fresh supplies of men, and thus was enabled to maintain his ground. Obtaining permission of Bragg, he changed position of his pieces, and then threw discharge after discharge of spherical case shot and shell among them.

The effect was magical. The right of the enemy broke and fled, the centre followed, then the left wing; and charging along the whole line the Confederate Army swept through the camps of the enemy, capturing three thousand, and driving the Federal force cowering beneath the shelter of the iron-clad gunboats. Then and there, in the full fruition of success, the Kentucky Brigade and its general met for the first time during that bloody day since their separation in the morning, both covered with glory, both proud of and gratified with each other.

It will be observed that, more than is usually the case in battle, the fighting of the Kentucky troops, on these two momentous days, was by separate detachments. Regiments and batteries made a kind of individual record of their own; and it would be impossible, on that account, to enter into detailed notices of the many incidents, of various nature, connected with each, as this would require a volume of itself. The reader will find frequent allusions to them in the biographies and the short personal sketches and incidents that follow this chapter.

On Monday afternoon the great battle had been fought—and lost. The trials, responsibilities, and sufferings of the Kentuckians were not over, however. The brigade had preserved its organisation in such a remarkable degree that its services were in demand to do a greatly disproportionate part in the work of protecting the rear of the retreating army. In the language of Col. Trabue, "It was a great undertaking."

Encamping that night without shelter, in the rain and mud, upon the very verge of the battlefield, now held by a powerful and victorious enemy, officers and men lay upon their arms; and next day it moved out slowly, gathering up abandoned property and wounded men; halted again almost within cannon shot of the enemy, and went to work to bury the dead found along the road and at the field-hospital, and to send forward the wounded, the prisoners, and captured property; and at last withdrew under Gen. Breckinridge's orders to Corinth, arriving there Friday morning, one week from the time it had set out for Burnsville.

Many and many a noble heart that beat high with hope, and with the pride that the expectation of great achievements naturally inspires, was now stilled in death. These, our slain, lay in soldiers' graves, scattered promiscuously, and with no mark even so much as to name them, and say to future generations that such and such a one sleeps here. The victory that the very first blow promised, and that seemed, to all who lived till nightfall on the 6th, almost within their grasp, had been snatched from them, and their dead comrades were now mourned as those who shed their blood in vain.

The living had reached Corinth after almost unparalleled hardships, and, having witnessed the most heartrending scenes after the battle was over, in the suffering of the wounded, who were slowly and with extreme difficulty carried to that place by every means of conveyance at the command of the Confederate officers. The almost constant rain, the horrid condition of the roads, the absence of every comfort that a wounded man so much needs, made the lot of these poor sufferers dreadful beyond expression. To complete the discomfiture of the Army of the Mississippi, their great captain was no more; and they felt now that there had been a "giant in the land," and that there was no one left who could restore their broken strength as he could have done, nor lead them as he had led.

Just as light seemed to be about to dispel the darkness that for some months had been settling over the Confederacy, the hand of the Almighty wrote the doom of the new Republic. With Johnston here, and Lee in Virginia, unopposed by the decree of Him who rules the nations of the earth, no human power at the disposal of the United States Government could have stayed the onward and triumphant march of the Confederate Armies; but one touch—a ball sped perhaps at random—and one of the greatest generals of modern days, who seemed to hold the fate of a nation in his hand, dropped the reins of his charger some minutes after he had received a stroke that he had scarcely noticed, reeled into the arms of Gen. Preston, and was presently no more.

No studied disquisition is needed to portray the conduct of Kentuckians on that field, and the traits indicated by that conduct. However tried they had proved true, and displayed the highest soldierly qualities. Intelligent, well-trained, intrepid in action, steady under blows which they could not return, actively humane when good offices could be extended to a wounded enemy; bearing with unflinching fortitude the hardships of a week's marching and more than their share of labour and of watching by night and by day,—all this was seen and acknowledged by those in position to judge, and lauded by all capable of being both generous and just.

And what prouder names could the Confederacy boast than those who led them there? The Commander-in-chief was a Kentuckian— he who fell after he had won a victory the consequences of which, had he lived to hold it, would have been incalculable; and their general of division, Breckinridge,—what knightlier soldier had ridden in battle on this continent?

But why attempt to call the roll of all the honourable names that proudly maintained on that field Kentucky's old renown? The list is too long, and the attentive reader has already seen how well they did it.

At Corinth there was gloom among the survivors, but the darker hue of disgrace was no part of it. More than thirty-five *per cent.* of the brigade, including its batteries, had been killed or wounded, but very few were missing and unaccounted for.

On two great fields, now, had the Kentucky volunteers tried their strength, had proved their valour and their constancy, and the living who were not in prison or disabled by wounds were "present for duty." An enemy coming upon them now would have found them ready, even in their dejected state, to "stiffen the sinews and summon up the blood" for another conflict.

INCIDENTS AND ANECDOTES: ON THE MARCH; ALSO, AT AND AFTER SHILOH.

1. "The Battle of Sunset."—I am indebted to that gallant and steady soldier and faithful comrade, Thomas Owens, of Co. I, Fourth Kentucky, for the following account of the false alarm referred to in the preceding chapter:

The First Kentucky Brigade—now famous as the Orphan Brigade—had been in camp at Oakland Station, on the Louisville and Nashville railroad, twelve miles north of Bowling Green, Ky., since December 12th, 1861. The monotony and discipline of camp life had become irksome to the boys, and occasional rumours of an early call to active service were hailed with delight. After the fall of Fort Henry on the 6th day of February, 1862, we were in daily expectation of marching orders, which came at last on the 12th of February. After rapidly packing knapsacks and striking tents we turned our faces towards Nashville.

By forced marches we arrived on the evening of the second day within a couple of miles of the intersection of the Russellville and Glasgow turnpike with the pike running south into Tennessee on which we had been marching for two days. The weather was extremely cold, and we had that day marched more than twenty miles. We were all footsore and nearly exhausted when, late in the afternoon, Capt. Jack Allen, who was then acting *aide* to Gen. Breckinridge, rode back along the column in a gallop, shouting, 'Close up, men, close up; the enemy is directly in front of us!' This announcement instantly banished all sense of fatigue, and the column was quickly closed up, halted, and directed to load.

It must not be supposed that this manoeuvre of loading was accomplished with the same cool deliberation as on drill; on the contrary, many of us showed considerable trepidation as we brought the cartridge to the muzzle of the gun. This done, however, the order, 'forward, double-quick; march,' rang out along the line, and we moved forward at a rapid pace, listening every moment for the boom of cannon or the rattle of musketry at the front. Nothing of the kind was heard, however, and we soon began to suspect it was a false alarm; and so, it proved to be.

The squad of cavalry acting as a vanguard for our little army had reached the crossing of the two roads above mentioned, and seeing a body of cavalry coming down the Glasgow road, took it to be a part of the Federal force then at Mill Spring, and, without waiting to learn the truth of it, rode back and reported the fact to Gen. Breckinridge. The reported enemy turned out to be Helm's regiment of cavalry, a gallant body of Confederates, which had been watching the movements of the Federal Army then lying in the vicinity of Mill Spring, and were on their way to join our force. The battle (in anticipation) came to an end about the setting of the sun; and it was then christened the 'Battle of Sunset,' a name by which it was ever afterwards known.

2. Alabamians—A Noble and Appreciative People.—All who remember the incidents of that trying retreat can but recall with a glow of admiration the cordial, even enthusiastic greeting extended to the brigade by the people of Alabama, as it passed through the State. Waving of handkerchiefs, cheers, words of welcome and encouragement, met them from the time they entered it till they were encamped on the left bank of the Tennessee River, and were no more among them, as the infantry was conveyed by rail from Decatur to Burnsville in the night. At Huntsville a stand of colours was presented to the Sixth Regiment by the ladies of that place, and as much enthusiasm prevailed as though Gen. Johnston had been marching northward after a victory. This is the more worthy of note, too, from the fact that they were the same in the latter years of the war.

Reverses, apparently failing fortunes, and the raggedness of the bronzed Kentucky soldier never deterred them from nocking to the roadside when this command, or any portion of it, was passing, and from contributing something to their wants. The last private gift to them was from the ladies of Lowndes county, of that State—some boxes of clothing, which came opportunely, and were issued to them in July, 1864, during the defence of Atlanta.

3. A Camp Struck by a Southern Hurricane at Night.—A storm, which occurred on the night of the 14th of March, just before the brigade reached Decatur, somewhat varied the monotony of the wearisome days, and afforded much matter for laughter and fun, though it was of itself a serious thing. The infantry had encamped in a pasture, to the right of the road, and along a skirt of enclosed woodland. The companies had each been supplied with about seven Sibley tents, and these were pitched in order, as the clouded atmosphere betokened rain. A short time after the evening meal had been dispatched, and all who had concluded to spend the night at home were sitting around in their tents, passing their time in the various ways of which soldiers alone can conceive, when a low sound, at first as of falling rain, then of approaching wind, arrested attention.

It grew more furious every second, until it struck the encampments as with a mighty blow, and created such a stir as no one who was present can ever forget. Officers and men sprang up and seized the centre poles of their Sibleys, in the vain hope of holding them to the ground; but the wind was so violent that they were bounced up and down like puppets on a string, and quicker than it can be told almost every tent in the brigade was torn up and blown away or sprawled over, and some thousands of men were uncovered at once to the fury of a Southern hurricane. In some instances, where less care had been taken to fasten the tents down securely, they were blown loose from cords and pins, and flew about to the danger and discomfiture of all who chanced to stand in their course.

Blankets, hats and clothing darted suddenly from their rightful owners—tin-cups, spoons, crockery, sheet-iron vessels, rattled their accompaniment to the din as they were blown or kicked about—everything was jumbled up in a disorderly mass. To add to the dire confusion, a drove of cattle had been turned into the pasture, and at dark were at the far end of the field, keeping a very respectful distance from the tented quarter; but when the wind struck them they were frightened into instant action, and came sweeping round with a noise that was appalling, as they appeared to be charging directly upon the encampment, and were calculated to do more mischief than a battle. No one relished the idea of dying by the inglorious means of either a bullock's horns or his hoofs.

But by some means they were turned somewhat, or turned themselves, and passed with thundering tread, in a body, straight along the outer line of the mass of men and things that formed a medley of what had been quite a cheerful and comfortable little city, with spires looking modestly out from a conical canvas. Some sought the covered wagons for shelter, as the rain was now pouring down as though all the drops of old ocean had been distilled into clouds for that special occasion. Some fled to neighbouring gin-houses, guided on their way by the almost constant and vivid flashes of lightning—and some lost their way to the gin-houses and went to Decatur, where they forthwith proceeded to have "a time."

A few, more calm and collected under difficulties, or more opposed to violent exertion, waited patiently for the storm to abate, when they stirred around and managed to raise a shelter and pass the night among the debris of the camp. The party that found the gin-houses came in next morning thickly covered with bits of cotton that had adhered to them in the night, as they burrowed among the bales or the loose-picked. A facetious friend who made one of the unfortunate number that found themselves at Decatur afterward explained that the shelter and refreshments were so grateful to their feelings that it was nearly day before they could tear themselves away and set out on their return to camp—and that, taking the railroad after they got over the footbridge they left a man in every cow-gap between the river and the plantation where they had last seen their less adventurous comrades, since they could find these holes in the road only by having the advance man of the party incontinently pitch into one as he strode along in the dark. From all which those who know a soldier's proneness to "wet up" when it is apparent to others that he is already wet enough may draw what conclusions they please.

4. Who Led the Brigade's First Skirmishes on the Battlefield?—For some time after this, the first great battle for all but the Second Kentucky, there was a friendly contention as to who was the first sent out to deploy the enemy on Sunday morning—both Lieut. Rogers, of Co. A, Fourth Kentucky, and Lieut. Weller, of Co. D, same regiment, claiming this honour; but it was finally decided that each commanded a skirmish party, and deployed in somewhat different directions at the same time.

5. Wasn't Quite So Angry Now.—After the brigade had formed line of battle Sunday morning, as previously noticed, and marched some distance through the forest, it was halted and ordered to rest at will. Some of the men stood by their arms, while others sat down on the leaves, logs, stumps—whatever came convenient; the officers walked about and conversed with each other. I chanced to be near John Crawford, a gallant young fellow, as he proved, a member of Co. H, Sixth Kentucky. Hardee's cannons were booming in front, and we were near enough for other reverberations of the initiatory conflict to reach us.

Crawford sat listening awhile, and then broke out with "What does all this mean, anyhow?" "What are you talking about?" "This fighting—this war; what's it all about?" Of course, the tension of the nerves which precedes expected conflict was not proof against a laugh from those in hearing, and Crawford wound up with "I'm not half so angry as I was, I tell you!" We were presently ordered forward, and before noon of the next day the brave boy was dead—killed while the Kentuckians were fighting so desperately to keep back Buell's overpowering force as Beauregard's broken army retreated.

6. The First Work of the Fourth Kentucky on Sunday Morning.— When Col. Trabue formed line of battle, to march in supporting distance of Gen. Polk, the line of march brought the Fourth Regiment, on the extreme left, into a depressed place in a field, where it halted awhile; then the brigade moved by the left flank, which threw this regiment in the woods and at the base of a small hill or bank, where it again halted and was faced to the front. Here Lieut. John Bird Rogers, with a platoon of Co. A, and Lieut. John H. Weller, with a platoon of Co. D, were thrown out as skirmishers. Deploying, they marched over the hill; through a camp of the enemy which had been abandoned in confusion; passed dead and wounded Federals as they pressed to the farther edge of this encampment, and found themselves in the rear of a Confederate line of battle, in range of spent balls and the shot and shell designed for the troops in front. While halted here one of the regiments engaged broke and ran back through the line of Kentuckians.

This, with the flying bullets, bursting shells, and plunging cannon shot would have demoralised any ordinary troops; but even the bugle that now sounded the recall failed to budge them, as they were afraid they had not heard aright, and would be put down, if they should retreat, as having fled with the demoralised regiment which had run over them. The order to retreat must be unmistakable or they would die there. Maj. Monroe had to send an officer with a verbal order to withdraw. This is a sample of the stuff the regiment was made of. Shortly after this the attention of acting Maj. Nuckols was called to a long line of muskets glistening through the trees to the left of the regiment and moving to its front.

Tall, and sitting on horseback, he could see that a Federal regiment was there and forming at an angle to the Fourth Kentucky. He reported to Maj. Monroe, commanding, who quickly apprehended the necessary movement, and gave the order "Change front to rear on first company!" his was promptly executed, and as promptly a battle was raging with the Forty-Sixth Ohio. This was presently reinforced by another regiment, seeing which the Fourth Kentucky charged and drove them out of the woods, when it halted, and the brigade's lines were readjusted. It was a brilliant and audacious piece of work.

7. Putting on a New Uniform in Time of Action.—About the time the Louisiana regiment referred to by Col. Trabue appeared on the left front of the brigade, some Confederate troops had sent a volley of minie-balls among them, having mistaken them for Federals. This made them advance their crescent battle-flag into view in a hurry; and they afterward appeared in a peculiar uniform, made by turning their coats inside out.

8. An Unconquerable Irishman.—Hugh McVey, member of Company D, Fourth Kentucky, had served in the British Army when young; but he was a modest and quiet man, now past middle age, and indisposed to parade his exploits. On the morning of the second day at Shiloh he was struck by a ball. It did not fell him, but Lieutenant (afterward Captain) Weller, seeing that he bled, told him to go back to the surgeon and have his wound dressed. "No, Leftenant," he answered, pronouncing the word in that old way, "no, I'll die on the faild!" and stood to the line. Not long afterward he was again hit, and Weller urged him to go back, but he still plied his rifle and answered as before. In a little while the noble fellow died "on the faild" which he had helped to make famous for Kentuckians; a third shot killed him instantly.

9. How the "Desperadoes" All Died.—Lieut. Harris, of Company C, Ninth Kentucky, picked up, sometime during the first day's fight at Shiloh, a handsome silk banner, on one side of which was painted the Goddess of Liberty, with the motto, "We Will Die for Our Country," and on the other side was inscribed "The Chickasaha Desperadoes," and "Victory or Death." Col. Hunt, noticing it afterward, said that "the entire command must have been killed, for they surely could not have thrown away their colors after going in to win or die." The Ninth appropriated the staff, as their own had been shot in two, but the flag itself was given to Gen. Breckinridge, and was hung up at his headquarters, at Corinth, perhaps elsewhere.

10. He Expected to be Murdered.—Mistaken or malicious speakers and writers, in their efforts to fire the northern heart, early in 1861, dealt in the grossest misrepresentations of the Southern people, and the effects of these attempts to arouse sectional hate were in keeping with their wicked purpose. One peculiarly odious slander was to the effect that Southern men were such blood-thirsty barbarians that they would not respect the usages of civilized warfare, and were capable of butchering wounded men and helpless prisoners. On Sunday forenoon, at Shiloh, when the Sixth Kentucky was ordered to relieve the Fourth, as described elsewhere, on its run to the edge of the open field through which the enemy had been driven, the writer, with others, passed near a Federal soldier who had a broken leg doubled back under him in a way that seemed to make his sufferings the more excruciating.

He evidently expected to be bayoneted as he lay, for he said pleadingly, "Don't kill me!" The regiment was halted for orders a few yards beyond, and as if by one impulse, Capt. Crewdson and the writer stepped back to place him in a more comfortable position. But he still mistrusted and again begged not to be killed.

"Poor fellow!" we replied, as we straightened him out and did what we could to make him easier till he could be reached by the infirmary corps, "we're trying to help you. We don't kill men who are down." The grateful and somewhat puzzled look which he gave us with his thanks was a thing to be remembered. Many a time that day, judging by individual observation, did the Kentuckians, who had things pretty much their own way till night, divide water and food during the lulls of the storm, with wounded Federals strewn over the field, and render such little assistance as they could, and this, of course, was done by the other Confederate forces.

11. Armed for Close Fighting.—Old soldiers recall with a smile the erroneous impressions that obtained at the beginning of the war and the character of certain arms with which men were provided or thought it well to provide themselves. Gov. Joe Brown's pikes are in point; but many Kentuckians carried from the State and expected to use a long heavy knife, that in a hand-to-hand conflict would have been as terrible as the Cuban machete. Stories told about the first battle of Manassas, that had their foundation chiefly in the fertile brains of war correspondents, gave some colour to the prevailing impression that close-quarter engagements were not at all improbable.

Big knives, made as a rule out of the heavy steel files or rasps used by blacksmiths, were borne in many a cartridge belt up to the very opening of the Battle of Shiloh. When the men had orders to divest themselves of knapsacks and extra blankets and pile them preparatory to engaging the enemy, most of these long knives went with them, as they saw that with the Enfield and Belgian rifle, which most of them now had, and which would kill at a thousand yards, there was small prospect of even a stand-up fight with bayonets. A few were afterward found in the camps, but they were debased to the level of butchers' cleavers or took the hatchet's place in sharpening tent-pins and cutting kindling wood.

12. Bee Stung.—First experiences and impressions in battle were diversified and often peculiar, and manifestations were frequently ludicrous. John Philpot, a Cumberland county man, belonging to Co. F, Sixth Kentucky, was quiet and rather abstracted, attending to his duties in a composed and matter-of-fact way, and fighting in the same manner; but when, in the heat of the battle at Shiloh, on Monday, a bullet cut his scalp without knocking him over, he lost his wits. Throwing down his gun he began striking and scratching furiously about his head with both hands, jerking his hat off—in the manner of a man fighting bees and apparently pretty badly stung and very much afraid of bees, anyhow. But he quickly recovered his senses, and seemed to realise that he had been making a spectacle of himself. Looking at his comrades in a sort of shame-faced way, he replaced his hat, grabbed his rifle, and resumed firing; but subsequently the men guyed him a good deal about not knowing the difference between a bullet and a honey-bee or a hornet.

13. Southern Man Ran the Wrong Way.—Unscrupulous enlisting officers doubtless played some scurvy tricks on foreigners to induce them to swell the ranks of the Northern Army, as an instance at Shiloh indicated. One of the Kentucky regiments captured among others a German soldier, who was at first angry and sullen and required some sharp talk and some threatening demonstrations to induce him to move along as required. He was evidently new to the country, as his English was bad and had a touch of his native tongue. One of the men tried to jolly him a little, which brought out the fact that he had been deceived. "Hans," said his interlocuter, "what are you doing here, anyhow? What do you want to fight the South for?"

"Py himmel!" he blurted out, "I vish I didn't!" Then he showed how he had been taken in: "Zey dell me to zay boo! at the Southern man unt he runs off. I zay boo! and shoots; but py tarn! Southern man he runs the wrong vay!"

14. Gov. Johnson Taking the Oath as a Private Soldier.—

Dr. John O. Scott, on duty with Byrne's battery at Shiloh, thus tells of the scene and what followed: "He and his private secretary, Samuel Gray, had rested Sunday night under an oak tree near the bivouac of the Kentucky Brigade. I can never forget loaning him a pocket comb Monday morning; how politely he thanked me when he returned it; and how my heart warmed when he spoke of his love for my father. After a hurried breakfast we were reminded by the sound of the bugle that we must go to arms again. Glancing toward a distant hill we saw rank upon rank of Federal soldiers, with fixed bayonets glittering in the sunlight, filing rapidly to our right in front of Shiloh church. Gen. Breckinridge was in sight, sitting on his impatient war-horse.

At this moment Gov. Johnson asked Capt. Ben Monroe, of the Fourth Regiment, to swear him as a private in his company, and the boy Captain, with uplifted cap and sword unsheathed, asked the Governor of Kentucky to raise his right hand, and with it uplifted to heaven, in witness of the sincerity of his devotion to the cause for which he fought, he took the oath; then fell into the ranks of Co. E. Fighting to protect our battery, when it stood to fight, and to keep it from capture when forced to fall back, Gov. Johnson and Maj. Monroe were killed, and Burnley, Dudley, Steele, Tom Price, Capt. Monroe and others were wounded."

15. Too Late to Pray.—Nat Crain, of Co. F, Sixth Kentucky, then less than eighteen years old, was the son of an eminent Methodist minister, but he was full of fun and could be ludicrous even in "the imminent deadly breach." As the brigade was being pushed back from point to point on the second day at Shiloh, Nat came into line, at one of the rallying places, near a small black-jack tree, behind which a comrade had already established himself, lying flat on the ground, his head and body so disposed that the tree afforded him some protection. He was loading and firing, as he had been drilled to do in this posture, and was praying so audibly as to be heard by those near him in spite of the noise of battle. This struck Crain as he took position, standing, beside him, and he pushed him with his foot and shouted: "Get up here, Will! what's the use in praying when the devil's done come?"

16. The Little Book Saved His Life.—Among the many instances in which small articles, as books, belt-buckles, etc., stopped or deflected bullets, was that of John L. Marshall, Sergeant-Major of the Fourth Kentucky. During the first year, especially, it was common for the men to have at least one pocket in the front of the coloured shirts worn, and if but one this was on the left breast, and fell naturally over the heart. At Shiloh Marshall had in his shirt pocket a small testament which he had brought from home, (given him, presumably by his mother, sister, or sweet-heart, as they never forgot to arm their warriors with a copy of the Scriptures). During the battle an Enfield ball imbedded itself in the book, and he received only a shock and a bruise, whereas without this obstacle the bullet would have gone through his heart. He took a gallant part in nearly every engagement of his regiment, great or small, but was never again struck.

17. The Kentucky Artillery: Byrne and His Men Cheered.—An eye-witness furnished this account of the artillery action referred to by Gen. Hodge:

> Capt. Byrne opened on them at a thousand yards. He had eight pieces, and they worked on the enemy's right. Gen. Breckinridge was driving him on his left, and the retreating column had to pass in front of the battery. Capt. Byrne sat on his horse, giving his orders; Gen. Ruggles, Col. Baird, and Capt. Ellis (of Bragg's staff), and Lieut. Robinson (of Trabue's staff) came up.

Col. Baird gave a cheer—this was taken up by the artillerists and then by the commands on the right. Never did men work harder and faster, and never did enemy fall thicker before the same number of guns. Col. Baird, in his enthusiasm, got down and put his hand on one of the pieces, remarking, as he did so, that he '*wanted to feel it!*'

18. Coolly "Picked His Flint" Under Fire.—About the time the above-described incident occurred, James W. Nelson, of Co. F, Fourth Kentucky, found that the tube of his Enfield was choked, and seeing no other rifle in reach except in the hands of his comrades, he sat down by a tree, picked the tube, recapped it, then rose and resumed firing—all this with as much apparent coolness as though he were deaf to the roar of the artillery, the whistle of bullets that flew by, and the thud of those that struck. He missed no chance to get hurt from the first morning of Shiloh to the closing days of the brigade's service below Camden, S. C, April, 1865; but he received only a single wound, and that in the last fight in which his company engaged.

19. A Double Duel, Fatal to at Least One Man.—On one of the lines occupied by the Brigade, Monday forenoon, Elliott W. Thompson and Nathan B. Thompson, of Co. F, Sixth Kentucky, found themselves in the rear of an abandoned gun carriage and knelt behind the heavy wheels for such protection as wheels and axles would afford. The Federals had pressed so closely that their strong lines were but little concealed by the woods; and these two young men had hardly opened fire from their partial shelter before they discovered that two Federal soldiers had "treed" within rifle range and were firing at them point blank. Several shots were exchanged without fatal effect upon either side, when Nathan Thompson became impatient, and said to his companion in the desperate game: "Let's stand out; then we can fetch 'em!"

They instantly agreed as to which particular combatant each should aim at, jumped to their feet, and drew upon their adversaries; but at the crack of their rifles Nathan fell dead—his enemy's bullet had struck him square in the forehead. At the instant the line broke under orders to find another position from which to renew the fearfully unequal strife; and there was no time to determine whether their shots had taken effect.

20. "No Detail! Ask for Volunteers."—When Byrne's battery was placed on the little eminence back of the field where he fought it so splendidly for four hours, supported by the Kentucky Brigade, he at once drew the fire of several of the enemy's guns, and for part of the time three of their batteries were playing upon him, while their infantry kept up a continuous fire; but they could not move him or any part of his indomitable support. About one-third of the cannoniers had been killed or wounded, and as the ridge was very sandy the recoil of the guns threw the carriages back, and they had constantly to be moved up by the hand. Many of the men were consequently completely exhausted.

Col. Lewis was sitting near Capt. Byrne, who asked him for a detail to assist in working the guns, when John B. Spurrier, of the Sixth Regiment, stepped forward and cried out, "No detail! Call for volunteers, and we are there!" And they were there. The gallant Spurrier acted number one at a piece until he went down, dangerously wounded, about an hour after having volunteered. Gen. Bragg sent twice by his *aides-de-camp*, Col. Walton and Lieut. Parker, ordering Capt. Byrne to use spherical case or canister on the right of the enemy, as they were moving up through the undergrowth, but he had already given them plenty of spherical case. The Kentucky Brigade was now ordered to go to the right, as the enemy's guns appeared to have been silenced. Byrne's battery was moved about eight hundred yards further, and as they came up to Gen. Bragg, he took his sleek cap off and saluted them.

21. A Tuneful Voice Heard in the Uproar.—Perhaps no more thrilling circumstance took place during the "noise of battle and the shouting" that day than the singing of a song which had been our favourite while recruiting went on in 1861. At one point in the line arose the music of a voice or voices, mingling with the rattle and crash of musketry, the sharp tones of command, the groans of the stricken and mangled, for the moment diverting the thoughts of fighting men from their bloody work—

> *Cheer, boys, cheer, we'll march away to battle;*
> *Cheer, boys, cheer, for our sweethearts and our wives;*
> *Cheer, boys, cheer, we'll nobly do our duty;*
> *And give to Kentucky our hearts, our arms, our lives!*

22.—"Devil Dick."—As the Fourth Kentucky was making its way back to Corinth under command of Lieut.-Col. Hynes, a supper was gotten up one evening from commissaries found on the road. Among others who partook of the meal with the commander's extemporized mess was John W. Slusser, of Co. D. He was a rollicking blade, nearly always cheerful and full of humour, and, though by no means a bad man nor deserving of any soubriquet that would convey such an imputation, he was known as Devil Dick. He was so designated throughout the war, and though everybody in the brigade knew Devil Dick, few knew his real name. Hynes and others were talking over their supper about the many incidents of the battle, their feelings, their views of this their first great conflict, when Slusser, who had been quietly listening, broke in with: "Well, I feel as though I shall live through this war. When I'm an old man, I'll take my grandchildren on my knee and tell them that I was in the great battle of Shiloh, and what I saw and what I did. They'll think of course that grandpap was a hero, because the little things can never know how bad the old man wanted to get away from there!"

23. Some of His Teeth Had Lost Their Edge at Shiloh.—Among other drolleries of Nat Crain's, to whom reference is made above, he declared when he enlisted that he was a "roaring tiger, with double rows of teeth—one for vegetation and one for Yankees;" and occasionally afterward he would sing it out, especially when it seemed that he ought to emulate Mark Tapley and be jolly under creditable circumstances: "I'm a roaring tiger, etc.!" After the brigade had gotten back to Corinth and the men, having smoothed their ruffled feathers a little, were trying to make the best of a bad business, it occurred to Nat one day to cry his slogan, so he put on as much of a savage aspect as he could assume, and began with a raised voice; but he seemed suddenly to recall that there had been trouble over about Pittsburg Landing, in which he was mixed up, and his speech took a peculiar turn: "I'm a roaring tiger with double rows of teeth—one for vegetation, but *none* for Yankees!"

24. The Preaching Didn't Suit Him.—John Conner, of Co. C, Second Kentucky, was a son of the Green Isle, a good fellow and a good fighter, with a mind that is best described as both witty and humorous. Meeting the writer the week after the brigade got back, he said: "We went to church last Sunday week, didn't we?"

"Yes, to Shiloh Church."

"Well, I'm not going anymore; I don't like the sermons they preach there."

25. Shiloh Not Conclusive as to Whether One of Us Could Whip Five Yankees.—A little gathering of the Kentuckians who had tried conclusions with Grant and Buell were talking over things during the time of serious reflection that followed, when one remarked: "You know we set out from home to whip five Yankees apiece."

"Yes."

"Over yonder last week, now— we didn't do it, did we?"

"Oh," rejoined another, "they were not Yankees; they were Western men—men like we are!"

Then a shadow fell over the little squad that had come out to whip five apiece, as though their would-be comforter had given them a cold potato. They could but reflect that from Canada to the coast of Florida the woods were still full of "Western men like we are."

26. What a Reserve Corps Is.—The brigade's experience on the field and on retreat furnished abundant food for thought during the weeks of comparative quiet that followed, and the unique, piquant, and humorous ones that found expression among the Kentuckians would fill a volume. Some reference having been made to the reserve corps of which the Orphans constituted an important part, one of them remarked that before the battle he didn't know what a reserve force was. Questioned as to whether he now knew, he replied: "Yes; it means the best body of men that can be found to go in early, stay all the time, and afterward hold back the enemy for two or three days till the rest can get away with themselves and their impedimenta. It's a funny term, though—reserve." The part played by the Kentuckians during that eventful week seemed to justify his conclusions.

27. The Street Bully in Battle.—To many, one of the singular revelations of the war was the fact that in nearly every instance the men who were known to have been quarrelsome, overbearing, and addicted to personal brawls and fistic combats, were arrant cowards. Of course, the oldest soldiers, whose experience with men and study of character had led them to form just conclusions, mistrusted bluster, and understood that Jack Falstaff was a fair type, in the matter of real courage, of the pot-valiant of every age and nation; but to the young it was a matter of astonishment that the man whose boast was that he "could whip his weight in wild-cats," and was always looking out for insults and professedly ready to shoot or stick or pound anyone who should "tread on his toes," suddenly lost his ferocity when cannon balls began to smash and crash around him and bullets were finding their targets in human flesh and bones.

It would doubtless be hard for those who served faithfully throughout the war to recall instances in which these men made thoroughly reliable soldiers. They were a nuisance in camp, when they did not choose to run away altogether, and a disappointment on the field. Notwithstanding the orders which officers had to prevent straggling and those to file-closers to shoot any who should endanger the steadiness of a line by breaking in time of action, these fellows could get away; and if they stayed in the army afterward, to run on another day, it was notorious that they knew vastly more about the battle than the men who were in it, and in general they had the cheek to tell marvellous stories about the part they played.

CHAPTER 5.

Siege of Vicksburgh

In a short time, the work of reorganising the army throughout was begun, and the remainder of the month of April was spent in getting it in proper shape to render it available for attack or defence. Halleck, who had now assumed in person the command of the combined armies of Buell and Grant, delayed his movement on Corinth for a similar purpose; and even when he began his approaches, it was in a manner so cautious that it was not until the 2nd of May that Beauregard deemed an engagement imminent. Confederate cavalry watched him closely while the work of preparation was going on at Corinth.

But, to come more particularly to the troops of Kentucky and their leaders: Shortly after the battle of Shiloh, Breckinridge was commissioned a major-general, and assigned to the permanent command of the division which had led with such distinguished skill and valour on and from its first field. Some changes took place, however, and additions were made. Colonels Preston and Helm received notification of promotion to the rank of brigadier-general, and were ordered to report to Gen. Breckinridge for duty. The Kentucky troops were now separated and made part of two commands. One brigade was assigned to Brig.-Gen. J. M. Hawes, who had been promoted in the summer or autumn of 1861, and consisted of the Fourth and Ninth Kentucky Regiments, Hale's Alabama Regiment, Clifton's Alabama Battalion, and Byrne's Battery.

Owing to resignation of the officers of Byrne's Battery, and the consequent breaking up of the company, a change was made in the artillery of this brigade, on the 2nd of May, Hudson's Battery being substituted for Byrne's. Gen. Hawes soon relinquished his command for service in the Department of the Trans-Mississippi, and Gen. Ben Hardin Helm was placed in charge of his brigade, which was so modified as to consist of the following: Fourth and Ninth Kentucky Regiments, Thirty-first Alabama Regiment, Fourth Alabama Battalion, Thirty-first Mississippi Regiment, and the Hudson Battery.

One brigade was assigned to Brig.-Gen. William Preston, and consisted of the Third, Sixth, and Seventh Kentucky Regiments, Thirty-Fifth Alabama Regiment, and Cobb's Battery.

The Seventh Kentucky fought at Shiloh, in another command, and did not report to Gen. Breckinridge until after the arrival at Corinth. Its first colonel (Wickliffe) had been killed there, and it was now commanded by Col. Ed Crossland.

These two brigades and two under Bowen and Statham respectively, with two cavalry companies, now constituted Breckinridge's division. It will be noted that this was an organisation composed of Kentuckians, Alabamians, Missourians and Mississippians; and this ill-advised arrangement prevailed till the following September, when the Second Kentucky returned from prison, and preparations were being made to join the army under Bragg, when the Kentucky regiments were all thrown together, and the title became once more appropriate in every sense. The Third and Seventh were detached, with a view of moving them into Kentucky, by way of Jackson, Tenn., and were not again connected with the main body, but there were four regiments still together, under the title of First Kentucky Brigade, until the autumn of 1861, when the Fifth Kentucky Infantry was added, or rather substituted for the Forty-First Alabama, and no further change took place in the organisation.

Though not strictly pertinent to the history of the Kentucky regiments and artillery composing these brigades, it is not amiss to note the staff announced by Gen. Breckinridge after his promotion to MajorGeneral, as they were nearly all Kentuckians, and saw much service with the Kentucky infantry during the next twenty months. This staff was at first about as follows, though frequent changes afterward occurred—some of which are referred to below: Capt. George B. Hodge, A. A. G.; Capt. John S. Hope, A. I. G.; Maj. Alfred Boyd, Chief Quartermaster; Capt. Clint McClarty, Chief Commissary; Lieut.-Col. D. Beltzhoover, Chief of Artillery; Lieut. James Wilson, Ordnance Officer; Dr. B. W. Avent, Medical Director; Col. T. T. Hawkins, *aide-de-camp;* and Col. Jack Allen, Capt. A. Keene Richards, Capt. F. Lousdale, and Capt. Charles J. Mastin, volunteer *aides-de-camp.*

Col. O'Hara, who had hitherto been announced as *aide*, was still with him, but was recommended to the Government for promotion, and assignment to a command of cavalry, and was not included among the regularly appointed staff. He did not receive the proposed promotion, however, and so continued to serve with Gen. Breckinridge in various capacity. It may be proper to remark, also, that other officers of the staff, who were with him during the battle of Shiloh, were highly complimented in dispatches to the War Department, and recommended for promotion to higher rank. Of these, in addition to O'Hara, Hodge, Hawkins and McClarty were thus mentioned.

Capt. Hodge resigned on the 2nd of May, being a member of Congress, and the duties of A. A. G. devolved on others of the staff till June 3rd, when Maj. John T. Pickett was appointed. He served in this capacity till July, when he was ordered to Richmond, for service with Gen. Cooper, after which Col. John A. Buckner was made A. A. G. Capt. Hodge was afterward promoted to Brigadier-General of Cavalry, and, re-entering the field, served till the close of the war.

Col. O'Hara had served on the staff of Gen. Albert Sidney Johnston till the death of that officer. At Shiloh, he conducted himself with that noble bearing which had been exhibited on the fields of Mexico and Cuba.

The staff of Brig.-Gen. Hawes was announced to be as follows: Capt. Joe Linden Robertson, A. A. G.; Capt. Wm. M. Cargill, A. Q. M.; Maj. A. P. Barbour, *Aide-de-camp*; and Lieut. J. Cabell Breckinridge, volunteer *aides*. The duties of inspection and the commissariat were performed by other officers not included in the order of announcement in our possession, and whom we cannot now recall to mind.

The order announcing staff of Brig.-Gen. Preston has been lost, but the following officers are remembered to have served with him at different times: Major (afterward Lieutenant-Colonel) James W. Hewitt, having escaped capture at Donelson, was some time Acting Adjutant-General, also Capt. Nat Wickliffe; and on the 29th of August, Captain (afterward Major) R. W. Woolley was appointed to that position. Capt. William Stanley was his Inspector General during the summer, Maj. John R. Throckmorton, Chief Quartermaster, and Maj. Alex. Evans, Chief Commissary.

The staff of Brig. Gen. Helm, after he succeeded to the command of the brigade in which the Fourth and Ninth Kentucky were included, consisted of: Capt. G. W. McCauley, A. A. G.; Maj. Thomas H. Hays, A. I. G.; Maj. G. W. Triplett, A. Q. M.; Maj. Silas M. Moorman, A. C. S.; Lieut. G. M. Ryals, Ordnance Officer, and Lieut. Alexander H. Todd, *Aide-de-camp*.

Changes occurred, too, in the regiments themselves, and particularly in the Sixth and Ninth, which had been enlisted for twelve months only; whereas the others were originally three-year men. The two twelve-months regiments reorganised early in May, making their term of service co-extensive with that of the others—elections being held for officers throughout, except those of each regimental staff, who, of course, were to be the appointees of the respective colonels chosen.

Officers who preferred remaining in the service with the rank then held, but in a different field or different capacity, were to report to the commanding general for assignment; such as chose to relinquish their rank could be discharged from the service by simply refusing to appear as candidates; and such as should be defeated were to be thus divested of rank—the two classes last named to be held subject to the provisions of the conscription bill, provided they failed to select some arm of the service and reenlist. Such of the field and staff officers as appeared for the suffrages of the men were retained in their old positions, and, in most cases, the officers of the line also. In some few instances the officers in commission under the old organisation declined to have their names used, and a few were rejected. Some of those who entered other departments of the service distinguished themselves in different fields.

The companies which had been reduced below the minimum were ordered to be consolidated in such manner as to give the organisations that were retained their full quota of men, in pursuance of which the new regiments were made to consist of but eight instead of ten companies each. The Ninth chose a lieutenant-colonel and a major, none having been previously appointed, and its organisation was thus perfected after it had passed through the ordeal of battle.

Among the officers elect, some few were rejected by the examining board, as being disqualified by want of a sufficient knowledge of tactics and general regulations. At this juncture, Bragg, who assumed command of the army on the 6th of May, stepped in to remedy defects, and began the appointment of officers to fill vacancies. The men selected in these cases were, for the most part, worthy of position; and, indeed, some most excellent ones were assigned to duty in the line by authority of the general commanding—talented, courageous, and faithful—but after six months, or more, during which time these officers had discharged the duties, borne the responsibilities, and met the expenses incidental to their position—and that, too, under the evident displeasure of those whom they commanded, because not the men of their own election—Bragg's action was declared illegal, and they were returned to the ranks without having their pay-claims allowed; and the temper of the men was henceforth humoured by suffering them to choose for themselves who should wield the authority that they considered as rightfully in their gift.

The month of May was spent for the most part in moving to and fro along the line of defence in front of Halleck, who, with spade and pick, gradually drew nearer. Indications were frequent that battle would be joined, but further than the customary picketing in force, skirmishing between the outposts, occasional battle-orders, and formation to meet an attack, nothing of moment occurred during the entire month of May. About the middle of that month the enemy was known to be near the Confederate line of defence, and everybody was vigilant, and on the 20th the medical officers received orders to prepare for the care of wounded. On the 22nd it was thought that the crisis had come, and the army, having made all necessary preparations, marched out in full expectation of battle, but no general attack was made by either party, and that afternoon the old camps were reoccupied.

On the 28th of May, the encampment was finally broken up; the troops took position in the entrenchments; the various wagon trains were sent out on the Kossuth road four miles, to await orders. The Confederate general made the impression on Halleck that he could seriously resist his advance, and was thus enabled to withdraw on the night of the 29th, without loss of men or stores.

The circumstances attending this retreat require to be noticed somewhat in detail because of the important part played by the Kentucky troops—now regarded as thoroughly reliable in cases of emergency.

Of the Reserve Corps, (as Breckinridge's Division had been designated,) the special rear-guard of infantry was the Ninth Kentucky and a Mississippi regiment, with Cobb's Battery, the whole force under command of Col. Hunt. The Mississippians and a section of the battery passed over during the night, and bivouacked beyond the swamp that lies along the stream on each side; but the Ninth was not withdrawn from its position at the front till about midnight, and the darkness was so profound, in the deep forest through which they had to move, and the road still so rough for the remaining two pieces of artillery, that Corinth was still in view when daylight dawned upon them. They passed over the Tuscumbia, however, at an early hour, and joined the remainder of the force with which Col. Hunt was expected to dispute the passage of the bridge.

On the morning of the 1st, Federal cavalry attacked the picket, stationed some distance back toward Corinth, under command of Lieut. Charles Semple, but they were repulsed, with slight loss to the Confederates.

On the afternoon of June 1st, the main body of the army having now had ample time to reach a position of comparative safety, Col. Hunt resumed his march. He continued to press forward till midnight, when information was received that the train of sick, which had been started from Corinth on the 28th, had been captured at Booneville, and that the Federal cavalry was between him and the main body of the army—a considerable force being then in bivouac, it was said, half a mile to his left. Having halted, that the men might have an hour's rest and sleep, he again moved forward, slowly, but steadily, almost constantly, till noon, when, within three miles of Black Land, he again halted; and as it had been rumoured and was apprehended that a Federal force now occupied that place, he consulted with the commanders of the Mississippi regiment, the battery, and others who had been left on similar service for other commands, and at other crossings of the Tuscumbia, as to what course they should pursue.

There was a difference of opinion about the measures best to be adopted, and he cut the matter short by announcing that he would march his own regiment straight forward, as the most expedient course. He accordingly assumed immediate command of the Ninth and the artillery, and moved on. The Mississippians and others followed, and they fortunately passed through Black Land just after a body of Federal cavalry had left it. At sundown that afternoon Col. Hunt reported to Gen. Breckinridge, and rejoined the main body of the Reserve Corps, near Baldwin, whither it had preceded him.

He had almost been given up for lost; but after a long and perilous march, extending through thirty hours from the time of leaving Tuscumbia bridge, with but little rest, and no sleep that was worth the name, he restored the component parts of the guard, almost perfectly intact, to their places in the corps.

From this point the army marched to Tupelo—the Reserve Corps leaving Baldwin on the 6th of June. The transportation had now been reduced, and tents and baggage curtailed to such an extent that but little transportation was needed, and the command reached Tupelo on the 7th and 8th without loss or molestation, though it was constantly rumoured, from the time that Corinth was out of sight, that the Federals were advancing in force, and the utmost caution and vigilance were exercised daily.

Having arrived at Tupelo, the Reserve Corps was encamped from four to seven miles west of the village, on the wagon road to Pontotoc, and near the little Coonewah Creek. They had suffered with hunger, heat, and dust, hard marching and want of sleep and rest on the retreat, but the new encampment gave little promise of refreshing repose. In open fields, beside a dusty road, water so scarce that the digging of wells had to be resorted to, and a June sun, in Mississippi, beaming down upon almost unprotected heads—all this was not calculated to inspire one with the idea of comfort, and still less was the system of regular drilling in an unshaded, parching desert of a place, that was kept up while the army remained there.

On the 19th of June, this corps, increased by a brigade of Missouri infantry under Gen. Parsons, was detached from the main army, and marched westward, by way of Pontotoc, to the neighbourhood of the Tallahatchie bridge, on the Mississippi Central Railroad, a Federal advance being apprehended from the direction of Grand Junction. The expedition was under command of Gen. Wm. Preston, (Gen. Breckinridge having obtained a short leave of absence to visit Louisiana), and on the 22nd he had encamped the troops within four miles of Abbeville, and was prepared to meet the contemplated movement, having, however, but about ten thousand effective men at his disposal. He was likewise to remove all government stores from Oxford and Grenada, southward, which he speedily effected.

The Federal columns did not advance as had been anticipated, and Gen. Preston was ordered to the relief of Van Dorn, at Vicksburg. The movement began on the 25th, the troops, baggage, and camp equipage to go by rail, and the wagon train to start empty across the country, for the purpose of gathering up supplies for the now beleaguered "Bluff City." Owing to scarcity of rolling stock, and the difficulty that even so early in the war attended railroad transportation on many of the lines, the entire command had not reached Vicksburg before the 30th.

The division went into camp in a low, narrow valley just opposite and below the "four-mile bridge," on the right, and Gen. Breckinridge was soon in command again.

Maj.-Gen. Van Dorn, charged with the defence of the city against the combined fleets of Admirals Farragut and Porter, had, besides the division of Gen. Breckinridge, from one to two thousand infantry and a small artillery force in charge of heavy ordnance and some field guns in battery—the whole force not exceeding ten thousand men of all arms. He assigned Gen. M. L. Smith to the immediate command of the city and its defensive works, and Gen. Breckinridge to that of the entire reserve force, and the execution of measures designed to guard the river front, above and below, against the landing of Federal troops, that were held in readiness, on transports, to be thrown into the city by whatever means should appear most practicable.

Almost the entire month of July was passed here, in a clime and under circumstances most adverse to the troops of Kentucky; they suffered greatly by reason of disease, though they withstood the effects of heat, malarious influences, want of wholesome supplies and pure water even better than the native soldiers. None were exempt, and toward the latter part of the month the sickness became alarming; but its relative influence on the combatants was in favour of the Confederates, as the Federal troops, despite all their sanitary precautions, abundant medical stores, and well-supplied commissariat, were daily falling victims by hundreds to the pestilent demon.

After the departure of Gen. Hawes, Col. Hunt was in command of his brigade, and when Gen. Breckinridge returned, Preston resumed command of his own. The first dispositions of Breckinridge's division looking to the repulse of any attempt by the Federals to land troops and occupy the city, were made on the 1st of July. The orders to the brigades of Preston and Hunt specified that they should keep forty rounds of cartridges in boxes, and one day's cooked rations constantly on hand; that full regimental guards should be posted in advantageous positions, with instructions to watch for rocket signals from Vicksburg—the signal for movement to be three rockets from the city, following each other rapidly, and a fourth after a short interval.

The moment the signals were given, these brigades were to form without knapsacks, and march rapidly along the Jackson road to Vicksburg, without further orders—commanding officers to acquaint themselves with the route from their encampments, and be able to move promptly by day or night.

On the 2nd, the mortar fleets began the bombardment of the city, which was kept up with scarcely a day's intermission, until the evening of the 25th. The city presented a sad scene when the shells began to burst over and within its limits. The heroic people had expressed their preference for risking its destruction to its occupation by the Federal forces, and, with no adequate means of removing their personal property, or even themselves, many families yet occupied their homes. When the upper fleet opened fire, some retired from the city, while others took refuge in the cellars and other places that promised protection.

In some instances, excavations were made in the sides of the hills with which the city abounds, and the inhabitants sought, in these, refuge from the storm. Moving out on foot, during that first week of the enemy's operations, might be seen the old and decrepit, and frequently a mother with her family of little children, whose father was, perhaps, in the far-off Army of Virginia, and happily unconscious of the deadly peril of his beloved, and the hard fate that awaited them as refugees from their homes.

A different arrangement of the forces was made on the 3rd. The brigade of Col. Hunt was disposed in the following order: Two regiments were placed in the deep railroad cut under the bridge nearest the river, and in the lower part of the city, with two companies at the mouth of the cut, near a field battery known as Starling's, and sentinels close down to the river. The rest of the brigade was held in reserve south of the railroad cut, in the valley in rear of Smede's house.

Gen. Preston took position in supporting distance of the upper batteries. Two regiments were to be constantly on duty near the batteries, and the others held in reserve, close at hand. Both brigades were to leave sufficient force, under command of officers, in the camps first established, to guard them, and cook and carry rations to the outpost. One-third of the force at the front were to return alternately to the old camps, for the purpose of washing clothes and persons.

The general plan, as it regarded the Kentucky troops, though with various modifications, prevailed during the siege. On the 5th of July, the Fourth Kentucky and a battery were detached and sent down to the crossing of the Big Bayou below Warrenton, to prevent the approach of Federals from that direction for a land attack, where they remained for about a week. (See end of chapter).

On the 8th of July Gen. Helm assumed command of Hawes' brigade, and Col. Hunt returned to his regiment.

The incidents of most peculiar moment which transpired during the time that Gen. Breckinridge remained there, was the attack upon the enemy's fleet by the *Arkansas*; an engagement between the Confederate batteries and the upper fleet; on the evening of the same day, the 15th, and the attempt to destroy the *Arkansas*. The enemy at no time made a direct attempt to land, but the troops were kept always in readiness, and were always more or less exposed to the furious shelling that took place regularly in the forenoon and afternoon of each day. A few casualties occurred among the Kentuckians, which are referred to in the latter part of the work.

One attack upon the *Arkansas* occurred on the morning of the 22nd, shortly after sunrise. The *Essex* came down to where the ram lay, at the levee, and having given it a furious broadside, attempted to grapple and board it, but was foiled, and withdrew. A detail from Helm's and Preston's brigades had been made to supply the place, temporarily, of those who had been killed and wounded, on the morning of the 15th. Some of them were on board and assisted in repelling the attack of the *Essex*; and one, Caleb W. Allen, distinguished himself by his exertions and intrepidity in working a heavy gun, and anticipating the movements of a Federal officer who attempted to enter a port-hole during a pause between discharges of his piece, and whom he killed with a pistol-shot.

A plan for floating a submarine battery from the city front to be fired under the lower fleet was conceived by one McDaniel, of Allen county, Kentucky, and it appeared so plausible that he obtained the ear of the authorities, and was furnished with the means of carrying it into effect. Some twelve or fifteen men of one of Preston's Kentucky regiments were named by McDaniel himself, and permitted to volunteer for the occasion; and everything was being rapidly put in readiness one dark night, when some break or other mishap occurred, which so materially crippled his arrangements as to defeat the entire plan, and no further effort was made to test it during the siege.

The conduct of the Kentucky troops here, though marked by none of those more brilliant passages in the life of a soldier that characterize great battles, was one, nevertheless, of constant danger; and the manner in which they discharged their duties, whether as pickets, sharpshooters, or drawn out in full force to repel anticipated efforts to disembark Federal forces—bearing at all times cheerfully the trial of being exposed to the enemy's artillery fire without engaging in active resistance—won the confidence of the general commanding department, and confirmed among the Southern people the reputation won at Shiloh.

Gen. Van Dorn, on the 18th of July, issued a congratulatory order to the troops defending Vicksburg, from which we make the following extract:

> Your conduct thus far, under the circumstances which surround you, has won the admiration of your countrymen. Cool and self-possessed under the concentrated fire of more than forty vessels of war and mortar-boats, you have given assurances

that the city intrusted to your keeping will not be given up to the blustering demands of cannon nor the noisy threatenings of bombshells.

To have been among the defenders of Vicksburg will be the boast hereafter of those who shall bear your names, and a living joy by your hearthstones forever.

Here the command remained till July 27th, when in pursuance of orders, Gen. Breckinridge set out to reduce the Federal garrison at Baton Rouge, an account of which expedition will be found in the following chapter.

INCIDENTS AND ANECDOTES.

1. Breckinridge and Van Dorn.—When Breckinridge's division was ordered to the defence of Vicksburg against the fleets lying both above and below, Van Dorn was in command of the department, with headquarters then at Vicksburg, and of course Breckinridge was subject to his orders. Soon after the division went into camp about the city, an Orphan had occasion one day to visit department headquarters, where he saw Van Dorn for the first time, and with him was Gen. Breckinridge. The contrast between the men was very great, and it struck the observer. He had not been in service long enough to reconcile him to the incongruity of having the finest-looking man in the Confederacy, and that man a Kentuckian, subordinate to one so apparently inferior in every way.

Our Orphan transacted his business and was busy meanwhile taking notes. He wondered, and still his wonder grew, till he got back to camp, by which time he was ready to explode. Being a man of some volubility and fair descriptive powers, he made an impression that was never erased from the minds of his hearers. Coxcomb, dandy, fop, ballroom *beau*—and such a thing of paint, perfume, and feathers to command our Breckinridge—and us! The thing was so preposterous in his sight that it seemed to call in question the wisdom of a military establishment that allowed rank to take priority to men. We learned a good deal afterwards as to Van Dorn's ability and fighting qualities, but, for the time he seemed to be almost as odious to our critic as the "thing that smelt so sweet" was to Hotspur.

2. Celebrating the 4th of July During the Siege; Expedition of the Fourth Regiment Down the River.—On the morning of the 4th day of July, 1862, we naturally supposed the Federals would celebrate the day by an extraordinary bombardment of the city, and thus make things somewhat lively for us. The sun arose with unusual splendour; expectation was on tiptoe; but to our surprise a silence, profound as death, rested upon the combatants until just at noon, when both fleets opened fire with every gun. They rent the heavens with the fury of exploding shells; the shore batteries instantly responded, and for half an hour these tremendous engines of death vomited forth their horrible contents, and then ceased as suddenly as they began, not another gun being fired during the day.

On the following day the Fourth Regiment, with a battery, was ordered to a point on the Mississippi River just below Warrenton, fourteen miles from Vicksburg. This place was a wide, swampy bottom on the east side of the river, and occupied a bend in the river, which, with the bluffs on the east, enclosed several hundred acres. This bottom had been overflowed, and the cottonwood trees which grew on a considerable portion of it had caught and held large quantities of brush, drift wood, etc. Our mission was to conceal ourselves and our battery in this drift, near the river, and pounce upon any steamer which might undertake to pass up the river. It did not take us long to conceal ourselves in this wilderness and plant our guns along the river bank. Of course, they were nicely masked. Sentinels were posted down the river. Five days passed in the pleasant occupations of eating, sleeping, and fighting mosquitoes without a single alarm or sign of the enemy. On the fifth day the pickets sent in information that a small craft, with several men in it, was crossing the river from the Louisiana shore, a mile or so below us.

The colonel immediately ordered a sergeant to select a squad of six men to investigate the movement. This was done and we proceeded down the river as fast as possible, and concealed ourselves in the bushes, near the point which the batteaux seemed to be making for. The moment it struck shore we sprang from our hiding places, with cocked guns, and demanded a surrender. The enemy consisted of four lusty negro men and one woman. With these we captured several bundles of old clothing, bed-quilts, and other trumpery prized by negroes. Had we dropped from the clouds, out of a clap of thunder, the poor darkies could not have been more astonished and terrified. With dilated eyes and trembling limbs they awaited death, which they evidently thought was at hand.

In answer to the sergeant's inquiry, "Who are you? Where are you going?" one of them answered supplicatingly.

"We'se nothing but poor n——rs, massa, trying to git wid our

folks on dis side of de river." Ordering them to shoulder their baggage, we led them to the colonel, who gathered from them that they were the slaves of a Louisiana planter, who had fled from his home on the approach of the Yankees, leaving them to take care of themselves; and they, being scarcely less terrified at the name of Yankee than their master, were seeking to reach their friends and relatives in Mississippi. The colonel sent them on their way.

On the morning of the 12th day of our ambush, about an hour before dawn, the pickets reported a steamboat coming up the river. When she had arrived nearly opposite the battery the guns opened on her with shot and shell. Her lights were almost instantly extinguished, and her speed increased; but before she could get out of range a number of shot struck, as we could distinctly hear them crashing through her timbers. They failed, however, to disable her, and she sped on her way up the river. It was now apparent that our longer stay would be useless. The Federals would almost certainly send a gunboat to investigate and avenge the insult if possible.

We had no particular desire to tackle one of these monsters, so we limbered up and pulled out about dawn, and in a few hours had gained the summit of the high bluffs back of Warrenton, a few miles nearer the city, where we had a fine view of the river. As we came into view a flat, black, villainous-looking gunboat was just squaring herself in the river opposite our recent hiding place; and it was with some satisfaction that we contemplated our safe distance as she poured a broadside from her heavy guns into the unoccupied timber.—Thomas Owens (Fourth Kentucky).

3. *Dodd's Unequal but Gallant Fight.*— In the Brief History of Individuals will be found various allusions to the officers who took other service when the Kentucky regiments were reorganised. The experience of one of them, Lieut. Thomas L. Dodd, of Glasgow, deserves special mention. He was soon afterward appointed lieutenant of artillery, and assigned to duty with the famous Morgan Battery, with others, whom he had assisted in recruiting a company for that arm. The battery was given them by Gen. Leonidas Polk, and they were attached with it to the Fourth Battalion Tennessee Cavalry, Morgan's Brigade. The battalion was then doing duty on the Kentucky border as a separate command, and while there, was attacked by an entire brigade of Federal cavalry, and a large part of it killed, captured, and scattered.

He remained with the battery and strove to rally the command in the face of the enemy; but they were new and undisciplined troops, and being almost surrounded by overwhelming numbers, they retreated in confusion. With a few faithful men he attempted to cover the retreat and prevent the entire destruction of the command, but the men were killed or disabled, with the exception of Private Gilleland; and the charging column demanded their surrender. Gilleland escaped into the bushes, and Dodd, determined to make the attempt on his horse, fired his pistol at the pursuers, wheeled into the forest, and after a furious ride, distanced his foes, and rejoined such of the command as had gotten together.

For his conduct on this occasion, he was promoted to captain of cavalry, and served with Gen. Debrell, in Forrest's campaigns in East Tennessee, and at the battle of Chickamauga, where he was complimented by his commander for gallant conduct. He was shortly afterward severely wounded, but measurably recovered (though the ball was permitted to remain imbedded in his right shoulder). Having been disabled for active field duty, he afterward did various service till the close of the war, in command of provost force at Covington, Ga., and of two companies for the protection of Atlanta from raiding parties that might operate from Dalton, in the winter of 1864-5. He was, meanwhile, recommended by Gen. Howell Cobb for promotion to provost marshal-general of Georgia, but the war terminated before the application was acted upon.

4. Graphic Description of a Sublime Spectacle.—The following allusion to the affair of July 15th, referred to in preceding chapter, is from the journal of John S. Jackman, Ninth Kentucky:

> Late in the afternoon we marched to our old position, about the railroad cut. Just as we were filing off the railroad, up a street, where there was a high bluff that would protect us in a measure from the shells, all the upper batteries opened, and were replied to by the upper fleet, as it dropped down before the city. The first intimation we had of this movement was when one of these long, conical shells—two feet in length and ten inches in diameter—came shrieking over our heads, making something like the noise of a man screaming in agony. Soon the fight became general. The mortar fleets, above and below, filled the air with bursting shells; the fleets vomited forth both iron and flame; our batteries thundered till the very earth trembled; the enemy's hot shot were flying through the air, mimicking the forked-tongued lightning; and flashes of artillery made

the night as light as day. To heighten the grand scene, some buildings up town took fire from the hot missiles, and a pillow or flame pierced the very heavens. As the storm-cloud passes, so did this. Soon a perfect silence brooded over the city—the whole affair lasted, perhaps, an hour—and we went to sleep.

5. Starving Him Into Terms.—Old soldiers can recall occasional experiences with men who would do guard, picket, and special duty, and go to battle, but draw the line at mess-work, and could hardly be driven to do their share of providing water and fuel and taking a turn at preparing meals. I am indebted to Smith E. Winn, one of the non-commissioned officers of Co. D, Sixth Kentucky, a scholar and a gentleman, and as good a soldier as ever shouldered a gun, for the following: Pryor Murphy, of that company, was notoriously delinquent in the particular alluded to, and made a very undesirable mess-mate. During the first siege of Vicksburg, Murphy became one of Winn's mess, and the latter was a man who wouldn't be imposed on three times a day for all the days in the week, and by agreement with the others he read the law to Mr. Murphy: If he wouldn't work he shouldn't eat.

At the first breakfast afterward he was unceremoniously shouldered out; but he seemed to feel that his refusal to work was a matter of principle, and he declined to give in during the day, so that tattoo found him unquestionably very hungry, since no other mess had enough to spare to be charitably disposed and to encourage a do-nothing policy. The mess had a tent at that time, and when they chose to take shelter under it, the front curtains were fastened back to admit the air. During the night Winn chanced to wake up and find the interior of the tent flooded with light. Somewhat astonished, he rose to a sitting posture and discovered Murphy seated a little in front, with a bright fire on each hand. He called out: "Pry, what are you doing there?"

Now the offending soul had a lisp and no use for initial j's or s's, and he replied with emphasis: "Thmith, I'm thess a-runnin' two fires!" Further investigation showed that he had gone to a country cornpatch and provided himself with a lot of roasting ears, which he now had reclining on end before his two fires, and he was intently engaged in preparing "to fill a long-felt want," independently of his comrades and of the regimental commissary.

CHAPTER 6

The Battle of Baton Rouge

The enemy now held Baton Rouge, (the capital of Louisiana), with a land force of about thirty-five hundred men and four or five gunboats with accompanying transports. Communication with Vicksburg by way of the Red River was thus cut off, and the garrison deprived of much-needed supplies, which were abundant in the regions drained by that river and hard to be obtained from other quarters. Van Dorn deemed it important to reduce Baton Rouge, for this and other military reasons, and so open the navigation of Red River and the Mississippi to Vicksburg. He therefore ordered Gen. Breckinridge to move upon the place with five thousand picked men, among them the five Kentucky regiments in his division, including Cobb's Battery, constituting much the greater part of his force.

When he moved, however, he had in hand but about four thousand of all arms; but at Camp Moore a small force under Gen. Ruggles was added to these. The ram *Arkansas*, which had been repaired after the conflict noticed in preceding chapter, was to cooperate with the land forces by simultaneously attacking the gunboats before Baton Rouge.

The conduct of the expedition and the immediate result are best given in the reports of the commanding general and the officers who led the various organisations. The ultimate result, as will also be seen, was that after the partial failure of the attack, Gen. Breckinridge retired to the Comite River, leaving a force of observation near the town; the enemy ceased to send out marauding parties, to despoil the country and annoy the citizens; in a few days a detachment under Ruggles was sent to occupy Port Hudson, a strong point on the Mississippi below the mouth of Red River; and the Federal garrison abandoned Baton Rouge, so that there was now communication by that important route with a field as yet rich in supplies.

Headquarters Breckinridge's Division,
September 30, 1862.

Major M. M. Kimmel, Assistant Adjutant-General—

Sir: I have the honour to report the operations of a portion of my division, recently ordered from Vicksburg to Camp Moore and Baton Rouge, La., by Maj.-Gen. Van Dorn:

I left Vicksburg on the 27th of July, with somewhat less than four thousand men, and arrived at Camp Moore the evening of the 28th. The major-general commanding the district, having received intelligence that the enemy was threatening Camp Moore in force, the movement was made suddenly and rapidly by railroad, and, having but few cars, nothing could be transported except the troops, with their arms and ammunition. Brig.-Gen. Charles Clarke, who had reported for duty but a few days before our departure from Vicksburg, promptly and kindly consented to accompany the expedition. Brig.-Gen. Ruggles was already at Camp Moore, in command of a small force, with which he had kept the enemy in check. The troops were immediately organised in two divisions, Gen. Clarke taking command of the first, and Gen. Ruggles of the second. The rumour of an advance of the enemy upon Camp Moore proved to be unfounded.

On the 30th of July, in obedience to a dispatch of the 29th from the major-general commanding the district, the troops were put in motion for Baton Rouge. During the march I received information that the effective force of the enemy was not less than five thousand men, and that the ground was commanded by three gunboats lying in the river. My own troops having suffered severely from the effects of exposure at Vicksburg, from heavy rains, without shelter, and from the extreme heat, did not now number more than thirty-four hundred men. Under these circumstances, I determined not to make the attack unless we could be relieved from the fire of the fleet.

Accordingly, I telegraphed to the major-general commanding the condition and number of the troops and the reported strength of the enemy; but said I would undertake to capture the garrison if the *Arkansas* could be sent down to clear the river, or divert the fire of the gunboats. He promptly answered that the *Arkansas* would be ready to cooperate at daylight on Tuesday morning, the 5th of August.

On the afternoon of Monday, the command having reached the Comite River, ten miles from Baton Rouge; and learning by an express messenger that the *Arkansas* had passed Bayou Sara in time to arrive at the proper moment, preparations were made to advance that night.

The sickness had been appalling. The morning report of the 4th showed but three thousand effective, and deducting those taken sick during the day, and the number that fell out from weakness on the night march, I did not carry into the action more than twenty-six hundred men. This estimate does not include some two hundred Partisan Rangers, who had performed efficient service in picketing the different roads, but who, from the nature of the ground, took no part in the action; nor about the same number of militia, hastily collected by Col. Hardee, in the neighbourhood of Clinton, who, though making every effort, could not arrive in time to participate.

The command left the Comite at 11 o'clock p. m., and reached the vicinity of Baton Rouge a little before daybreak on the morning of the 5th. Some hours before the main body moved, a small force of infantry, with a section of Semmes' Battery, under Lieut. Fauntleroy, the whole commanded by Lieut.-Col. Shields, of the Thirtieth Louisiana, was sent, by a circuitous route, to the road leading from Clinton to Baton Rouge, with orders to drive in any pickets of the enemy, and attack his left as soon as the action should begin in front. This service was well performed; but for details reference is made to the report of Brig.-Gen. Ruggles, from whose command the force was detached.

While waiting for daylight to make the attack, an accident occurred, which deprived us of several excellent officers and enlisted men and two pieces of artillery.

The Partisan Rangers were placed in rear of the artillery and infantry, yet, during the darkness, a few of them leaked through, and, riding forward, encountered the enemy, causing exchange of shots between the pickets. Galloping back, they produced some confusion, which led to rapid firing for a few moments, during which Brig.-Gen. Helm was dangerously wounded by the fall of his horse; Lieut. Alexander Todd, his *aide-de-camp*, was killed; Capt. Roberts, of the Fourth Kentucky, was severely wounded; several enlisted men were killed and wounded, and two of Capt. Cobb's three guns were rendered, for a time, wholly useless. After Gen. Helm was disabled, Col. Tho. H. Hunt assumed command of his brigade. (Lieut. Col. John W. Caldwell also had his horse killed, and was much hurt by being thrown against a gun carriage as the horse rushed back headlong and fell.)

Order was soon restored, and the force placed in position on the right and left of the Greenwell Springs road. I was obliged to content myself with a single line of battle, and a small regiment of infantry with one piece of artillery to each division as a reserve. The enemy (expecting the attack) was drawn up in two lines, or, rather, in one line, with strong reserves distributed at intervals. At the moment there was light enough our troops moved rapidly forward. Gen. Ruggles, commanding the left, brought on the engagement with four pieces of Semmes' Battery, the Fourth and Thirtieth Louisiana, and Boyd's Louisiana Battalion, under the command of Col. Allen, of the Fourth Louisiana; and the Third, Sixth and Seventh Kentucky, and the Thirty-Fifth Alabama, under the command of Col. Thompson, of the Third Kentucky. These troops moved forward with great impetuosity, driving the enemy before them, while their ringing cheers inspired all our little command. The Louisiana troops charged a battery and captured two pieces.

At this point, Col. Allen, commanding the brigade, while pressing forward with the colours in his hand, had both legs shattered, and Lieut.-Col. Boyd received a severe wound. This produced confusion, and the enemy at the same moment throwing forward a strong re-enforcement, the brigade was forced back in some disorder. It was rallied by the efforts of Col. Breaux, Lieut.-Col. Hunter, and other officers, and although it did not further participate in the assault, it maintained its position under a fire from the gunboats and land batteries of the enemy. During this time Thompson's brigade, which composed the right of Ruggles' division, was behaving with great gallantry. After driving back superior forces, toward the close of the action it took part in the final struggle from a position immediately on the left of the First Division. Col. Thompson being severely wounded in a charge, the command devolved upon Col. Robertson, of the Thirty-Fifth Alabama, whose conduct fully justified the confidence of his troops.

The Louisiana Battery, Capt. Semmes, was admirably handled throughout. The First Division, under Gen. Clarke, being the Second Brigade, composed of the Fourth and Ninth Kentucky, Thirty-First Mississippi, and Fourth Alabama, commanded by Col. Hunt, of the Ninth Kentucky, and the Fourth Brigade, composed of the Fifteenth and Twenty-Second Mississippi, and the Nineteenth, Twentieth, Twenty-Eighth, and Forty-Fifth Tennessee, consolidated into one battalion, commanded by Col. Smith, of the Twentieth Tennessee, together with the Hudson Battery, Lieut. Sweeney, and one piece of Cobb's Battery, advanced to the right of the Greenwell Springs road.

On the right as on the left, the enemy was constantly pressed back, until, after several hours of fighting, he was driven to his last encampment in a large grove just in rear of the penitentiary. Here the contest was hot and obstinate, and it was here that the First Division suffered the greatest loss. Col. Hunt was shot down, and, upon the fall of that excellent officer, at the suggestion of Gen. Clarke, and with the consent of the officers concerned, I placed Capt. John A. Buckner, assistant adjutant-general on my staff, in command of the Second Brigade. In the management of his command he displayed so high a degree of skill and courage, that I commend him especially to the notice of the government.

Gen. Clarke pressed the attack at this point with great vigour, until he received a wound which was supposed to be mortal, when, through some misapprehension, the brigade began to fall back down the slope, but without confusion. Capt. Buckner, learning, upon inquiry from me, that I did not desire a retrograde movement, immediately, aided by Maj. Wickliffe, of the Ninth Kentucky (Lieut.-Col. Caldwell, who was injured by the accident of the preceding night, having been obliged to retire), and other regimental commanders, faced the brigade about and renewed the attack. At the same time Col. Smith, commanding the Fourth Brigade, composed of the consolidated Tennessee regiments and the Twenty-Second Mississippi, Capt. Hughes, were ordered forward, and moved against the enemy in fine style. In a few moments Capt. Hughes received a mortal wound at the head of his regiment.

Observing some troops on the left, partially sheltered by a shallow cut in the road, who proved to be the remnant of Thompson's brigade, and out of ammunition, I ordered them to advance to the support of the First Division with the bayonet. The order was promptly obeyed, and in executing it, I happened to observe, as distinguished for alacrity, Col. Crossland, of the Seventh Kentucky, Lieut.-Col. Goodwin, of the Thirty-fifth Alabama, and Lieut. Terry, of the Eighth Kentucky, on duty with sharpshooters. At this critical point, Maj. Brown, chief commissary, and Capt. Richards, one of my *aides*, were conspicuous in urging on the troops. In this assault we suffered considerably from the fire of the fleet, until the opposing lines approached each other so closely that a regard for their own friends obliged them to suspend.

The contest at and around this last encampment was bloody, but at the end of it the enemy were completely routed, some of our men pursuing and firing at them some distance down the street, running in front of the arsenal and barracks. They did not re-appear during the day. It was now 10 o'clock. We had listened in vain for the guns of the *Arkansas*. I saw around me not more than one thousand exhausted men, who had been unable to procure water since we had left the Comite River. The enemy had several batteries commanding the approaches to the arsenal and barracks, and the gunboats had already re-opened upon us with a direct fire. Under these circumstances, although the troops showed the utmost indifference to danger and death, and were even reluctant to retire,

I did not deem it prudent to pursue the victory further. Having scarcely any transportation, I ordered all the camps and stores of the enemy to be destroyed; and, directing Capt. Buckner to place one section of Semmes' Battery, supported by the Seventh Kentucky, in a certain position on the field, withdrew the rest of the troops about one mile, to Ward's Creek, with a hope of obtaining water. But finding none there fit for man or beast, I moved the command back to the field of battle, and procured a very imperfect supply from some cisterns in the suburbs of the town. This position we occupied for the rest of the day. The citizens of the surrounding and thinly-settled country exhibited the warmest patriotism; and, with their assistance, conveyances enough were procured to carry off all our wounded who could bear removal. A few citizens, armed with shot-guns and other weapons, had been able to reach the field in time to join in the attack. Having neither picks nor shovels, we were unable to dig graves for the burial of the dead.

I still hoped for the cooperation of the *Arkansas*, and, in that event, intended to renew the attack. But late in the afternoon I learned by express that before daylight, and within four miles of Baton Rouge, the machinery had become disabled, and she lay helpless on the right bank of the river. Upon receiving this intelligence, I returned with my command to the Comite River, leaving a force of observation near the suburbs of the town. The Hudson Battery, Lieut. Sweeney, and Cobb's one piece, under charge of Sergt. Frank Peak, played their part well.

I am unable to give the exact force of the enemy, but by comparing all my information with the number and size of their camps, and the extent and weight of their fire, I do not think they brought into action less than 4,500 men. We had eleven pieces of field artillery. They brought to bear on us not less than eighteen pieces, exclusive of the guns of the fleet. In one respect, the contrast between the opposing forces was very striking. The enemy were well clothed, and their encampments showed the presence of every comfort, and even luxury. Our men had little transportation, indifferent food, and no shelter. Half of them had no coats, and hundreds of them were without either shoes or socks. Yet no troops ever behaved with greater gallantry, and even reckless audacity. What can make this difference, unless it be the sublime courage inspired by a just cause?

The wound of Brig.-Gen. Clarke being thought mortal, and the least motion causing great agony, he was left on the field, in a comfortable cottage, at his own request—his *aide*, Lieut. Yerger, remaining with him. The next morning, they gave themselves up to the enemy. I cannot speak in terms too strong of the skill, coolness, and courage of Gen. Clarke. He played the part of a perfect soldier.

Brig.-Gen. Ruggles conducted the attack on the left with uncommon rapidity and precision, and exhibited throughout the qualities of a brave and experienced officer.

In addition to the officers of my staff already mentioned, I desire to express my acknowledgment of the zeal and gallantry of Maj. Wilson, chief of artillery; Maj. Hope, inspector-general, whose horse was shot under him; Capt. Nocquet, chief of engineers; Lieut. Breckinridge, *aide-de-camp*, and Dr. Pendleton, medical director, assisted by Dr. Weatherly, on temporary service. A number of gentlemen from Louisiana and elsewhere rendered efficient service as volunteers, among whom were Lieut.-Col. Pinkney, Mr. Addison, and Capt. Bird, of Louisiana; Lieut.-Col. Brewer, of Kentucky, and Mr. William B. Hamilton, of Mississippi. The thanks of the army are also due to Hon. Thomas G. Davidson for his attention to the hospitals; and to all the inhabitants of that part of Louisiana, for their devotion to our sick and wounded. Col. Pond and Maj. De Baum, in command of Partisan Rangers, were efficient both before and after the battle in observing and harassing the enemy.

The inability of Gen. Clarke, and failure of several officers, to make reports, may prevent full justice to the conduct of the First Division. Any omission here will, when brought to my notice, be embodied in a supplemental report. The report of Gen. Ruggles is very full as to all that occurred on the left. I send herewith a list of the officers and men specially mentioned in the division, brigade and regimental reports, for gallant conduct, with the request that it be published, and the names brought to the favourable notice of the government. I transmit, also, the reports of the subordinate commanders, and the returns of the killed and wounded. It will be seen that our casualties amount to 467.

I have reason to believe that the loss of the enemy was much greater. We captured two flags and a few prisoners. Nothing was left by us except one caisson, which was so much injured as to be wholly unserviceable—one of the enemy's being taken in its place. After the battle the enemy, who had previously been plundering, burning houses and other property, stealing negroes, and seizing citizens, through a large region of country, never ventured to send out another marauding force. Our pickets continued to extend to the immediate vicinity of Baton Rouge, and very soon the enemy abandoned the place and retired to New Orleans. A few days after the engagement, knowing the desire of the major-general commanding to secure a strong position on the Mississippi below the mouth of Red River, I occupied Port Hudson, with a portion of the troops under the command of Brig.-Gen. Ruggles. The next day I received orders to remove all the troops to that point. Brig.-Gen. Bowen, who had just arrived, was left with his command on the Comite River, to observe Baton Rouge from that quarter, to protect our hospitals, and to cover the line of communication between Clinton and Camp Moore.

I directed Gen. Ruggles to select eligible positions at Port Hudson for heavy batteries, and ordered Capt. Nocquet, chief of engineers, to report to him temporarily for this duty. Upon my arrival there I found that rapid progress had been made, and some of the works, under charge of Capt. Nocquet, were ready to receive the guns, which, the Major-General commanding wrote me, were on the way.

Port Hudson is one of the strongest points on the Mississippi River (which Baton Rouge is not), and batteries there will command the river more completely than at Vicksburg.

On the 19th day of August, in obedience to orders from the headquarters of the department, I moved from Port Hudson for Jackson, Mississippi, with a portion of the force, leaving Brig.-Gen. Ruggles in command with the remainder.

In concluding this report, I have to express my obligations for the prompt and cordial support which I received, at all times, from the major-general commanding the department.

Very respectfully, your obedient servant,

John C. Breckinridge,
Major-General.

I omitted to mention that the Fifteenth Mississippi, Maj. Binford, was not brought into action. This admirable regiment, much reduced by long and gallant service, was held in reserve.

J. C. B.

It will be observed that a temporary organisation of the entire forces under his command was made by Gen. Breckinridge for the occasion, and that the allusions to brigades, in reports of the battle, are made with reference to that special organisation and not to the designations they bore at Vicksburg. We herewith publish the report of Gen. Ruggles, in whose division were included three of the Kentucky regiments. Where he and Gen. Breckinridge speak of "Thompson's Brigade," it must be borne in mind that they allude to the brigade of Gen. Preston, that officer having been compelled by sickness to leave the division before its departure for Vicksburg, when the command devolved upon Col. Albert P. Thompson:

Headquarters Second Division, First District,
Army East of the Mississippi,
Camp Breckinridge, August 9, 1862.

Sir: I have the honour to submit, for the consideration of the major-general commanding the forces, the following report of the part taken by my division in the action of the 5th inst., at Baton Rouge. The Second Division was composed of two brigades: The first consisting of the Third Kentucky Regiment, Capt. Bowman; Sixth Kentucky, Lieut.-Col. Cofer; Seventh Kentucky, Col. Crossland; and Thirty-Fifth Alabama, Col. Robertson. The Second Brigade, of the Fourth Louisiana Regiment, Lieut.-Col. Hunter; battalion of Thirtieth Louisiana Regiment, Col. S. H. Breaux; battalion of Stewart's Legion, Lieut. Col. Boyd; and Confederate Light Battery, Capt. O. J. Semmes, with two companies mounted men and some two hundred and fifty Partisan Rangers detached on scouting and outpost service.

On the night of the 4th August, the division proceeded from Comite bridge, marching left in front; Semmes' Light Battery in the rear of left battalion Fourth Louisiana Volunteers, a detachment commanded by Lieut.-Col. Shields; Thirtieth Louisiana Volunteers, consisting of one company from his regiment, commanded by Capt. Boyle; one company of Partisan Rangers, commanded by Capt. Anuker; one company mounted rangers, and a section of Semmes' Battery, under Lieut. Fauntleroy, had preceded the march of the division, having left camp at four and a half p.m., to operate on the plank road leading from Baton Rouge to Clinton, on our extreme right.

The head of the division column, preceded by a company of mounted rangers and advanced guard, reached Ward's Creek bridge, on the Greenwell Springs and Baton Rouge road, about 3 o'clock a. m., where a temporary halt was called, preparatory to the formation of the division line of battle. During this halt, while the advance was driving in the enemy's pickets, some stragglers from the column were mistaken for enemy's pickets and fired on. The mistake being mutual, in the darkness a few shots were exchanged, unfortunately disabling Gen. Helm and killing Lieut. Todd. This necessarily caused some confusion.

Order, however, was soon restored, and the column marched to the point whence the deployment was to begin. The line was formed a little before daylight. Col. Thompson's brigade (the first), with the right resting near the Greenwell Springs road, Col. Allen's brigade (the second) on the left, his left extending through a wood, and resting on a large field. Semmes' Battery (four pieces) in the centre, occupying the space between the two brigades; a squadron of cavalry, under command of Capt. Augustus Scott, was ordered to proceed to the extreme left of the line, to observe and endeavour to prevent any attempt to outflank us in that direction.

At a little after daylight, during the prevalence of a thick fog, the order was given to advance. The line proceeded but a few hundred yards before it encountered a brisk fire from the enemy's skirmishers, strongly posted on our extreme right, in some houses surrounded by trees and picket fences. Almost simultaneously a battery of the enemy opened on our line from the same direction. Semmes' Battery was ordered forward to our indicated position, to drive off the skirmishers and silence the enemy's battery, and the whole line moved rapidly forward firing and cheering. The effect was instantaneous. The enemy's skirmishers fled, and his battery was compelled to change position and seek shelter under the guns of the arsenal to prevent being captured, where it remained, continuing to fire on our advancing line. Semmes' Battery took position on the right of the division, to keep up the engagement with the battery of the enemy.

Col. Thompson's brigade continued to advance, under an occasional fire, across an open field and through some cornfields, just beyond which they encountered a heavy fire from the enemy, strongly posted in a wood. Here the contest was warmly maintained on both sides for a considerable time, during which the First Division succeeded in entering a regimental camp on our right. The enemy were finally driven back into and through another camp immediately in our front. The enemy at this period were strongly re-enforced, and a heavy battery a little to the left of the centre opened an oblique fire on both brigades. About the same time the enemy attempted to break our centre, by pushing a column between the two brigades. This movement being discovered, Semmes' Battery was ordered forward and opened on this column at short range, with grape and canister, with marked effect, for a few rapid discharges scattered the enemy and drove him back in confusion.

A similar attempt was made on the right of the division, which was defeated with equal success by a timely and well-directed fire from the Thirty-Fifth Alabama and Sixth Kentucky Regiments. The two brigades, which, from the nature of the ground, had become separated, were ordered, in advancing, to gain ground, to the right and left respectively, in order to subject the enemy's position in front to a converging fire. In executing this movement, the First Brigade met a portion of the First Division falling back in some disorder. Col. Thompson halted, and was attempting to reform them when he was informed by a mounted officer that the order was for the whole line to fall back. In obedience to this supposed order he fell back a short distance, but soon reformed his line and charged the enemy under a galling fire.

Unfortunately, while leading his men in this charge, Col. Thompson fell, severely wounded, and was borne from the field; and about the same time Col. Allen also fell, dangerously wounded, while leading, with unsurpassed gallantry, his brigade against a battery of the enemy. These circumstances prevented the further prosecution of this movement. About this time the major-general commanding arrived upon this part of the field, and directed the final charge upon the enemy, which drove him in confusion through his last regimental encampment to the river, under the protection of his gunboats.

His camps, containing a large quantity of personal property, commissary stores and clothing, were destroyed. Finding it fruitless to remain longer under the fire of the gunboats, and disappointed in the expected cooperation of the *Arkansas*, the exhausted troops were withdrawn in good order to the suburbs of the town—the Seventh Kentucky Regiment and a section of Semmes' artillery being left on the field to protect the collection of the stragglers and wounded, which was thoroughly accomplished.

Col. Allen's brigade, on the left, moved forward through a wood and into some cornfields. They soon encountered the enemy in superior force, protected by houses and fences. They successively charged these positions, driving the enemy steadily back until within a few hundred yards of the river, where they were subjected to a destructive fire from the batteries before mentioned and the enemy's gunboats. They charged and took a section from one of the enemy's batteries, Col. Allen leading the advance with the colours of one of his battalions in his hand. It was at this critical juncture that, as before stated, this gallant soldier fell from his horse severely wounded, and, during the confusion which followed this misfortune, the enemy succeeded in recapturing the pieces.

The enemy pressed heavily upon this brigade, and poured into it such a galling fire from infantry and artillery that it fell back in some disorder. Col. Breaux, who assumed command upon the fall of Col. Allen, succeeded, with the aid of officers of the brigade and two officers connected with the staff, who were sent to his assistance, in rallying a sufficient number to show front to the enemy, until Semmes' Battery was brought up, as already stated, to their support, and succeeded, by a well-directed fire, in preventing the enemy's advance. This position was maintained despite the heavy firing on the brigade from the enemy's gunboats and land batteries, until the troops were withdrawn, with the rest of the army, to the suburbs of the town.

Lieut.-Col. Shields had been ordered, as already stated, to take position on the plank road leading from Clinton to Baton Rouge, and as soon as he heard the fire of our main body, to attack a battery of the enemy, said to be stationed at the junction of the Clinton and Bayou Sara roads. This service was promptly and gallantly performed. He drove in the enemy's pickets, followed them up, and opened fire on a regimental encampment to the right of the Greenwell Springs road, driving the enemy from it. He was here met by two regiments of the enemy, but succeeded in holding them at bay till he was fired upon by our own artillery, fortunately without injury.

Four of the artillery horses being disabled, and the infantry unable to withstand the heavy fire of the enemy, he withdrew to his original position, where the wounded horses were replaced by others, when he returned to his advanced position, which he held till Gen. Clarke's division came up on his left, when the two companies of infantry were, by order of the major-general commanding, attached to the Twenty-second Mississippi Regiment. The section of artillery under his command retained its position until the army retired, when it rejoined the battery in the suburbs of the town.

In concluding this report of the battle, I have the satisfaction of stating that the conduct of both officers and men was gallant and daring, every movement being performed with characteriztic promptitude. I respectfully commend the reports of the commanders of brigades, as well as those of regiments, battalions, and independent companies, to the special consideration of the commanding general, and also recommend the following officers and soldiers, specially named in these reports, to favourable consideration:

Col. A. P. Thompson and Col. H. W. Allen, brigade commanders, both severely wounded. Third Kentucky, commanded by Capt. Bowman. Seventh Kentucky, Col. Crossland, and his colour-bearer, James Rollins. Sixth Kentucky, Lieut.-Col. Cofer; Captains Isaac Smith, Gran Utterback, and Thomas Page, and First Lieut. Frank Harned. Thirty-Fifth Alabama, Col. Robertson and Lieut.-Col. Goodwin. Of the Second Brigade, the Fourth Louisiana, Lieut.-Col. Hunter. In this regiment, Lieut. Corkern, Co. B; Lieut. Jeter, Co. H, and Sergt.-Maj. Daniels. Battalion of Stewart's Legion, commanded by Lieut.-Col. Samuel Boyd, who was disabled by a severe flesh wound in the arm. Capt. Chum also was wounded. The command devolved upon Capt. Tom Bynum, who acted with gallantry.

The battalion, Thirtieth Regiment of Louisiana Volunteers, commanded by Col. J. A. Breaux, who speaks in high terms of the officers and men of his regiment, especially Capt. N. Trepagnier and Lieut. Dapremont, both wounded. Lieut.-Col. Shields, Thirtieth Louisiana, commanding separate detachment, who speaks in high terms of the intrepidity of Lieut. Fauntleroy, commanding section of guns in his detachment. Capt. Semmes, commanding battery, and his officers, Lieutenants Barnes and J. A. West, performed gallant service. Capt. Blount, brigade inspector of Second Brigade, rendered gallant service in the field, where it is believed he has fallen, as nothing has been heard of him since.

I also have the gratification to name the members of my staff, who served with me on this occasion, *viz.*: Lieut. L. D. Sandidge, corps artillery, Confederate States Army, A. A. A. and inspector-general; Capt. George Whitfield, chief quartermaster; Maj. E. S. Ruggles, acting ordnance officer; and acting chief commissary of subsistence, First Lieut. M. B. Ruggles, *aide-de-camp*. Lieut.-Col. Charles Jones, who was severely wounded, and Col. J. O. Fuqua, district judge advocate and provost marshal-general, were all distinguished for their efficiency, coolness, and gallantry throughout the conflict.

The following officers, attached to the general staff, also rendered gallant service: Capt. Sam Bard, on special service; Lieut. A. B. DeSaulles, engineers; Lieut. H. H. Price and Lieut. H. C. Holt. Other officers on special services, among whom were Capt. Augustus Scott, commanding squadron on temporary service; Captains Curry, Kinderson, and Behorn, as volunteer aides for the occasion, and Capt. J. M. Taylor served with zeal and gallantry. The entire division entering the fight numbered about nineteen hundred and fifty, infantry and artillery, with a few irregular cavalry and Partisan Rangers, numbering in all some three hundred and fifty or four hundred. The casualties, killed, wounded, and missing, being two hundred and seventy-seven.

 Very respectfully, your obedient servant,

Daniel Ruggles,
Brigadier-General Commanding Second Division.

Capt. John A. Buckner, A. A. General.

 The following is the report of Col. Buckner, who conducted the movements of Helm's brigade after Col. Hunt was wounded, as noticed in the report of Gen. Breckinridge:

Headquarters in the Field,
Comite River, August 9, 1862.

General: In compliance with your request, I have the honour to submit the following report of the late engagement at Baton Rouge, so far as the First Brigade of First Division was concerned, after its commanders, Brig.-Gen. Helm, and, subsequently, Col. Thomas H. Hunt, were wounded, and I had the honour to receive the command at your hands:

 The enemy had been repulsed from one of his encampments, and the different regiments constituting the First Brigade were drawn up in line of his camps, not, however, fully deployed. After moving the two regiments on the left of the brigade, by the flank to the left, the whole were formed in line of battle, and were ordered to advance.

 The movement was made with spirit up to the second encampment, through a somewhat sharp volley of musketry, in as good style as the broken and confined limits of the ground would admit, and immediately the enemy was hotly and determinedly engaged. After a few volleys, I ordered the brigade forward, which order was being properly obeyed by the Fourth and Ninth Kentucky, the other regiments being just in the act of advancing, when I received, from Gen. Clarke, the order to face about and retreat. This order was then given by myself and by Col. Clarke's *aides*. The troops fell back reluctantly, and not in very good order, the general himself and a number of others being wounded in the retreat.

 I reported immediately to you to know whether you had ordered the retreat, and was informed that you had not. The Second Brigade of this division was then ordered by yourself to advance. It went up in good style—Capt. Hughes, commanding Twenty-Second Mississippi

Regiment, leading them gallantly. By your presence and assistance, the First Brigade was rallied and led by yourself, in person, to the same position from which it had fallen back, when it joined with the Second Brigade, and moved conjointly through the second encampment, driving the enemy before them through the third and last of their camps to the river, under cover of their gunboats.

This being accomplished, which was all that was expected of the land force, the *Arkansas* failing to make her appearance, nothing remained but to destroy what had been captured, (inasmuch as no arrangement had been made for bearing it off, though the battlefield was in our possession sufficiently long,) and retire from the range of the enemy's batteries on the river. Accordingly, you gave me the order to withdraw the division out of range of the fire of the fleet, to await the movements of the gunboat *Arkansas*.

This was done in good order, though with some degree of reluctance, the cause of the movement not being fully understood. Your order to fire the enemy's tents and stores was well executed. Their loss must have been very heavy in quartermaster and commissary supplies, and particularly so in sutlers' stores, considerable quantities of new goods and general equipments being burned. The position in which you left me near the house where Gen. Clarke lay wounded was held more than two hours after the main body of the troops were withdrawn, with a section of Semmes' Battery and the remnant of the Seventh Kentucky Regiment, Col. Crossland commanding, as support.

Learning that Cobb's Battery had left its position and been ordered to the rear, the section, with its support under my command, was moved to occupy the better position left by Capt. Cobb, at which point it remained a half hour, and would have remained the whole evening, but for the erroneous information of the enemy's advance in force being given by a surgeon who was moving rapidly to the rear. Leaving the pickets at this point, just in the edge of town, I withdrew the artillery and its support slowly back to the point at which you found me. A flag of truce was hoisted early in the evening by the enemy, and, on being met by an officer whom I sent to the front, the privilege of bearing off the dead and wounded was requested and granted for four hours by yourself, upon condition that the agreement be reduced to writing. No communication being received in writing for some time, twenty minutes longer were given, shortly after the expiration of which time a note was received, signed by the commanding officer at Baton Rouge, disclaiming the flag of truce.

I cannot conclude my report without speaking of the cool courage and efficient skill with which Brig.-Gen. Charles Clarke led his command into the action, and the valuable assistance rendered him by his aids, Lieutenants Spooner and Yerger; of the efficiency of Maj. H. E. Topp, of the Thirty-First Mississippi, in leading his regiment, (a Kentuckian, Capt. John B. Pirtle, was in command of right wing of the Thirty-First Mississippi that day); of Maj. Brown, chief commissary of the division, whose fearless exposure of himself, where the contest was hottest, in urging on the troops to a charge; of Capt. J. H. Millett, commanding Fourth Kentucky Regiment, who displayed conspicuous gallantry in leading it; of Col. Crossland, commanding Seventh Kentucky Regiment, whose regiment, after being in front and assisting in bearing the brunt of the battle, remained upon the field while the shells from the enemy's gunboats were falling thickly around them; and of the valuable service rendered me by Maj. J. C. Wickliffe, of the Ninth Kentucky, toward the close of the engagement, where his constant presence, at the head of his regiment, inspired confidence and courage, not only among his own men, but all who were near him in the closing contest, which decided the engagement so favourably and so gloriously for the Confederate arms. For list of casualties I would refer you to papers "A" and "B" concerning late battle.

I have the honour to be, general,
Very respectfully, your obedient servant,
John A. Buckner, A. A. G.

Col. J. W. Robertson commanded Preston's brigade after the fall of Col. Thompson, and reported its entire action through the day, as follows:

Headquarters First Brigade, Second Division,
Camp on Comite River, August 7, 1862.
To Capt. L. D. Sandidge, A. A. G., Second Division—

Captain: On receiving the order to report the part taken in the action of the 5th inst., by the First Brigade, I referred the order to Col. A. P. Thompson, who commanded the brigade during the action with the exception of the closing half hour that the troops were under fire, when he was borne from the field severely wounded; and I submit, by his request, the following report:

On reaching the angle of the main road leading into Baton Rouge, the brigade was formed in line of battle, in a common to the left of the main road, the right of the brigade resting on that road, and the left near a dense forest, into which Col. Allen's brigade had passed. The brigade was composed of the following regiments, positioned from right to left in the order named: Third Kentucky, Capt. J. H. Bowman commanding; Seventh Kentucky, Col. Ed Crossland commanding; Thirty-Fifth Alabama, Col. J. W. Robertson commanding; and the Sixth Kentucky, Lieut.-Col. M. H. Cofer commanding. As soon as the line was established, the command "forward" was given by Gen. Ruggles in person, which was promptly obeyed by the brigade, moving forward beyond the dwelling-house immediately to the front. The line was at this time found to be somewhat deranged, caused by the numerous fences and houses over and around which the troops had to pass.

    The brigade was consequently halted and the alignment rectified, when the command "forward" was again given. The brigade moved directly to the front, parallel to the main road, preceded by a company of sharpshooters deployed as skirmishers, and commanded by Lieut. G. C. Hubbard. At this point the firing began first, the line of the enemy having been unmasked by the skirmishers. The firing was continued but a short time when an order was received for the brigade to charge, and the troops rushed forward with a cheer, the enemy breaking before them. Having reached the middle of the field, the brigade was exposed to a fire from the right, which could not be returned without exposing the troops of Gen. Clarke's division to the fire of the brigade, and was consequently halted until the firing ceased. An advance was made, skirmishers covering the front.

    The second line of the enemy was thus unmasked and exposed to the fire of the brigade. They gave way precipitately before the steady advance of our troops. On clearing the fields and reaching the enemy's encampment, the right wing was found to be covered by a portion of Gen. Clarke's division. An officer approached from the right and stated that friends were exposed to our fire, when the firing ceased and the charge ordered by Col. Thompson, he leading the brigade into the encampment of the enemy to the left, which was nearly cleared by this brigade, when troops were met on the right returning without any apparent cause, and were ordered by Col. Thompson to halt and advance, when a mounted officer informed Col. Thompson that it was the order for all the troops to fall back.

    This movement became general in the brigade. In retiring, the Thirty-Fifth Alabama and Sixth Kentucky, forming the left wing, became separated from the right, and occupied a position in line one hundred yards to the left and rear. The enemy reformed in heavy force behind their tents, rapidly advancing, firing and cheering. The Third and Seventh Kentucky Regiments were thrown under cover and met this advance with a steady fire. The Thirty-Fifth Alabama and Sixth Kentucky were ordered forward, but advanced before the order reached them, opening a heavy fire upon the enemy, whose advance was thus checked.

At this point, Col. Thompson was severely wounded and taken to the rear. The command devolved upon Col. Robertson, who being, from complete exhaustion, in no condition at that time to assume command, and finding the right wing separated from the left, placed Col. Crossland in command of the right, and Lieut.-Col. E. Goodwin in command of the left, with orders to maintain the line, which was firmly held for nearly an hour, in the face of a terrible fire from musketry and artillery, when the charge, which closed the action, was made in person by the major-general commanding. It is the request of Col. Thompson, that his entire approbation of the conduct of all the field and acting field officers engaged, and Capt. W. P. Wallace and Lieut. Charles Semple, *aides*, and Acting Adjt. R. B. L. Soery, of the Third Kentucky, be specially expressed in this report.

To the deportment of the Thirty-Fifth Alabama Regiment he desires attention to be called. This regiment, although for the first time under fire on the 5th inst., proved itself a worthy comrade for the Third, Sixth and Seventh Kentucky Regiments, who, in this action, sustained the enviable reputation won by them on the field of Shiloh. Col. Robertson would call special attention to the gallant conduct of Col. Ed Crossland and Lieut.-Col. E. Goodwin, who, the first with his regimental colours in hand, and the second with his hat on his sword, led the brigade in the final charge.

To the reports of regimental commanders, you are referred for notices of gallant conduct in other members of the command. The medical staff deserve the highest praise for their prompt and unceasing attention to the wounded.

J. W. Robertson,
Colonel Commanding First Brigade,
Second Division.

Headquarters First Brigade,
August 8, 1862.

To Captain L. D. Sandidge, A. A. G., Second Division—

Captain: Col. Robertson desires me to say that he wishes to amend his report by stating that Maj. John R. Throckmorton (of Kentucky), A. Q. M., rendered very efficient service in taking off the wounded from the field, showing great fearlessness of personal danger in the discharge of his duties.

G. C. Hubbard, A. A. G.

The following are the reports of the various officers who commanded the six Kentucky regiments:

Headquarters Third Kentucky Regiment,
August 7, 1862.

Lieutenant George C. Hubbard, A. A. G.—

Lieutenant: In obedience to an order from your office, I return the following statement of the action of the Third Kentucky Regiment in the battle of Baton Rouge, on the 5th:

The brigade was formed in an open field, the Third Kentucky Regiment on the right flank, and ordered to march forward. The Third crossing a lawn into a field, received a fire from the enemy's skirmishers, when we were ordered to charge. The skirmishers were routed, and the regiment halted in a pea patch, and ordered to lie down here. We received a heavy fire, killing one man and wounding five. We were again ordered forward and to charge, which order was executed in gallant style.

Passing over the ground occupied by the enemy, we saw the bodies of a few of their dead. Another charge brought us into a road near the enemy's camp, through which we charged and halted, and remained for some time; and seeing that our line to the left was not up on line with us, I placed Capt. Edward in command temporarily, until I went to the rear to see where to form the line, with instructions to remain in position until I could return. After obtaining the necessary information, I started on my return, with the regiment falling back in good order. When I demanded to know the cause, I was informed it was by order of Brig.-Gen. Clarke. I then resumed command and formed on line with the brigade.

Soon Col. Thompson ordered me to fall back to a cut in the road, which order was promptly executed. We remained in this position for nearly one hour, firing nearly thirty rounds of ammunition at the enemy, at times they being in short range of our rifles. The regiment was then ordered to charge forward by Col. Crossland, which was done, and again we passed through their encampment, and were ordered to fall back, which order was executed without any confusion or excitement. Without a single exception, the officers of the regiment bore themselves gallantly, and too much cannot be said in praise of the conduct of the men. Our infirmary corps kept close on our heels, and promptly removed and took care of our wounded.

J. H. Bowman,
Captain Commanding Third Kentucky Regiment.

Camp near Comite River,
August 7, 1862.

Captain John A. Buckner—

Sir: Through an unfortunate circumstance, I was placed in command of the Fourth Kentucky, at about three o'clock a. m., on the 5th instant. After being placed in line, our brigade moved forward until it reached the outskirts of Baton Rouge, when we moved by the left flank, as far as the camp of the Fourteenth Maine Regiment. We then moved forward. The smoke being so dense, my command was here separated from the brigade. Having thrown out my right company as skirmishers, I continued to move forward, but, discovering that the enemy were on my left, supported by a battery, all concealed by the houses and fences, and not being able to change direction without placing my regiment immediately under the fire of our own troops, I rejoined the brigade.

I had just taken my position on the right when you took command and ordered us forward. I moved my regiment obliquely to the left until my right had cleared the fence in front, when I ordered them forward in the direction of the enemy's camp, which they did with a cheer.

We had advanced, probably, two hundred yards when an *aide*, whom I took to be on Gen. Clarke's staff (not being personally acquainted with any of them), ordered me to fall back. Seeing the balance of the brigade retiring, I gave the command to my regiment, which they were very unwilling to execute, seeing the enemy retiring from their camps. After reforming my regiment, I was again ordered by you to advance.

In this charge the enemy were driven completely from their camps. It is not necessary, captain, for me to say how my command acted in this charge. You, being in front of my left, could judge for yourself. I think that you will agree that they did not abuse the confidence the commanding general has in "ragged Kentuckians." The Fourth Kentucky lost, in—

Killed	5
Wounded	14
Missing	1
Total	20

Respectfully,

J. H. Millett,
Captain Co. K. Commanding Fourth Kentucky.

Headquarters Sixth Kentucky Regiment Volunteers,
Comite River, August 7, 1862.

To G. C. Hubbard, First Lieutenant and A. A. G.—

Sir: Pursuant to circular order, just received, I have the honour to submit the following report of the part taken by the Sixth Regiment Kentucky Volunteers in the battle of the 5th instant, and the orders received from the commanding generals. This regiment occupied the extreme left of the First Brigade, Second Division, Col. A. P. Thompson commanding. At a little before daylight the troops were drawn up in line, this regiment in the open field, the left resting about two hundred yards to the right of a dense forest, in which Col. Allen's brigade was formed. At daylight the command, "forward," was given by Gen. Ruggles, and we moved forward a short distance and halted by the order of the same officer, who was present in person.

We were very soon ordered forward again, when we moved, encountering rough ground, hedges, fences, ditches, and a luxuriant growth of weeds and grass, altogether rendering even tolerable alignment and steady marching impossible.

Passing on over this character of ground for nearly one mile, the enemy's skirmishers fired on us, doing no injury, but falling back as we advanced, until we arrived immediately in front of the enemy's camp. Here he engaged us warmly from a strong position in a heavy forest, but, charging forward, we drove him from his position, and my regiment passed nearly through the camp, when we observed a battery on our left, say one hundred yards, and a little in front. This battery was nearly silenced by an oblique fire from my left wing, and would have been easily taken but for the fact that the right of the brigade was retiring. Seeing no cause for the retreat, on account of any movement or fire of the enemy, the regiment was ordered back, presuming the brigade was ordered to retire, which I have since learned to have been the case.

This retreat enabled the enemy to regain his battery, which he did promptly, and opened a furious fire with grape, canister, and shrapnel on our flank. From the nearness of the guns, he did no serious damage. We continued to move to the rear some two hundred yards, when we reformed and returned to a fence in front of a graveyard, where we halted and opened fire on the enemy, who had reformed and reoccupied his original position, from which we had just driven him. This position both parties held with great stubbornness, and an almost incessant fire was kept up for one hour. At this place I sustained nearly all the loss of the day. My position was very much exposed during this time, having no shelter but a thin picket fence, and being on ground elevated some eighteen inches above any ground in front between my line and the enemy.

This position was maintained until an order to charge was given, and the enemy driven under his gunboats, when the regiment returned with the brigade to camp, having sustained a loss of five killed and seventy-three wounded, several mortally. I cannot allow this opportunity to pass without returning my thanks to the officers and men of the regiment for the gallant manner in which they bore themselves during the whole engagement. From a want of commissioned officers, I caused the eight companies of the regiment to be consolidated into four companies, placed respectively under Captains Isaac Smith, Gran Utterback, and Thomas G. Page, and First Lieutenant Frank Harned. It is proper for me to say that I was not in the last charge, having been carried off the field too much exhausted to be able to go forward.

I have the honour to be, sir, your obedient servant,

M. H. Cofer,
Lieutenant-Colonel Commanding
Sixth Kentucky Regiment.

Headquarters Seventh Kentucky Regiment,
August 7, 1862.

Lieut. G. C. Hubbard, A. A. A. General—

Lieutenant: In obedience to an order from your office, I return the following statements of the action of my regiment, in the battle at Baton Rouge, on the 5th. The brigade was formed in an open field, and ordered to "march forward." My regiment crossed a lawn into a field, and received a fire from the enemy's skirmishers, when we were ordered to charge. The skirmishers were routed, and the regiment halted in a pea patch, and ordered to lie down. Here we received a heavy fire, wounding three men. We were again ordered forward and to charge, which order was executed in gallant style. Passing over the ground occupied by the enemy, we saw the bodies of two dead and three wounded. Another charge brought us into a road near the enemy's camp, through which we charged, and were halted and ordered to fall back by Capt. Buckner, of Gen. Breckinridge's staff, who received the order from Gen. Clarke, which would have been done in order, but for a regiment in advance of our right, which broke in wild confusion through my regiment, which caught the panic and retired confusedly for a short distance.

Aided, however, by the coolness of my company officers and adjutant, I succeeded promptly in rallying and reforming them in front of the road. Col. Thompson ordered me to fall back to the road, where we opened fire on the enemy, then advancing from their camps, and kept it up briskly for an hour. The enemy advanced cautiously from their camp, under cover of a grove of timber, with the evident intention of turning our left flank. I saw two lines of infantry, with cavalry in rear. They charged, and the Thirty-Fifth Alabama regiment opened and kept up a hot fire from our left, which broke the enemy's lines, and they retired in confusion.

Our ammunition was nearly exhausted, the wagons not having come up. Gen. Breckinridge came up on our right, and I reported the want of ammunition to him, when he ordered me to charge the camp with my regiment and the Third Kentucky. We went through the camp and were halted by Capt. Buckner, and ordered to retire, which was done in good style. Capt. Buckner, by order of Gen. Breckinridge, ordered my regiment to remain and support a section of Semmes' Battery, which was posted, and remained to protect those engaged in recovery of the wounded and retreat of the stragglers. Capt. Wess Jetton, with five men, was sent back to fire the camps. A cloud of smoke soon told that his mission of destruction had been faithfully executed. He reports the burning of large quantities commissary stores and quartermaster stores, together with numerous boxes of guns and valuable camp equipage.

Without a single exception the officers bore themselves gallantly, and too much cannot be said in praise of the conduct of the men. Our Infirmary Corps kept close at our heels, and promptly removed and took care of the wounded. I beg to mention the gallant conduct of Joseph Rollins, our colour bearer

Edward Crossland,
Colonel Commanding Seventh Kentucky Regiment.

Headquarters Ninth Kentucky Regiment,
Camp Near Comite River, La.,
August 7, 1862.

Sir: I have the honour of submitting to you the following report of the part taken by the Ninth Kentucky Regiment, in the action of the 5th inst., at Baton Rouge. (Maj. Wickliffe assumed command after Col. Caldwell was disabled.)

The Ninth Kentucky, with the other commands of the brigade, was placed in line of battle early on the morning of the 5th of August. The line was advanced toward Baton Rouge steadily. In obedience to an order of my brigade commander my regiment was held as a support to the battery attached to this brigade, where it remained until I received an order, in person, from Maj.-Gen. Breckinridge, to post one company, as pickets, to the right and at some distance from the arsenal. In obedience to this order, I placed Capt. Gillum, with his company, consisting of one lieutenant, four sergeants, one corporal, and twenty-four men, upon the ground designated by the general; and, in obedience to another order from him, left Capt. Gillum there, when my command was ordered to join the brigade and engage the enemy in their camps.

Capt. Gillum remained at his post until ordered away, when the brigade retired to the point where the line of battle was first formed. Thus, this company was prevented from engaging in the battle, and this will account why none was killed or wounded in Co. A, of this regiment. When ordered by Maj.-Gen. Breckinridge to join the brigade to which my regiment is attached, I was placed on the left of the Fourth Kentucky Regiment, which was the first regiment in the brigade.

Immediately after this an order from you was given to advance. My command did so, and until the fire was drawn from the enemy, who were secreted in and about the tents of the third and last encampment. The fire was immediately returned by the men under my command. It continued warm and heavy for about twenty or twenty-five minutes, our line, as far as I could see, advancing very little, but steadily, and the enemy as slowly retreating. At this time an order was given by Brig.-Gen. Clarke, commanding the division, to fall back to a small ravine, a short distance in the rear, and reform, which was done in proper manner. In a few moments we were again ordered to advance, and did so, never halting until the enemy had been driven from the last of their encampments.

After the brigade line had been formed, in obedience to an order from you we retired slowly and in good order. My command numbered two hundred and twenty-two, rank and file. From this deduct Co. A, numbering thirty-one officers and men, and seven detailed to carry off the wounded, thus reducing the number of men actually engaged in the fight, under my command, to one hundred and eighty-four men.

The following is a list of the casualties which occurred in my regiment:

In Co. A, none. In Co. B, L. P. Smith, mortally wounded and since dead; H. Osborne, slightly. In Co. C, Lieut. H. H. Harris, wounded; private R. S. Brooks, killed; privates J. S. Jackson, J. T. Taylor, D. Tinsley, and J. B. Young, wounded. In Co. D, Lieut. Oscar Kennard, wounded; private William Hicks, killed; privates John Estill and John Henry, wounded. In Co. E, Sergt. R. M. Hague, wounded; privates James Bowers and Isaac Rutledge, killed; privates Elbert Gramor, B. Logan, and J. L. Thompson, wounded. In Co. F, A. P. Fowler, W. P. Ratliff, J. Leach, J. W. Wallace, and D. P. Howell, wounded. In Co. G, Lieut. P. V. Daniel, privates William Beauchamp, Thomas Stith, Michael Meardin, Allen Dereberry, Frank Keith, Green Woorley, and M. S. Newman, wounded. In Co. H, Sergt. John H. Hughes, Corporal Moses Lassiter, privates Alexander Barry, Charles Freeburg, and Thomas Lively, killed; Sergt. L. H. Atwell, privates Edmond Elliott, Peter Fritz, James Hunt, G. Polfus, L. Holtsenburgh, A. J. Williams, and W. McFatridge, wounded.

I cannot close this report without stating that the officers and men under my command discharged their duties, in the action at Baton Rouge, in a manner creditable alike to themselves and the cause for which they are battling. Very respectfully,

J. C. Wickliffe,
Major Commanding Ninth Kentucky Regiment,

CHAPTER 7

Return to Murfreesboro'

After the operations at Baton Rouge and Port Hudson noticed in the preceding chapter, and particularly in the report of Gen. Breckinridge, the Reserve Corps returned to Jackson, Miss., arriving there on the night of the 22nd of August.

The sick who had been left at Vicksburg and other points, unable to accompany the expedition to Baton Rouge, had recovered somewhat, in considerable numbers, and, preceding the main body to Jackson, had established an encampment six miles out on the Brandon road, whither the various regiments marched on the 23rd.

If the condition of the command had been bad when it went to Baton Rouge, no words are adequate to express its real condition now, as far as destitution and physical condition were concerned. Great numbers were perfectly barefoot, and had been so for such a length of time that they could even track the burning sand like ostriches, and instead of blistered feet, seemed to have on an improved style of moccasin from the skins of salamanders. As for clothing, the "human form divine" shone through in so many places, that the whole combination had the appearance of very bad patchwork, and impressed one with the idea that the clothes and men would look better in separate bundles. Some had shirts and some did not, and the latter managed to cover the upper portions of their bodies with ragged jackets; while those with shirts on were considered as indulging in superfluity if they had jackets too. And the pants they wore are a painful subject to contemplate.

The imagination of the reader must supply the place of description; and, if he can conceive of anything better suited to exhibit naked muscle while the wearer has answered the demands of modesty by doing his best to be covered, he is welcome to draw his picture, and write under it, "These are the breeches Kentuckians wore at Jackson." Passing through the streets, they were amused at astonished gazers, and could not resist the temptation that always beset them when anything could be made to serve a humorous turn. They inquired of wonder-stricken beholders how they liked the style of pantaloons, and declared, in mock serious ness, that, in their opinion, it was the best military dress—"so light and cool."

But preparations were now being made to join the expedition of Bragg into Kentucky, and there was no sign of demoralisation—no lack of that spirit which characterizes the true soldier. Once again encamped, too, in a pleasant locality, with better food and better water, the tone of health rapidly improved, and the ranks were daily swelled by the return of those who had been unable to withstand the effects of the climate, the rainy weather that had prevailed during August, and the hardships attendant upon the movements in Louisiana.

On the 11th of August, the senior surgeon of Preston's brigade, Dr. J.W. Thompson, had made a report, in which he remarked, that when they arrived at Vicksburg, their health was better than at any other time during the service, but that they had been there but a short time when the malarious atmosphere began its work. On the 28th of June, the number of men of that brigade for duty was 1,822; on the 27th of July, 1,252; and on the 11th of August, at Comite River, only 584, showing a reduction, by sickness, wounds and death of 1,238 men in seven weeks, or more than sixty-seven *per cent.* of its whole strength; and this is but an average instance of the whole division.

Remaining at this place more than two weeks, the men were clothed and everything was put in readiness for a movement. Some doubt was entertained by Gen. Van Dorn as to the nature of the order upon which Gen. Breckinridge proposed to move; and as he wished to retain the division in his department, there was unnecessary, but, to Gen. Breckinridge unavoidable, delay in setting out to join the army in Kentucky.

The division moved by rail, on the 10th of September, up the Mississippi Central to Cold Water Creek, from ten to twenty miles above Holly Springs, disembarking at that point on the morning of the 11th. It remained here until the 19th. Meanwhile the order had been made imperative by President Davis, and Gen. Breckinridge relinquished command of all the troops heretofore under his orders, except the Fourth, Sixth and Ninth Kentucky Infantry, Blackburn's, Biggs' and Roberts' companies of cavalry, a brigade of Tennessee infantry, and the light artillery of Cobb and McClung. The Third and Seventh Kentucky Regiments, having been recruited mainly in the lower part of the State, were permitted to move by way of Jackson, Tenn., thence by the Mobile and Ohio road, in the hope that they might receive large accessions of recruits to their ranks as they marched to join the army now threatening Louisville. They were thus finally separated from their major-general, and were no more connected with any portion of the Kentucky troops which they left at Cold Water. They were afterward mounted, and subsequently participated in the brilliant campaigns of Gen. Forrest, proving themselves second to none of that redoubtable corps in deeds of valour and warm devotion to the cause which they defended.

The remaining Kentucky troops were thrown together, forming a temporary organisation, under command of Col. Trabue. Gen. Helm, it will be remembered, was absent, suffering from his hurt received at Baton Rouge; and Gen. Preston had been relieved of the command of his brigade at his own request, and had gone into Kentucky for the purpose of fighting in a field that now promised much, in the redemption of his old State from Federal rule, and general good to the Confederate cause.

The hearts of Kentuckians now beat high with hope. To them the promised return to Kentucky assumed the character of a triumphal march. They had been tried in fiery ordeals, and had come out with honour, if not with the other fruits of victory. Sometime in August Gen. Breckinridge had called their attention to orders from Richmond relative to the inscription of the names of battles in which they had been engaged on their banners, and wrote in connection therewith as follows:

> The major-general refers, with peculiar pride and gratification, to the action of his troops in the battles of Shiloh and Baton Rouge, and in the successful defence of the city of Vicksburg. Through every difficulty, over every obstacle, with a climate exceedingly hostile, with a scanty supply of clothing, and, at times, of food, you have marched by day and night, oftentimes with bare feet, upon heated sands and rugged roads, without a murmur, and with a heroism worthy of the veteran soldiers of many years. You have won for yourselves, in all your trials and noble daring, the grateful remembrance of your whole country; and in after years the names of Shiloh, Vicksburg and Baton Rouge will awaken within your breasts a thrill of pride and delight that will heighten the pleasures of your future life, and be a constant

source of gratification to your friends, who have watched with such deep solicitude your progress through the many struggles you have encountered in defence of your country.

The troops of his old brigade to whom, in common with others of his division, these words were addressed, were on the point, as they fondly believed, of appearing before their friends at home with so proud a record, and under banners whose inscriptions were the titles to renown.

The troops designated as those who were to remain under command of Gen. Breckinridge, took the cars at Cold Water on the 19th, and went back to Jackson; thence to Meridian, afterward to York Station, the terminus, at that time, of the railroad from Meridian to Demopolis; then it was decided that the wagon train should go out empty across the country, while the men and baggage should be shipped by way of Mobile, Montgomery and Atlanta to Chattanooga, from which point it was expected the march would be made into Kentucky. After a tedious and disagreeable trip from York Station, by railway and river, the command pitched tents at Knoxville, on the 3rd of October, having been eight days and nights *en route*.

Here the Second Regiment and the artillery company of the gallant Graves were reunited with the comrades they had left at Bowling Green on the 22nd of January before, and Col. Hanson, being senior, was placed in command.

These prisoners, with the exception of the officers, had left Camp Morton and elsewhere on the 26th of August, and were joined at Vicksburg by the latter, where exchange was duly effected. They went thence to Jackson, where the work of reorganising, and, as far as possible, equipping, was effected in the case of the various troops captured in the Western department and exchanged under the provisions of the cartel which had finally been agreed upon. Thence they proceeded to Chattanooga, but reported to Gen. Breckinridge after his arrival at Knoxville, and the heroes of Donelson were thenceforth closely identified with those of Shiloh and Baton Rouge.

By the 15th of October, Gen. Breckinridge had succeeded in procuring the necessary transportation and supplies, though much difficulty was encountered, and it was not without great and constant effort that the command was placed in a condition to justify the advance, which was now to be made by way of Cumberland Gap. He had under his command the four Kentucky regiments, and something over five thousand miscellaneous troops, which he found at Knoxville under Gen. Maxey—the whole, with the artillery of Cobb and Graves, amounting, perhaps, to seven thousand men. The Tennessee brigade had been relinquished, under orders from Richmond, to Gen. Sam Jones, commanding Department of East Tennessee.

Gen. Maxey marched on the 12th with the greater force, and on the morning of the 15th Col. Hanson set out with his brigade of Kentuckians, Gen. Breckinridge accompanying them.

For two days the march was uninterrupted, the weather was beautiful, the hearts of all were buoyant, even joyous, and the remembrance of past hardships, and dangers, and dearth of affection faded away in anticipation of treading once more the soil of their own State, and of meeting, perhaps, those for whom they now yearned with almost the tenderness of children. On the evening of the 16th the brigade encamped in fields on each side of the Tazewell road, three miles beyond Maynardville.

On the morning of the 17th the reveille was sounded early, and all hastened to prepare the morning meal, after which the command was formed, and with even more than their wonted vivacity, began the march, but the head of the column from the field on the left had scarcely turned into the road when a halt was ordered, then they were faced about and marched back to the camping ground of the night before. Now the wildest rumours got afloat, and every heart was sinking, however much the various hopeful ones tried to construe the pause to mean anything than a foreboding of evil. One hour a faint hope would be kindled that the march would be resumed on the morrow, in the direction of home; the next, it would be destroyed, by some fact which eager inquirers pretended to have elicited.

Thus, the day wore on, and a painful day it was, too, as may well be conceived. Before night the sad truth seemed to have been impressed upon every one, though as yet no authoritative announcement of the real condition of affairs had been made. The dress parade of the old brigade on that afternoon is remembered as one of the peculiar incidents in its career. The Second Regiment, on the right of the road, made the call by bugle at the usual hour, and formed in sight of the Fourth, Sixth, and Ninth, on the left. The proximity of these three enabled them to form one almost continuous line, little space intervening.

The silence that prevailed in the ranks then was not the silence of restraint—it was the silence of stern manhood bowed down by bitter disappointment. No one chose even to whisper. But they were erect, steady, scrupulously exact in formation, and handled their arms with a promptness and a precision that seemed to speak a manly determination that nothing could conquer—that could resist a siren song as readily as an attack of the foe. The burden of every tune from the regimental bands was "home;" and to say that tears found their way down many and many a bronzed cheek, is but to say that soldiers are not always provided with hearts of stone.

Immediately after having received the dispatch by courier on the morning of the 17th, Gen. Breckinridge sent to halt Maxey, who, as we have seen, was now far ahead. A letter received from Bragg, dated two days later than the order by courier, instructed him to return to Knoxville, and, assuming command of all forces that could be made available in the defence of Middle Tennessee, proceed thence to Chattanooga, and take such steps as might seem to him best adapted to that end. He was first, however, to send all surplus supplies to Cumberland Gap, to meet the army now rapidly retreating from Kentucky.

The return march to Knoxville began on the morning of Oct. 19th, and on the evening of the 20th the brigade was encamped on the same ground occupied the week before. The retrograde movement was as sad a one as ever marked the career of the Kentucky Brigade; but the failure of Bragg to maintain himself, the consequent trouble he had created for their friends there, and their own bitter disappointment, but served to bring out, in bolder relief, their striking soldierly qualities. On turning their faces toward Knoxville, they sent up a mighty shout—half in desperation, half in defiance; and once again committed to the fate of service away from home the gloom soon gave way to a degree of cheerfulness.

Breckinridge removed his command to Chattanooga, or rather to Shell Mound, some distance out on the Nashville Railroad, and it encamped there on the 23rd. Bragg had by that time reached Knoxville in person, and Breckinridge was ordered to proceed to Murfreesboro', and assume direction of military operations there, as it was apprehended that Buell, who was now on the march for Nashville, might endeavour to occupy a more advanced position. After much trouble in crossing the river at Bridgeport—the bridge there having been destroyed—and everything having to be ferried over the two arms of the river, and carried upon the men's shoulders across the island which cuts the stream at that point, the command reached Murfreesboro' on the 28th, just eight months from the time of having left it with Gen. Johnston, and encamped in the same locality—some of the regiments on the same ground.

Breckinridge now had command of all the advance forces, which he retained until the arrival of Bragg in November. Changes had been constantly taking place in his staff, and we note here, as part of the record affecting Kentuckians, that, after the arrival at Murfreesboro', the following officers were announced: Lieut. Col. John A. Buckner, A. A. G.; Maj. Calhoun Benham and Maj. James Wilson, Assistant Inspectors-General; Maj. Rice E. Graves, Chief of Artillery; Dr. L. T. Pim, Medical Director; Maj. George W. Triplett, Chief Quartermaster; Col. T. T. Hawkins and Lieut. J. Cabell Breckinridge, *Aides-de-camp*; and Captains Keene Richards and Richard C. Morgan, volunteer aides. Maj. Brown was still Chief Commissary.

Associated with him at various times during the summer and autumn, in addition to those named heretofore, had been Maj. Sullins, Quartermaster; Maj. Clarence J. Prentice, aide; Capt. James Nocquet, Chief Engineer; Dr. Cary N. Hawes, Medical Director, and Maj. Alexander Evans—the latter of whom was made Post Commissary after the arrival at Murfreesboro'. Maj. Throckmorton was made Post Quartermaster, and Maj. Boyd had been some time engaged in the pay department, but was thereafter again immediately connected with the staff of Gen. Breckinridge.

A new division was formed for him in December, which consisted of Hanson's, Preston's, Adams', and Brown's brigades.

But we recur to events connected more particularly with the Kentucky Brigade. This now consisted of the Second, Fourth, Sixth, and Ninth Kentucky Regiments, the Forty-First Alabama Regiment, and Cobb's Battery. The cavalry company of Capt. B. E. Roberts was also connected with it till ordered to report to Gen. Buford in January, 1863. Col. Hanson was assigned to the permanent command of it, and recommended for promotion, which he received on the 13th of December. The officers of his staff were Capt. John S. Hope, A. A. G.; Capt. Thomas E. Stake, A. I. G.; Maj. John R. Viley, Chief Quartermaster; Maj. S. M. Moorman, Chief Commissary; Lieut. Presley Trabue, Ordnance Officer, and Lieut. Joe Benedict, *aide-de-camp*.

******

Capt. (afterward Lieut.-Col.) S. F. Chipley was acting A. A. G. during the week's fighting on Stone River, and with Col. Hanson in the final charge of Friday, January 2, 1863.

Maj. Viley was Chief Quartermaster of Brigade till December, 1863, after which he was assigned to similar duty on the staff of Gen. Bate.

Maj. Moorman was nominally Chief Commissary of brigade till February, 1864, when he was relieved by Capt. C. W. Helm, and assigned to post duty at LaGrange, Georgia, where he afterward died of disease.

✶✶✶✶✶✶

Gen. Hanson at once devoted himself, with his usual energy and ability, to the work of discipline and the attainment of the highest order and efficiency; and early in November a division inspection report showed clearly that the Kentucky troops were in better condition and in better tone than any others then available for the defence of the advanced position.

Breckinridge had now but a small infantry force at his command, and it was late in November before Bragg had succeeded in concentrating all the troops subject to his orders at that point. The enemy had arrived at Nashville, and was prepared to advance before Bragg was in any condition to meet him; but from some cause remained quietly on the Cumberland until near the close of the year. General Rosecrans had succeeded to the command of the Federal Army there, and though he adopted such measures at once as threatened Murfreesboro' at an early day, nothing occurred immediately affecting the infantry at that point till the battle of Hartsville, excepting a march toward Nashville, designed by Breckinridge as a feint, both to hide his own weakness and to enable Morgan to destroy a large amount of rolling stock collected in Edgefield.

The cavalry of Generals Morgan, Forrest, and Wheeler was actively engaged between Murfreesboro' and Nashville, and on the flanks of the Federal position; and frequent engagements of minor importance were taking place between this arm and the enemy's outposts. The plan alluded to was communicated to Morgan by Gen. Breckinridge early in November, and the time was fixed for the morning of the 5th of that month. Forrest, supported by the infantry troops under Breckinridge was to approach as nearly as possible to Nashville, and to make as strong a demonstration as he could not to bring on a general engagement; and it was hoped that, in the excitement of the moment, Morgan could destroy the cars at Edgefield before the enemy should become sufficiently aware of the object to defeat it.

Accordingly, on the morning of the 4th of November, Breckinridge set out. At nightfall there was a pause at Hart's Springs, where the troops rested till 9 o'clock p. m., when the march was resumed and continued till 3 in the morning, at which time the infantry was within five miles of Nashville, with the cavalry in advance. Here they rested till the dawn of day, when Forrest drove in the Federal pickets, and sharp skirmishing began, the infantry following at convenient distance to be rendered available in case of emergency. In a few minutes the Federal batteries opened on the east of Nashville, which announced to those who were advised of the plan that Morgan had arrived promptly and begun his work. Some cavalrymen were wounded, but the infantry did not come under fire, and the whole force soon retired.

The Kentucky Brigade was allowed to rest and sleep in the grounds of the Lunatic Asylum, when they had reached that point on the return, till the afternoon, when they marched back to Hart's Springs, and encamped for the night. Next day they returned to their tents at Murfreesboro'. It was afterward ascertained that Morgan was only partially successful, as the enemy too soon became aware of his object, and, after opening the batteries on him from Capitol Hill, had marched out in strong infantry force, so that, though the train was fired, he had not time to make thorough work of it.

As remarked heretofore, there is no necessity that we should enter at length into the history of the armies at this point. The situation, relative forces, importance to either cause of the coming struggle between Bragg and Rosecrans—all these may be found in works of greater scope.

The next considerable action in which the Kentucky troops took part was the battle of Hartsville, and this was pre-eminently a Kentucky fight. Rosecrans had stationed small forces at Gallatin, Castalian Springs and Hartsville, with the ostensible design of protecting that portion of Tennessee from the incursions of cavalry, and to prevent the withdrawal of supplies therefrom for the Confederate Army. Morgan, who was now operating on that flank, conceived the design of capturing the force at Hartsville.

After having procured as accurate information as possible relative to its strength and position, he communicated his plan to Bragg, whose consent he finally obtained, and the expedition was organised, which resulted, after a sharp conflict on the morning of the 7th of December, in the capture of the entire garrison who were not killed and wounded in the action. The following reports of Bragg, Morgan and the officers who commanded the infantry forces on the occasion, with explanatory notes, disclose the nature of the undertaking, the gallant conduct of all concerned, and the result:

Headquarters Army of Tennessee,
Murfreesboro', Tennessee, December 22, 1862.
General S. Cooper, Adjutant and Inspector-General, Richmond, Va.—
Sir: Having been informed by acting Brig.-Gen. John H. Morgan, whose cavalry brigade covered my front in direction of Hartsville, Tenn., that the enemy's force at that point was somewhat isolated, I yielded to his request and organised an expedition under him for their attack. On the 5th instant Hanson's brigade, of Breckinridge's division, was moved forward on the road toward Hartsville and halted at Baird's Mills, a point nearly due east from Nashville, and half way to Hartsville, when it was joined by Morgan's cavalry force. Two regiments, the Second and Ninth Kentucky Infantry, with Cobb's Kentucky Artillery, moved from this point, with the cavalry, at 10 p. m., on the 6th, to attack the enemy at Hartsville. Early on the morning of the same day, Hanson, with the remainder of his brigade, moved as directed on the road toward Nashville, for the purpose of a reconnoissance and to cause a diversion.

At the same time the troops above named left their camps near here, Maj.-Gen. Cheatham, with two brigades, moved out on the Nashville road, halted at night at Lavergne, fifteen miles, and, on the next day, in conjunction with Gen. Wheeler's cavalry, made a strong demonstration on the enemy's front.

These movements had the desired effect, and completely distracted the enemy's attention from the real point of attack. Learning that a foraging train of the enemy was on his right flank, Cheatham detached Wheeler with a cavalry force to attack it, which he did in his usual dashing and successful manner, capturing eleven wagons and fifty-seven prisoners. Under cover of these feints, Morgan, by an extraordinary night march, reached the point of his destination about sunrise, and in a short but warmly contested engagement, killed, wounded and captured the entire command of more than 2,000 officers and men.

I enclose herewith the reports of Gen. Morgan and the subordinate commanders, and take great pleasure in commending the fortitude, endurance and gallantry of all engaged in this remarkable expedition. It is a source of personal and official gratification to perceive that the department has recognised the services of the gallant and meritorious soldier who led the expedition by confirming my previous nomination of him as a brigadier-general.

Two sets of infantry colours and one artillery guidon, taken at Hartsville, are also forwarded with this report. A third set of infantry colours was presented by its captors to the President on his recent visit to this place.

I am, sir, very respectfully, your obedient servant,

Braxton Bragg,
General Commanding.

Morgan's Headquarters, Cross-roads
near Murfreesboro', December 9, 1862.

Colonel Brent, Chief of Staff—

Sir: I have the honour to lay before you, for the information of the general commanding, a report of the expedition against the Federal force at Hartsville.

I left these headquarters at 10 a. m., on the 6th instant, with one thousand four hundred men of my own command, under the orders of Col. Duke; the Second and Ninth Kentucky Infantry, commanded by Col. Hunt; Capt. Cobb's battery of artillery, and two small howitzers and two rifled Ellsworth guns, belonging to my own command.

At Lebanon I received information that no change had been made in the number of the Federals at Hartsville, their number being still about nine hundred infantry and four hundred cavalry, with two pieces of artillery. I found afterward that their force had been considerably underrated.

I proceeded with the infantry and artillery to Purcell Ferry, on the Cumberland River, sending the cavalry, under the orders of Col. Duke, to pass at a ford some seven miles below the point where we were to rendezvous. I passed my troops with great difficulty, there being but one boat; and about half-past five on the morning of the 7th, I arrived at Hague Shops, two miles from the Federal camp.

I found that Col. Duke, with his cavalry, had only just marched up, having crossed the ford with difficulty, and that one regiment of his command, five hundred strong (Col. Gano's), had not yet reported. Maj. Stoner's battalion had been left on the other side of the Cumberland, with two mountain howitzers, to prevent the escape of the enemy by the Lebanon road; and Col. Bennett's regiment had been ordered to proceed to Hartsville to picket the road leading to Gallatin, and to attack any of the Federals they might find in that town, to take possession of the Castalian Springs, Lafayette, and Carthage roads, so as to prevent the escape of the enemy.

This reduced my force considerably; but I determined to attack, and that at once. There was no time to be lost, day was breaking, and the enemy might expect strong reinforcements from Castalian Springs should my arrival be known. Advancing, therefore, with the cavalry, closely followed by the artillery and infantry, I approached the enemy's position. The pickets were found and shot down. The Yankee bivouac first appeared to cover a long line of ground, and gave me to suppose that their number was much greater than I anticipated.

On nearing the camp, the alarm was sounded, and I could distinctly see and hear the officers ordering their men to fall in, preparing for resistance. Col. Duke then dismounted Col. Cluke's and Col. Chenault's regiments, in all about seven hundred and fifty men, drawing them up in line in a large field in the front, and a little to the right of the enemy's line, which was then forming; and seeing that the artillery and infantry were in position, he ordered his men to advance at the double-quick, and directed Col. Chenault, who was on the left, to oblique so as to march on the enemy's flank.

His men then pressed forward, driving the Federals for nearly half a mile, without a check, before them, until their right wing was forced back upon their own left wing and centre.

Duke then ordered a halt until the infantry had begun their attack on the Federal left wing, which caused a retreat of the whole line. At this juncture, Lieut.-Col. Huffman and Maj. Steele, of Gano's regiment, came up with about one hundred men of that regiment, who had succeeded in crossing the ford, and threw their small force into the fight. My dismounted cavalry, under Duke, had been skirmishing, previously to this, for only about twenty minutes; but seeing that Col. Hunt, with the infantry, was pressing hard upon the Federal left, he ordered an advance upon the right wing and flank of their new line. It gave way and ceased firing, and soon after surrendered.

Col. Duke reports that his men fought with a courage and coolness which could not be surpassed.

Cluke and Chenault led on their men with the most determined bravery, encouraging them by voice and example.

The timely arrival of Lieut.-Col. Huffman and Maj. Steele, and the gallant manner in which they threw themselves into the fight, had a very decided effect upon the battle at the point of which they entered. The artillery, under Capt. Cobb, did most excellent service, and suffered severely from the enemy's battery, which fired with great precision, blowing up one of his caissons and inflicting a severe loss on that arm.

The infantry conducted themselves most gallantly—the Second

Kentucky suffering most severely.

Col. Bennett's regiment, as I said before, was not in the fight, having been sent on special service, which was most efficiently performed, four hundred and fifty prisoners having been taken by them, and twelve Federals killed.

Thus, sir, in one hour and a half, the troops under my command, consisting of five hundred cavalry (Col. Gano's, Col. Bennett's regiments, and Maj. Stoner's command not participating in the fight), seven hundred infantry, with a battery of artillery—in all about one thousand three hundred strong—defeated and captured three well-disciplined and well-formed regiments of infantry with a regiment of cavalry, and took two rifled cannon, the whole encamped on their own ground, and in a very strong position, taking about eighteen hundred prisoners, eighteen hundred stand of arms, a quantity of ammunition, clothing, quartermaster's stores, and sixteen wagons. The battle was now over.

The result exceeded my own expectations, but I felt that my position was a most perilous one, being within four miles in a direct line and only eight by the main Gallatin road of an enemy's force of at least eight thousand men, consisting of infantry, cavalry, and artillery, who would naturally march to the aid of their comrades on hearing the report of our guns. I, therefore, with the assistance of my staff, got together all the empty wagons left by the enemy, loaded them with arms, ammunition, and stores, and directed them immediately to Hart's Ferry.

There was no time to be lost. The pickets placed by my assistant adjutant-general on the Castalian Springs road sent to report the advance of a strong body of Federals, estimated at five thousand men.

I sent Cluke's regiment to make a show of resistance, ordering Gano's regiment, which had arrived, in support. In the meantime, I pressed the passage of the ford to the utmost.

This show of force caused a delay in the advance of the enemy, who had no idea of the number of my men, and probably greatly overrated my strength and gave me time to pass the ford with infantry, artillery, and baggage wagons. The horses of my cavalry being sent back from the other side of the Cumberland River, to carry over the infantry regiments, it was time to retreat. The enemy attacked our rear, but was kept at bay by the two regiments before specified, aided by four guns I had previously ordered to be placed in position on the south side of the Cumberland, looking forward to what was now taking place.

The banks of the river, on both sides, are precipitous, and the stream breast deep, but our retreat was effected in excellent order. We lost not a man, except three badly wounded, that I was reluctantly forced to leave behind. Cavalry, infantry, guns and baggage train safely crossed, with the exception of four wagons, which had been sent by another route, and which are still safely hidden in the woods, according to accounts received today.

In justice to my brave command, I would respectfully bring to the notice of the general commanding the names of those officers who contributed, by their undaunted bravery and soldier-like conduct, to the brilliant success which crowned the efforts of the Confederate arms.

To Col. Hunt, of the Ninth Kentucky, commanding the infantry, I am deeply indebted for his valuable assistance. His conduct, and that of his brave regiment, was perfect, and their steadiness under fire remarkable.

The Second Kentucky also behaved most gallantly, and suffered severely. Sixty-five men killed and wounded, and three regimental officers left dead on the field, sufficiently testified to their share in the fight, and the resistance they had to encounter.

Cluke's regiment paid also a high price for its devotion. It went into the field two hundred and thirty strong, had six officers with twenty-one non-commissioned officers and privates killed and wounded, besides six missing.

Duke, commanding the cavalry, was, as he always has been, "the right man in the right place". Wise in council, gallant in the field, his services have ever been invaluable to me.

I was informed by my adjutant-general that Col. Bennett, in the execution of the special service confided to him, and in which he so entirely succeeded, gave proofs of great gallantly and contempt of danger.

I owe much to my personal staff, Maj. Llewellyn, Captains Charlton Morgan and Williams, and Lieut. Bob Tyler, acting as my *aides-de-camp*, gave proof of great devotion, being everywhere in the hottest fire; and Maj. Llewellyn received the sword of Col. Stewart, and the surrender of his regiment. Capt. Morgan's and Capt. Williams' horses were killed under them, and Lieut. Tyler was severely wounded. My orderly sergeant, Craven Peyton, received a shot in his hip and had his horse killed by my side. (Young Peyton died of his wound.)

I must have forgiveness if I add, with a soldier's pride, that the conduct of my whole command deserved my highest gratitude and commendation.

Three Federal regimental standards and five cavalry guidons fluttered over my brave column on their return from the expedition. I have the honour to be, sir, with respect,
Your most obedient servant,
John H. Morgan,
Brigadier-General.

Headquarters Breckinridge's Division,
December 11, 1862.

Maj. Thos. M. Jack, A. A. General—

Sir: I have the honour to forward a report from Col. R. W. Hanson, commanding First Brigade of my division, covering the report of Col. Thomas H. Hunt, who commanded the Second and Ninth Kentucky Regiments and Cobb's Battery, in the recent expedition (under command of Brig.-Gen. Morgan) against Hartsville; and also the reports of Maj. Hewitt and Capt. Morehead, commanding, respectively, the Second and Ninth Kentucky.

I beg to call attention to the officers and men specially named for gallantry, and to suggest, respectfully, that the troops engaged in this expedition deserve mention in orders for conduct, which, in fortitude and daring, has not been surpassed during the war.

Very respectfully,
John C. Breckinridge,
Major-General Commanding.

Headquarters First Brigade,
Camp Near Murfreesboro',
December 11, 1862.

Col. Buckner, A. A. General—

In pursuance of the order of Gen. Bragg, I proceeded with my command, on the 5th instant, to Baird's Mill, and remained two days, making, as directed, reconnoissance toward Nashville. Gen. Morgan designated the Second and Ninth Kentucky, and Cobb's Battery, as the troops he desired to accompany him upon the Hartsville expedition. They were detached under command of Col. Hunt. (It was Morgan's request that Col. Hunt should command the infantry selected to join in the expedition.) I enclose, herewith, his report of the battle of Hartsville, and the reports of his subordinate officers.

I wish to call attention to the honourable mention that is made in Maj. Hewitt's and Col. Hunt's reports of the gallant conduct of Sergt. Oldham, of the Second Kentucky Regiment, with the hope that the proper steps may be taken to procure for him the reward of his conduct. Sergt. Oldham was the colour-bearer of the Second Kentucky at the Battle of Donelson, and acted with great gallantry upon that occasion. He is a suitable man for a lieutenancy, being well qualified, as well as truly brave.

R. W. Hanson,
Colonel Commanding Brigade.

Headquarters Ninth Kentucky Regiment,
Camp near Murfreesboro', December 9, 1862.

To Captain John S. Hope, A. A. A. G.—

Captain: I have the honour to report that the detachment from the First Brigade, Breckinridge's division—consisting of the Second Kentucky Regiment, Maj. James W. Hewitt, commanding, three hundred and seventy-five strong; Ninth Kentucky Regiment, Capt. James T. Morehead, commanding, three hundred and twenty strong; and Cobb's Battery,—placed under my command, as senior officer, with orders to report to Morgan, left Baird's Mill, where the brigade was in bivouac, on Saturday, the 6th instant, about one and a half o'clock, p. m. Marching in the rear of the cavalry force until we arrived in the vicinity of Lebanon, an exchange was made, when the infantry mounted the horses and rode five or six miles.

The command reached Cumberland River about ten o'clock. The infantry, artillery, and a small portion of cavalry crossed at Purcell Ferry, the balance of the cavalry crossing at a ford a few miles lower down the river. The two boats used for crossing were of small capacity and in miserable condition, but by constant bailing they were kept afloat, and by five o'clock in the morning the command was safe over.

The march of five miles to Hartsville (where the battle was fought), yet to make, over bad roads for artillery, was not accomplished until after sunrise, and the purpose of Morgan to surprise the enemy was defeated. When we approached in sight of their camp, we found their infantry already formed, occupying a very strong position on the crest of a hill, with a deep ravine in front, and their artillery in battery. The troops under my command were placed in position west of the enemy's camp, while under a heavy fire from their battery, and sharpshooters thrown out from their right, but these latter were quickly driven in by the dismounted cavalry.

The Second Regiment having been formed on the left of the Ninth, was now ordered forward to support and follow up the success gained by the cavalry skirmishers. That they had hot work to accomplish this is shown by their heavy loss in killed and wounded.

In the meantime, Capt. Cobb, with his battery, was not idle. He was doing good execution, and the enemy responded with effect, one of their shells striking and blowing up a caisson. As the ground was cleared of the enemy opposite our left, he (Capt. Cobb) was ordered to take a new position with his battery in that direction, and at the same time the Ninth Kentucky Regiment was ordered forward to engage the enemy's left.

My whole command was now engaged. The crest of the hill was reached, and here began a desperate struggle, as the contestants were only from thirty to fifty paces apart, where they fought for the space of ten minutes, when the order to charge was given, and most nobly was the command responded to. The enemy broke and were driven to the river cliff, where they were completely surrounded by my force in front, and the dismounted cavalry on their flanks and rear, and where they surrendered at discretion.

It was a continued success from the beginning. In about one and a half hours from the time the first gun was fired, they surrendered, and more prisoners were brought off than we had men in action. Large quantities of commissary and quartermaster stores were also secured, and a section of artillery and a large number of small arms, with the usual supply of ammunition.

Morgan had made most skilful disposition, which, with the good fighting qualities of the troops engaged, secured success. I cannot speak in too high terms of praise of the troops, and I scarcely know which most to admire, their patient endurance on the march or courage in the battle. They marched fifty miles in cold, winter weather, the ground covered with snow, crossed and recrossed the Cumberland River, fought a largely superior force strongly posted within six miles of their supports, and brought off the prisoners, all within the space of thirty hours.

Capt. Cobb, with his officers and men, had a most laborious time in getting their pieces and horses across the river, and it was only by the best directed exertions they succeeded at all. Where officers and men all behaved so well, it is impossible for me to single out individual cases as peculiarly worthy of commendation. I cannot, however, refrain from mentioning Lieut. Joseph Benedict, who acted as my *aide* on the occasion. He was the right man in the right place.

I enclose, herewith, copies of the reports of Maj. Hewitt and Capt.

Morehead, and would bring to your attention the fact that the former commends Colour-Sergt. John Oldham for his gallant bravery.

The following is a summary of the loss sustained by my command:

Command.	Killed.	Wounded	Missing
Second Kentucky Regiment	8	54	3
Ninth Kentucky Regiment	7	10	1
Cobb's Battery	3	7	0
Total	18	71	4

Included in the above, are, of the Second Kentucky Regiment, Charles H. Thomas, first lieutenant, and John W. Rogers, second lieutenant, Co. C, killed; T. M. Home, first lieutenant, Co. A, mortally wounded; A. J. Pryor, second lieutenant Co. D, and Lieut. Harding, Co. K, wounded.

Of Ninth Kentucky, Dandridge Crockett, second lieutenant killed; J. W. Cleveland, first lieutenant wounded.

I am, sir, very respectfully, your obedient servant,

Thomas H. Hunt,
Colonel Commanding Detachment.

Headquarters Second Kentucky Regiment,
Camp Murfreesboro', December 9, 1862.

Colonel Thomas H. Hunt—

Sir: I have the honour to report that, in pursuance of your orders, I formed my regiment on the left of the Ninth Kentucky, opposite the enemy's camp, near Hartsville, a portion of Morgan's cavalry being at the same time on my left. When the order came for me to advance, I ordered my regiment forward; and, after passing the fence, the nature of the ground was such that I deemed it advisable to deploy my regiment, and, therefore, gave the order to deploy. In this way we drove the enemy from their first camp, and continued to drive them until they surrendered.

The officers, without an exception, behaved in the most gallant style. They were continually in advance of their men, urging them forward; and, where all behaved so well, it would be impossible to particularise.

Each seemed to vie with the other in deeds of gallantry. The whole command, I am pleased to say, behaved in a most unexceptionable manner. I cannot conclude my report without reference to Colour-Sergt. John Oldham, whose conduct and courage during the whole engagement elicited the encomiums of both officers and men.

Your obedient servant,

James W. Hewitt,
Major Commanding Second Kentucky Regiment.

Ninth Kentucky Regiment,
Camp near Murfreesboro', December 10, 1862.

To Colonel Thomas H. Hunt, Commanding Infantry—

Sir: At twelve o'clock on Saturday, the sixth instant, I, as senior captain, was placed, by your orders, in command of the Ninth Kentucky Regiment, which had, the day before, moved to Baird's Mills, eighteen miles from Murfreesboro', and was, at that time, about to march against the enemy, reported to be at Hartsville, Tennessee.

The weather was excessively cold, the snow having fallen the day before to some depth, and the road was very rough, notwithstanding which the men marched steadily during the day and night, and reached the immediate neighbourhood of the enemy's camp, near Hartsville, at sunrise. The enemy occupied a strong position in front of his encampment, his line of battle stretching along the crest of a hill, which was separated from our forces by an intervening hollow or ravine. Our line of battle was formed with Cobb's Battery on the right, supported by the Ninth Kentucky Regiment directly in its rear. On our immediate left was the Second Kentucky Regiment, and still further to the left a portion of two regiments of dismounted cavalry, under Col. Duke.

The enemy occupied, with his sharpshooters, the woods and ravines in front of the left wing of our line, and opened a brisk fire on us. Against them the dismounted cavalry deployed as skirmishers, and soon succeeded in dislodging and driving them back upon the main body of the enemy. The Second Kentucky Regiment was ordered forward, and the Ninth left in support of the battery. In a few minutes after, I was ordered to advance, and moved the regiment, in double quick, in the direction of the main body of the enemy, going over, in our route, very rough ground, and through a deep ravine. Ascending the hill, the regiment advanced to the right of the Second Kentucky, halted, and immediately became engaged, at less than fifty paces, with the enemy.

After fighting for a short time, I ordered a charge, which was made with such gallantry by the regiment that the left wing of the enemy's line gave way and began retreating in confusion. Pressed closely by the Ninth Kentucky, they passed through their camps and took refuge under the brow of a hill on the bank of the river and in rear of their artillery. The regiment continued to move rapidly on, and captured the two pieces of artillery and a stand of colours; then charged the line of the enemy and drove them to the brink of the river, compelling their immediate surrender. Here we captured Col. Moore, commanding brigade, who, in reply to a question from Capt. Crouch, answered that he surrendered himself and all the men around him, meaning the whole force.

The battle was now fairly won, the firing had ceased, save a few scattering shots here and there. I immediately formed the regiment again in line of battle, had order restored, stragglers collected, and the men kept in their places. I sent details from all the companies to look after the dead and wounded, and detailed Co. H, Capt. Bosche, to guard the One Hundred and Sixth Ohio Regiment, captured by us. The prisoners being collected, I was ordered to detail Cos. A and C to guard them, and afterward Co. G. The regiment recrossed the river, and began its march toward Lebanon, Tennessee. Too much praise cannot be given to the officers and men for their spirit and patient endurance under a march of almost unexampled hardship and rapidity, and for their gallantry and good conduct in action.

The regiment had in battle three hundred and twenty men, and the loss was eighteen—seven killed, ten wounded, and one missing.

Respectfully, your obedient servant,

James T. Morehead,
Captain Commanding Ninth Kentucky Regiment.

INCIDENTS AND ANECDOTES: AT MURFREESBORO; AND AT AND AFTER HARTSVILLE.

1. Splendid Fighting of the Second and Ninth Regiments, Infantry.—Gen. Duke, who from his position in command of the Second Cavalry, saw Hunt come into action with his two regiments and battery says:

> The infantry had marched quite thirty miles, over slippery roads, and through the chilling cold, and I saw some of them stumble (as they charged), with fatigue and numbness; but the brave boys rushed in as if they were going to a frolic. The Second Kentucky dashed over the ravine, and as they emerged in some disorder, an unfortunate order to halt and dress was given them. There was no necessity for it—the regiment was within fifty yards of the enemy, who were recoiling and dropping before their fire. Several officers sprang to the front and

countermanded the order—it was a matter of doubt who gave it—and Capt. Joyce, seizing the colours, shouted to the men to follow him.

The regiment rushed on again, but in that brief halt sustained nearly all its loss. Just then, the Ninth Kentucky came to its support,—the men yelling and gliding over the ground like panthers. The enemy gave way in confusion, and were pressed again on their right and rear by Cluke and Chenault, who were at this juncture re-enforced by seventy-five men of Gano's regiment, who came up under Lieut.-Col. Huffman, commanding the regiment in Gano's absence, and Maj. Steele, and at once went into the fight. A few minutes then sufficed to finish the affair. The enemy were crowded together in a narrow space, and were dropping like sheep. The white flag was hoisted in an hour after the first shot was fired. Our loss in killed and wounded was one hundred and twenty-five, of which the Second Kentucky lost sixty-five, the Ninth eighteen, the cavalry thirty-two and Cobb's Battery ten.

2. The Blue and the Gray Meet and Greet.—The fortunes of war often furnished touchstones of character by which the combatants learned to know, and, in many instances, to honour each other's manly traits. Dr. John O. Scott, left at Hartsville in charge of the wounded, has told of an occurrence in point. Shortly after Hunt and Morgan had withdrawn from the battleground and hurried across the Cumberland with their prisoners and captured munition of war, a Federal force arrived, having set off hastily from their camp, only eight miles distant by the Lebanon road, as soon as the continuous artillery firing indicated that an attack had been made on Moore. Scott and his nurses, busily engaged with their wounded men at Mrs. Halliburton's, received an order to report to the commander of the newly-arrived troops. They responded promptly, but were uncertain as to what was in store for them, and feared some interference with the attention now so important to the sufferers.

Approaching the commanding officer, however, one of the detail recognised him, and ventured to call out familiarly, "How are you, John?" That dispelled the cloud. "John" was Gen. John M. Harlan, of Kentucky, and he responded cordially. Mutual inquiries were made about old friends and acquaintances back in the State and in the Confederate Army; (i the wall of partition was broken down "for the time;

and the Federal commander addressed himself at once to the business of providing medical and food supplies, and otherwise contributing to the relief of the suffering Confederates as well as of Col. Moore's men.

3. *"Cunny" Fooled Them.*—The Second Kentucky had a man named Cunningham, who so far resembled Cassius that he had at least a "lean and hungry look." It is to be presumed that after a year and a half of army life, of which nearly seven months were spent in a Federal prison, he looked a good deal hungrier than the old Roman. The men called him "Cunny," and they declared that Cunny could never get a flesh wound. At Hartsville, however, a bullet found muscle enough on one of his legs to go through without breaking a bone, and he had the laugh on them—declaring that "Cunny did get a flesh wound and a good furlough."

4. *Scenes on the Battlefield.*—The explosion of Cobb's caisson was frightful. It scattered men and horses with a horrible noise that hushed the din of battle. Near this spot we found the body of Watts, of Paducah. He was shockingly disfigured. He was riding the caisson when it blew up. A little further on towards the crest of the hill was Lieut. Charlie Thomas, of the Second Kentucky, wounded in the left breast—the blood spurting from the wound; and near him, dead, lay his handsome mess-mate, Lieut. Rogers. This was the spot where some confusion occurred in the charge up the hill in the face of a galling fire, when Moss, McDowell, Lee, Joyce, Higgins and other officers rushed forward and by command and cheer renewed the charge.

At the hospital we gathered about one hundred and fifty wounded men, Confederate and Federal; and when too late for glory or John Morgan the enemy captured our men. I remember one unsoldierly act: a member of Stokes's cavalry took a United States blanket from Craven Peyton, Col. Morgan's orderly, who had been badly wounded, remarking, as he did so: "I guess that's our'n;" but he did not see the fine ivory-mounted pistol Morgan had given him.

Gen. Harlan went with us to Mrs. Halliburton's house, after we reported to him, and ordered sugar, coffee, and other rations for our wounded; also, ambulances and a surgeon, and they were taken to Hartsville, about a mile from the field. The ladies entered heartily into the work of caring for them. Mrs. Hart had Craven Peyton carried to her house, where he afterward died. Hodges, of Bourbon County, had his leg amputated, but he never rallied from the effects of the chloroform. Young Edwards, Second Kentucky, wounded through the lungs, believed himself dying and asked a nurse to pray for him. Instead of doing so he rushed off after Father Pickett. He came and prayed there in the dead of night over the dying soldier—a solemn scene. When the wounded were all cared for, I and my nurses returned to Murfreesboro' and reported to Gen. Hanson. When I told him how kind Gen. Harlan had been, he appreciated it, of course, but he simply asked, "And did he tell you what he was fighting for?"—Dr. John O. Scott.

5. How We Took Nashville.—Jim Wilson, of Co. E, Sixth Kentucky, was one of our wags whose pranks and speeches enlivened hours that might otherwise have been monotonous and very trying. On the march towards Nashville, November 4th, 1862, to divert attention from Morgan's operations north of the Cumberland, the rank and file were of course ignorant of what was in view; and when we were marching back two days afterward, without having fired a gun, and being still in some doubt as to whether anything had been accomplished, we were not in the most comfortable frame of mind. Wilson was grum, but not entirely speechless, and occasionally stirred up his part of the column a little.

One sally is worth recording: As we passed a large residence near the pike, on the portico of which a number of persons stood observing us, a lady called out eagerly, "Did you take Nashville?" Wilson was quick to reply, "Oh—yes, yes: we took Nashville—but we couldn't bring it with us!" Our friends at the house joined in the laugh that followed, and Jim trudged on with the air of a man who with a single sentence had explained everything connected with the expedition.

6. How Jap Got and Kept the Mule.—Sergt. Jasper Anderson, Co. B, Ninth Kentucky, familiarly known as "Jap," had the distinction, among others, of being the only "web-foot" who ever beat a Morgan man when property rights were to be considered. He was accused by some of those rough riders of having stolen one of their mules, and they said that a man who could steal a mule from them "made a record."

After Morgan and Hunt had compelled the Federal outpost at Hartsville to surrender, as noticed in preceding chapter, and the Confederates were hastily gathering up arms, and other property with which the encampment abounded, preparatory to a hasty and successful retreat which followed, Jap found a red mule, with a blind bridle on, roaming around, and took possession of him. He seemed to have had a quick eye for the supply and medical departments, as being most promising, and soon had his mule loaded with a dozen large United States blankets, about thirty pounds of coffee, and a dozen canteens of apple brandy—a keg or barrel of which he had scented while nosing around, and from which he filled all the canteens he could lay hands on.

Having mounted and set out for the ferry, he was halted by a cavalryman, who demanded the mule, under order of Gen. Morgan that all infantry-men should be promptly dismounted. Anderson replied that the mule belonged to headquarters, and that they would have to go to Capt. Morehead, then in command of the Ninth Regiment, to see what he had to say about it.

When Morehead was found he said that Gen. Morgan had ordered all animals to be given up, and that he would have to comply. "But," said Jap, "I can't do that, captain. I have a valuable cargo here, and I can't carry it myself."

"What have you?"

"Well, these blankets, as you see, and a big lot of coffee, and something in the canteens. Try a canteen."

The captain took a taste and a new light broke in on him. "Why, Jap, this is good apple brandy!" Then he took another pull or two and wound up with: "Jap, you keep that mule, and stay along with headquarters. Shoot the first cavalryman that tries to take him away from you." And to the man who was waiting to dismount Anderson: "You tell John Morgan that this is my mule; he can't have him." The provident and persuasive web-foot said afterward that he rode that mule right along in front, like a staff-officer, slept at headquarters that night, and rode him to Murfreesboro' next day—at last turning him loose only when he had nothing for him to carry.

7. *After Many Years: A Singular Occurrence.*—After that noble young fellow, Sergt. Thomas Maddox, of Co. E, Second Kentucky, was killed, one of his lieutenants, the Rev. G. B. Overton, embraced the first opportunity which seemed to promise success in getting a letter through the lines to his parents, notifying them of his death and the manner of it, as well as the character which he had maintained as a man and a soldier.

Two and a half years more of the exciting events of war, the disappointment brought by the final overthrow of the Confederacy, and the exacting duties of the life that followed, led him to forget that he had ever written it. Thirty-five years afterward, however, while as Presiding Elder he was holding a quarterly meeting at Jeffersontown, Ky., he was invited to the home of Mrs. Buchanan, Maddox's sister, who brought vividly to his mind the mournful circumstance by giving him the letter, which she had carefully preserved. The following is a copy:

Camp near Murfreesboro', Tenn.
December 13, 1862.

Mr. and Mrs. Maddox—

Dear Sir and Madam: It is my painful duty to announce to you the death of your son, Thos. Maddox, a sergeant of Second Kentucky Regiment.

He was killed in the Battle of Hartsville, December 7, 1862. One ball entered his arm, another his breast, and a third his mouth, which being partly opened did not in the least disfigure his face.

I have known Tom well and intimately ever since he entered the army. I never knew a better boy nor one whom I loved more. The contamination of camp life never reached his pure and lofty spirit. I never knew him to do a wrong. I never heard him speak an unkind word. He lived in the fear of God and kept His commandments.

He was as brave as the bravest; and a smile of heavenly sweetness rested on his countenance in death.

As sure as the Bible is true and religion a divine reality, his spirit rests with the sacramental host of God's elect. I bid you not sorrow as those that have no hope, for he shall live again when the light of the resurrection morn illumines the earth. Death shall restore him immortal. May this blessed hope console your hearts in your sad bereavement. May the God of all grace comfort your hearts as only He can.

Yours respectfully,

G. B. Overton,
Sometime Chaplain Second Kentucky,
now a Lieut. of Co. E.

Chapter 8
Battle of Stone River

On the afternoon of the 8th December the brigade again took up its quarters at Murfreesboro', and the ordinary business attendant upon camp life engaged attention, with little to vary the monotony till near the close of the month. Daily drill was practiced; and all that concerned their welfare and their training was inquired into by their ever-vigilant commander. An order, which had been received on the 18th of July, while Breckinridge's division was at Vicksburg, to discharge all soldiers who should be under eighteen or over thirty-five years of age, at the expiration of the term for which they had originally enlisted, required some attention here, both before and after the battle of Hartsville; and a few of this class of soldiers were discharged from the Sixth and Ninth Regiments.

On the 13th of December, President Davis visited the army at this point and reviewed the troops. Occasionally an old familiar face would appear in the various camps, fresh from Kentucky, and news from home would contribute its mite of joy or sadness.

The weather was generally fair, and seemed rather to invite to active operations; but, aside from the constant movements and skirmishes of the cavalry, all was quiet enough, and, as far as warfare may be, generally pleasant enough, too. The troops now had as many tents as were really needed, and to these little chimneys had been constructed, which rendered them almost as snug, even in the worst weather, as the cabins usually prepared for winter quarters. They were better fed and better clothed than they had been before since leaving Bowling Green; and thus, Christmas came on, with its thousand memories and associations; but with it came news of trouble at the front.

On the afternoon of December 26th, it was rumoured that Rosecrans was advancing with a heavy and well-appointed force. The forenoon had been dark, rainy, and disagreeable; but about one o'clock the rain ceased, the afternoon was brighter, and there was more animation in the widely extended encampments. Towards night the distant boom of artillery was heard, and was kept up steadily for a short period, as at the opening of a regular engagement. It was the Twenty-First Corps, under Gen. Crittenden, engaged with the Confederate outposts in the vicinity of La Vergne. This corps was advancing directly on Bragg's centre, by way of the Nashville and Murfreesboro' pike, with Thomas and McCook (Fourteenth and Twentieth Corps), on his right, proceeding by way of the Franklin and Nolensville roads. The advance of these corps was also contested, and their artillery was frequently brought into play before night.

Crittenden encamped about nightfall near La Vergne. Rain fell again during the night. It ceased before daylight of the 27th, but there was a deep fog in the morning, which did not lift until about nine o'clock, when Hascall's Brigade was able to move upon the Confederate force occupying La Vergne, which it compelled to retire. The corps then resumed its march; but soon the cold and driving rain set in, and continued almost without cessation during the remainder of the day. After some desultory fighting, as the Confederate outposts gradually retired, it encamped that night near Stewart's creek, within ten miles of Murfreesboro'—with the Confederate pickets, however, still between it and the stream.

At Murfreesboro' the main army of Bragg lay quiet throughout the day, and there was little or no preparation looking to a battle. Rumour was there, with her "thousand tongues;" but at nightfall nothing definite seemed to have been learned with regard to the real design of the Federal general,—or, if he had learned anything about it, Bragg appears to have been over confident of his strength, and rather desirous of courting battle upon an open field than of securing himself from defeat by fortifying his position.

Just before sunset the season of rain and dreariness seemed to be ended. The sun came out, and the sky began to clear; and though the night was dark with lingering clouds, the next morning was serene and bright— a beautiful Sabbath morning, opening a week big with fate to the contending hosts and to the country. Bragg was at last aroused, and orders were issued at an early hour for the army to take position, which it did during the day, December 28th, and early on the morning of the next.

For the better understanding of allusions in the reports which we herewith publish, we may state that the army had been divided into two corps, commanded respectively by Lieutenant-Generals Polk and Hardee. The extreme right of the position chosen terminated on the Lebanon pike, two miles, perhaps, from Murfreesboro', the extreme left beyond or west of the Franklin road. Hardee's corps was to form right wing, extending from the Lebanon road to Stone River, nearly opposite Cowan's house, or the famous "burnt house," so much referred to in descriptions of that engagement.

Polk's corps was to form left wing, touching Stone River, opposite Hardee, and extending to the left across the Nashville pike, the Nashville Railroad and on toward the Franklin road. In addition to the two divisions each of Polk's and Hardee's corps, the division of Maj.-Gen. McCown, of Gen. Kirby Smith's corps, was present.

The cavalry was in two divisions, under Major-Generals Wheeler and Wharton, with a smaller command under Pegram. The cavalry commanders were to watch their opportunity to make a circuitous march, dash upon Rosecrans' wagon train, and interfere with his arrangements in the rear as much as possible, after which Wheeler and Wharton were to watch a flank each, and Pegram was to be held in reserve by the commanding general.

When the formation was first made, Hardee's corps was placed wholly on the right of Stone River, Breckinridge's division constituting first line, Cleburne second, while Maj.-Gen. McCown's was held as a reserve force.

During the forenoon, Breckinridge's division, consisting of four brigades and their meagre compliment of artillery, was formed on the right bank of Stone River, almost perpendicularly with the stream at that point—its right resting on the Lebanon pike, and its left on or near the river, a short distance below the crossing of the Nashville pike. The Kentucky Brigade, then under command of Brig.-Gen. Roger W. Hanson, occupied Breckinridge's extreme left. Brig.-Gen. J. R. Jackson's command of cavalry, temporarily reporting to Breckinridge, was held in reserve on the right flank, east of the Lebanon road. Cleburne's division formed the second line, in easy supporting distance, and Maj.-Gen. McCown, of Kirby Smith's corps, being then with Bragg, was held with his divisions as reserve.

Thus, it will be seen, the preponderance of forces was at first on the right—plainly indicating that Bragg anticipated the heaviest blow from that quarter, to which view he was doubtless led by the fact that the dense wood on the left offered such an obstacle to successful advance or retreat as would most likely determine Rosecrans to strike at a less obstructed point.

The day was passed in almost unbroken quiet—the men cooking their rations in the afternoon, and preparing for active work. The next morning was clear, but crisp and chilly; but as the sun rose it became spring-like in its mildness. The army remained in position; but the formation of the previous day was essentially modified during the forenoon, when it was ascertained that the heavier Federal force was approaching by the lower roads. The divisions of Cleburne and McCown were transferred to the left, leaving Breckinridge alone to hold the right, with his own division and Jackson's cavalry. The cannonading, though distant, announced that the enemy was advancing.

Steadily he came on, while the Confederate officers were busy all the forenoon inspecting the ground—studying the field so soon to become historic in the annals of America. There was an eminence, six or eight hundred yards in advance of Breckinridge's line, commanding the river on the left and in the front, sloping gradually to the water's edge; and this it was deemed necessary to occupy. It was also considered important that the right of the division should continue to rest on, or very near the Lebanon pike, while the left should be in easy supporting distance of the right of Polk's corps, and convenient to the ford near the ruins of the bridge on the Nashville railroad.

The force assigned to this part of the line was not sufficient, however,, to fill out the space from the river to the road, should the whole be advanced so as to cover the hill in question, without weakening the support; and it was determined to detach the Kentucky Brigade. This was accordingly thrown forward; and before sundown the battery of light artillery, under command of Capt. Robert Cobb, (attached to this brigade from the time of its organisation till just before the battle of Mission Ridge), was posted upon the crest of the hill, with the infantry in close supporting distance. Hanson was now completely isolated—being considerably in advance of the right of Polk's corps, as well as the remaining brigades of Breckinridge's division.

In the afternoon, a large brick house near the intersection of the railroad and the Nashville pike, almost directly in front of Hanson's position, was fired, by order of Bragg, to prevent its occupancy by Crittenden's sharpshooters.

The flames had scarcely ceased to rage, when the advance of the Federal Army appeared along the front, on each side of the turnpike, and bivouacked in line of battle—Wood's division and Grose's brigade, of Palmer's division, touching upon the left and the right of the road respectively, and just beyond the burnt house. As night drew on, the skies became again over-clouded, and the air exceedingly raw and disagreeable. Without tents, without fires, and, on the Confederate side, without adequate protection in the way of blankets and clothing, the troops prepared to sleep in line of battle.

An incident now occurred which is worthy of record, as probably never having been fully understood in all its bearings by the Federal troops concerned in it. A heavy picket force had been thrown out in front of the Kentucky Brigade, occupying this advanced and isolated position as before explained. The remainder of the command were endeavouring to make themselves as comfortable as possible, some thirty yards back from the crest of the hill,—some of them having already lain down to sleep,—when they were suddenly aroused by rapid firing in the vicinity of the burnt house. They sprang to arms, but had not completed formation when the flash of rifles was seen along the little eminence, and bullets came whistling over and among them. The pickets had been driven in, closely followed by the Federals, who were now upon the main body of the brigade,—in what force it was impossible to determine, and the situation was critical in the extreme.

Knowing their own weakness, being apprehensive of the strength of the attacking force, and conscious at first thought that their shots might be far more destructive to the retreating pickets than to the enemy, there was no alternative for the Confederates but to fall back under fire, in the now total darkness, and prepare for action, or else break into a rout and leave the field precipitately. It was a trying moment; but the officers were equal to the emergency, and the command was speedily aligned and prepared for resistance. It directly appeared, however, that the assailing force had no disposition to press the attack, as only a few straggling shots were fired after the first near volley or two—the greater portion of the enemy withdrawing at once to their supporting force beyond the river.

It was afterward stated that some misapprehension had arisen in the mind of Rosecrans, owing to false or misinterpreted signals, leading him to suppose that the Confederate right had been withdrawn; whereupon he had ordered a portion of the Twenty-First Corps to advance and occupy the town. In compliance with this order, Hascall's brigade actually crossed the river, and, as we have seen, encountered and drove in the pickets, and part of it dashed up to the very muzzles of Cobb's guns, and almost within bayonet reach of the infantry. One man ran up so close to the battery that the fire from his rifle singed and powder-burnt one of the gunners; but in the darkness and confusion he made his escape.

When the enemy retired, the brigade was withdrawn some three or four hundred yards, fearing to advance, lest they come suddenly upon the enemy lying in wait, and being apprehensive of an attack in force should they remain in position there. The loss inflicted upon the main body of these troops was inconsiderable; but a number of the pickets had been wounded—some of whom fell into Federal hands,—besides two or three killed. The Forty-first Alabama Infantry, which had lately been attached to this brigade, lost one of its best officers, who was commanding the picket force and fell when the onset was first made.

Thus, it will be seen, this important position, the loss of which would have thoroughly disconcerted all the plans of the Confederate general, and changed the entire aspect of the battle, hung for a moment in the wavering of a balance.

The Federals being once established upon it, the natural strength of Bragg's position would have been rendered nugatory. It would have given the Federal Army three of the strongest positions possible to have been attained on that memorable field; namely, that which Gen. Sheridan occupied on Tuesday evening, and from which he could scarcely be driven at all on Wednesday, though the other divisions of that corps had been pushed back and left him doubly exposed; the celebrated "Round Forest," in the centre, where Negley and Rousseau withstood successive dashes of the storm, and over which the contending armies continued to struggle, at times, till after Bragg had brought about the denouement by sacrificing Breckinridge on Friday afternoon; and this, the key to the Confederate position, and which would have rendered practicable the original plan of the battle which Rosecrans proposed to himself.

It was one of those peculiar circumstances of war beyond which men cannot see—of which the prudent cannot avail themselves, but which sometimes serve to give blind and heedless leaders an extrinsic greatness. A venturesome dash upon the place that night would have put it under Federal control. Even a conflict in the darkness, with the weak force by which it was held, could scarcely have resulted in anything else, had the assailants been strong enough to cover the line while the temporary confusion prevailed; but there was really no need for this, as, after the skirmishers retired, the main body of Hascall's troops could hardly have reached it so soon as not to find it abandoned. It seems, however, to have been decreed that the battle should not be lightly won by either of the belligerents; and the night passed, with this bone of contention lying alone, midway between them.

After having withdrawn to such distance as to be comparatively safe from the shots that might be fired from this hill, Hanson's command lay in line of battle in an open field. Early next morning, however, it occupied the line of the day before—indeed, one of the regiments had moved up an hour or two before dawn, the rest following as soon as it was light.

The weather had now set in windy, cloudy and cold, and the situation of the men was trying beyond conception. During the whole of that day they lay quiet, under frequent and furious shelling, to which they could reply with only an occasional shot from the battery. It was much of the danger without any of the excitement of battle. Fires were forbidden; and so, damp, cold and in much anxiety and suspense, they passed the time.

Meanwhile, McCook had fought himself into position on the extreme right of the Federal line. Not satisfied with merely getting up, he pressed heavily upon Polk's left flank, just before night, and endeavoured to take one of his batteries. But after a short and sanguinary conflict, he was driven back, and the opposing hosts bivouacked in order of battle, so close to each other that the Federal bugle and drum calls were plainly heard by the Confederates—whom the Federal bands also taunted by playing "Dixie" for a long time, and with uncommon pathos, and following this with two airs which the southerners were trying their best to forget—"Yankee Doodle" and "Hail Columbia."

Temporary earth-works had been constructed along the crest of the hill of which we have been speaking, extending from the left of Cobb's Battery down the slope to the right, behind which lay the Kentucky Brigade; while the remainder of Breckinridge's division and Jackson's-cavalry kept their places as originally formed.

Indications were now plain that the great struggle was close at hand. For five days the Federal Army had been advancing, skirmishing and reconnoitring, and Rosecrans had perfected his plan of battle. It was afterward known, (and Bragg seems for once to have divined the purposes of his antagonist and to have frustrated his schemes by a timely blow), that these were in the first place, to throw Crittenden upon Breckinridge—who, as has been seen, was covering Murfreesboro' with his right in constant jeopardy from any troops who might advance by the Lebanon pike,—holding Thomas in the centre, ready to support him, and Negley's division in reserve to Thomas, to maintain connection between the right and left, in case the main body of the Fourteenth Corps should find it necessary to unite with Crittenden in turning and breaking the Confederate right.

In the next place, and meanwhile, McCook was to hold the left in check, if possible, until Crittenden, or he and Thomas united, had performed the part allotted to that wing—that of driving the Confederate right back upon its left. This would have turned every natural advantage against the Confederates, and, with Murfreesboro' in possession of the Federals, the entire supplies of Bragg within their grasp, and his army thrown for the most part into a quadrangle, three sides formed by the lines of the Federal forces and Stone River, with its rugged bluffs, defeat would have been almost certain destruction.

The dawn of the fateful day, Wednesday, December 31, 1862, was ushered in with a deep fog; this gave way, as the sun came up, to clouds less dense; then this veil of nature was entirely lifted, the sun shone bright, and the air was balmy, till the contending hosts had rushed to the shock, and the smoke and stench of carnage began to rise upon the erewhile gentle breeze.

A little after sunrise the battle opened in earnest on the left of the Confederate line, (north bank of Stone River), and raged throughout the day, with occasional lulls in the storm. So terrible was the onset of the Confederates upon McCook—coming, too, at a time when he had been lulled into a false security by the failure of Hardee to attack at daylight—that the battle assumed an unfavourable aspect to the Federal Army within half an hour; and soon the right was hopelessly broken, and the right centre engaged in a deadly struggle—so that the condition of affairs determined that Crittenden should not attack at all. This relieved Breckinridge from the present hazard; and, weak as was his force, in view of the line to be covered, portions of the division were transferred, from time to time during the day, to the left, to meet such exigencies as arose in the course of the battle.

A portion of the Kentucky Brigade (the Sixth Regiment) was removed, in the beginning of the engagement, to the left of the position hitherto described, and stationed immediately on the south bank of the river, a little in rear of a right line with the rifle-pits on the hill, and slightly in advance of Polk's right flank. The plain immediately beyond—an old cotton held, skirted by a dense cedar wood—was in full view of this regiment, while to the troops about the battery the position in front of McCook was more or less plainly visible; and much of the dire conflict of that day was witnessed by this command, as it lay there, watching the issue of the struggle, and ready to contest the passage of the river, should the Federal arms prove victorious on the left and threaten Breckinridge from that quarter.

But the grand events of that day have passed into history. The excellent plan of battle determined upon by the Federal general, by which natural obstacles were to be turned into advantages; the unaccountable false security of McCook, at a moment when vigilance was most to be expected, and by which the fine divisions of Davis and Johnson were quickly driven back, with frightful slaughter, while Sheridan suffered scarcely less; the attack of Polk, (supported by troops from Breckinridge), first upon Negley and Rousseau, then upon the entire Fourteenth Corps; the obstinately contested field; the terrible carnage; and at last the uncertainty of the issue, when night fell upon the scene,—these things have constituted the themes of many pens, and we need not attempt to treat more fully of them here.

It is of one of the minor events in the great drama of the week, and its attendant circumstances, that we have principally to do—illustrating in a striking manner a peculiar phase of blindness which now, for the second or third time during the war, lost to Bragg the opportunity to strike a decisive blow for the cause of which he was one of the chosen leaders.

Sometime before night the detached regiment of Kentuckians returned to its place on the right of the battery; and, with the exception of a few artillery shots fired from an eminence on the right of the burnt house, Hanson was not, nor indeed was any part of the division, subjected to annoyance during the evening.

The next day, (Thursday, January 1, 1863), was spent in almost profound quiet, the monotony being relieved only by the sound of distant cavalry fighting, an occasional artillery shot, and once in a while desultory firing of pickets. The Federals had been re-formed during the night; but their movements were concealed by the nature of the ground and by forests—at least from eyes so easily dazzled by the prospect of victory as to be insensible to the possibility of an American general's recovering from the effects of a disaster, and wresting triumph from defeat; and Bragg, probably deceived by the withdrawal of Hazen's brigade from the position which it had held in Crittenden's front line, and being under the impression that the Union Army was ruinously cut up and retreating, telegraphed to Richmond that the enemy had yielded his strong point and was falling back; that the Confederates occupied the whole field; that, in short, the victory was his.

But the suspense among the troops was dreadful. Knowing less than Bragg pretended to know, but suspecting more, they felt that the issue of the battle was not yet determined: and they waited anxiously for further developments. It became plain, early in the day, that, though repulsed on the left, the Federal Army, or at least a large portion of it, was in the Confederate right front; and though a thousand rumours were afloat, to the effect that the show of organised strength was but for the purpose of enabling the main body of the army to draw off in safety, none of them gained credence to any considerable extent; for the dilatoriness and want of decisive action on the part of the commanding general argued doubt and perplexity rather than the consciousness of victory.

This gloomy New Year's Day went by with the Confederate troops thus inactive; and even before its noon the golden opportunity that comes so seldom to the leaders of armies had passed away. from Gen. Bragg, and the mark of waning fortune was again upon the cause which he represented. The dispositions of the troops of Rosecrans were completed—the snare was laid; and as the Federal Army had nothing to lose but everything to gain by waiting, it waited—but meanwhile it worked. The Confederate Army waited, and—hoped. About nightfall it was reported that some Federal artillery had been put in battery on a bluff, a little to the right of Breckinridge's centre; and an order came from Bragg that Hanson must move up and take it.

This, as was known to officers of the division, would necessitate the crossing of the river, and the ascent of the bluff beyond, against what odds it was impossible to tell; and that, too, in the gloom of night—all upon insufficient knowledge of the exact topography of the position to be assaulted by this handful of men. Some explanations were vouchsafed to the commanding general, and the order was countermanded. There were perhaps at that moment fifty-eight pieces of ordnance in position along that bluff, with heavy supporting columns; and Van Cleve's division was then south of the river and between Hanson and the point to be stormed.

Grose's brigade, of Palmer's division, had been sent over in the morning to support Van Cleve, (or rather, Col. Beatty, who was commanding in Van Cleve's absence); but Grose was withdrawn before sundown, to bivouac in the forest beyond—and this was probably magnified by the scouts and spies into the statement that the whole advance force had been withdrawn, thus inducing Bragg to order a forward movement.

The next morning, Friday, was dull, cold, cloudy, and as peculiarly dreary as the day before had been. Not a shot was to be heard along the extended space which had marked the lines of the contending armies two days before, and which, in part, they still occupied. There were few signs of animation in the Confederate ranks, and none that could be discovered among the Federals. Pickets and skirmishers were relieved in a measured and deliberate way, as though it were but the form that must be kept up in the presence of an enemy,—there being nothing to indicate to the rank and file that upon the vigilance of the moment depended the safety of the troops and perhaps the fate of a cause.

In the Orphan Brigade—as perhaps in all the rest—the morning meal was leisurely dispatched, and the men relapsed into that half-stupid and half-restless state that is observed to pervade a body of troops under arms but without active employment. Some lay upon their blankets and gazed vacantly upon the scene; others sat in groups and talked in a dull and listless manner.

The more unquiet wandered from company to company—as far as was consistent with the orders of the day; and all seemed oppressed by the sense of dreariness and uncertainty, and that partial freedom from the perils of impending battle which does not entirely remove from the thoughts the anticipations of the dreadful ordeal, but is still sufficient to allow of *ennui*.

Before noon it began to drizzle rain, and fitful showers—cold and benumbing—imparted increased gloom and discomfort. But about 1 o'clock came signs of a general waking up. There were shots at intervals along the line of pickets, and officers were riding out for reconnoissance. It was reported before 2 o'clock that Beatty's picket line had been pushed up to a certain old house, near a fence, forward and somewhat to the right of the battery to which we have before alluded. The skirmishers of the brigade were relieved by detail at 2 o'clock.

The special detail of the Sixth Regiment of Kentucky Infantry was put under command of Capt. Gran Utterback, who had orders to force his way up to the house in question, and burn it. He moved off promptly; the old skirmishers were relieved; and he found the Federal advance already up to the fence, just in rear of the house, and also to the right of it, in his front. A detail from the Twenty-first Kentucky Regiment, infantry, United States Army, were throwing the fence down, preparatory to a forward movement, or to prevent the Confederates from sheltering behind it. The captain began at once a vigorous attack, pushed back the enemy's line, and set fire to the building; but in the course of the action he was mortally wounded. Meanwhile an order had come to Gen. Breckinridge directing, in substance, that he must promptly move upon the position occupied by Beatty, plant his artillery upon that hill, and hold it. Grose had come back now, it must be borne in mind, and, with a strong brigade, was posted on and about Beatty's left flank—for what purpose, and to what effect, in this attempt of the Confederate general to recover by one desperate venture, the advantages lost by delay, will be adverted to hereafter.

Such was the train of events which had their emphatic denouement in the charge of Breckinridge's division on Friday afternoon of that terrible week in front of Murfreesboro.'

This officer had now about forty-five hundred men, infantry and artillery, exclusive of Pegram's cavalry, which was ordered to cooperate with the movement, and of one infantry regiment and Cobb's Battery which were left to hold Hanson's old position against the possibility of being taken by troops that might approach by turning or avoiding the left flank of the assailing force, or the right of those corps now held in observation north of the river.

The main body of cavalry which had been ordered to join in the attack failed to come up in time; but the order to Gen. Breckinridge was of such a nature that he did not deem himself allowed that discretionary power which would justify delay; and he made his dispositions at once. The infantry, two batteries of the artillery, and the cavalry present, were put under arms, and the order to march was given.

The point to be assailed lay obliquely to the right of Hanson, and his regiments were turned and advanced by the right flank across an open field, into some woodland, probably half a mile from the original position. Here the main body of the division had come up, and the whole was halted and aligned. Hanson occupied the extreme left, and his left was designed to touch upon the river bluff at the point of attack. When the alignment was made, this brigade stood in an open space—a bit of depressed fallow land in an angle of a field. Intervening between it and the enemy was an uncleared space, covered, for the most part, with sassafras and other brushwood, and with briars, and a little ahead was another open plat of ground, descending from the bushes, for some distance, then ascending to the line upon which the enemy lay. The general character of the ground along the whole division was undulating and broken by thickets, forest trees and patches of briars.

The formation was but fairly completed when Hanson rode up, having just left Gen. Breckinridge, and, accosting the colonel of the Sixth Kentucky, (which was to move in front of the extreme left), gave the order of advance to this regiment in person, in full hearing of the soldiers, who stood grimly waiting, at an order arms, for the next act in the drama. "Colonel," he said, "the order is to load, fix bayonets and march through this brushwood. Then charge at double-quick to within a hundred yards of the enemy, deliver fire, and go at him with the bayonet."

"Attention!" rang out the voice of the officer addressed—a man whom such an hour served always to prove far greater in every respect than in his ordinary seeming—"attention!" and pulses beat quick and the men nerved themselves for the struggle, knowing that the decisive moment had come.

Then came the loading,—that act in a soldier's life fraught with so terrible a significance—then the order to carry arms and march, and they stepped off in line of battle. With low, cautionary commands, as the officers exerted themselves to preserve formation, the brushwood was passed, the line was dressed, the pieces were brought to a "charge bayonet," and then the order was heard along the line, caught up and repeated by field, staff and company officers, "Forward! Double-quick! March!" and they dashed down the declivity. An obstacle, in the shape of a pond of water of unknown depth, threatened to check the progress of the left; but, by a quick command to avoid it by one of those dexterous movements known to military men, and which was handsomely executed, they cleared the pond, closed ranks on the opposite side, sprang forward up the hill a few paces, and delivered fire. Then, with a loud shout, they rushed at the Federal advance.

The latter replied with a volley, having held their fire for close work; and as the assailants became partially broken by the fence to which we have referred, and which they struck obliquely, there was a momentary delay, which the Federals on that part of the line improved by reloading and firing again upon the advancing columns. The first volley of the Confederates, however, had been deadly, and the onset was so fierce, that the front line now broke and retreated on the second, by which time the pursuers were bearing down upon them in full career, and could not then be checked.

But at this point some Federal artillery began a cautious but well-directed and steady fire upon the advancing columns, avoiding their own troops, and yet doing execution among the Confederates; and, among others, Gen. Hanson fell mortally wounded. But heedless alike of those who were falling now, and of the sure destruction awaiting them at the front, they rushed on—firing as fast as they could load, and cheered amid the carnage and the din by the thought that perhaps now, even now, they were dealing the finishing blow to what had been begun on Wednesday, and that the disastrous effects of Perryville and the retreat from Kentucky were about to be retrieved. The left wing of the Kentucky Brigade, striking the river first, as it ran obliquely and made a turn, so that, some hundreds of yards ahead, it came around almost directly in front, dashed into the stream, and reached the opposite bank, where some of them were captured, some killed and others escaped by striking abruptly off to the left and returning up the river when they found into what kind of toils they had been led.

In the madness of pursuit all order and discipline were forgotten. In one instance a reserve regiment having full view of the manner in which the attack was made, became almost ungovernable through excitement, and begged to join in the fray, which, from some mistaken notion of duty or misapprehension of orders, was allowed, and they came tearing down the slope by the river and intermingled with the front line. This proved in the end to be a most unfortunate circumstance. The turn of the river had the natural effect of crowding the ranks back towards the right and mingling them; and so, with the reserve troops that were thus thrown untimely forward, there was, in a few minutes, a mass of men huddled together upon this flank wholly disproportioned to the strength of the entire force.

As the bluff beyond the stream began to be plainly visible, the Confederates were met by a well-directed oblique fire from the Eighty-Fourth Illinois and Sixth Ohio regiments, of Grose's brigade, which had been stationed by that officer farthest in the rear, or, rather, so as to have formed the left of his line had the attack come from the quarter where it was most expected—the extreme right of the Confederate position. As soon, too, as the retiring Federals had well cleared the front, the Third Wisconsin Battery, also put in position by Grose near the regiments last named, opened furiously. As Beatty's Division was disappearing over the hill beyond, and the main body of the Confederates were on the point of dashing wildly into the river, the very earth trembled as with an exploded mine, and a mass of iron hail was hurled upon them.

The concentrated fire of more than sixty pieces of ordnance—including the Third Wisconsin Battery—was dealing death and destruction among them. Negley's Division had come up solidly to the front, along the line of the Federal batteries, and was pouring steady volleys into the disorganised and struggling mass. The rushing host had been checked in mid-career, and now staggered back. The artillery bellowed forth such thunders that the men were stunned and could not distinguish sounds. There were falling timbers, crashing arms, the whirring of missiles of every description, the bursting of the dreadful shell, the groans of the wounded, the shouts of the officers, mingled in one horrid din that beggars description. In fact, no general description can convey to the reader an idea of the terrible reality.

It is only the minute details of personal experience, through which single small bodies of troops pass, or in isolated facts, as the reader bears in mind that these, or something similar, were experienced by thousands of others, can he be impressed with the nature of the conflict that raged there, and the manner in which men inured to arms conduct themselves in the midst of such horrors.

At a point near where such of Hanson's left wing as had not crossed the river were brought to a stand, there stood two great oaks, close to each other, and behind these a few men naturally sought shelter; but they had scarcely done so when bullets were cutting the bark from them at every cardinal point of the compass. The assailants, having pressed to the right, in following the course of the river, instead of taking it squarely as they came up, had now passed so far forward as to be abreast of where one of Crittenden's right regiments had a number of sharpshooters concealed in some old houses on the opposite bank, and these gave them a raking fire of small arms; so that, front and flank, the air was literally burdened with flying projectiles.

It seemed impossible for a man to live a minute in such a horrid hail of shot and shell; but there they stood, plying their rifles eagerly, while so dire was the confusion, so thunderous was the cannonade, that the long line of Federal rifles on the bluff, as they poured forth their volleys, could not be heard, nor could the whistle of their bullets, so close were the Confederates to the oncoming enemy. They knew of the flying missiles only as they struck into trees and men, or tore up the ground around them. There was a composure there as the composure of despair. Men put on their ordinary seeming after the first stagger—it was the sober state succeeding the intoxication of the pursuit so suddenly checked.

The wounded who were not wholly stricken down spoke calmly of their hurts and walked composedly away. The survivors looked upon the dead, and spoke to one another of their fall. It was, for a few moments, one of those appalling storms in which humanity sometimes finds itself without the hope of escape; against which it has no visible protection; and yet, in which men nevertheless move and speak and from which many are finally saved. It is one of the unaccountable things of war how *so many* live and so few fall under some of the most desperate circumstances in which soldiers can be placed.

To endeavour to press forward now was folly, to remain was madness, and the order was given to retreat. Some rushed back precipitately, while others walked away with deliberation, and some even slowly and doggedly, as though they scorned the danger or had become indifferent to life. But they paid toll at every step back over that ground which they had just passed with the shout of victors. In addition to the execution done by the main body of the Federals, who had now become pursuers, they were terribly galled by Grose, who, in the main, had held his ground, and was pouring a destructive enfilade fire into the shattered column.

Near the line where Beatty's division received the charge, the Confederates rallied and re-formed; but the Federals were in too close pursuit, and the new formation was too weak to offer any effectual resistance, so it presently broke, leaving a part of the batteries for want of horses to carry them from the field. Cannoniers and animals had been almost entirely destroyed by the Federal artillery, whose fire they had attracted early in the action; and retreat was so suddenly necessitated as to preclude the possibility of their being replaced in time to move the guns.

When the Confederate troops had reached the line of rifle pits from which they had first started, and which were still held, in part, by Cobb's battery and the Ninth Kentucky Infantry, they rallied again and the pursuit ceased—the Federals following but little beyond the original line of Beatty.

It was now near nightfall and the evening was so cloudy that darkness soon came on—precluding the practicability of further active operations. The actual combat had lasted less than an hour. Gen. Breckinridge gave the whole time of the action as having been eighty minutes. It was stated by a participant that the time from the giving of the command "Charge bayonets" till the Confederates had been driven back to that line was forty-two minutes. But, in proportion to the number of combatants among whom the shock first occurred, the slaughter had been terrible.

The Confederate loss was almost unparalleled in the annals of war; while that of the Federals, as shown by their reports, was more than ordinarily heavy, considering the time that they were exposed to fire. But if the advance Federal division suffered in the onset, it was fearfully avenged at the last; for, in the short space of time mentioned, and chiefly during the last fifteen minutes, Breckinridge's loss, as stated by himself, was seventeen hundred men—more than thirty-seven *per cent.*

The Federal loss would doubtless have been far greater had it not been for the excellent disposition of Grose's men, which was so posted as to protect Beatty's left flank in case of a heavy assault there; to reinforce his whole line conveniently, could he have withstood the first shock; or, in case of a repulse, to cover the retreat and check pursuit. After a temporary confusion, and the sudden flight of Beatty's division, as the Confederate right partially covered and bore down upon this brigade, it poured in a destructive and well-maintained fire, which had the effect of pressing the Confederate right wing back towards the centre,—much the same as was produced by the turn in the river on the left and causing an attempt to push obliquely past him after the retiring division.

When the Kentucky Brigade had formed on the original ground, near Cobb's Battery, a hasty roll-call followed, and it was afterward ascertained that nearly every unhurt man of that renowned command was present to answer—a remarkable and noteworthy fact, that even veteran troops should be so little affected by such a terrible reverse. An officer says:

> Here, we were joined by Gen. Breckinridge, who had come around from the right front, where he had gone to direct in person some movement near the old mill on that flank. I never, at any time, saw him more visibly moved. He was raging like a wounded lion, as he passed the different commands from right to left; but tears broke from his eyes when he beheld the little remnant of his own old brigade—his personal friends and fellow-countrymen; and a sorrowful exclamation escaped his lips, to find, as he said, his 'poor Orphan Brigade torn to pieces.'

Bragg at once made his dispositions to retire with as little loss of men, munitions, and subsistence as possible; and Saturday night the evacuation began. Breckinridge's division remained upon the old line until the preparations were completed and the remainder of the infantry had begun the march southward. When the movement of this division began, the Kentucky Brigade was selected as a special rearguard of infantry, and did not abandon the line until daylight Sunday morning. Thus, terminated the great Battle of Stone River.

The official reports of Gen. Breckinridge and Col. Trabue are appended. The first gives, with sufficient minuteness, the operations of the whole division, of which the Kentucky Brigade formed so important a part, and makes mention of gallant Kentuckians who were serving on his staff, and were otherwise directly under his orders and his observation. That of Col. Trabue is a concise history of the brigade during the week.

Headquarters Breckinridge's Division,
January, 1863.

Maj. T. B. Roy, Assistant Adjutant-General—

Sir: I have the honour to report the operations of this division, of Lieut.-Gen. Hardee's corps, in the recent battles of Stone River, in front of Murfreesboro'.

The character and course of Stone River, and the nature of the ground in front of the two, are well known; and as the report of the general commanding will, no doubt, be accompanied by a sketch, it is not necessary to describe them here.

On the morning of Sunday, the 28th of December, the brigades moved from their encampments and took up lines of battle about one and a half miles from Murfreesboro' in the following order: Adams' brigade on the right, with its right resting on the Lebanon road, and its left extending toward the ford over Stone River, a short distance below the destroyed bridge, on the Nashville turnpike; Preston on the left of Adams, Palmer on the left of Preston, and Hanson forming the left of the line, with his left resting on the right bank of the river, near the ford. The right of Maj.-Gen. Withers, of Lieut. Gen. Polk's corps, rested near the left bank of the river and slightly in advance of Hanson's left.

Brig.-Gen. Jackson, having reported to me with his command, was placed, by the direction of the lieutenant-general commanding, upon the east side of the Lebanon road, on commanding ground, a little in advance of the right of Brig.-Gen. Adams. My division formed the front line of the right wing of the army; Maj.-Gen. Cleburne's division, drawn up some six hundred yards in rear, formed the second line of the same wing; while the division of Maj.-Gen. McCown, under the immediate direction of the general commanding, composed the reserve.

My line extended from left to right, along the edge of a forest, save an open space of four hundred yards, which was occupied by Wright's Battery, of Preston's brigade, with the Twentieth Tennessee in reserve to support it. An open field, eight hundred yards in width, extended along nearly the whole front of the line, and was bounded on the opposite side by a line of forest similar to that occupied by us. In the opinion of the lieutenant-general commanding, who had twice ridden carefully over the ground with me, and the general commanding, who had personally inspected the lines, it was the strongest position the nature of the ground would allow.

About six hundred yards in front of Hanson's centre was an eminence, which it was deemed important to hold. It commanded the ground sloping toward the river, in its front and on its left, and also the plain on the west bank, occupied by the right of Withers' line. Col. Hunt, with the Forty-first Alabama, the Sixth and Ninth Kentucky, and Cobb's Battery, all of Hanson's brigade, was ordered to take and hold this hill, which he did, repulsing several brisk attacks of the enemy, and losing some excellent officers and men. A few hundred yards to the left and rear of this position, a small earth-work, thrown up under the direction of Maj. Graves, my chief of artillery, was held during a part of the operations by Semple's Battery of Napoleon guns.

In the afternoon of Tuesday, the 30th, I received intelligence from Lieut.-Gen. Hardee, that the divisions of Cleburne and McCown were to be transferred to the extreme left, and soon after an order came to me, from the general commanding, to hold the hill at all hazards. I immediately moved the remainder of Hanson's brigade to the hill, and strengthened Cobb's Battery with a section from Lumsden's Battery and a section from Slocum's Washington Artillery. At the same time, Adams' brigade was moved from the right, and formed on the ground originally occupied by Hanson's brigade. Jackson was moved to the west side of the Lebanon road, to connect with the general line of battle.

All the ground east of Stone River was now to be held by one division, which, in a single line, did not extend from the ford to the Lebanon road. I did not change my general line, since a position in advance, besides being less favourable in other respects, would have widened considerably the interval between my right and the Lebanon road. The enemy did not again attack the hill with infantry, but our troops there continued to suffer, during all the operations, from heavy shelling. Our artillery at that position often did good service, in diverting the enemy's fire from our attacking lines of infantry; and especially on Wednesday, the 31st, succeeded in breaking several of their formations on the west bank of the river.

On the morning of Wednesday, the 31st, the battle opened on our left. From my front, information came to me from Pegram's cavalry force, in advance, that the enemy, having crossed at the fords below, were moving on my position in line of battle. This proved to be incorrect: and it is to be regretted that sufficient care was not taken by the authors of the report to discriminate rumour from fact.

About half-past ten o'clock a. m., I received, through Col. J. Stoddard Johnston, a suggestion from the general commanding, to move against the enemy instead of awaiting his attack. (I find that Col. Johnston regarded it as an order, but as I moved at once, it is not material.) I prepared to fight on the ground I then occupied, but supposing that the object of the general was to create a diversion in favour of our left, my line, except Hanson's brigade, was put in motion in the direction from which the enemy was supposed to be advancing.

We had marched about half a mile, when I received, through Col. Johnston, an order from the general commanding, to send at least one brigade to the support of Lieut.-Gen. Polk, who was hard pressed, and, as I recollect, two, if I could spare them. I immediately sent Adams and Jackson, and at the same suspended my movement, and sent forward Capt. Blackburn with several of my escort, to Capt. Coleman and Lieut. Darragh, of my staff, with orders to find and report, with certainty, the position and movements of the enemy.

Soon after an order came from the general commanding to continue the movement. The line again advanced, but had not proceeded far when I received an order from the general commanding, through Col. Johnston, repeated by Col. Grenfell, to leave Hanson in position on the hill, and with the remainder of my command to report at once to Lieut.-Gen. Polk. The brigades of Preston and Palmer were immediately moved by the flank, toward the ford before referred to, and the order of the general executed with great rapidity. In the meantime, riding forward to the position occupied by the general commanding and Lieut.-Gen. Polk, near the west bank of the river and a little below the ford, I arrived in time to see, at a distance, the brigades of Jackson and Adams recoiling from a very hot fire of the enemy.

I was directed by Lieut.-Gen. Polk to form my line, with its right resting on the river and its left extending across the open field, crossing the Nashville turnpike almost at a right angle. While my troops were crossing the river and getting into line, I rode forward with a portion of my staff, assisted by gentlemen of the staffs of Generals

Bragg and Polk, to rally and form Adams' brigade, which was falling back chiefly between the turnpike and the river.

Jackson, much cut up, had retired farther toward our left. The brigade of Brig.-Gen. Adams was rallied and placed in the line across the field, behind a low and very imperfect breastwork of earth and rails. These brigades did not again enter the action that day, (which indeed closed soon after with the charge of Preston and Palmer.) They had suffered severely in an attack upon superior numbers, very strongly posted, and sustained by numerous and powerful batteries which had repulsed all preceding assaults. The list of casualties shows the courage and determination of these troops.

Gen. Adams, having received a wound while gallantly leading his brigade, the command devolved upon Col. R. L. Gibson, who discharged its duties throughout with courage and skill.

Preston and Palmer being now in line, Preston on the right, Lieut. Gen. Polk directed me to advance across the plain until I encountered the enemy. The right of my line rested on the river (and from the course of the stream would, in advancing, rest on or very near it), while the left touched a skirt of woods from which the enemy had been driven during the day. At the opposite extremity of the plain a cedar brake extended in front of Palmer's whole line, and two-thirds of Preston's line, the remaining space to the river being comparatively open, with commanding swells, and through this ran the railroad and turnpike nearly side by side. It was supposed that the enemy's line was parallel to ours, but the result showed that, in advancing, our right and his left, at the point of contact, would form an acute angle.

These two brigades, passing over the troops lying behind the rails, moved across the plain in very fine order, under the fire of the enemy's artillery. We had advanced but a short distance when Col. O'Hara (my acting adjutant-general) called my attention to a new battery in the act of taking position in front of our right, between the turnpike and the river. I immediately sent him back to find some artillery to engage the enemy's battery. He found and placed in position the Washington Artillery. About the same time, Capt. E. P. Byrne reported his battery to me, and received an order to take the best position he could find, and engage the enemy. He succeeded in opening on them after our line had passed forward.

A number of officers and men were killed along the whole line, but in this charge the chief loss fell upon Preston's right and centre. His casualties amounted to one hundred and fifty-five. The Twentieth

Tennessee, after driving the enemy on the right of the turnpike and taking twenty-five prisoners, was compelled to fall back before a very heavy artillery and musketry fire—Col. Smith commanding, being severely wounded—but it kept the prisoners, and soon rejoined the command. The Fourth Florida and Sixtieth North Carolina encountered serious difficulty at a burnt house (Cowan's) on the left of the turnpike, from fences and other obstacles, and were for a little while thrown into some confusion. Here, for several minutes, they were exposed to a destructive and partially enfilading fire at short range of artillery and infantry. But they were soon rallied by their gallant brigade commander, and, rushing with cheers across the intervening space, entered the cedar glade. The enemy had retired from the cedars, and was in position in a field to the front and right.

By changing the front of the command slightly forward to the right, my line was brought parallel to that of the enemy, and was formed near the edge of the cedars. About this time, meeting Lieut.-Gen. Hardee, we went together to the edge of the field to examine the position of the enemy, and found him strongly posted in two lines of battle, supported by numerous batteries. One of his lines had the protection of the railroad cut, forming an excellent breastwork. We had no artillery, the nature of the ground forbidding its use.

It was deemed reckless to attack with the force present. Night was now approaching. Presently the remainder of Lieut.-Gen. Hardee's Corps came up on the left, and with McCown's command and a part of Cheatham's prolonged the line of battle in that direction. Adams' Brigade also appeared and formed on the right of Preston. The troops bivouacked in position.

The commanding general, expecting an attack upon his right the next morning, ordered me during the night to recross the river with Palmer's Brigade. Before daylight, Thursday morning, Palmer was in position on the right of Hanson. No general engagement occurred on this day, the troops generally being employed in replenishing the ammunition, cooking rations, and obtaining some repose.

On Friday, the 2nd of January, being desirous to ascertain if the enemy was establishing himself on the east bank of the river, Lieut. Col. Buckner and Maj. Graves, with Capt. Byrne's Battery and a portion of the Washington Artillery, under Lieut. D. C. Vaught, went forward to our line of skirmishers toward the right, and engaged those of the enemy who had advanced, perhaps a thousand yards, from the east bank of the river. They soon revealed a strong line of skirmishers, which was driven back a considerable distance by our sharpshooters and artillery, the latter firing several houses in the fields, in which the enemy had taken shelter.

At the same time, accompanied by Maj. Pickett, of Lieut.-Gen. Hardee's staff, and by Maj. Wilson, Col. O'Hara, and Lieut. Breckinridge of my own, I proceeded toward the left of our line of skirmishers, which passed through a thick wood, about five hundred yards in front of Hanson's position, and extended to the river. Directing Capt. Bosche, of the Ninth, and Capt. Steele, of the Fourth Kentucky, to drive back the enemy's skirmishers, we were enabled to see that he was occupying, with infantry and artillery, the crest of a gentle slope on the east bank of the river. The course of the crest formed a little less than a right angle with Hanson's line, from which the centre of the position I was afterward ordered to attack was distant about sixteen hundred yards. It extended along ground part open and part woodland.

While we were endeavouring to ascertain the force of the enemy, and the relation of the ground on the east bank to that on the west bank of the river, I received an order from the commanding general to report to him in person. I found him on the west bank, near the ford below the bridge, and received from him an order to form my division in two lines, and take the crest I have just described with the infantry. After doing this, I was to bring up the artillery and establish it on the crest, so as at once to hold it and enfilade the enemy's lines on the other side of the river. Pegram and Wharton, who, with some cavalry and a battery, were beyond the point where my right would rest, when the new line of battle should be formed, were directed, as the general informed me, to protect my right, and cooperate in the attack. Capt. Robertson was ordered to report to me with his own and Semple's batteries of Napoleon guns.

Capt. Wright, who, with his battery, had been detached some days before, was ordered to join his brigade (Preston's). The brigades of Adams and Preston, which were left on the west side of the river Wednesday night, had been ordered to rejoin me. At the moment of my advance, our artillery in the centre and on the left was to open on the enemy. One gun from our centre was the signal for the attack. The commanding general desired that the movement should be made with the least possible delay.

It was now 2:30 p. m. Two of the brigades had to march about two miles, the other about one mile.

Brig.-Gen. Pillow having reported for duty, was assigned by the commanding general to Palmer's brigade, and that fine officer resumed command of his regiment, and was three times wounded in the ensuing engagement. The Ninth Kentucky and Cobb's Battery, under the command of Col. Hunt, were left to hold the hill so often referred to.

The division, after deducting the losses of Wednesday, the troops left on the hill, and companies on special service, consisted of some forty-five hundred men. It was drawn up in two lines—the first in a narrow skirt of woods, the second two hundred yards in rear. Pillow and Hanson formed the first line; Pillow on the right, Preston supported Pillow; and Adams' brigade (commanded by Col. Gibson), supported Hanson. The artillery was placed in rear of the second line, under orders to move with it and occupy the summit of the slope as soon as the infantry should rout the enemy.

Feeling anxious about my right, I sent two staff officers in succession to communicate with Pegram and Wharton, but received no intelligence up to the moment of assault. The interval between my left and the troops on the hill was already too great, but I had a battery to watch it, with a small infantry support. There was nothing to prevent the enemy from observing nearly all our movements and preparations. To reach him it was necessary to cross an open space six or seven hundred yards in width, with a gentle ascent. The river was several hundred yards in rear of his position, but departed from it considerably as it flowed toward his left. I had informed the commanding general that we would be ready to advance at 4 o'clock, and precisely at that hour the signal gun was heard from our centre. Instantly the troops moved forward at a quick step, and in admirable order. The front line had bayonets fixed, with orders to deliver one volley and then use the bayonet.

The fire of the enemy's artillery on both sides of the river began as soon as the troops entered the open ground. When less than half the distance across the field, the quick eye of Col. O'Hara discovered a force extending considerably beyond our right. I immediately directing Maj. Graves to move a battery to our right and open on them. He at once advanced Wright's Battery, and effectually checked their movements. Before our line reached the enemy's position, his artillery fire had become heavy, accurate and destructive. Many officers and men fell before we closed with their infantry, yet our brave fellows rushed forward with the utmost determination; and after a brief, but bloody conflict, routed both the opposing lines, took four hundred prisoners, several flags, and drove their artillery and the great body of their infantry across the river. Many were killed at the water's edge. Their artillery took time by the forelock in crossing the stream. A few of our men, in their ardour, actually crossed over before they could be prevented, most of whom, subsequently moving up under the west bank, recrossed at a ford three-quarters of a mile above.

The second line had halted when the first engaged the enemy's infantry, and laid down under orders; but very soon the casualties in the first line, the fact that the artillery on the opposite bank was more fatal to the second line than the first, and the eagerness of the troops impelled them forward, and at the decisive moment when the opposing infantry was routed, the two lines had mingled into one, the only practical inconvenience of which was that at several points the ranks were deeper than is allowed by a proper military formation.

A strong force of the enemy beyond our extreme right yet remained on the east side of the river. Presently a new line of battle appeared on the west bank directly opposite our troops, and opened fire, while at the same time large masses crossed in front of our right, and advanced to the attack. We were compelled to fall back. As soon as our infantry had won the ridge, Maj. Graves advanced the artillery of the division and opened fire; at the same Capt. Robertson threw forward Semple's Battery toward our right, which did excellent service. He did not advance his own battery (which was to have taken position on the left), supposing that that part of the field had not been cleared of the enemy's infantry. Although mistaken in this, since the enemy had been driven across the river, yet I regard it as fortunate that the battery was not brought forward. It would have been a vain contest.

It now appeared that the ground we had won was commanded by the enemy's batteries, within easy range, on better ground upon the other side of the river. I know not how many guns he had. He had enough to sweep the whole position from the front, the left, and the right, and to render it wholly untenable by our force present of artillery and infantry. The infantry, after passing the crest and descending the slope toward the river, were in some measure protected, and suffered less at this period of the action than the artillery. We lost three guns, nearly all the horses being killed, and not having the. time or men to draw them off by hand. One was lost because there was but one boy left (private Wright, of Wright's Battery) to limber the piece, and his strength was unequal to it.

The command fell back in some disorder, but without the slightest appearance of panic, and reformed behind Robertson's Battery, in the narrow skirt of timber from which we emerged to the assault. The enemy did not advance beyond the position in which he received our attack. My skirmishers continued to occupy a part of the field over which we advanced until the army retired from Murfreesboro'. The action lasted about one hour and twenty minutes. As our lines advanced to the attack, several rounds of artillery were heard from our centre, apparently directed against the enemy on the west bank of the river.

About twilight Brig.-Gen. Anderson reported to me with his brigade, and remained in position with me until the army retired. I took up line of battle for the night a little in rear of the field over which we advanced to the assault, and Capt. Robertson, at my request, disposed the artillery in the positions indicated for it. Many of the reports do not discriminate between the losses of Wednesday and Friday. The total loss in my division, exclusive of Jackson's command, is two thousand one hundred and forty, of which I think one thousand seven hundred occurred on Friday. The loss of the enemy on this day was, I think, greater than our own, since he suffered immense slaughter between the ridge and the river.

I cannot forbear to express my admiration for the courage and constancy of the troops, exhibited even after it became apparent that the main object could not be accomplished. Beyond the general good conduct, a number of enlisted men displayed, at different periods of the action, the most heroic bravery. I respectfully suggest that authority be given to select a certain number of the most distinguished in each brigade, to be recommended to the President for promotion.

I cannot enumerate all the brave officers who fell, nor the living, who nobly did their duty. Yet I may be permitted to lament, in common with the army, the premature death of Brig.-Gen. Hanson, who received a mortal wound at the moment the enemy began to give way. Endeared to his friends by his private virtues, and to his command by the vigilance with which he guarded its interest and honour, he was, by the universal testimony of his military associates, one of the finest officers that adorned the service of the Confederate States. Upon his fall the command devolved on Col. Trabue, who, in another organisation, had long and ably commanded most of the regiments composing the brigade.

I cannot close without expressing my obligations to the gentlemen of my staff. This is no formal acknowledgment. I can never forget that during all the operations they were ever prompt and cheerful, by night and day, in conveying orders, conducting to their positions regiments and brigades, rallying troops on the field, and, indeed, in the discharge of every duty. It gives me pleasure to name Lieut.-Col. Buckner, assistant adjutant-general, who was absent on leave, but returned upon the first rumour of battle; Col. O'Hara, acting adjutant-general; Lieut. Breckinridge, *aide-de-camp*; Maj. Graves, chief of artillery, twice wounded and his horse shot under him; Maj. Wilson, assistant inspector-general, horse shot; Capt. Semple, ordnance officer; Lieut. Darragh, severely wounded. Captains Mastin and Coleman, of my volunteer staff, were active and efficient. The former had his horse killed under him.

Doctors Heustis and Pendleton, chief surgeon and medical inspector, were unremitting in attention to the wounded. Dr. Stanhope Breckinridge, assistant surgeon, accompanied my headquarters, and pursued his duties through the fire of Wednesday. Mr. Buckner and Mr. Zantzinger, of Kentucky, attached themselves to me for the occasion, and were active and zealous. Capt. Blackburn, commanding my escort, ever cool and vigilant, rendered essential service, and made several bold reconnoissances. Charles Choutard, of the escort, acting as my orderly on Wednesday, displayed much gallantry and intelligence.

The army retired before daybreak on the morning of the 4th of January. My division, moving on the Manchester road, was the rear of Hardee's Corps. The Ninth Kentucky, Forty-first Alabama, and Cobb's Battery, all under the command of Col. Hunt, formed a special rearguard. The enemy did not follow us.

My acknowledgments are due to Col. J. Stoddard Johnston, Lieut. Col. Brent, and Lieut.-Col. Garner, of Gen. Bragg's staff, and to Maj. Pickett, of Lieut.-Gen. Hardee's staff, for services on Friday, the 2nd of January.

Respectfully, your obedient servant,
John C. Breckinridge,
Major-General, C. S. A,

Headquarters Kentucky Brigade,
Tullahoma, Jan. 15, 1863.

Col. T. O'Hara, A. A. G—

Sir: The untimely fall of the gallant and lamented Hanson, brigadier-general commanding this brigade, in the engagement on Friday, the 2nd instant, at Stone River, imposes on me the duty of reporting, to the extent of my knowledge, the operations of the brigade prior to and after his fall, in the battle before that place.

On Sunday, the brigade having received orders to that effect, marched from their camp in rear of Murfreesboro', at eight o'clock a.m., to the position in the front line of battle indicated for our occupation. This brigade formed the left of Gen. Breckinridge's Division, and in line rested with its left on or near Stone River, extending eastward until the right was united to Col. Palmer's Brigade. The position first taken up (the exact line not having been pointed out) was along the skirt of woods in rear of the open fields, east and south of Stone River, which afforded, by the existence of a small ridge running parallel with the front, and a consequent depression in rear, very good protection against the enemy's long-range artillery.

On Monday, Semple's Battery of six Napoleon guns, furnished by the chief of artillery, was placed on the crest immediately in front of the right wing, and Cobb's Battery was held to be placed later. Thus, formed in line, the Fourth Kentucky was on the right; Second Kentucky, Maj. Hewitt, second; Forty-First Alabama, Col. Talbird, third; Sixth Kentucky, Col. Lewis, fourth; and Ninth Kentucky on the left, Col. Hunt.

On Monday evening it was perceived that the enemy meant to occupy immediately all the advantageous positions in our front, of which he could possess himself, for artillery. A prominent elevation existed one thousand yards in front of our left, which Gen. Breckinridge desired we should hold, notwithstanding it was liable to assault, being isolated one thousand yards in front of our lines. To this end, Col. Hunt, with the Ninth Kentucky; Col. Lewis, Sixth Kentucky; Lieut.-Col. Stansil, Forty-First Alabama, and Cobb's Battery, were ordered to occupy it. Throwing out skirmishers, they were soon engaged with those of the enemy.

The force above named was then moved up to the front, in support of the skirmishers, and succeeded in establishing Cobb's Battery on the eminence. This was not accomplished without the loss of two valuable officers, Lieutenants Beale and Kennard, of Co. D, Ninth Kentucky—the former severely, the latter slightly wounded.

By this time it was dark, when the enemy endeavoured, in a spirited effort, to retake the position, rapidly driving in our skirmishers, and approaching to within a few yards of the battery. This attempt was frustrated by promptly advancing the Forty-First Alabama, under Lieut. Col. Stansil, when the enemy were driven off in confusion, leaving two of their dead near the battery. Our loss here amounted to not less than ten wounded, falling mainly on the Sixth Kentucky and Cobb's Battery, among whom was Lieut. Holman, Sixth Kentucky.

On Tuesday night these regiments were withdrawn, and I, with the Second and Fourth Kentucky, and Cobb's Battery, occupied this position. It was deemed of the last importance to hold this hill, and orders were received to do so at all hazards, it being called the key of the battlefield.

On Wednesday evening the entire brigade was brought up, having been re-enforced by a section of Lumsden's Battery, commanded by Lieut. Chalaron, and a section of the Washington Artillery, commanded by Lieut. Tarrant; and Semple's Battery, having taken up a position six hundred yards in rear and left of us, a section of this battery replaced, for one night, Cobb's Battery.

During the week which followed, we were kept here bivouacking in the mud and rain, and exposed to an incessant fire from the enemy's batteries and sharpshooters. A temporary and slight entrenchment was made, which, to some extent, protected the batteries, but the casualties at this place were not inconsiderable, amounting to fifty men, as stated above, and as will appear by reference to regimental reports.

During the engagement of Wednesday time and again did the gallant Cobb, aided by his not less gallant lieutenants, and the three sections before referred to, disperse the enemy's columns as they endeavoured to succour that part of their force engaged with the right of the left wing of the army. Indeed, during every day of our occupation of this hill, our battery did signal service, frequently driving the enemy's artillery away, and often dispersing his infantry. All this while the brigade covered more than a mile of front, with skirmishers and pickets, using for that purpose from six to ten companies daily.

These advanced to within one hundred yards of the enemy, in many places, and were hourly engaged. On this hill Cobb's Battery lost eight men. Col. Hunt, Ninth Kentucky, lost a most excellent officer killed—his adjutant, Henry M. Curd—whose death all lament; and wounded, Capt. Joe Desha, whose subsequent conduct elicited universal praise, together with Lieut. Lewis, Co. A, and Buchanan, Co. H, wounded, and three other officers and twenty-three privates. Col. Lewis, Sixth Kentucky, lost slightly here. Lieut.-Col. Stansil, Forty-First Alabama, lost here two of his best officers and several men. The Second and Fourth Kentucky, though equally exposed, lost less at this point.

On Friday, the 2nd instant, at three o'clock, the order came to move to the right and front, and form the left of the front line of Breckinridge's Division, to attack that portion of the enemy's left which was posted in the woods and ravines on the south side of Stone

River, opposite the extreme right of our army, which was done. Col. Hunt, with his regiment, remained at the hill, ordered to support the battery, and six companies were kept out as before, on picket duty, thus leaving us for the fight about twelve hundred men. Stone River, in front of this new position, runs nearly parallel with the new line, but inclined to the point occupied by the right of this brigade, when by a change of direction to the north, it runs for some distance nearly perpendicularly from the front of our line.

At this point, whence the river changes its direction northward, is a skirt of woods and an elevated ridge, behind which, and in the ravines and woods, the enemy lay concealed. To the right of our line the enemy were likewise posted in a wood, thus outflanking us. A thousand yards in the front from this first skirt of woods is a ford of the river, while the bank of the river opposite us, between the ford and point of attack, overlooks the south and east bank. One mile further down the river is another ford, as I have since learned. This topography, as well as the enemy's strength, were wholly unknown to us.

The two lines of the division having been formed, the signal for attack was sounded at four p.m., when the brigade, in line, moved steadily forward to the attack, with arms loaded and bayonets fixed, instructed to fire once and then charge with the bayonet. The peculiar nature of the ground and direction of the river, and the eagerness of the troops, caused the lines of Pillow's (formerly Palmer's) brigade and this brigade to lap on the crest of the hill, but the fury of the charge and the effective fire of the lines, put the enemy at once to flight.

All in front of us that were not killed or captured ran across the river at the ford, and out of range of our fire, as did a battery which had been posted off to our right; and many of the infantry mentioned before as being on the right likewise fled across this ford. A part, however, of this force, double-quicking toward the ford, from their position, finding they would be cut off, formed in line to our right on a ridge, and not being assailed, held this ground meanwhile; and from the moment of beginning the attack the enemy's artillery from the opposite side of the river directed on us a most destructive fire. Very soon, too, the crests of the opposite side of the river swarmed with infantry, whose fire was terrible.

Thus, exposed to the fire seemingly of all his artillery, and a large portion of his infantry, from unassailable positions, as well as to the flanking fire from the right, it was deemed prudent to withdraw. This was done slowly, though not in the best order, resulting mainly from the confusion consequent upon the too early advance of the second line into ground already too much crowded by the first. The lines were reformed about six hundred yards in rear of the river, and near the line from which we advanced to the attack.

While thus engaged in reforming my own regiment, I received intelligence of the fall of Gen. Hanson, when I took command of the brigade, the other regiments of which had likewise been reformed. This brigade in the battle having advanced to within eighty yards of the ford, part of Col. Lewis' Sixth Kentucky, and part of the Second Kentucky, having crossed the river a little to the left, when near the ford, slightly protected by a picket fence on this side, they fought the enemy across the river, until the rear having fallen back, made it necessary to withdraw them also. I obtained returns on the field, showing still in line more than half the men with which we started, notwithstanding a loss of thirty-three *per cent.* killed and wounded.

I remained in line until 9 o'clock, having replenished the cartridge-boxes, when I received orders to return to my original position on the hill, which was obeyed. We remained in this position until Sunday morning at 1 o'clock, when, having been assigned the duty of bringing up the rear, we moved off with Col. Hunt's Ninth Kentucky, Forty-First Alabama, Lieut.-Col. Stansil, and Cobb's Battery, being detailed as special rear-guard. My pickets were withdrawn at 3 o'clock a.m., by Capt. Bosche, of the Ninth Kentucky, under direction of Capt. Martin, of Gen. Breckinridge's staff.

I have thus briefly given you a report of the part taken by this brigade, omitting many details and incidents creditable to individuals and the command.

In the absence of a report from my own regiment, Fourth Kentucky, prior to the time when I took command of the brigade, I will state simply that both officers and men did their duty. Willis Roberts, major, was killed early in the action, by a grape-shot. Than he, there was not a more gallant officer; he had not recovered from wounds received at Baton Rouge. Lieut.-Col. Nuckols was wounded in shoulder near the picket fence; Capt. Bramlett, First Lieut. Burnley, Second Lieut. Higginson, Second Lieut. Clayton and Second Lieut. Dunn were killed; and Lieutenants Dudley, Robert Moore (since said to have died), John B. Moore, Lashbrook, and Thomson were wounded, together with privates and non-commissioned officers. One company, Capt. Trice's, being on picket duty, was not in the engagement.

The colour-bearer, Robert Lindsay, being wounded, refused to allow anyone to accompany him to the rear, although bleeding at the mouth and nose. He handed the colours, on return, to private Jones, who was killed, when they were borne to the last by Joseph Nichols, of Company F.

Thus, it will be seen that of twenty-three officers of this regiment who went into the fight, seven were killed and six wounded. The command of the regiment was, on my assuming command of the brigade, turned over to Capt. Tho. W. Thompson.

The detailed statement heretofore furnished show the casualties to have been as follows:

	Killed.	Wounded.	Missing.
Second Kentucky	14	70	24
Fourth Kentucky	12	47	11
Sixth Kentucky	2	60	14
Ninth Kentucky	1	28	0
Forty-first Alabama	18	89	35
Cobb's Battery	3	3	0
Total	50	297	84

Total loss, 431.

The conduct of Col. Lewis, Sixth Kentucky, and Lieut.-Col. Stansil, Forty-first Alabama; Maj. James Hewitt, Second Kentucky; Lieut.-Col. Nuckols and Capt. Thompson, of Fourth Kentucky, as well as that of the other field and company officers engaged, was gallant in the highest degree, and the men repeated, also, the steadiness and courage which characterized them at Donelson, Shiloh, Baton Rouge, Vicksburg, and Hartsville. Lieutenants Stake, Benedict and Capt. Chipley, of Gen. Hanson's staff, bore themselves with exemplary courage. My thanks are due, too, to the medical staff, and to Capt. Semple, division ordnance officer, and acting Lieut. Presley Trabue, brigade ordnance officer, for their promptness in bringing up supplies of ammunition; and to my adjutant, Robert Williams, of Fourth Kentucky.

I cannot close this report without more especial mention of one whose gallantry and capacity we all witnessed with pride, and whose loss we and the whole army sincerely deplore—I mean the gallant Gen. Hanson, who fell in the pride of his manhood, in the thickest of the fight, nobly doing his duty. His wound was mortal, and death ensued on Sunday morning at 5 o'clock.

Col. Hunt, Ninth Kentucky, though not in the engagement of Friday, deserves commendation for his conduct, prior and subsequent to that time, as do the other officers and men of his regiment.

    Respectfully,

                 R. P. Trabue,
             Colonel Commanding Brigade.

 P. S. The missing were those who went into the engagement but who were not seen to come out, and must have been killed or wounded. I find, also, I have omitted to mention that Lieut.-Col. Stansil received a severe wound in the leg, but did not quit the field, and still commands his regiment.

It will be observed that Col. Trabue, having led his own regiment up to near the close of the engagement, and witnessed its casualties, mentions his wounded officers, in advance of regimental report from the commander who led it from the field. Speaking of the affair with the enemy's skirmishers on the evening of December 29th, alluded to in the preceding report, a staff officer remarks, that:

> About four o'clock on Monday afternoon, the enemy's skirmishers appeared, and Col. Hunt was ordered to move forward with Cobb's Battery, supported by his own regiment and two others, and hold a hill which was the real key of Bragg's position. At dusk, our skirmishers met the enemy and were driven back upon our line. A brisk encounter ensued, with the loss of several officers and men. The Federals approached so near that a member of Cobb's Battery was severely burned by the powder from a gun, from the discharge of which he was wounded, as he stood with his hand resting upon the limber of his piece. At this critical moment, Col. Hunt ordered a charge, which he led in person, and drove what afterward proved to be a Federal brigade across Stone River.
>
> Night closed in, enveloping our line in darkness—not a fire being kindled. An order came about ten o'clock for Col. Hunt to abandon the hill occupied, and take a new line farther back. I had known much of him, but never before saw him so restless and excited when not under the observation of the men. Just over the hill which loomed above us could be heard the busy axes of the Federal troops; and who, for a moment, imagined that, with the coming dawn, they would neglect to occupy a position, the possession of which would render our line untenable? About four o'clock next morning he sent repeatedly for

permission to reoccupy the hill, and not receiving a prompt reply, he assumed the responsibility, advanced, and formed upon it. When daylight came, it was obvious to all observing men that the movement had saved our position.

A Federal account of the action says, that the number of guns massed on the bluff was fifty-eight, and that for full fifteen minutes they continued to pour their storm of shot and shell into the now broken division.

INCIDENTS AND ANECDOTES: AT MURFREESBORO; AND AT AND AFTER STONE RIVER.

1. Preston's Coolness and Heroism.—When Gen. Preston's brigade, in connection with Palmer's, made the attack on the enemy's left, December 31st, as noticed by Gen. Breckinridge, having been ordered forward after the repulse of Jackson and Adams, it was on the right of Palmer, and nearest the river. It moved forward across the open field, with its flank exposed to the fire of twenty pieces of artillery, and the strongest position of the enemy's line. Preston ordered the Twentieth Tennessee to make a half-wheel to the right beyond the railroad, and it attacked with such dashing courage that it drew away the fire from his iine advancing across the plain.

The brigade rapidly passed the plain, and, dauntlessly moving under the fire of the artillery, carried the wood. Preston had a staff officer (Ewing) killed by his side, and another (Lieut. Whitefield) severely wounded, who fell across his horse, covering him with his blood. The general's cap was struck with a shell, but he escaped without a wound. One of the regiments had broken; but Preston seized the colours and rode before the line toward the enemy—when, rallied by its officers, and by Whitefield, the standard-bearer seized his colours again, and the regiment dashed forward over the plain and into the wood.

2. Suffering with Cold.—After Sunday, December 28th, the week at Stone River was almost constantly inclement, and the suffering was great, particularly among those who at different times constituted the picket force that covered the position at night. On the night of Tuesday, December 30th, it was extremely cold; and as it was impossible to kindle even the smallest fire without attracting the enemy's attention, the pickets suffered almost to absolute freezing, as they quietly waited and watched, nearly motionless, for indications of the foe. "I thought," said one, describing his experience, "that I had been cold before; but I never suffered on account of wintry weather as I did that night."

3. A Surgeon's Experience on the Field at Stone River.—On Wednesday afternoon Capt. Jo Desha was brought to my ambulance corps like a man dead from a shell wound. I ordered the nurse to put a cold-water compress to his head. I was so engaged for an hour that I could not give him my personal attention, but at the end of that time I went to look after my patient. He was gone; had hurried back to the front and resumed command of his company.—Corporal Hawes, of one of Cobb's guns, had been detailed to serve with me as druggist for the Second Kentucky. When the firing began, he left me, saying: "Doctor, I must go to my gun. If I get killed, tell my sweetheart that I died like a hero."

In two hours after that a cannon ball took his head off. He has buried on Whayne's Hill, where he fell.—Shortly after Breckinridge had made the desperate charge of Friday afternoon, a staff-officer on a black horse dashed up to the field hospital with an order: "Move up your ambulances at double-quick to yonder woodland," pointing to where the Orphans had gone in. There was now a mingled roar of continuous musketry and the thunder of artillery. An ambulance was hurried to Gen. Hanson. A brave surgeon of Louisiana artillery had found him near Graves's Battery, wounded with the cone of a shell. A cord was used as tourniquet, and he was hurriedly driven towards Murfreesboro'.

I met his ambulance and gave him a stimulant; his *aide*, Capt. Steve Chipley, was trying to control the artery; Lieut. Payne was holding his head; Gen. Breckinridge rode up—a few hurried but pathetic words passed between him and his wounded brigadier—and then he dashed away to look after his lines. Hanson did not utter a groan or speak a complaining word. When I had done the little it was possible to do there, he asked me to leave him with Chipley and go to the help of his wounded men.—About this time we found Lieut. Geo. Burnley with his leg all shattered; and as he could not then be moved we put him in a sink-hole to keep him from being torn to pieces with the enemy's shot and shell.—Dr. John O. Scott, (Second Kentucky).

4. "That's Our Flag!"—As the Second and Sixth Regiments retired from the river (and from the opposite side, where those who struck the stream first had gotten), Col. Lewis, directed an officer of the Sixth Kentucky, in answer to a question, to try to rally the men and make a stand just north of where Semple's five Napoleons were then in battery. The subaltern endeavoured to execute the order, and called on the few men then on that part of the field to dress on a flag with which a brave colour-bearer was faced to the front and standing fast. While the officer, within a feet of him, was directing attention to a body of the enemy coming up the slope a little to the left front, he heard a snap as of a blow against hard wood, and a glance at the colour-bearer showed that a splinter had been knocked from the staff and the man was pitching over as though desperately hurt.

He ran and seized the colours, but had hardly raised them when a soldier who had stood, firing, a little to his right, ran up saying, "That's our flag!" "Whose flag?" "It belongs to the Second Kentucky, sir, and I'll carry it!" It was promptly placed in the hands of the brave fellow; but as the officer was knocked over in a minute afterward, and was soon after a prisoner, he saw nothing more of the colours or the man. The flag of the Second Kentucky was carried off the field, after four colour-bearers had been killed within a space of about thirty feet, but whether this was the fifth man who took the banner and saved it, or whether he mistook somebody else's for his own, has not been determined, though inquiry has often been made.

5. *Must Be Killed With Due Formality.*—The following horrid parody of the form of sentence usually passed by courts-martial upon offenders condemned to death was perpetrated at Murfreesboro' in the autumn of 1862 by three officers of the Sixth Kentucky, who had been detailed to examine and report upon the condition of a diseased mule:

> We, the undersigned, a board appointed to examine a sick mule, respectfully report that in our opinion the said mule will never be fit for duty, and we do hereby recommend that he be shot to death in the presence of the wagoners.

6. *Sententious as Suvaroff.*—James P. Tolle, the chief musician of the Sixth Kentucky, had for one of his drummers John C. Valcour, of Co. G. He was a hard-headed, refractory soul, and one morning Tolle became exasperated and shut off the wind of his nimble-sticks for an indefinite and threatening length of time. This was reported to headquarters, whereupon came an order, duly headed, numbered and signed, to this effect:

> The Chief Musician is hereby placed under arrest for choking Valcour.

7. *Our One Military Execution.*—About the 4th of December, 1862, while the brigade was encamped near Murfreesboro', after its arrival from Knoxville, a young man of the Sixth Kentucky was found to be absent without leave. In a few days he was brought in under ar-

rest, having been captured between that point and Kentucky. He was one of the corporals of his company; had fought gallantly at Shiloh, Vicksburg, and Baton Rouge; and was every way a good and efficient soldier. Before a general court-martial convened in Polk's corps, December 1st, and still in session when he was arrested, he was arraigned for trial on a charge of desertion.

In the course of this trial it was brought out that in September or October, 1861, he enlisted for but one year, and that he did not hold the action of the regiment in reorganising for the remainder of the war as binding on those who did not individually re-enlist, which he claimed he had not done; that he was the son of an estimable widow with three daughters, for whose support and protection he had toiled—living with them and making them his chief care; that when he deemed it his duty to enter the army he provided for them a year's subsistence and left them all the money he could command; that he had expressed much solicitude concerning them, and had at last told his messmates that he meant to go home and make further provision for them, after which he would return and resume his place in the regiment; and that his conduct up to this time had been exemplary.

In spite of all this, however, and though ably represented by counsel, he was found guilty and adjudged to suffer death at such time and in such manner as the commanding general might direct. On the 20th of December, Bragg issued an order approving the action of the court, and fixing Friday, December 26th, as the day on which he should be executed by shooting in the presence of the brigade. Personal pleading on the part of his officers and friends was of no avail, and on the 25th a petition was filed with the commanding general, asking suspension of sentence pending an appeal to the President. This was signed by most of the commissioned officers of the brigade: but Bragg refused to grant it, alleging that desertions were frequent in his army and that the law must be rigidly enforced.

Gen. Breckinridge visited the condemned man in the Murfreesboro' jail that night, and told him that his efforts and those of others had proved unavailing; and to Breckinridge he gave his pocketbook, requesting him to give it to his brother. Col. (afterward General) Lewis, and his captain and first lieutenant visited him on the morning of the fatal day, to have some last talk with him as his feet stood now upon the brink of eternity. Knowing him and feeling a comrade's interest in him, what a dreadful interview was that! With a yet lingering hope, but without communicating it to him, the three went again to Gen.

Breckinridge to learn whether it were possible to move the commander; but they found that Bragg was inexorable. The field officer of the day, charged with the execution of the sentence, had detailed from the brigade guard one lieutenant, one non-commissioned officer, and fifteen men (three from each of the five regiments).

Three of the fifteen rifles were loaded with blank cartridges, so that there were twelve containing balls, and out of the fifteen men twelve were selected and given a rifle, but no one of the detail knew whether his contained a bullet. A circumstance should be related here, as at least one of the actors is yet living, and his conduct that day should be recorded, that now and henceforth he may be known and honoured of those who still believe that mercy should have been extended to this erring man. Two or three lieutenants were designated successively to command the men who were to do the shooting, as one after another begged not to be peremptorily ordered to do so, and was excused. At length that noble soldier and Christian gentleman, Lieut. G. B. Overton, of Co. E, Second Kentucky, was called and told that he must do it. "Colonel," he answered, "I'll give up my sword before I'll command that detail!" He was allowed to go and another was found.

The morning was cloudy, and at ten o'clock the rain began to fall heavily. At eleven, the hour fixed, the brigade was marched to its drill ground and aligned to make three sides of a hollow square. The clouds were lowering and the rain still fell, adding dreariness to the horrid scene. The condemned man was brought out in an open wagon, surrounded by his executioners. A hearse with coffin followed; then came the brigade officer of the day and some other officers on horseback. As the wagon passed near me, I could see the pale but firm countenance; the somewhat unnatural glare of his eyes when he looked upon those fellow-Kentuckians with whom he had fought and suffered as bravely as the best; and the sternly closed lips. He was placed standing with his back to the open space; his hands were bound, but he asked to be spared that last indignity, blindfolding, and so he stood looking full at the file of executioners ten paces in front of him.

Gen. Breckinridge dismounted and went and talked with him a little, then bade him goodbye, remounted his horse, and rode out of the lines. The lieutenant of the Guard, on horseback, a few paces in the rear, called out, "Ready!" The guns were brought in position for cocking, and *click! click! click!* went the hammers. Then the order, "Aim!" and a dozen rifles were levelled at the breast of our poor comrade. "Fire!" The sudden crash reverberated over the field, and he fell back dead. He was placed in the coffin, and the company buried him in accordance with his request, beside a cousin who had died at Murfreesboro' in the spring of 1862, when the brigade stopped there on its way to Corinth.

It was a horrifying spectacle. It was said that when the young man fell Gen. Breckinridge was seized with a deathly sickness, dropped forward on the neck of his horse, and had to be caught by some of his staff. If so, it was to the credit of the knightly leader whose presence on the field of battle was an inspiration. "The brave are ever kind," and only the desperately obdurate can look on with cold indifference when a fellow-soldier is shackled and shot down like a common malefactor.

8. *Col. Trabue at Stone River.*—As an instance of Trabue's perfect self-possession under the most trying circumstances, Capt. John B. Moore, of Greensburg, related the following: "When the brigade, reeling out of the fight, had reached the top of the hill from which the first lines of the enemy had been driven, a storm of shot and shell from more than fifty pieces of artillery, parked on the bluffs near the ford, was sweeping the ridge, and death to every man seemed imminent. Col. Trabue sat here on his horse, and while giving some directions he chanced to see a Yankee bugle lying on the ground nearby. 'There,' said he to one of my men, 'pick that up, Nichols. We'll need that.' And near this point, too, is said to have occurred a rather humorous incident, as such things would, even in the most trying hours.

"A soldier who seemed to have held on near the river a little longer than others, was now observed coming out, with rifle trailed, in a long gallop. His line of march naturally brought him near the colonel, who exclaimed: 'Halt, sir! don't run. You're in just as much danger running as you would be in a walk.' The man stopped a moment, and, looking up rather quizzically, bawled out in the uproar, 'Oh, yes, Colonel, I know that; but then, you see, we get away so much quicker.' and instantly set forward with even accelerated speed for a more eligible base upon which to rally."

9. *Not a "Butternut Cap'n."*—Occasional instances occurred in which the Kentuckians rather involuntarily made it manifest that they did not want to be mistaken for other people. Whenever the Orphans became convinced that this or that body of troops was thoroughly reliable and could be trusted to stand fast to their flank, or come promptly and gallantly to their relief in a crisis, their admiration was quickly kindled, and their praise unstinted, no matter what State such troops

came from. The term "butternut" was applied to the walnut-dyed jeans which was much worn by the Confederate soldiers in the Army of Tennessee, and by a natural metonymy the men themselves were "butternuts." (This, by the way of explaining what follows.) One afternoon soon after the Battle of Stone River, a young and rather gasconading Federal surgeon came into the temporary hospital, where Dr. Lytle was dressing the wound of Lieut. Frank Tryon, of the Second Kentucky.

The wound was a dreadful one, and the surgeon's work, albeit as carefully done as though the patient were one of his own blue-coats, was so painful that the sufferer seemed to be grinding his teeth, while his face was almost livid, though not a groan escaped him. The visiting surgeon, standing with his back to the fire, with his legs apart like the Colossus, stopped his general chatter long enough to ask: "Doctor, is that a butternut cap'n?"

Tryon forget his misery for the moment and turned his eyes on the questioner, and they flashed as he jerked out angrily, "No, sir! I'm none of your butternuts!"

Lytle, who was a thorough gentleman, was quick to apprehend, and he answered soothingly, "Oh, no! this is a Kentuckian."

That, of course, was to the point, and the sufferer relapsed into quiescence under his hands. Poor Frank! the sore place that a sight of his aspect and his misery made on my heart as he lay near me, and where he died soon after, remains with me, though the years of a generation have passed since then.

Chapter 9

Battle of Chickamauga

After the disastrous repulse of Friday evening, the weary night was passed, by the survivors, in the cold rain, at the old position, extending the line of Col. Hunt to the right—the men hovering over a little lire, except the line of pickets, or wrapped in wet, some in bloody blankets, while those of their wounded comrades who had fallen last were left to suffer the horrors of a long winter night, in their clotted gore, alone and unattended, perhaps to die, or to fall into the hands of their enemies,—little less to be dreaded than death. The morning that dawned upon the armies was scarcely less gloomy and cheerless to the Confederates than the night had been.

The day passed almost listlessly; then the enemy's advance, for the purpose of feeling the position, on the night of the 3rd, varied humdrum misery by putting the Confederate troops under arms. Then, on the early morning of the 4th, the retrograde movement began, under dispositions of the Kentucky Brigade mentioned by Col. Trabue.

Breckinridge's Division proceeded to Allisonia; thence, on the 8th of January, to Tullahoma, with the exception of the Ninth Kentucky, which was left at Manchester, and remained there some weeks alone, when the other regiments were sent back to that place.

Pending the decision of the War Department as to the promotion of Col. Trabue, to succeed Gen. Hanson, Gen. Marcus J. Wright was assigned to the command of the brigade, on the 17th of January. He continued with it but a short time, however, till it was ordered to Manchester, February 3, where it was under command of Col. Hunt till the arrival of Gen. Helm, who had been some time on post duty, on account of accident at Baton Rouge, but had now recovered sufficiently to take the field, and had been relieved from duty at Pollard, Alabama, to report to Gen. Breckinridge for assignment. He took command of the brigade on the 16th of February, and announced the following staff: Capt. G: W. McCawley, A. A. G.; Maj. Thomas H. Hays, A.I.G.; Maj. John R. Viley, Chief Quartermaster; Maj. S. M. Moorman, Chief Commissary; Lieut. L. E. Payne, Ordnance Officer; and Capt. S. B. Shepp and Lieut. William Wallace Herr, *aides-de-camp*. Capt. Fayette Hewitt, was added to the staff, on the 13th of May following, as A. and I. G.

There was now a long period of comparative inaction. From the time of arrival at Manchester and Tullahoma little occurred to vary the monotony of camp life, save the expedients resorted to by the men to kill time with a certain amount of what they denominated enjoyment. The routine of drill and guard service, picket and police, by day; dancing frolics with the girls in the neighbourhood at night, or theatricals and concerts in town, with the various amusements of the camp itself—these duties were performed and these pleasures enjoyed according to the tastes and dispositions of the men; and these, for the most part, constituted the life of more than three months there.

One little incident happened to create a more than momentary interest—the capture of McMinnville, and some of a hundred men of the brigade, who had been sent there on the 20th of March to guard stores—but military actions were rare with the infantry, and military achievements none. The cavalry under Forrest and Van Dorn was active, and, at Thompson's Station and Brentwood, in March, killed, wounded and captured almost the entire command of Col. Straight; but, up to sometime in April, the infantry was allowed to rest; and when movements began, they were simply marchings and countermarchings, initiatory, as it proved, to the final abandoning of that line of defence, and even of Tennessee.

Bragg's position was continually threatened, and picketing in force, with occasional movements apparently with a view to battle, took place during April and May. On the 23rd of April, the Kentucky Brigade was sent forward to Beech Grove, twelve miles in the direction of Murfreesboro', and remained here till the first of May, when Gen. Helm was ordered to take position at Jacobs' store, in the vicinity of Hoover's Gap—Hardee's whole corps having been advanced in that direction.

While here, the most noteworthy incident connected with the Kentucky Brigade was its trial drill with the brigade of Gen. Dan Adams. A challenge had been made by Gen. Adams, and accepted by Gen. Helm, and it was arranged that four regiments of each should be drilled against each other, beginning on the 19th of May, in the order of seniority of colonels. Matters were accordingly arranged, and, on the 19th, the Sixth Kentucky and Sixteenth Louisiana; on the 20th, the Second Kentucky and the Thirteenth and Twentieth Louisiana (consolidated); on the 21st, the Fourth Kentucky and Nineteenth Louisiana; and on the 22nd, the Ninth Kentucky and Thirty-Second Alabama were to contend for the championship of the army—not simply of the division, as it was matter of remark among Louisianians that Adams' brigade was the best drilled in the Army of Tennessee, while Kentuckians retorted that they themselves could beat the world on anything required of soldiers.

This kind of badgering naturally produced great, but friendly emulation, and on the day of trial each strove to do his best, and show all his strong points to the greatest advantage. The Second, Fourth, and Sixth met their respective regiments, and vanquished them—the judges, who were the mutual choice of the parties, deciding, in every instance, for "old Kentucky." The Ninth was deprived of trial, as a movement was inaugurated before the day on which it was to occur, but no doubt existed as to favourable decision in its case.

On these drill days a large concourse of people assembled to witness the display, and everything assumed, for the time, a gala-day air of lively enjoyment. The generals of the Army of Tennessee looked on with pleased admiration as the splendid movements were executed; while the citizens, men, women, and children, manifested a most enthusiastic interest.

On the 24th of May, Gen. Breckinridge marched, under orders, to Wartrace, where he was to take the cars for Mississippi, with all his force except the Tennesseans, for the purpose of re-enforcing Gen. Johnston in the attempt to relieve Pemberton, now closely besieged at Vicksburg.

Orders had been issued that the men should have three days' cooked rations in haversacks, and the Kentucky Brigade became impressed with the idea, by some means, that they were to go to Mississippi, though as yet no one not intimate at headquarters of division knew their destination. Their displeasure at the prospect of a return to a region where they had known little but want and suffering, in addition to the dangers they were always prepared to encounter, was great, and found vent in many expressions rather antithetical to good wishes for either Mississippi or Gen. Bragg. Gen. Breckinridge, knowing their feelings, appealed to Bragg to know whether he could not give him a brigade of Mississippians, who would naturally desire to return to their own State, and let the Kentucky Brigade remain where it would at least have the assurance of reaching Kentucky in case of a success to the Confederate arms.

Bragg left the matter to be decided by Gen. Breckinridge himself, and in this dilemma, he appealed to the brigade to know their choice. Having had them to assemble near his quarters, he explained to them the true state of the case. Though he made no allusion to the unpleasant feelings known to have been existing between himself and Bragg ever since the battle of Stone River—on account of Bragg's attempt to shift the loss of the battle to the shoulders of Gen. Breckinridge—the men seemed naturally to take this view of the case—that to stay was to decide for Bragg, whom they really despised, while to go would be to sustain their own general; and when called upon they voted without dissent to accompany him, and made their vote emphatic by the most enthusiastic cheering for Breckinridge, and expressions of their determination to stand by him through good and evil.

They accordingly took the train on the morning of May 25th, and were transported to Jackson, Mississippi, in common with the rest of the division, where they encamped on the 3rd of June, having previously remained, however, three or four days six miles from the city, at the point to which the railroad had been torn up some time previously by Gen. Grant.

The entire division of Breckinridge was encamped at Jackson, while the rest of the forces, then under immediate command of Johnston, for the relief of Vicksburg—the divisions of Loring, Walker, and French—were stationed in the neighbourhood of Canton.

Gen. Johnston was now making the most strenuous efforts to get sufficient force in hand to raise the siege of Vicksburg, but the condition of Bragg in Tennessee was such as precluded the practicability of having reinforcements from that army, while affairs in Virginia no less demanded the presence of all the troops now in that department, so that he was compelled to labour long and under many disadvantages to gather up a detachment here, another there, and little by little collect even enough with which to make a hazardous venture beyond the Big Black, for an attack upon the land force investing Vicksburg.

Breckinridge's division spent the whole month of June in the vicinity of Jackson, picketing, fortifying, and in little else than the commonplace routine. The condition of Gen. Pemberton had now become so critical, however, that delay was disaster, and though an advance on the part of Gen. Johnston was but a forlorn hope, it was resolved upon, and on the first day of July his troops were ordered forward. The march of fourteen miles that day was the most trying ever made by the command. The day was hot, almost to suffocation, and to add to the extreme difficulty with which the movement was effected, the roads were dry, and the sand rose in clouds to envelop the heated, panting column. Water was so scarce that even a reasonable supply could not be procured, and extreme thirst contributed to the fatigue and discomfort otherwise endured. Many fell out exhausted by the way, and some died of sunstroke. No one of the Kentuckians, however, suffered to that extreme.

The command encamped that afternoon two miles west of Clinton, but resumed the march at three o'clock on the morning of the 2nd, and went to Bolton's Station, where it was again halted, and encamped early in the day. Then there was no further movement till the evening of the 5th, at which time the division was moved six miles down the railroad and bivouacked in line of battle at Champion Hill; but next morning, Gen. Johnston having received information of the fall of Vicksburg, the return to Jackson began, and, on the afternoon of the 7th, the Kentucky Brigade went into camp on Pearl River, two miles below Jackson.

On the morning of the 9th, the approach of the Federals having been announced, the troops were placed in position, Breckinridge's division occupying the works between the Clinton road and the river, below Jackson, the Kentucky Brigade on the left of division, with its left flank resting on the river. The enemy appeared on the 10th, and besieged the place. The Confederates improved their half-finished works, and the sharpshooters and artillery of both armies were thenceforth engaged, more or less constantly till the 17th. Skirmishes between the advanced lines took place almost daily, and once during the week in which Gen. Johnston maintained his position there a heavy column of Federal troops made an attempt to break Breckinridge's centre, occupied by Stovall's brigade, supporting Cobb's Battery.

They were allowed to approach within short musket range, when Cobb opened upon them with grape and canister. Slocomb's Washington Artillery, of Adams' brigade, on the right, was also in position to rake the enemy's left. The right of the Kentucky Brigade, as well as the left of Adams', and the entire front of Gen. Stovall, began an irregular fire of musketry; but the dreadful discharges of the artillery could not be withstood. The enemy was instantly staggered, and, unable to advance, became confused, while the sweeping hail from the batteries mowed them down remorselessly till the living had escaped out of its deadly range, or made signs of surrender, to escape destruction. The only casualties to the Confederates were nine men of Cobb's Battery and three of Stovall's brigade, wounded; while the enemy lost two hundred killed outright, and two hundred and fifty wounded and prisoners. Five stands of colours fell into the hands of Stovall's brigade, and of the men of Cobb's and Slocomb's batteries.

An attempt was made immediately to bring off the wounded and bury the dead, but even the litter-bearers were fired on, and it was not till the 14th that the Federal commander would consent to a short truce for the burial of his dead, when the horrid task of interring two hundred mangled and now bloated corpses, the stench of which, at that hot season, was almost insufferable, devolved upon parties detailed from the various commands of Breckinridge's division.

The enemy gradually extended his lines and assumed a more and more threatening attitude; heavy skirmishing and artillery fire, having excellent range, occurring on both the 13th and 16th. Gen. Johnston, knowing his own weakness, and having ascertained the strength of the enemy, which he was not prepared to withstand, had taken the necessary precautions, and on the 16th withdrew by pontoon (the bridge having been destroyed) to the left bank of Pearl River, and began his march to Morton. The Kentucky Brigade was the rear-guard of the little army, but was not attacked, as the enemy did not press the pursuit in force, evidently inspired with caution, lest Gen. Johnston, whom they always seemed to suspect of some deep design, even when he was performing a most perilous feat of escaping from the toils of an overwhelming and well-appointed force, should inveigle them into a snare.

On the 18th, the brigade was encamped on Dead River, and remained there till the 21st, then moved about nine miles, encamping four miles east of Morton, and, a little subsequently, to the spot, some four miles from that point, which was afterward known as "Camp Hurricane."

This march of forty or fifty miles was, on the whole, a wretchedly disagreeable one, both on account of the warm and sometimes rainy weather, and the extreme scarcity of wholesome water, as well as the nature of the country through which the march was made. Gen. Helm, in a private letter to his wife, wrote, on the 22nd:

> As usual, we are on a grand retreat, the sufferings of which, so far as I am personally concerned, are unparalleled in the war. We have to drink water that, in ordinary times, you wouldn't

offer your horse; and I have hardly slept out of a swamp since we left Jackson. This is the sixth day, and we have not come much over forty miles. Our retreat is very slow and deliberate. The enemy have not annoyed us.

Here a month of inaction followed; the quietest, and with least duty to perform, ever enjoyed by the Kentucky Brigade. Gen. Breckinridge was then ordered to re-enforce Bragg at Chattanooga. The division left Camp Hurricane on the 26th of August, and proceeded by rail and steamer, by way of Mobile, to Chattanooga, or rather to Tyner's Station, where the brigade went into camp on the 2nd of September.

The health of the troops was now bad, and many of the division were consigned to hospitals; but those who were able for duty began; on the 8th of September, the initiatory movements to their part of the great Battle of Chickamauga; and after having marched and countermarched even more than is usually the case preliminary to an engagement, they found themselves, on the 18th, in bivouac near the Chickamauga River, which was to be made classic on the next two days by a sanguinary contest scarcely paralleled in the annals of civilized man. As in previous instances, it is wholly impracticable to enter into minute inquiry as to the entire conduct of that battle, and the actions of various troops engaged.

And even did the limits of our work admit, it would not be desirable, since we aspire to nothing of so comprehensive a nature. The following report of Gen. Breckinridge will enable the reader to understand the relative position of his division to the other divisions of the corps during the two days' fighting, as also the position of the Kentucky Brigade of that division; while the report of Gen. Lewis, following, records the special action of the brigade in question. It may be observed, however, that in August, Lieut.-Gen. D. H. Hill had reported for duty in the Army of Tennessee, and was placed in command of the corps of which Breckinridge's division formed a part.

Headquarters, Breckinridge's Division,
D. H. Hill's Corps, October, 1863.

Lieut.-Col. Archer Anderson, A. A. G. of Hill's Corps—

Sir: I have the honour to report the operations of my division in the Battle of Chickamauga on the 19th and 20th of September last.

It was composed of the Second, Fourth, Sixth, and Ninth Kentucky, and Forty-First Alabama Regiments, with Cobb's Battery, under the command of Brig.-Gen. B. H. Helm; the Thirteenth, Twentieth, Sixteenth, Twenty-Fifth, and Nineteenth Louisiana, Thirty-Second Alabama, and Austin's Battalion of Sharpshooters, with Slocomb's Battery (Fifth Washington Artillery), under the command of Brig.-Gen. Daniel Adams, (a native of Frankfort, Ky.); the First, Third, and Fourth Florida, Forty-Seventh Georgia, and Sixtieth North Carolina Regiments, with Mebane's Battery, under the command of Brig.-Gen. M. A. Stovall.

My effective strength was, of enlisted men, three thousand three hundred and ninety-five. Total, three thousand seven hundred and sixty-nine.

At daylight of the 18th my command moved from Catlett's Gap, and that neighbourhood, in the Pigeon Mountain, and the same afternoon took position on the east bank of the Chickamauga, near Glass's Mill, and composed the extreme left of the infantry of the army. I immediately threw the Second Kentucky across the ford to skirmish with the enemy and reveal his position, the Sixth Kentucky being placed in close supporting distance at the mill. Adams' brigade was sent by order of Lieut.-Gen. D. H. Hill to a ford a mile and a half above, where the enemy, as the cavalry reported, threatened to cross. It was so late when these dispositions were made that nothing satisfactory was developed that night.

On the morning of the 19th Slocomb, with four guns, Cobb, with two, and the remainder of Helm's brigade, were moved across Glass's Ford to ascertain the position of the enemy, while the two rifled pieces of Slocomb's Battery, under Lieut. Vaught, took position on a bluff upon the east side of the stream. An artillery engagement ensued much to our advantage, until the enemy, who occupied the better position, brought forward a number of heavy guns, and showed the greater weight of metal. (This was the celebrated artillery duel of Maj. Graves.) While the engagement was progressing, I received an order from Lieut.-Gen. Hill to withdraw my command, if it could be done without too great peril, and take position about three miles south of Lee and Gordon's Mill, on the road leading from Chattanooga to Lafayette, and so as to cover the approach to that road from Glass's Mill and the ford above; leaving a regiment and section of artillery to observe those crossings.

The movement was made in good order, Col. Dilworth, with the First and Third (consolidated) Florida, and a section of Cobb's Battery being left in observation. Our casualties, which fell upon Slocomb, Cobb and Helm, were twenty-two killed and wounded. The loss of the enemy in killed alone, as shown by an examination of the ground after the 20th, was nearly equal to the sum of our casualties. Although the enemy was in considerable strength at the fords above referred to, the result showed that it was a covering force to columns passing down the valley to unite with the centre and left of his army.

Soon after taking up the new position, I was ordered to relieve Brig.-Gen. Patton Anderson's division, which was facing the enemy opposite Lee and Gordon's Mill. The troops marched rapidly, yet it was late in the afternoon before this movement was completed. The division was hardly in position when I received an order from the general commanding the army to move to the right, cross the Chickamauga at a point farther down, and occupy a position to be indicated. The division crossed at Alexander's bridge, and arriving between ten and eleven o'clock at night at a field about a mile and a half in the rear of the right of our line of battle, bivouacked there by order of Lieut.-Gen. Polk.

Remaining some time at Lieut.-Gen. Polk's campfire, I left there two hours before daylight (the 20th) to place my command in position. During the night Gen. Polk informed me that I was to prolong the line of battle upon the right of Maj.-Gen. Cleburne. Conducted by an officer of his staff and Lieut. Reid, *aide-de-camp* to Gen. Hill, my division reached Cleburne's right a little after daybreak. Upon the readjustment of his line, I formed on his right, and became the extreme right of the general line of battle. Helm was on the left of my line, Stovall in the centre, and Adams on the right, the last extending across a country road leading from Reid's bridge and striking the Chattanooga road at a place called Glenn's farm. The country was wooded, with small openings, and the ground unknown to me. Our skirmishers, a few hundred yards in advance, confronted those of the enemy. Our line was supposed to be parallel with the Chattanooga road.

Soon after sunrise, I received a note from Lieut.-Gen. Polk directing me to advance, and about the same time Maj.-Gen. Cleburne, who happened to be with me, received one of the same tenor. Lieut.-Gen. Hill having arrived, the notes were placed in his hands; by his order the movement was delayed for the troops to get their rations, and on other accounts.

Dilworth, who had been relieved by a cavalry force late the preceding evening, and who had marched all night, now arrived and took his place in line. At half-past nine a.m., by order of Lieut.-Gen. Hill, I moved my division forward in search of the enemy. At a distance of seven hundred yards we came upon him in force, and the battle was opened by Helm's brigade with great fury.

The Second and Ninth Kentucky, with three companies of the Forty-first Alabama Regiment, encountered the left of a line of breastworks before reaching the Chattanooga road, and though assailing them with great courage, were compelled to pause. From some cause, the line of my left had not advanced simultaneously with my division, and in consequence, from the form of the enemy's works, these brave troops were at first, in addition to the fire in front, subjected to a severe enfilading fire from the left. The rest of Helm's brigade, in whose front there were no works, after a short but sharp engagement, routed a line of the enemy, pursued it across the Chattanooga road, and captured a section of artillery posted in the centre of the road.

This portion of the brigade was now brought under a heavy front and enfilading fire, and being separated from its left and without support, I ordered Col. Joseph H. Lewis, of the Sixth Kentucky, who succeeded to the command upon the fall of Gen. Helm, to withdraw the troops some two hundred yards to the rear, reunite the brigade, and change his front slightly to meet the new order of things, by throwing forward his right and retiring his left. The movement was made without panic or confusion.

This was one of the bloodiest encounters of the day. Here Gen. Helm, ever ready for action, and endeared to his command by his many virtues, received a mortal wound while in the heroic discharge of his duty. Col. Hewitt, of the Second Kentucky, was killed, acting gallantly at the head of his regiment. Captains Madeira, Rogers, and Dedman, of the Second, Capt. Daniel, of the Ninth Kentucky, and many other officers and men met their deaths before the enemy's works; while Col. Nuckols, of the Fourth Kentucky, Col. Caldwell, of the Ninth, and many more officers and men were wounded. (Col. Nuckols received his wound while leading the Fourth, as skirmishers, and in conflict with a strong force of the enemy, sometime before.)

In the meantime, Adams and Stovall advanced steadily, driving back two lines of skirmishers. Stovall halted at the Chattanooga road. Adams, after dispersing a regiment and capturing a battery, crossed at Glenn's farm, and halted a short distance beyond in an open field.

When Helm's Brigade was checked, and I had given Col. Lewis orders in reference to his new position, I rode to the commands of Adams and Stovall on the right. It was now evident, from the comparatively slight resistance they had encountered, and the fact that they were not threatened in front, that our line extended beyond the enemy's left. I at once ordered these brigades to change front perpendicularly to the original line of battle, and with the left of Adams and the right of Stovall resting on the Chattanooga road, to advance upon the flank of the enemy. Slocomb's Battery, which had previously done good service, was posted on favourable ground on the west of the road to support the movement.

The brigades advanced in fine order over a field, and entered the woods beyond. Stovall soon encountered the extreme left of the enemy's works, which, retiring from the general north and south direction of his entrenchments, extended westwardly nearly to the Chattanooga road. After a severe and well contested conflict, he was checked and forced to retire. Adams, on the west of the road, met two lines of the enemy, who had improved the short time to bring reinforcements and reform nearly at a right angle to the troops in his main line of works.

The first line was routed, but it was found impossible to break the second, aided as it was by artillery; and after a sanguinary contest, which reflected high honour on the brigade, it was forced back in some confusion. Here Gen. Adams, who is as remarkable for his judgment on the field as for his courage, was severely wounded, and fell into the hands of the enemy.

Lieut.-Col. Turner, of the Nineteenth Louisiana, was wounded, and the gallant Maj. Butler, of the same regiment, was killed.

Stovall had gained a point beyond the angle of the enemy's main line of works; Adams had advanced still farther, being actually in rear of his entrenchments. A good supporting line of my division at this moment would probably have produced decisive results. As it was, the engagement on our right had inflicted heavy losses, and compelled him to weaken other parts of the line to hold his vital point. Adams' Brigade reformed behind Slocomb's Battery, which repulsed the enemy by a rapid and well-directed fire, rendering, on this occasion, important and distinguished service.

By order of Lieut.-Gen. Hill, my division was withdrawn a short distance to recruit, while the troops of Maj.-Gen. Walker engaged the enemy. My new line was about six hundred yards in advance of the position on which I formed first in the morning, with a slight change of direction, which brought my right relatively nearer the Chattanooga road. Soon after taking this position, an attack was reported on our right flank. It proved to be Granger's corps coming up from Rossville, and threatening our right with a part of his force.

At the request of Brig.-Gen. Forrest, I sent him a section of Cobb's Battery, under the command of Lieut. Gracey, who assisted handsomely in repulsing the enemy.

At the request of the brigade commanders, the artillery of the division had been ordered to report to the brigades with which they were accustomed to serve. Cobb's Battery, from the nature of the ground, could not participate to its accustomed extent, yet, as opportunity offered, it displayed its usual gallantry. The excellent battery of Capt. Mebane, for the same reason, was able to take little part in the action.

The afternoon was waning, and the enemy still obstinately confronted us in his entrenchments.

I received permission from Lieut.-Gen. Hill to make another charge. A line of troops on my right, and covering a part of my front, advanced at the same time. A portion of these troops obliqued to the right, and my line passed through the rest, who seemed to be out of ammunition, so that after moving a few hundred yards, the enemy alone was in my front. The division advanced with intrepidity, under a severe fire, and dashed over the left of the entrenchments. In passing them I saw on my left the right of Maj.-Gen. Cleburne, whose brave division stormed the centre.

Several hundred of the enemy ran through our lines to the rear, the rest were pursued several hundred yards and beyond the Chattanooga road; of these some were killed, and a good many taken prisoners, but most of them escaped through the darkness. It was now night; pursuit. was stopped by order of Lieut.-Gen. Hill, and, throwing out pickets, I bivouacked in line near the road.

The prisoners taken by my command, of whom there was a considerable number, were allowed to go to the rear, since details could not be spared for them, and it was known they would be gathered up there.

The division captured nine pieces of artillery. I am aware that it is usually the whole army, not a part of it, that takes guns from the enemy, and that often the troops who obtain possession of them owe their good fortune quite as much to fire from the right and left as to their own efforts. Yet I think it due to my command to say that in regard to six at least of these guns such considerations do not apply, and that they were taken without assistance from any other troops.

My total casualties, as shown by official reports, were twelve hundred and forty, of which number one hundred and sixty-six were killed, nine hundred and nine wounded, and one hundred and sixty-five missing.

To Brig.-Gen. Stovall, to Col. Lewis, who succeeded to the command of Helm's brigade, and to Col. Randall L. Gibson, (a native of

Woodford county, Ky.), who succeeded to the command of Adams' brigade, the country is indebted for the courage and skill with which they discharged their arduous duties.

The officers and men of the division, with exceptions so rare as to place in striking contrast to them the general good conduct sustained their former reputation, and were alike worthy of each other.

To the gentlemen of my staff I feel sincere gratitude for the prompt, fearless, and cheerful manner in which they discharged their duties.

Maj. Wilson, assistant adjutant-general; Col. Von Zinken, A. I. General, who had two horses shot under him; Capt. Mastin, A. I, General, who received a contusion from a grape-shot; Lieut. Breckinridge, *aide-de-camp*, whose horse was shot; Capt. Semple, ordnance officer; Lieut. Berties (Twentieth Louisiana), A. A. I. G.; Dr. Heustis, chief surgeon; Dr. Kratz, on duty in the field, and Messrs. McGehee, Coleman, Mitchell, and Clay, volunteers on my staff, performed their duties in a manner to command my confidence and regard.

One member of my staff I cannot thank. Maj. R. E. Graves, chief of artillery, received a mortal wound in the action of Sunday, the 20th. Although a very young man, he had won eminence in arms, and gave promise of the highest distinction. A truer friend, a purer patriot, a better soldier never lived.

I am, colonel, very respectfully, your obedient servant,

John C. Breckinridge,
Major-General, P. A., C. S.

Indorsement of Report.

In speaking of the final attack on the afternoon of the 20th, Gen. Breckinridge employs a phrase in a different sense from its ordinary meaning. He says: "I received permission from Lieut.-Gen. Hill to make another charge." The facts in the case are simply these: About 3:30 p. m., or it may be a little later, I ordered another major-general, not of my corps, but who had been sent to report to me, to make the attack, telling him that Breckinridge's men, after their repulse, were scarcely in a condition to make another charge. He replied, "My division was sent by Gen. Polk as a support to Gen. Breckinridge, and, under my orders, I can do nothing more than support him." I then returned to Gen. Breckinridge, told him of this conversation, and asked him if his troops were ready to renew the attack. He answered, "Yes, I think they are."

I then added, "Well, then, move promptly, and strike hard."

The division responded to the order with a cheer, moved off in beautiful style, and made a most glorious charge.

D. H. Hill, Lieutenant-General.

Headquarters Helm's Brigade,
Before Chattanooga, September 30, 1863.

Major James Wilson, Assistant Adjutant General—

Sir: The death of Brig.-Gen. B. H. Helm makes it my duty, as senior colonel commanding, to report the part taken by this brigade in the action of the 19th and 20th instants:

On the afternoon of the 18th, the brigade took position on the right bank of West Chickamauga, near Glass's Mill, except the Second Kentucky Regiment, deployed on the opposite side as skirmishers.

On the morning of the 19th, the command, with Cobb's Battery, crossed the stream. About nine a.m., a shot from the battery, into a house about five hundred yards off, where the enemy's skirmishers were concealed, excited an immediate response from the enemy further to the right, followed soon after by a spirited artillery duel, in which Slocomb's Battery, also, which had, in the meantime, crossed over, participated, resulting in silencing the enemy. Soon, however, another battery of the enemy opened fire still farther to the right. In a short time, orders having been issued from Maj.-Gen. Breckinridge to that effect, the whole command recrossed the stream and moved to the Chattanooga road. Fourteen men of this brigade were killed and wounded on this occasion.

From thence we moved toward Chattanooga, to the position held by and relieving Deas' brigade. About two hours after nightfall we reached a point one and one-half miles beyond Alexander's bridge, where we bivouacked until three a.m., 20th instant, when we were ordered to our position in line of battle one mile or more beyond and on the left of the division. We got into position and were ready to advance by about half-past five a.m. Soon after getting into position, one company from each regiment was, under command of Lieut.-Col. Wickliffe, of the Ninth Kentucky, deployed two hundred and fifty yards in advance as skirmishers. Becoming hotly engaged with the enemy, the Fourth Kentucky Regiment, Col. Nuckols commanding, was ordered to their support. The skirmishers of the enemy, having the advantage in position, showed determination and kept up a rapid fire, wounding several officers and men before the advance of the brigade. Among others severely wounded was Col. Nuckols, by which his command was thereafter deprived of the services of this gallant and meritorious officer.

Between nine and ten a.m., the brigade advanced in the following order, *viz*.: the Sixth Kentucky, Col. Lewis, and the Second Kentucky, Lieut.-Col. Hewitt commanding, on the extreme right and left respectively. The Fourth Kentucky, Maj. Thompson, and Ninth Kentucky, Col. Caldwell commanding, on the right and left centre respectively, and the Forty-First Alabama, Col. Stansil commanding, in the centre.

The enemy's fortifications did not extend the entire length of the brigade front, but the Sixth and Fourth, and seven companies of the Forty-First, in advancing, passed to the right and clear of them, consequently fighting the foe on something like equal terms. This portion of the command, with but a momentary halt and no hesitation, steadily drove the enemy back to within one hundred yards of the Chattanooga road, when I discovered a battery of two Napoleon guns fifty yards beyond the road. Here I also discovered, for the first time, what the thicker growth of timber had prevented me from observing before, that the left of the brigade was considerably in rear. Neither a halt nor retreat at this time was, in my judgment, proper or allowable. So, the command was given to take the battery, and it was done. Soon after crossing the road, Capt. McCawley, of Gen. Helm's staff, informed me that the general had been mortally wounded, near the position occupied by the left of the brigade.

The right not being then under fire, I left it in command of Lieut. Col. Cofer, and started, on Capt. McCawley's horse, to where the other portion of the brigade was. I encountered considerable difficulty in reuniting the brigade, on account of the distance apart and the want of staff aid, having no one with me but Capt. Hewitt, and not him immediately, on account of the loss of his horse. Although not personally cognisant of the behaviour of the left of the brigade previous to assuming command, yet I am warranted, by information of an entirely satisfactory kind, in speaking of it. Justice to the living, and affectionate memory of the dead, make it a duty and a pleasure to allude to their conduct in terms of praise.

After advancing about four hundred yards, they encountered a heavy musketry and artillery fire in front, and also an enfilading fire from the left, which the failure of the command to their left, to advance simultaneously with Breckinridge's division, enabled the enemy to pour into their ranks. Besides, I am satisfied they were subjected to a fire on their right from the two pieces subsequently captured by the right of the brigade. Yet three several times this devoted little band charged the enemy, securely fortified and in a favourable position. Though necessarily repulsed, their frightful loss shows their constancy and bravery.

Here the kind, pure, brave Brig.-Gen. B. H. Helm was mortally wounded, heroically doing his duty. Lieut.-Col. James W. Hewitt, in advance of his regiment, and showing a devotion and daring entitled to the highest commendation, was killed. Col. Caldwell was severely wounded, as usual, in his place, doing his duty. Robert C. Anderson, colour-sergeant Second Kentucky, was killed upon the enemy's works, after having planted his colours thereon. Here fell many another officer and soldier, life images of Kentucky's old, renowned, and valiant soldiers, true men. The blood of her sons also attest Alabama's chivalry and manhood.

As soon as I ascertained the exact position of the left, I caused it to be moved, by the right flank, to the right, and in advance of where it was then, till the right of the brigade, under command of Lieut.-Col. Cofer, was met—he having recrossed the road—when I formed the brigade in line of battle nearly perpendicular to the road and to the enemy's works. About this time, I received orders from Lieut.-Gen. Hill, through one of his staff, not to advance, but to await the arrival of fresh troops. In a short time, Gist's brigade attacked the enemy, passing through my lines for that purpose, but was drawn back.

Ector's brigade then advanced, but, being unable to drive the enemy from his works, finally fell back, leaving this brigade again to confront the enemy. My men, though at this time nearly exhausted by several hours hard fighting, and suffering greatly for want of water, remained firm, no one leaving his place. After the repulse of the other two brigades, I was ordered to retire several hundred yards to the rear to rest the men, which was done in good order and without confusion.

Late in the afternoon Walker's division advanced against the enemy, a portion of it attacking the same point the left of this brigade did in the morning. Being with my command about four hundred yards in rear at that time, and out of sight of the combatants, I could not see with what result the attack was made, though a short time thereafter Cheatham's division moved to the attack over the same ground—Wright's brigade, of that division, passing through the lines of this brigade. After some time had elapsed, and it appearing from the firing that no appreciable advantage had been gained, this brigade was moved forward, being on the left of the division.

In advancing, it was discovered that the centre brigade of the division lapped on mine, making it necessary for me to oblique to the left about two hundred yards. It was also necessary to advance the left more rapidly than the right wing, in order to get on a line more parallel with the enemy. Both these difficult movements were executed while marching through the woods, without any material derangement of the line, the command moving steadily and unfalteringly forward.

Upon arriving in sight of the enemy's fortifications, the brigade rapidly charged upon them, driving them from their stronghold, in confusion, toward the Chattanooga road. The pursuit was continued across an open field till the road was reached, when, it being dark, I judged it prudent to halt, which met the approval of Lieut.-Gen. Hill, who, close after us, immediately came up. In passing through the fortifications, a number of prisoners were captured and sent, to the rear. We also captured two pieces of artillery in the road, which our rapid pursuit of the enemy prevented their carrying off—one Napoleon and one James rifle. The nature of the ground (woodland) prevented Cobb's Battery performing the important part in this action he and his gallant company have so often done, and knew so well how to do—though, in the afternoon, one section, under the gallant and faithful Gracey, was placed in position under Gen. Forrest. I refer you to Capt. Cobb's report for an account of their behaviour on that occasion.

I am not enabled to state the exact number engaged in the actions of the 19th and 20th. But one thousand three hundred is the approximate number of officers and men, including Cobb's Battery. The whole number of casualties were sixty-three killed and four hundred and eight wounded.

It would afford me pleasure to designate, by name, the officers and men who so gallantly fought on these two occasions, for, with very few exceptions, all did their duty; but to do so would swell this report to an inordinate size. However, I feel it to be my duty, and take pleasure in the performance of it, to call attention to the conduct of the field officers of the different regiments. Lieut.-Col. Cofer, in command of the Sixth, after I took command of the brigade; Maj. Clark, of the same regiment; Maj. Thompson, in command of the Fourth, after Col. Nuckols was wounded; Capt. Millet, senior captain, acting field officer, of the same regiment; and Maj. Nash, in command of the seven companies of the Forty-first Alabama, all came under my observation.

In each I remarked constancy, gallantry, and coolness. In the afternoon, Col. Stansil, of the Forty-first; Lieut.-Col. Wickliffe, in command of the Ninth, after Col. Caldwell was wounded; and Capt. Gillam, acting field officer, of the same regiment, attracted my notice, and but confirmed the good account I had of them in the morning. Capt. Lee, of the Second Kentucky, though too unwell to endure the fatigue throughout the day, acted as field officer with his accustomed bravery in the charges made by the left in the morning.

It is the highest praise I can possibly bestow on the officers of the brigade, to say they proved themselves, in nearly every case, worthy of their commands.

Of the staff of Brig.-Gen. Helm, I take pleasure in bearing testimony in behalf of, and making special mention of Capt. Fayette Hewitt, assistant adjutant-general. As soon as he was enabled to do so, he reported to me, and throughout the entire action, after the death of Gen. Helm, as well as previous thereto, as I learn, he displayed coolness, gallantry, and judgment.

Capt. G. W. McCawley, assistant inspector-general, promptly reported to me the wounding of Gen. Helm, as before stated, at which time I got from him his horse, not having my own with me, when he returned to where Gen. Helm was wounded and remained with him. I am reliably informed that, previous thereto, he was in his place on the left, and acted bravely and efficiently.

Capt. Helm, acting commissary of subsistence, though not compelled to do so, went on the field and did his duty.

Lieut. William Wallace Herr, *aide-de-camp*, and Lieut. John B. Pirtle, acting *aide-de-camp*, reported to me as soon as the necessary attention to their wounded general allowed, and thereafter acted gallantly and faithfully.

I enclose the several reports of regimental and battery commanders, together with a list of killed and wounded.

I am, very respectfully, your obedient servant,

Joseph H. Lewis,
Colonel Commanding Helm's Brigade.

The Fifth Kentucky fought at Chickamauga in Kelley's brigade of Preston's division, and of course is not noticed in the preceding reports. It behaved with conspicuous courage and steadiness and received honourable mention from both its division and brigade commanders. A number of the officers were specially commended in reports. The following report of Col. Hiram Hawkins, commanding, is published here, as the connection of the Fifth with the other regiments of the brigade began substantially with this battle:

Headquarters Fifth Kentucky,
Near Chattanooga, October 20, 1863.

Lieut. Mastin, A. A. G., Reliefs Brigade:

Sir: As directed, I submit the following report of the operations of my command, on the 19th and 20th *ultimo*, in the Battle of Chickamauga:

My position was on the left of your brigade, in line of battle ready for action on the 19th; frequently shelled during the day.

On the 20th, marched in my position in line over the battlefield some three miles (frequently under fire and in range of shells and canister from the enemy's guns), when we came up to the enemy in strong position on a range of hills. We were immediately ordered to charge. My men rushed forward, reserving their fire until within a very short range, and, after a desperate struggle, drove the enemy before them, and crossed the bridge under a heavy cross-fire from the left and very direct, and a cross-fire from the right, at least eighty yards in advance of the brigade, driving the enemy from my front, when the command on my left rallied, moved forward, and drove the enemy from my left.

I then moved by the right flank and rejoined my brigade. The enemy, still firing on me from the right, soon with great fury assailed my front. I ordered my command forward, swinging a little to the right, and again drove the enemy and crossed the ridge some forty paces in advance of the brigade, and nearly silenced the fire in my front, and was directing my fire to the right when part of Col. Trigg's command passed to my left, covering part of my front. My ammunition being nearly exhausted, I ordered my men to fall back and rejoin the brigade, and replenish their boxes with ammunition from the dead and wounded, as far as practicable.

Col. Palmer, having been moved from the right to the left, placed my command in centre of the brigade, which was ordered forward by the colonel commanding. Changing direction to the right, (it then being near dusk), we moved but a short distance, when a line of battle was discovered forty to sixty yards distant, who first announced that they were friends and then that they surrendered. Stealing this advantage, they treacherously fired upon us, killing and wounding several of my men and officers. Among the killed was Lieut. Yates, a brave and gallant officer. The same volley shattered the leg of Capt. Calvert, who has since died.

My men, recovering from the temporary surprise caused by the treachery, reformed, and, with fixed bayonets, advanced on the enemy, joined by Maj. French, then by Col. Palmer, in conjunction with Col. Trigg, and captured two regiments of the enemy, who surrendered to Col. Trigg during Col. Kelley's temporary absence. As the column began moving with the prisoners a volley was fired into our ranks, causing a good deal of confusion, it then being nightfall. Many of the prisoners scattered. Col. Trigg's command moved off, leaving them. They would have made their escape had I not recaptured them (249, including three field officers). Moved them from the battleground and turned them over to Lieut.-Col. Wade, except the three field officers, who were sent by Col. Kelley to division headquarters.

My loss was fourteen killed on the field, seventy-five wounded, one captured, and one missing.

Maj. Mynheir fell severely wounded while urging the men forward in making first charge.

Capt. Jo Desha was wounded early in the action (shot through the arm near the shoulder); remained on the field with his company until the enemy was ours.

Although this was the first time, with few exceptions, that my officers or men were under fire, they behaved with becoming gallantry and courage, never faltering when ordered forward.

Lieut.-Col. G. W. Conner and Adjt. Thos. B. Cook displayed great gallantry and coolness, and deserve honourable mention.

My company officers and men, with few exceptions, seemed to vie with each other in deeds of gallantry.

Very respectfully,

H. Hawkins,
Colonel Commanding Regiment.

INCIDENTS AND ANECDOTES: FROM MURFREESBORO' TILL AFTER CHICKAMAUGA.

1. Danger in Loose Orders.—We are indebted to a member of the Ninth Regiment for the following little incident, which shows that our honoured corps commander, Gen. Hardee, entertained an idea that when danger was to be encountered, orders to Col. Hunt, at the head of Kentucky soldiers, should be cautiously worded, as, in case of doubt, he would be sure not to take counsel of fear, but would make things clear on that score, be the hazard what it might,:

While the brigade was at Beech Grove, Gen. Bragg directed Gen.

Hardee to send him out with his own and another regiment towards Murfreesboro', with orders "to proceed as far as he possibly could." Gen. Hardee transmitted the order, as in duty bound, but immediately rode over to Gen. Bragg's headquarters, and told him that it would never do to start Hunt with those Kentuckians towards Murfreesboro', with such an order as that, "for they wouldn't stop this side of hell!" The consequence was, that, about midnight, while the boys were busy cooking and preparing to take an early start for that uncertain point, the order was countermanded.

2. *The Best Drilled Regiments in the Army of Tennessee.*—At Beech Grove there was a beautiful piece of grassy bottom land surrounded by smoothest green bluffs, which was set apart and used for drilling purposes by the various military bodies in the vicinity. On this drill ground about the middle of May occurred a grand match drill between the First Kentucky Brigade, commanded then by Col. Trabue and the First Louisiana Brigade, commanded by Gen. Adams. A good deal of friendly rivalry had existed between the two brigades, and all things being propitious, a challenge was given and accepted. Each brigade had the same number of regiments, (five), and these were to match each other according to seniority, the contest to end with a match brigade drill. Col. John C. Brown, afterward Governor of Tennessee, and a colonel, whose name I have forgotten, were chosen judges, and Gen. W. J. Hardee, umpire.

The day appointed for the first contest arrived, and large numbers of the citizens in the country round about assembled on the grassy slopes, overlooking the drill field, to witness what was to be to them a strange spectacle—and so on from day to day. The boys, arrayed in their best uniforms, and officers with swords flashing in the sunshine, vied with each other in precision of step and celerity of movement in the evolutions taught in the "School of the Battalion." The contest was long and earnest, and finally resulted in the triumph of each of the Kentucky regiments over its competitor. (The Ninth Kentucky was deprived of trial by the brigades being moved before its day arrived, but it would have won.)

The victory was the more gratifying to the Kentuckians because of the excellency of their Louisiana competitors; for there was no other body of troops in the western army which rivalled the Louisiana brigade in soldierly accomplishments. The Fourth Kentucky Regiment, commanded by Col. Joseph P. Nuckols, was pitted against the Nineteenth Louisiana regiment, commanded by Col. Von Zinken, a

Prussian and a splendid soldier. His broken English on the drill-field was the source of much amusement to the boys. The intended drill between the two brigades was deferred from time to time, and finally declared off.—Thomas Owens, (Fourth Kentucky).

3. *Should Have "Stood Pat.*—Co. H, Sixth Kentucky, had among its non-commissioned officers James M. Lee, of Bullitt County, who was a wag, a good soldier, and a general favourite. This story will be appreciated by gentlemen who have indulged in a certain game sufficiently to understand the allusion: As Gen. Johnston's troops were returning from Big Black that hot July day, after the unsuccessful attempt to strike Grant's rear before he could compel the capitulation of Pemberton at Vicksburg, the Kentucky Brigade was marching as rapidly as possible with the expectation of camping somewhere near Clinton.

The sand was deep, the water very scarce, (as previously noticed); and as the men struggled forward, enveloped in a cloud of dust, and almost suffocated, they were naturally anxious to know, from time to time, something about how far the hoped-for resting-place was yet in the distance. Meeting a citizen riding alongside of the panting column, someone in hearing of Sergt. Lee asked him how far to Clinton. "Four miles," was the answer. Having gone some distance farther they met another, of whom the same man asked again how far to Clinton. "Six miles," answered this one. Jim couldn't keep silent under this, but yelled out, as he puffed with fatigue, while his eyes lighted up with a momentary interest under the coating of sand which had settled over and around them: "By me sowl, Patrick," (in imitation of an Irishman, though he was an unadulterated native), "by me sowl, Patrick, why didn't ye stand? He's raised you two!"

4. *After Jackson: in Danger of Surfeit.*—While the brigade was at Camp Hurricane, Miss., summer of 1863, a considerable part of the daily ration consisted of roasting ears, which the commissary procured by impressment or purchase from the surrounding plantations. This would have answered admirably if merely additional to a fair supply of other food; but when other food was deficient in quantity and quality, and even the roasting ears, though in excess of the rest, had to be doled out, the reader can easily conceive that the food was hardly sufficient to keep up the daily and nightly supply of blood which the persistent mosquito took not only without leave but in spite of bitter opposition. As usual, however, the men made merry over it instead of cursing their hard fate, and the cry, when rations had to be distributed, was, "Come, draw your corn!"—and neighing was resorted to as a

reminder that they were hungry. After a time, they came to complain with mock earnestness that they were not furnished oats, hay, or fodder—they were in danger of taking the equine disease of surfeit, they said, for want of "long forage."

5. *How They Jollied Kelley.*—On Johnston's retreat from Jackson, noticed in the preceding chapter, the Military Court of the army lost orderlies and baggage, and at Morton the fact was communicated to Gen. Hardee, who advised that inquiry be made by circular letter through the commanders of divisions. The following reached the headquarters of Gen. Breckinridge:

Morton, Miss, July 28th, 1863.
General: In the retreat from Jackson the wagon and orderlies of the Military Court of this army became separated from the court, and have not been found. At the suggestion of Gen. Hardee, I respectfully request that you have inquiry made for them through the limits of your command, and that, if found, you order them to report immediately to the court at Morton.

Very respectfully, your obedient servant,

Henry B. Kelley,
Colonel and Member Military Court.

Thereupon circular letters of inquiry were issued to each of Breckinridge's commanders, who sent them to their subordinates to be indorsed with such information as they might be able to give. The one that reached Gen. Helm, then commanding the Kentucky Brigade, started from his headquarters with the following endorsement:

Has anybody found a Military Court lying around loose?

Fayette Hewitt, A. A. G.

The regimental commanders also made merry over it, and it came back endorsed as follows:

If this court understands herself (and she think she do), she haint seen that court.

James W. Hewitt,
Lieutenant-Colonel Commanding
Second Kentucky Infantry.

Narry sich as that about the Fourth Regiment.

John A. Adair,
Colonel Commanding.

I hain't neither seen nor hearn of a thing like that.

John W. Caldwell,
Colonel Ninth Regiment.

6. *At Chickamauga: Too Big a Wood-Chopping for the Major.*—At one time during the battle, as the brigade was pressing forward under fire, some troops belonging to another organisation were coming back helter-skelter and meeting the Second Regiment, having met with such a reception from the Federal advance that they broke. Among them was a major whose appearance indicated that he was acting on the plan of every fellow for himself and let the enemy's bullets take the hindmost. He came plunging towards Col. McDowell, who threw out his arms and caught him (hugged him, the boys said), exclaiming, "Hello, major! This is the biggest wood-chopping you were ever at, ain't it?" Old soldiers will recall how the term woodchopping pretty fairly represents the repetition of volleys following each other in regular and pretty close succession.

7. *Supposing a Case.*—During the heat of engagement on the second day, Sergt. Wm. W. Franklin, of Co. E, Sixth Kentucky, discovered a man smartly in rear of the line, behind a tree, where his firing, if he fired at all, would endanger his own men. This man had previously made it apparent that he "wanted to live always," and Franklin objected to favouring him, so in pursuance of his duty as file closer, he ran and hauled him out, ordering him in no gentle terms to get into line. "Say!" cried the fellow, "didn't you see that cannon ball? Suppose it had hit me—it would have killed me!"

"Oh, suppose!" replied Franklin, as he drew him into place, "suppose you were a pig, rooting in a potato patch; but you're not!"

8. *Spoilt His Beauty and Enraged Him.*—Konshattountzchette, or Flying Cloud, of Co. H, Ninth Kentucky, the Mohawk Indian chief who seemed to have chosen the life of a soldier of fortune, was a handsome man—tall and symmetrical, with fairly good features. Occasionally he seemed to tire of conforming wholly to white men's ways, and would stalk about camp with his blanket over his shoulders and drawn about him Indian fashion, and wearing a head-gear of band and feathers.

Being something of a curiosity and a good soldier withal, he was a favourite with the Southern people wherever he chanced to make acquaintances, and was evidently a little vain of the attention bestowed upon him by ladies. At Chickamauga, he was so dreadfully wounded in the face—a considerable portion of the upper jaw being carried away—that his features became distorted and his aspect rather hideous, and this seems to have enraged him. It was long before he was able to rejoin the command, but when he did so he manifested such a savage hatred of Federal soldiers that it was deemed unsafe to entrust a prisoner to him, a responsibility which he seemed to court.

9. *The Sang Diggers.*—Before the Battle of Chickamauga, and while the Fifth Kentucky belonged to Kelley's Brigade, the men of the other Kentucky regiments occasionally saw it, and had their flings at what they considered a newer and less experienced organisation. There were jokes about their hurting themselves with army rifles and bayonets; they were squirrel hunters, butternuts, etc., and as most of them were from the mountain sections where ginseng at one time constituted a sort of staple of barter, they were dubbed Sang Diggers.

After Chickamauga, however, where the Fifth Regiment, officers and men, behaved like heroes of a hundred fights, the veterans gladly welcomed them as members of the brigade, and took them into full fellowship—the regiment being now transferred from Kelley to Lewis. Most of them had really seen much service; but Chickamauga was to them as to the major whom Col. McDowell momentarily checked, "the biggest wood-chopping they had ever been at," and here they proved themselves to be as good as the best. The term Sang Digger, however, stuck, because it seemed to strike the brave fellows themselves as being a good sort of designation; and to this day the survivors recognise it as their own. They made it be an honourable title.

10. *A Passage at Arms with Gen. Breckinridge.*—While Bragg was manoeuvring for position, preceding the Battle of Chickamauga, Breckinridge's division was encamped one day near a well-enclosed field, and its owner asked that its fences be spared. An order was issued accordingly; but soon another order came to prepare three days' rations within a prescribed short time.

The Kentuckians were poorly supplied with axes, and no suitable wood was in reach; so, considering the last order so imperative as to supersede the first, they promptly pounced on the fence and made the necessary fires. The citizen reported at headquarters and Gen. Breckinridge rode down to the bivouac in a white heat and scolded, in rather unmeasured terms, calling the men, as they thought, "a lot of vagabonds and thieves."

This was too much for the Kentuckians. They thought the exigences of the case justified the destruction of the fence, and they were angry—and they nursed their anger until late in the afternoon of the second day of the battle which soon occurred. When the brigade had made its last charge and taken the fine battery near the road which they struck when they went over the Federal position, some of them ran one of the guns forward, and just as Gen. Breckinridge and staff reached that point, elated over the victory and congratulating the men, Eph Smith, of the Fourth Kentucky, sprang astride one of the cannons, swung his cap over his head, and cried out: "Gen. Breckinridge, see what your thieves and vagabonds have stolen!"

This brought the general to a standstill and a shade to his brow, and he rejoined: "My brave boys,—you misunderstood me! I didn't say it. I said that people would consider you thieves and vagabonds!" That was enough. Breckinridge resumed his place in their affections.

CHAPTER 10

Battle of Mission Ridge

After the fighting had ceased on the 20th, as noticed in the preceding chapter, the command bivouacked in line, a little in advance of the scene of the last engagement. Next morning skirmishers were thrown out, and the fact that the enemy had retired to Chattanooga became certainly known. The day was spent in collecting and attending to the wounded, by details sent out for that purpose, till late in the afternoon, when the main body moved to within five miles of Chattanooga, leaving a detail to bury the dead. Next day, September 23rd, the division marched over Mission Ridge, and lay on arms that night. It was confidently believed that the Federal works would be stormed during the night, or next morning, but the troops were withdrawn during the 24th, to a position a little back over the crest of Mission Ridge, two or three miles from Chattanooga.

Here a weary, monotonous, and disagreeable period of two months was passed. The only shelter was, in most instances, a blanket stretched up in the manner of a tent-fly, while cold autumnal rains were frequent. Indeed, rainy, damp, and chilly weather prevailed nearly the whole time, and the gloom was oppressive. And generally, too, the poorest quality of food was issued, and in quantities that scarcely served to prevent the absolute gnawings of hunger.

In this condition, the Army of Tennessee, in the main, passed the entire period intervening between the 24th of September and the Battle of Mission Ridge; but the Kentuckians, happily for them, escaped more than a month of this extreme hardship at the front. Chickamauga Station had been made a depot of supplies for the troops in the field, and the brigade was sent back to Tyner's Station, at convenient distance from Chickamauga, to guard the public stores from destruction by either secret enemies or raiding parties of Federal cavalry.

The entire brigade went into camp at Tyner's Station, on the 21st of October, whence a regular guard, consisting of daily details from each regiment, was constantly on duty at Chickamauga till the 17th of November, when Col. Cofer was appointed to the command of the post at that place by Bragg, his own regiment to act as a special guard, and the Sixth was accordingly detached, and took up quarters near the latter depot. At both Tyner's and Chickamauga considerable preparations were made for protection against the inclemencies of the weather. The few tents that had been collected were supplied with simple chimneys (in the building of which the men had now become adepts), while those who could not be furnished with tents erected cabins, which were destined to serve them for but a brief period, though sufficiently comfortable for the coming winter.

Gen. Helm having fallen, Col. Lewis, who was not only senior, but had won an enviable reputation for gallantry and the most unfaltering devotion to the cause, had been promoted to brigadier-general, and assigned to the permanent command of the brigade. His staff, as announced on the 4th of October, consisted of—Capt. Fayette Hewitt, A. A. G.; Lieut. Sam. H. Buchanan, A. I. G.; Maj. John R. Viley, Chief Quartermaster; Maj. S. M. Moorman, Chief Commissary; Lieut. Lewis E. Payne, Ordnance Officer, and Lieut. H. Clay McKay, *aide-de-camp.*

Lieut. Buchanan had been recommended for promotion, and was afterward made Captain and A. A. G.; but he long continued to discharge the duties of inspector, while Capt. Hewitt, an assistant adjutant-general, P. A., C. S., performed the legitimate service of his department in connection with the Kentucky Brigade. Maj. Viley was assigned to the staff of Gen. Bate in December, when Capt. William S. Phillips, of the Fourth Regiment, was made chief quartermaster, and retained that position till the close of the war. During most of the time after Gen. Lewis assumed command, Maj. Moorman was absent on sick leave or post duty, and in such absence Lieut. D. C. Hughes was the acting chief commissary till Capt. Helm was assigned to that duty. And afterward, in the absence of Helm, Lieut. Fletcher Thompson was chief in that department of brigade.

About this period an order was issued from the War Department providing for organising the troops of the various States in separate commands, as far as possible, instead of the promiscuous arrangement heretofore existing. During the autumn and winter a number of individual Kentuckians, who had been serving elsewhere, were added, by transfer under this order, to the different regiments of Lewis' brigade.

At Tyner's Station, November 5, 1863, the Fifth Regiment Kentucky Infantry was transferred from Kelley's Brigade, Buckner's corps, to Gen. Lewis, taking the place of the Forty-first Alabama, which was transferred to the brigade of Gen. Gracie.

Some account of the recruiting and organisation of the Fifth Regiment will be found in the biographical sketch of Col. Hawkins. An account of the various field and staff officers of the first organisation may be seen elsewhere in this work, and in the same connection the field, staff, and line officers of the regiment after its reorganisation in the autumn of 1862. During the first year of the war it did constant arduous service in the Department of East Kentucky and West Tennessee, and a detachment of it fought at Ivy Mountain in the autumn of 1861. The entire regiment took a prominent part in the battle of Middle Creek, Kentucky, January, 1862, and, indeed, in all the operations of Gen. Humphrey Marshall's trying winter campaign at that period.

At the Battle of Princeton, Virginia, in which the Federals, under Brig.-Gen. Cox, were defeated, the Fifth Kentucky played a conspicuous part, and, indeed, virtually achieved the victory by one rapid and irresistible charge. We copy the following, from an account of the engagement which has fortunately fallen into our hands:

> In May, 1862, Gen. Marshall's command moved up to Jeffersonville, Virginia, and about a month afterward defeated a Federal force at Princeton. Gen. John S. Williams was in command of the advance, consisting of the Fifth Kentucky, Twenty-Ninth Virginia, and Fifty-Fourth Virginia Infantry, and a battalion of mounted men. When the battalion developed the position of the enemy, Gen. Williams ordered a halt, and directed the Fifth Kentucky to take the front of the infantry force, (another regiment being front in the order of march,) thus giving it the post of honour and of danger. Two companies were formed on the left of the road—Col. May moving down and directing the two thus formed, while the remaining eight were formed on the right of the road, under Col. Hawkins, and confronting the main force of the enemy. At the proper command, the Fifth Kentucky charged forward and drove the Federals from every position in such rapid succession that the other regiments did not get up in time to fire a gun until they had been driven into the limits of the town, a distance of nearly four miles.

After the order of Marshall, mustering out such of his twelve-months' troops as desired it, the ranks were again filled, as noticed in the sketch of Hawkins, and a new organisation took place on the 18th of November, 1862. From this time, it continued on duty in the Department of East Kentucky and West Virginia till July, 1863, when it left Abingdon with the other troops of Preston, and joined Buckner at Knoxville, in whose corps it remained until November, 1863, participating in the Battle of Chickamauga, when, as we have seen, it was transferred to and became a part of the Kentucky Brigade—in which no other organic changes took place, these five regiments surrendering together at the close of the war.

For the gallant manner in which the Fifth Regiment demeaned itself at Chickamauga, during the desperate fighting of Buckner's corps, the reader is referred to reports on preceding pages, where he will also find some striking facts connected with the final assault upon the stubborn Thomas, which, if more generally known, would redound greatly to the honour of the Kentucky soldiers engaged on that momentous day, and of the Kentucky generals commanding them and other troops. Buckner, immediately after the sanguinary but successful conflict of Preston's division, rode out beyond the enemy's works, and to the right, just in time to get a glimpse, in the deepening twilight, of Breckinridge's division already over the works of the last Federal force between Thomas' position and the Chattanooga road, and the battle closed with the magnificent, we might say, unsurpassed fighting of these commands.

On the evening of the 23rd of November, after Grant had begun unmistakably to show his intention to move on Bragg's position, the Kentucky Brigade (with the exception of the Sixth Regiment, left to guard Chickamauga and remove stores in case of accident,) marched to Mission Ridge, and bivouacked near the point which it had occupied previous to its removal to Chickamauga. Next day, it was moved somewhat farther to the left, and began the preparation of breastworks. Before day, on the morning of the 25th, it was again moved, and this time to the extreme right, as a support to Gen. Cleburne.

When the engagement began that day, the Kentucky Brigade was marched from one part of Cleburne's line to another, as danger threatened, with the exception of the Ninth Regiment, which was formed on the right of Smith's brigade, of Cleburne's division, to occupy open space between him and Gen. Liddell. The Federals advanced on this regiment, unprotected by works of any kind, but were repulsed, with a loss to the Ninth of three men wounded. The other regiments, though under fire, were not closely engaged, as Cleburne's division held its own, as usual. A desperate charge was made on Gen. Smith, just on the left of the Ninth Regiment, late in the afternoon, but the enemy, five lines deep, was repulsed with great loss.

But during the day the Federal forces succeeded in turning the left, and late in the evening broke the centre, and the retreat to Dalton began. Cleburne's division, to which the Kentucky Brigade was now attached, and with which it remained till they reached Dalton, was perfectly in hand, and fell back in excellent order, rendering important service in covering the retreat, and punishing the enemy whenever he came near enough. Several skirmishes took place during the 26th, as Cleburne moved so leisurely that it was dark before he had reached the little town of Graysville. He suffered little loss, however, of men or munitions, while he inflicted great loss on the enemy at Ringgold by masking batteries at a point from which they swept down the railroad, on which a strong column was advancing. No casualties whatever occurred in the Kentucky Brigade, though at one time a battery, just in the rear of it, was ambushed and fired into.

The brigade lost its battery on the evening of the 25th, when the Confederate centre was compelled to give way, but it was through no fault of Kentuckians, as it had been detached and was at no time during the day dependent upon them for support. The Confederate rear reached Dalton on the 28th of November,, the main body of the Federals retired into the valley of Chattanooga; and soon the infantry and artillery of both armies were quietly settled in winter quarters, while the cavalry forces watched each other on the outposts, and disturbed the general stillness by an occasional skirmish or a raid.

INCIDENTS AND ANECDOTES.

1. *"Where's Our Battery?"*—At no time after he set out on his Kentucky campaign, leaving the Kentuckians in Mississippi, was Gen. Bragg in favour with them; and matters grew worse with each succeeding failure of his to avail himself of the fruits of victory, which it cost them so many of the bravest and best to win. It was a lack of true generalship for which he himself severely condemned Gen. Beauregard after the Battle of Shiloh. At Mission Ridge the Kentucky Battery (Cobb's), commanded by Lieut. Frank P. Gracey after Capt. Cobb's promotion to be chief of artillery for division, was detached from the brigade and placed in position near Bragg's headquarters. It was supported by troops that had hitherto conducted themselves well on every field, but were

now among the first to give way before the Federal advance.

The battery thus fell into the hands of the enemy, while the men who would have defended it as long as there was a charge to fire or room to handle a bayonet were far on the right, and ignorant of its peril. Lieut. Gracey stood to his guns, fighting till the whole line was abandoned, and then walked off, slow and sullen. The men of the brigade had regarded the cannons composing the battery, which had been with them so long, with a species of attachment amounting almost to affection, and had even bestowed upon two of them the pet names of Lady Buckner and Lady Breckinridge. The abuse that was heaped upon those who lost them was perhaps out of proportion to the offense.

The Kentuckians believed themselves incapable of being routed from breast-works, even of the slightest kind, when their battery was to be defended, without leaving bloody evidences to show that there had been a fight. Bragg came in for his share of blame for entrusting it to other troops; and the story was current that they were so angered that as he passed a part of the command next day they hooted and otherwise manifested disrespect, and asked what he had done with their battery. A sight of those who had been placed to support, but had abandoned it, was sure to result in cries of "Where's our battery?" "What did you do with our battery?"

2. *What Jim Lee Thought of Bragg as a Strategist.*—Shortly after the battle of Mission Ridge, the conversation around the campfire of Sergt. Lee's mess at Dalton turned one night on religious subjects, and someone mentioned that Gen. Bragg was a member of one of the Protestant churches, whereupon Jim ejaculated, "What the devil's the use of that? If Bragg were now safe in heaven, he'd fall back in less than three days for a better position!"

3. *A Remarkable Incident.*—In the latter part of September, 1863, while we lay at the foot of Mission Ridge, a singular train of circumstances brought to my knowledge the fact that I had a brother in the Federal Army then occupying Chattanooga. It happened about that time that Bragg, having in mind a scheme—not now necessary to mention—required from Gen. Breckinridge a man from each of his Kentucky regiments for voluntary service in the furtherance of his said scheme.

It was my fortune to be chosen from the Fourth Regiment.

I have the relics of the pass given me by Bragg on that occasion, which I value highly as a memento of the war. I translate it, as a part of the writing is gone:

Mission Ridge, Oct. 7, 1863.

Sergt. Thomas Owens, Fourth Kentucky, has permission to pass our line of pickets and hold intercourse with the enemy. The officer to whom this is shown will keep it secret.

W. W. Mackall,
Chief of Staff

Having received passes, we went down to the picket lines and happened to strike that part of the Federal line where my brother was doing duty. By tacit agreement of the pickets on both sides there was no firing; and the boys met and mingled together in a very friendly manner. After giving the signal—the waving of a newspaper—I met half way between the lines a lieutenant of the Tenth Ohio, who, hearing from someone that I had a brother wearing the blue, went back to his own lines, hunted up my brother, and brought him out to me. Up to that time neither of us knew that the other was in service on either side.

As may be supposed, the meeting was a happy one. We remained together that day and the next two days, objects of great curiosity to the boys on both sides. The singularity of the circumstance was enhanced by the coincidence that I was a sergeant in Co. I, Fourth Kentucky Regiment, C. S. A., while he was a sergeant in Co. I, Fourth Kentucky Regiment, U. S. A. I am carrying a watch now which he gave me on that occasion. I may add that we are both living, and quite recently he spent a number of days at my house.—Thomas Owens, (Fourth Kentucky).

CHAPTER 11

The Army in Winter Quarters at Dalton

The condition of the army in general was now deplorable; but the Kentucky troops had maintained their morale admirably, notwithstanding the sore disappointments and privations of the last four months; and they went into winter quarters in fair condition as to health and spirits, though, in common with others, poorly provided with food, clothing and camp equipage. It has been maintained with much show of reason that want of even the ordinary comforts to which the Army of Tennessee had hitherto been accustomed had more to do with the loss of Mission Ridge and the giving up of Tennessee than the skill, courage and superior numbers of the enemy; and it is unquestionable that a state of demoralisation now existed to which it had hitherto been a stranger.

Bragg was relieved soon after reaching Dalton, and to other hands was entrusted the work of restoring its broken strength and rekindling its spirit. It is said that the permanent command was tendered to Gen. Hardee, who modestly, but firmly, declined to accept it. He assumed temporary command on the 3rd of December, and laboured successfully in gathering up the scattered fragments and reorganising, or, rather, restoring order, and rendering them available. On the 27th of December he was returned to the command of his old corps, and Gen. Johnston took immediate charge of the army. The scope of our subject forbids that we should enter into a minute description of the change that was wrought by this wonderful man, or the means employed to effect it.

From that time until he was relieved, near Atlanta, the Army of Tennessee grew and strengthened. Even after seventy days' fighting, on the

18th of July, when Gen. Flood took command, its strength was not impaired, and its spirit was wholly unaffected—indeed, the men seemed to grow more and more confident that Gen. Johnston would yet prove the destruction of Sherman and his apparently overwhelming host.

Life at Dalton, during that winter of 1863-4, had many phases peculiar to soldiers long established in quarters; but it would be impossible, even if consistent with the plan of the work, to describe in any reasonable space the employments and diversions, the scenes and incidents, relating to the Kentucky Brigade alone. This period is therefore only briefly sketched.

In February, 1864, Gen. Breckinridge was assigned to the command of some troops in Virginia, and Maj.-Gen. William B. Bate, of Tennessee, was placed in command of Breckinridge's old division. The men of the Kentucky Brigade were loath to part with their own major-general, and made earnest and repeated requests that they might accompany him to the Army of Virginia; but, owing, as it was said, to Gen. Johnston's high estimate of the command, and his determination not to part with it if he could possibly retain it, the request was never acceded to, and the campaign of 1864 was made under Bate.

Breckinridge himself, in a speech at the house of Mrs. Anderson, in Dalton, where they had collected one night to hear what he had to say about taking them along, told them that they themselves were the sole cause of being retained in the Army of Tennessee, as their good marching, great endurance, and gallant fighting had given them a position there that would be hard for any other brigade to fill.

About the 20th of February, Gen. Hardee was detached, with most of his corps, to assist Gen. Polk against Sherman, in Mississippi; and on the 23rd, Gen. Thomas, probably misinformed as to the extent to which Gen. Johnston had reduced his forces, advanced to Ringgold, and on the 24th drove in the Confederate outposts. Johnston met him promptly, and on the 25th some skirmishing took place at Millcreek Gap and Crow Valley, east of Rocky Face Mountain, in which the Confederates were successful. A Federal force had succeeded, however, in getting possession of Dug Gap, but on the morning of the 26th, Gen. Granbury drove them from that point.

On the night of the 26th, Thomas withdrew his forces; and on the 28th, the Confederates reoccupied their cabins around Dalton. The Kentucky Brigade had been posted in defensive attitude at Rocky Face Gap and on the ridge overlooking it, but was not at any time closely engaged, though one man of the Fourth Regiment was killed by the enemy's fire.

The army now lay quiet, in the main, until about the last of April, when the enemy began to press back the Confederate cavalry, on the Ringgold road, and on the 5th of May the Federal Army was in line between Ringgold and Tunnel Hill, skirmishing with Johnston's, advance.

INCIDENTS AND ANECDOTES: AT DALTON.

1. *Outwitting Col. Cofer.*—At Dalton the Orphans enjoyed almost uninterrupted rest and relaxation, as has already been intimated, from about the first of December, 1863, to May 7, 1864, more than five months, the longest by far in all their experience. The stories of their conduct during that time would fill a volume. Coming from Mission Ridge, where starvation and general discomfort in Bragg's army were no mean factors in losing the battle, they went into winter quarters with tightened belts, in other words, hungry, and but for a reasonable indulgence in "prowling," as they expressed it, there would have been almost unrelieved sameness in their bill of fare. Even "blue beef," bad as that was, was not abundant, and "grits," (cracked corn), though in fair quantity was of miserable quality. The men were not so conscienceless as to forage on the country without regard to the rights of the citizens; but the public stores were their own, at least in part, and it was not difficult for them to conceive that quartermasters and commissaries did not always do the best by them.

Another ground of complaint was the disadvantage of being so removed from home and friends that even occasional shipments of food and clothing to eke out government issues were out of the question. The consequence was that close watch had to be kept on depots of supplies, and on loaded trains; but with all the precautions taken by the authorities, the boldness and ingenuity of the men frequently made "trouble in the land," while the mess tables of the poor Orphans were not always suggestive of starvation.

Col. Cofer was provost-marshal, and he was a terror to evil-doers because of uncompromising devotion to duty, a keen circumspection, and an impartial temper that blinded his eyes when he had to deal with delinquents; he would have strung up one of "his own boys," as he called the men of the Sixth Regiment, as quickly as he would a Louisiana "Tiger." But not infrequently he found that bolts and bars and strong guards and strict orders were not wholly efficacious. For instance, it became known in one of the regiments one day that an unusually good lot of fresh beef had come in by train, and the boys, feeling their need, went after it. Two of them eluded the camp guard, one carrying his rifle, and went to Dalton. The man with the gun fixed bayonet and added himself to the regular detail then on guard and began to walk a beat which he had prescribed for himself, simply saying that he had been sent to strengthen the detail.

The other one watched his opportunity to cross the guard line, which he easily did by the connivance of his comrade, shouldered the best quarter of beef readily accessible, and started for camp. The self-constituted sentinel was the first to detect him (of course), and promptly took him in charge—abusing him meanwhile and vowing that he should suffer for his thievery. By this time others were attracted to the spot; but our extra watchman had neither eyes nor ears for them, though they highly approved his purpose to make an example of the rascal in hand. With bayonet alarmingly close to the man's body, (as spectators regarded it), he started him briskly towards the provost's office, but the sequel need hardly be told; at the first convenient point where they could dodge out of sight, they headed for camp, relieving each other on the way in carrying the very considerable load of fresh beef—and their company was for some days not wholly dependent upon the commissary.

2. *Misplaced Confidence.*—Among other tricks, of which the above is by no means the best sample of a job lot, Col. Cofer had a little experience which came particularly home to him, and eventually dumbfounded him. During almost their entire service the Orphans were in the main teetotallers. (Irreverent and degenerate sinners of this day will probably add "on compulsion," but their opinion is of no consequence.) At Dalton, however, as a member of the First Cavalry seemed to think was sometimes the case where his regiment encamped, "miasmatic conditions prevailed," and as quinine was generally scarce, the men thought it well to canvass the country round and use the railroad to some extent to supply themselves with enough brandy and whisky to ward off chills and fever.

Under order from headquarters these articles were contraband; and the grim provost, Cofer, was particularly intolerant of attempts to "run the blockade." He managed to compel all the regiments except his own, the Sixth Kentucky, to rely mostly on quinine; but, watch and scheme as he would, "his boys" seemed nearly always to have more whisky than malaria, and the notable way he had of showing his teeth under stress of mind seemed to grow on him. It was finally developed that they were supplying themselves through his office. The trick was to throw him off the scent by having their shipments made in boxes consigned to his care. The "innocents" would simply inform him that friends in Atlanta, or wherever they had their agents, would, at such and such a time, send them a box of creature comforts—would he please to take charge of it and have it in safe-keeping till called for, etc.?

Of course this appeared to be almost filial; they were relying on him as a father and friend; and as the poor fellows seemed to feel themselves in a wicked world, away from home, and in danger of being robbed, his heart went out to them; and under his fostering care and the protection of sawdust and strong nailing, the jug trade prospered. Had the survivors among these ingenious schemers turned their attention to "moonshining" after they came home, they would have used the United States Marshals to further their own thrift.

3. *Punishments in the Army.*—At Dalton we frequently witnessed the infliction of an ignominious penalty for various infractions of the military code, but it must be said to the credit of the brigade that no one of its men was ever subject to anything like it. There had been one execution in the command, as noticed elsewhere, but it was held by many to be substantially a military murder; and there were numerous executions at Dalton of men deserting from the army there and those of other commands who were hiding out and had been brought in by the cavalry, as the policy of Gen. Johnston and others high in authority was to enforce the law rigidly, as a preventive measure; but the keeping of men for hours in the stocks obtained during the winter and early spring, and the punishment seemed so disproportionate to minor crimes that it was regarded with much disfavour.

It was a species of torture—painful even to beholders. Three half circles were cut on an edge of each of two planks, so that when the edges were brought together there were round holes for the neck and wrists of the culprit. One of the planks was made fast at the ends in a vertical groove in each of two upright posts, so that the yoke would be between four and five feet from the ground, while the other was slipped into the grooves and left movable, that it might be raised to admit head and hands and then brought down and pinned, thus making the man utterly helpless in a painful posture.

In some instances the head was shaved, and the poor creature, so pinioned and so exposed (as the stocks were placed in open ground), would be kept there sometimes to the very limit of endurance. He adopted the only change of position possible, (and without some change even a strong man must have soon lost control of his muscles and suspended himself by neck and wrists), and that was to keep his feet in motion—raising and lowering them in a treadmill fashion. It was reported (though this cannot be vouched for) that occasionally one would faint and have to be removed.

It is needless to say that to Kentuckians this was odious and shocking and it is hardly probable that they would have quietly submitted, to it, had even a most unworthy comrade been the victim. Men were condemned to this who had deserted under what were considered palliating circumstances, and for other crimes for which no specific penalty was provided.

Another punishment had fallen under observation—that of the shaved head and barrel shirt, or a wooden placard fixed on the back and labelled "thief," bearing which a soldier convicted of base robbery would be drummed out of camp and dismissed as unworthy to bear arms; but no Kentuckian was ever subjected to this. It is not intimated that they were saints, or that they were always meekly subordinate. That would be too much to expect of high-headed and hotblooded men, whose opinion of official position amounted to something like this, that an officer was about as good as a private as long as he behaved himself.

Submissive to law and order, with the true old Anglo-Saxon spirit, they were nevertheless impatient of unnecessary restraint, and sometimes got into trouble on that account; but orders from headquarters and sentence of courts-martial seldom imposed more than short confinement, or extra duty, with the occasional superfluous but hard work of taking up a stump. They were very human, and pangs of hunger and the discomfort of scant clothing, especially when they contrasted their condition with that of people who lived fairly well while fighting only with their mouths, sometimes operated to obliterate nice distinctions as to property rights; and it was charged that in an emergency they could beguile a cook and steal a man's meal between the stove and dinnertable; but this was an invention of the wicked, and not to be credited.

Their experience in this particular extended no further than that of the irreverent sinner in Forrest's Cavalry, who, hungering for a Thanksgiving turkey, prayed for it the day before, and declared that about 11 o'clock that night his prayer was answered; but it was developed that he combined faith and works, and pulled the bird off the roost with his own hands.

4. *Guying Gen. Bate.*—When Bate succeeded Gen. Breckinridge in command of the division to which the Orphan Brigade belonged, there was a good deal of dissatisfaction—not that the men had any-

thing in particular against Bate, but that they were opposed to serving under any division general who was not a Kentuckian. Before the Dalton-Atlanta campaign was over, however, they came to know that their new leader had fine qualities and to admire his gallantry. Especially after he was wounded, they began to feel some attachment to him, and some visited him where he lay under a surgeon's care. At first, though, there were a good many who were not careful to conceal their displeasure; and a story was soon current that Gen. Bate complained to Gen. Lewis that his men were behaving badly towards him, to which Lewis replied: "General, I think I wouldn't pay any attention to that if I were you. My boys are always pestering some d—d fool!" This was thought to be so much like Gen. Lewis that it went the rounds, though it probably got its left-handed twist after it left him.

5. *Punishment for Desertion: One of the Saddest Features of the War.*— Thomas Owens thus describes a military execution which he witnessed:

> During the spring of 1864, while the army of Gen. Johnston was encamped near Dalton, Ga., there were several military executions. Desertions had become so frequent as seriously to threaten the integrity of the army; and it became necessary to make examples of the few, that the many might be deterred from committing so grave an offense.
> A soldier belonging to the regiment in Hardee's Corps, was arrested for desertion, tried, and condemned to be shot. In order that the awful example might have its full effect, the entire division was ordered out to the drill ground to be witnesses of the spectacle, and was formed into a hollow square of three sides facing inward, the fourth side being open.
> The culprit, surrounded by his spiritual advisers and an armed guard, was made to march around the entire square on the inside, and was then led to the middle of the open side, where a grave had been dug and a low cross had been erected near its edge. He was bound to the cross kneeling. His eyes were bandaged, and the officer in charge stepped off the regulation twelve paces, where he stationed the firing squad.
> A delay of some moments ensued, during which the officer stepped up to the doomed man, apparently for the purpose of adjusting the bandage over his eyes. The poor wretch gathered hope from this trivial circumstance, and quickly raised his head,

which had been before bowed upon his bosom, and strove to peer out from under the bandage. The buoyancy of hope stood out in every feature of his face. But it was brief—to him, O how brief—for a moment later the fatal order was given, "Ready, aim, fire," and the leaden bullets went crashing through his brain. The whole top of his head was blown off.

The division was then caused to march in double file past the body as it hung upon the low cross to view the ghastly spectacle, and thence back to camp to ponder on the horrors of war and 'man's inhumanity to man.'

6. *A Singular Death.*—In February, 1864, Rocky Face Ridge was occupied by Johnston as a signal station. The Fourth Kentucky was so deployed as to form a living telegraph line from the valley next to Dalton to the top and front face of the Ridge at a point where, next to the Federals, the ascent was perpendicular. From the top of this ridge the Federal Army was in full view. The next day after the formation of this line, there was a collision of the Federal and Confederate forces on the right of our line, and when the Federals would move, word was passed from man to man of the living telegraph, as, "Two more brigades advancing on such and such a point." The first night after the formation of the telegraph, the men slept at their posts.

The next morning George Disney, a private of Company B, arose to a sitting posture, after a night's sleep on the top of this height in the open air, and was in the act of gaping, as many men are wont to do on first awaking. He was seen suddenly to resume his recumbent position, as though resolved to take another nap; but after he had been so lying for an hour or two, men who tried to wake him found that life had departed. A careful examination at the time disclosed no wound, and it was conjectured that he had died from failure of the heart or other disease. Later, another examination was made, and while washing the face of the corpse, the hair on the back of his head was found stiff from clotted blood; and it was then clear that while gaping a minie ball from a Federal musket in the valley in front had entered the open mouth and crashed through the back of the head of the unfortunate soldier. He was a native of England.—Virginius Hutchen, (Fourth Kentucky).

7. *The Snowball Battle.*—When reveille was sounded on the morning of March 22nd, 1864, the soldiers encamped around Dalton were astonished on turning out to find the ground covered almost shoe-mouth deep with snow that had fallen during the night. Even for

north Georgia, in a somewhat mountainous section, it was quite an unusual thing, particularly at that time of year and to such depth. The Kentucky Brigade was stationed on the west of the Georgia railroad, about a mile north of town, with an open field extending northeast from the main encampment, which was used as drill ground.

The snow was of sufficient humidity to be readily made into balls; and about the middle of the forenoon a few of the Kentuckians were seen out on a rather high point of this ground pelting each other in a sort of lazy way; presently the crowd increased, and then there was calling over towards the east where some Tennesseans were quartered, presumably giving a challenge, which was promptly accepted, and it was but a few minutes till there were two pretty fair lines of battle and an exchange of showers of the white missiles. The fun was contagious, and soon about every well man in the brigade was out and the Tennesseans also came on in force. The excitement extended to field and staff officers, who hastily saddled up and rode out to take command; and then there was shouting of orders with words of encouragement as well as pelting.

Of course, each of the combatants did what he could to "bring-down" the officers of the other, after the manner of gunners; and even the Kentucky dog, Frank, rushed into the *mêlée*, where he found a Tennessee dog ready for battle. The two were quickly at it, tooth and nail, between the opposing lines. In their "official reports" both these four-footed warriors doubtless claimed the victory; but Frank had the best of it, in one particular at least—when his war was over, he went back to camp limping, having received an honourable wound while standing up to his friends. Occasionally something that seemed too solid for a snowball would hit a man, and of course there were charges that this or that side was violating the rules of civilized warfare by loading a little snow with a good deal of rock; but when all began to run short of ammunition, a treaty of peace was entered into by each side's withdrawing and gleefully explaining around the campfires how handsomely he had "used up" the other fellow.

CHAPTER 12

The Dalton-Atlanta Campaign, May 5th to September 8th, 1864

When the campaign opened, Bate's division consisted of the Kentucky Brigade, Tyler's (formerly Bate's) brigade of Tennesseans, and Finley's brigade of Floridans. The artillery of the army had been organised in two battalions, attached to the respective corps of Hardee and Hood. Polk's corps, then about in Mississippi, had its own quota of artillery there. One of these battalions was under command of Capt. Rob. Cobb, while Capt. Frank P. Gracey commanded the Kentucky Battery.

The Kentucky Brigade did not take final leave of winter quarters until May 7th, when it was marched out and took position—the Ninth Regiment in advance, and stationed on an eminence beyond Rocky Face Gap, north of Dalton, while the other regiments were held in reserve between two hills, also on the left of the railroad as was the Ninth. Cobb's battery was placed on the Bald Knob to the left of Mill Creek. The brigade was now engaged in moving from point to point about the Gap, first on one peak of the mountain, then another—skirmishing and sharpshooting most incessantly till the night of the 12th, when it was marched to Snake Creek Gap, and thence, next day, to Resaca.

A circumstance ought to be noted here that was far more remarkable in its consequences during the four-month campaign under consideration than was at all apparent in the outset, and they doubtless exceeded the expectations of those who suggested it: namely, the detailing and specially arming of a corps of sharpshooters. The services of these men day by day, on march and in battle, cannot be given in detail; and it is best to enter here a brief but comprehensive account, from which it may be understood that this little detachment of Kentucky marksmen was of itself almost as terrible to the Federal host as "an army with banners." For special and personal incidents, the reader is referred to subsequent pages.

In the winter of 1863-64, Gen. Breckinridge received eleven guns known as the Kerr rifle, which he allotted to his old brigade. It was said that an English friend presented them as a token of regard. It was a long-range muzzle-loading rifle, that would kill at the distance of a mile or more, requiring a peculiar powder; and there was some difficulty in charging it, so that it was not likely to be fully effective except in the hands of a cool and composed man. The use of ordinary powder made it necessary to swab out the barrel after every fourth or fifth shot.

There was a prolonged target practice in which a considerable number of the men engaged, and from these ten who had proved to be the best shots, and were known to be otherwise thoroughly reliable, were finally chosen. Lieut. George Hector Burton, Co. F, Fourth Kentucky, was not only a superior marksman but a dare-devil fighter, one of the few men known to any except braggadocios and closet-romancers who experienced what the old Romans really pretended to feel, "the joy of battle." He added to this the qualities without which even a fine soldier cannot possibly be a good leader—cool judgment, quick apprehension of whatever would give advantage of position, and a dogged resolution that made him proof against sore discomfort and unshaken by disaster. He was put in command and given only such orders as were so general in their nature that a large discretion was allowed him.

The most important of these was that he should not carry his men nearer the enemy's main line than within about a quarter of a mile—cautionary, and presumably designed to prevent him and his young bloods from taking questionable risks. Occasionally it was thought necessary to direct them to take position under cover of darkness between the Confederate and Federal lines, and so dispose themselves as to avoid fire from their own artillery and small arms. In general, they operated along Hardee's front; but if any other part of the army was annoyed by artillery, they went to its relief if they could be spared from their own corps.

When one man was killed or disabled, another volunteered from that man's regiment to take his place; and as four or five were killed and almost every one of the original ten, except the lieutenant, was wounded—some of them two, some of them three times—there were many calls for volunteers to take permanently the places of the dead and permanently disabled, and temporarily those of men only temporarily retired by wounds. It is probable that as many as twenty men served on the corps during the long campaign. It is known that seventeen different men were killed and wounded, though after Dallas there were but nine in the service at the same time.

It is to be regretted that no perfect list of the names was never made. The following are recalled by surviving members or have been found in a former history of the companies: George Hector Burton, Co. F, Fourth Kentucky; N. Frank Smith, Co. F, Second Kentucky; Thomas Owens, Co. I, Fourth Kentucky; Taylor McCoy, Co. A, Fourth Kentucky, Jerry Spalding, Co. K, Fifth Kentucky; Wm. H. VanMeter, Co. H, Sixth Kentucky; Wm. Ambrose, Co. B, Ninth Kentucky; Wm. H. Anderson, Co. E, Sixth Kentucky; John Y. Milton, Wm. H. Morgan and James Tennell, Co. A, Sixth Kentucky; and Steve Estill, Co. H, Second Kentucky.

This corps of sharpshooters was actively engaged every day of the one hundred and twenty except one. At one time it spent thirty-three consecutive days between the two armies, with an allowance of one canteen of water per day to each man. A detail of two was sent to fill the canteens and procure rations, the men alternating by couples. Without change of clothing, and with little opportunity to shelter themselves from rain, their condition soon became exceedingly uncomfortable by reason of dirt and vermin, and request was made repeatedly for a brief respite to wash clothing and bathe themselves, but in the great stress of difficulty and danger no attention was paid to this until Lieut. Burton went to Army headquarters and procured an order to suspend operations for this purpose one day.

The general plan was to work themselves at night between the lines, reconnoitre, fix upon a rallying base, and then cover the front of the army, and keep a lookout for opportunities to kill off pickets, men who exposed themselves along the lines of Federal breast-works, and officers who came in view beyond while directing the operations of their troops. A particular object was to note the position of batteries, and take post so as to pick off the gunners through the embrasures. Ordinarily, if these sharpshooters could place themselves in sight of the enemy's cannon, with fair cover, and within a quarter to a half mile, it was almost certain death or disabling for a Federal soldier to swab or load after each discharge, as he could not protect himself while his gun was in position.

It is unquestionable that the army was thus saved a vast deal of annoyance and much loss from Federal artillery. Sherman always kept his men abundantly supplied with ammunition, and to them the waste was nothing: so that it would often have been but a pleasant pastime to shell the woods all day long, even when the Confederate position was not definitely known, had not Burton, with his wide-awake and gallant fellows, taught them that the price of a useless shot from a battery was apt to be the loss of a cannonier. The consequence was that cannonading ceased to be a pastime, and was resorted to only when something definite and absolutely necessary was to be attempted.

The Federal sharpshooters had effective guns and many good marksmen; but the loss that these inflicted upon Kentuckians was comparatively trivial. One of their tricks was not much in favour with Burton; namely, taking position high up in the foliage of a tree. This had the disadvantage of more readily discovering a man by the smoke of his gun while he could not easily shift place and escape a shot aimed at the point where the whiff was seen. This was much resorted to by the Federals, and our men had had experience with them from Corinth to this time. Near Farmington, Miss., in April, 1862, one was brought down from an oak on a high point, and it was reported that he had clothed himself in green, so that he could not be distinguished from the tree-leaves, but he could not disguise his whiff of smoke.

In the pitched battles and charges of the brigade, the sharpshooters were not expected to be in line; they were to do all possible execution from their retired stations; but at Dallas, Burton thought he saw a better chance to be effective by joining in the mad charge, and they suffered grievously thereby—losing a man killed and a splendid rifle, and having three or four wounded, within twenty steps of that impassable Federal rampart.

From Federal prisoners it was learned that these men were a terror. It was current that summer that one was brought in who was curious to know what kind of a gun it was that killed a man at a distance of a mile or more. He declared, it is said, that his colonel had been killed by one of Burton's men while riding far in the rear of the Federal lines, and made the extravagant estimate that he was about three miles away. Some of these prisoners even represented that their troops were exasperated, and would kill a captured man if he was found with a Kerr rifle in hand.

When Gen. Polk was killed at Pine Mountain, this corps of sharpshooters quickly located the battery that fired the fatal shot, and in less than half an hour drove it from its place.

The experience of this little band is without a parallel. It is known that the lieutenant commanding subjected every man to a crucial test before he would trust him, so it is certain that those who stayed with him, original and substitutes, were men of stern courage and a Roman fortitude.

Their corps commander, Gen. Hardee, when about to part with them, complimented them in terms that confirm all that the writer has said of them; saying, among other things, that if all the men of Johnston's army had been proportionately as destructive as they, Sherman would not have had a sound man left.

On the 8th and 9th, the Kentucky Brigade of Cavalry which took a prominent part in all the operations of the spring, summer, and autumn, as will be found in the History of the First Regiment, in a subsequent part of this work, had fought at Dug Gap and Snake Creek Gap, and its splendid conduct at these two points had much to do in averting disaster from Johnston's army at the very outset of the campaign.

Late in the afternoon of the 9th these troops, after holding back Gen. McPherson from early morning, entered the fortifications at Resaca, previously constructed for the protection of Johnston's communications southward, and now held by a small brigade of infantry under Gen. Canty, which had been stopped there on its way from Rome when first intimation was had that a Federal force was marching by roads west of the Chattanooga mountains, with a view to debouching into the valley through Snake Creek Gap, and so placing himself in great strength in the rear of the Confederate Army. No determined assault was made upon these works until the 14th, though manned only by this little force of infantry and cavalry, while Gen. McPherson was within easy reach, with an infantry and artillery force of about twenty thousand men.

After reaching the vicinity of Snake Creek on the night of May 12th, as previously explained, the Confederate Army rested there till next day, when it took position at Resaca, the infantry and artillery being placed in the earth-works, and employed that afternoon, most of the night, and part of the next day in strengthening them.

It was eight o'clock on the evening of May 12th when Bate's division moved from Rocky Face Ridge, on the Sugar Valley road. It was ordered to bring up the rear of Hardee's corps, and, being retarded by troops in its front, did not reach Snake Creek Gap till about sun-up on the morning of the 13th. It was not till late in the afternoon that the division formed line of battle on the right of Hardee's corps. Bate occupied a cleared ridge between the Dalton and La Fayette roads.

In the formation at Resaca, above alluded to, the Kentucky brigade constituted the right of Bate's line, with Smith in reserve to support it, while half of Finley's brigade constituted his left, the other half being in reserve as support. At half-past nine on the morning of the 14th skirmishing began in front of Finley, and by ten o'clock there was skirmishing all along the line, which became more and more animated until noon, when five lines of battle emerged from the opposite wood and fiercely assaulted the whole of the division's entrenched line. They came up with banners flying, bands playing, and officers mounted, with drawn swords, in the most beautiful order; but when within short musket range the Confederates opened fire, and the host was staggered and thrown back in some confusion.

They rallied again and advanced, but were repulsed with slaughter, and retreated out of range of the small arms. This had not occupied more than twenty minutes. In this assault two regiments (the Fifth and Sixth Kentucky) reserved their fire until the enemy approached within seventy-five yards, when, with well-directed volleys, they instantly broke his lines and drove him back. At half-past one another assault by three lines was made and repulsed in like handsome manner, and with similar result. Another advance later in the day was easily repulsed. During the evening the Twentieth Tennessee and Fourth Georgia battalion of sharpshooters (Smith's brigade) participated in the fight.

The brunt of the attack on Bate had been sustained by Gen. Lewis. The major-general said of it:

> The burden of this fight fell upon Lewis' Kentucky brigade, which met and sustained it gallantly.

When the enemy's infantry had retired, his artillery opened a furious fire upon the works. Their batteries of rifled cannon had direct fire on the left regiments of the brigade, while it swept up in rear of those on the right of the line, which, after crossing the railroad, curved back toward the Oostanaula River. The works were, at best, so slight as to afford little protection, even from a front fire, and, while few suffered any injury whatever during the infantry attack, more than forty were killed and wounded by the artillery, which played upon them throughout the day.

Hotchkiss' Battalion of Artillery was posted on the right of Bate's line, and did, from the beginning to the end, most efficient service.

Slocomb's battery, Cobb's battalion, was posted in the line of Finley's brigade, and fired with much accuracy and effect on the advancing lines of the enemy. Heavy skirmishing continued until night-fall, when the pick and spade were resumed to repair breeches and strengthen and remodel our defences. The morning of the 15th was ushered in by heavy volleys of artillery, which, with constant fire from concealed sharpshooters, was kept up during the day.

The enemy occupied high wooded points opposite and to our left, from which he gave us an enfilading fire with artillery, which was not so fatal as would be supposed, because heavy traverses had been constructed in the flank along our trenches the previous night. Hotchkiss had two guns disabled, which were moved at night. Slocomb suffered much, also having two guns effectually disabled and one crippled; all of which, however, were brought off at dark. All the artillery engaged was well managed, and fought with much coolness and judgment in this engagement.

In proportion to the number of men constituting the division the loss during these two days was considerable, notwithstanding the partial protection afforded by the earthworks. Twenty-four were killed, two hundred and thirty-three wounded, and fifty-five missing. The latter were practically skirmishers left on the front as per order on the night of evacuating Resaca. An examination of the Brief History of Individuals will disclose that a disproportionate part of the loss was sustained by the Kentucky Brigade.

The losses of the enemy could not be accurately ascertained, as the command did not go out of the trenches. It was estimated to have been not less than fifteen hundred during the two days. Three battle-flags fell upon the disputed ground, which the Confederates were unable to get and the enemy could not regain them.

The division was ordered out and left the trenches at ten o'clock on the night of the 15th, leaving skirmishers on the line. Following Cleburne's division, it crossed the Oostanaula and marched out about five miles on the Calhoun road, where it bivouacked.

Early next morning the enemy was reported to be in front, in what force it could not be ascertained, and Bate was ordered to form line of battle and bring up the rear of Hardee's corps on the march to Calhoun; and near this place he took position to support Maj.-Gen. Walker. This position was maintained till half-past one o'clock that night, when the march was resumed, the Fifth Kentucky being detached from the Kentucky Brigade to strengthen Granbury as rearguard.

Arriving at Adairville at 7 o'clock on the morning of the 17th, the brigade, in common with other troops of the division, had a few hours' rest; but at two in the afternoon, line of battle was again formed—Bate extending the general line from Cleburne's left, where he remained in position until after dark, when he was ordered to guard a train to Kingston. It was not until eight o'clock on the morning of the 18th that the distance of ten or twelve miles was passed over, the march having proved the most disagreeable and exhausting of the campaign, so far. During the forenoon, line of battle was formed three and a half miles south of Kingston. The remainder of Hardee's corps came from Adairville during the 18th.

On the 19th of May, Gen. Johnston had decided to give battle. A stirring order to that effect was read to the troops at noon, and was responded to with the most enthusiastic cheers. The army of Gen. Johnston had now been re-enforced by Polk's entire corps from Mississippi—the last division having reached the front on the 18th. Gen. Johnston's plan, as he explains in his history of the campaign, was to attack the enemy when he could do so without encountering his whole strength; and this appeared the auspicious moment.

This was a turning point in the campaign, and though the Kentucky troops were no more concerned in it than the rest, it is not amiss to give, in connection with their service, Johnston's account of his purpose, his plan, and the unhappy circumstance which thwarted him and deprived the Confederate Army of a victory which would have so crippled Sherman as to throw him back upon his base, if it had not proved his destruction. In the exultation with which the battle-order was received, as he narrates, there were no more hearty cheers than those which went up from the Kentuckians, of all arms, and Hardee, knowing the temper of his corps, of which these Kentuckians formed so material a part, remained unalterable in his belief that he could hold the position assigned him.

> Two roads lead southward from Adairville—one following the railroad through Kingston, and, like it, turning almost at right angles to the east at that place; the other, quite direct to the Etowah railroad bridge, passing through Cassville, where it is met by the first. The probability that the Federal Army would divide—a column following each road—gave me a hope of engaging and defeating one of them before it could receive aid from the other. In that connection the intelligent engineer officer who had sur-

veyed that section, Lieut. Buchanan, was questioned minutely over the map as to the character of ground, in the presence of Lieutenant-Generals Polk and Hood, who had been informed of my object. He described the country on the direct road as open, and unusually favourable for attack. It was evident, from the map, that the distance between the two Federal columns would be greatest when that following the railroad should be near Kingston. Lieut. Buchanan thought that the communications between the columns at this part of their march would be eight or nine miles, by narrow and crooked country roads.

In the morning of the 18th, Hardee's corps marched to Kingston; and Polk's and Hood's, following the direct road, halted within a mile of Cassville—the former deployed in two lines, crossing the road and facing Adairville; the latter halted on its right. Jackson's division observed the Federal columns on the Kingston road, and Wheeler's troops those that were moving towards Cassville. Those two officers were instructed to keep me accurately informed of the enemy's progress.

French's division of Polk's corps joined the army from Mississippi in the afternoon.

Next morning, when Brig.-Gen. Jackson's report showed that the head of the Federal column following the railroad was near Kingston, Lieut.-Gen. Hood was directed to move with his force to a country road about a mile to the east of that from Adairville, and parallel to it, and to march northward on that road, right in front. Polk's corps, as then formed, was to advance to meet and engage the enemy approaching from Adairville; and it was expected that Hood would be in position to fall upon the left flank of those troops as soon as Polk attacked them in front. An order was read to each regiment, announcing that we were about to give battle to the enemy. It was received with exultation.

When Gen. Hood's column had moved two or three miles, that officer received a report from a member of his staff, to the effect that the enemy was approaching on the Canton road in the rear of the right of the position from which he had just marched. Instead of transmitting this report to me, and moving on in obedience to his orders, he fell back to that road and formed his corps across it, facing to our right and rear, toward Canton, without informing me of this strange departure from the instructions he had received. I heard of this erratic movement after it had caused such loss of time as to make the attack intended impracticable; for its success depended on accuracy in timing it. The intention was therefore abandoned.

The sound of the artillery of the Federal column following Hardee's corps, and that of the skirmishers of Wheeler's troops with the other, made it evident in an hour that the Federal forces would soon be united before us, and indicated that an attack by them was imminent. To be prepared for it, the Confederate Army was drawn up in a position that I remember as the best that I saw occupied during the war—the ridge immediately south of Cassville, with a broad, open, elevated valley in front of it completely commanded by the fire of troops occupying its crest.

The eastern end of this ridge is perhaps a mile to the east of Cassville. Its southwest end is near the railroad, a little to the west of the Cassville Station. Its length was just sufficient for Hood's and Polk's corps; and half of Hardee's, prolonging this line, was southwest of the railroad, on undulating ground on which they had only such advantage as their own labour, directed by engineering, could give them. They worked with great spirit, however, and were evidently full of confidence. This gave me assurance of success on the right and in the centre, where we had a very decided advantage of ground.

Brig.-Gen. Shoupe, chief of artillery, had pointed out to me what he thought a weak point near Gen. Polk's right, a space of one hundred and fifty or two hundred yards, which, in his opinion, might be enfiladed by artillery placed on a hill more than a mile off, beyond the front of our right—so far, it seemed to me, as to make the danger trifling. Still, he was requested to instruct the officers commanding there to guard against such a chance by the construction of traverses, and to impress upon him that no attack of infantry could be combined with a fire of distant artillery, and that his infantry might safely occupy some ravines immediately in rear of this position during any such fire of artillery.

The Federal artillery began firing upon Hood's and Polk's troops soon after they were formed, and continued the cannonade until night.

"On reaching my tent soon after dark, I found in it an invitation to meet the lieutenant-generals at Gen. Polk's headquarters. Gen. Hood was with him, but not Gen. Hardee. The two officers, Gen. Hood taking the lead, expressed the opinion very positively that neither of their corps would be able to hold its position next day; because, they said, a part of each was enfiladed by Federal artillery. The part of Gen. Polk's corps referred to was that of which I had conversed with Brig.-Gen. Shoupe. On that account they urged me to abandon the ground immediately, and cross the Etowah.

A discussion of more than an hour followed in which they very earnestly and decidedly expressed the opinion, or conviction rather, that when the Federal artillery opened upon them next day it would render their position untenable in an hour or two. Although the position was the best we had occupied, I yielded at last, in the belief that the confidence of the commanders of two of the three corps of the army of their inability to resist the enemy would inevitably be communicated to their troops, and produce that inability. Lieut.-Gen. Hardee, who arrived after this decision remonstrated against it strongly, and was confident that his corps could hold its ground, although less favourably posted. The error was adhered to, however, and the position abandoned before daybreak.

Hardee was near Kingston, as will have been seen, when the order was received to fall back by way of Cartersville to Cass Station, to join in the offensive movement. Bate had been skirmishing from noon till about 2 o'clock of the 19th when the order was received, and he fell back in the face of the enemy successfully, and reached Cass Station about 4 o'clock, where he was placed in support of Cleburne, but was moved within an hour to the extreme left of the Confederate position, to hold himself as a reserve, and guard against a flank movement which the cavalry might be unable to check. Here the Kentucky Brigade worked in constructing defences till 11 o'clock in the night, when an order was received to withdraw across Etowah River, and at 1:30 the movement began. The division crossed and encamped about three miles out on the Altoona road, near the Etowah ironworks.

This was the morning of May 21st, and the army remained in camp here until the 23rd. At 2 o'clock in the afternoon Bate took up line of march in the rear of Gen. Walker, and at night went into bivouac a mile west of Dr. Smith's, on the Dallas and Altoona road. Before midnight he received orders to move at 2 o'clock to New Hope Church and guard the approach on Johnston's right flank until the remainder of the army passed; after which he was to bring up the rear till near Powder Spring and halt there. When the division arrived at New Hope, the Kentucky Brigade, with one section of artillery, was formed in line of battle across the Burnt Hickory road. Smith, with one section of artillery, was advanced to Dallas to support our cavalry, the Florida Brigade and two batteries of Cobb's battalion held in reserve.

Here, (May 24th), there was some fighting. Smith became engaged and was re-enforced by two of Finley's regiments. A double line of skirmishers was thrown out, and the enemy was driven back a half mile, with a slight loss to the Tennesseans.

At half-past one o'clock that afternoon, he was ordered to withdraw to the vicinity of Dallas, and by noon of the next day the division was encamped in line of battle a mile and a half east of that place. Before four o'clock the enemy's infantry, cavalry, and artillery were at Dallas, the Confederate cavalry falling back before their advance. Defensive works were promptly begun, as usual, and this work was pressed until daylight next morning, May 26th, but the position was subjected to artillery fire before night of the 25th, and skirmishing occurred along Bate's front. During the night of the 26th, a strong skirmish force of the enemy (some have reported this to have been five infantry regiments) gained a foothold on the heights commanding the right of the division's main line.

When this was communicated to Gen. Johnston, he ordered Cheatham to storm the position at daylight next morning; but Gen. Bate took the responsibility of preparing to retake the hill in case Cheatham (several miles distant) should not arrive in time. Gen. Lewis was directed to take two of his regiments, the Second and Fifth Kentucky, and the Fifteenth and Thirty-Seventh Tennessee, Smith's brigade, and take it by storm at daylight, 27th. It was handsomely done, with the loss, however, of a noble and gallant captain (Richard B. Donaldson) killed, and four wounded. In this dash Lewis drove the enemy from the heights with such rapidity as to forbid the capture of more than six or eight. Seven or eight were killed or wounded. Gen. Cheatham arrived soon after and took position on the right of Bate's line, his left occupying this height. Gen. Walker's division, the same day, was placed in prolongation of his left.

INCIDENTS AND ANECDOTES: DURING THE DALTON-ATLANTA CAMPAIGN.

1. They All Say That.—Sometime during the night of May 15th, after the army had crossed the Oostenaula, the brigade was making the best of its way in the dark towards Adairville, when some horsemen, coming up to the rear of the column, tried to proceed by keeping to the road, which was too full of men on foot to allow of easy passage. One of them seemed to be a little too bold and persistent in getting straight forward, when it was thought he might feel his way along the flank through the woods. This aroused the ire of a web-foot who was being made uncomfortable, and he began saying words to the offender that wouldn't look well in print, and at the same time struck the horse along the side a furious blow with his rifle, that threatened if it did not hurt the rider's leg.

Thereupon the man ordered him in an angry tone to desist and allow him to pass on, saying, "I am Gen. Bate!" That made matters no better. "Oh!" cried the wrathful soldier, still using his gun, "I know. You can't play it on me that way. Every scoundrel that wants to ride over us says he's Gen. Bate!" Whoever it was had to hunt a route to the head of the column by a flank movement, as nobody's name given in the dark could have secured immunity from rough usage at the hands of the men he was trying to press out of his path.

2. *"Two Minutes to Get to Your Holes."*—Many stories are current illustrating with what facility the men of the Confederate and Federal armies fraternised, even during the bitterest years of the war; and they do credit to American manhood, albeit some of them indicate a certain disregard of military discipline. The real soldiers quickly learned to respect and trust each other, and, when not engaged in the dreadful pastime of killing, were inclined to chaff across the interval between picket lines, even to meet for the purpose of talking over matters and swapping articles which one had to spare and the other needed. The staples of trade were chiefly coffee and tobacco—the northern men being well supplied with coffee while short on tobacco, and the southerner having tobacco to smoke and chew, while coffee (a most valuable article in army life) could hardly be procured at all after the blockade was established.

This story indicates the nature of these odd little episodes in the great drama, as well as the sententious style of the officer who broke up the meeting: On the Dalton-Atlanta campaign, busy as the two armies usually kept each other, the respective out-guards sometimes had their long range passage of words as well as shots, and sometimes met. One morning (this I have at second hand, but every old Orphan will recognise it as true to life if not to particulars), Col. Hervey McDowell went out with a detail to relieve the brigade's picket. His approach was not perceived until he was right upon their night base, and there he found a squad of blues and grays gathered around a blanket and absorbed in a game of cards, whether for stakes or in a trial of skill is not stated.

The Confederates knew McDowell's grim fashion of demanding conformity to the articles of war, and of course they were as much disconcerted as the Federals; but he quickly dispelled the fears of the latter by giving them honourable terms. Drawing his watch, he said to them: "Boys, two minutes now to get to your holes!" It is hardly necessary to say that they made such use of those two minutes that they had snatched up their weapons and were at their posts and ready for duty before the time had expired.

3. *War Could Not Make Them Inhuman.*—Familiarity with scenes of blood during years spent in the savage occupation of killing enemies could not destroy the sensibilities and demonize true men. Gen. Hewitt gives a case in point, in connection with our corps of sharpshooters above alluded to. Taylor McCoy, Co. A, Fourth Kentucky, was apparently an unsentimental devil-may-care man, full of fight, and always on hand when his regiment went into battle. Nobody seemed to suspect that the shooting of a Federal soldier could disturb him in the least. On the Dalton-Atlanta campaign, he came in one day after the corps had been engaged forward along the front, and was observed to be sitting around moody and abstracted. Hewitt asked him what was the matter with him.

"Oh, nothing—nothing." As he continued quiet and grum, however, his questioner saw that there was some trouble, and he went to him again: "Taylor, are you sick?" "No, not sick;" then he added: "Well, I'll tell you. I did not want to kill the fellow. On the line this morning someone picked me out and began shooting at me. I watched my chance for a shot, and got it. I struck him, and he screamed. It was the cry of a boy! I don't like to think of having killed a boy!" This, notwithstanding the boy had on a blue uniform and was trying to kill him.

4. *Wouldn't Be Checked Off Till His Time Came.*—All Presbyterians have of course a more or less positive belief in predestination; but it does not regulate the conduct of every one in time of difficulty and danger. Col. McDowell, however, seems to have accepted the doctrine so literally as to feel that his destiny was by no means in his own keeping, and that on the battlefield any special effort at self-preservation was unnecessary. One day on the Dalton-Atlanta campaign, while the brigade was in reserve and awaiting orders under a pretty heavy fire, he appeared to the men to be rather unnecessarily exposing himself,

and some of them suggested that he get behind a tree. He declined the well-meant advice, however, replying in his positive way that he would not be killed till his time came, no matter which side of the tree he was on.

5. *Frank, the Soldier Dog.*—Among the singular circumstances attending the life of soldiers, few are more deserving of special mention than the facts in connection with this representative of the canine species in the army of the Confederacy. The peculiar ties existing between men and dogs—the strong and constant attachment of the animal for his master—have long been the subject of song and story. The noble Newfoundlander, in the snows of the Alps, seeking the benighted and storm-caught traveller, presents to our minds the image of a benevolent: intelligence; and the poet has made "Old Dog Tray" the embodiment of unselfish love, and fidelity, for which man seeks in vain among his fellows, and not always finds, even in woman, after he leaves the sacred precincts of his childhood home, and the domain that is lighted by the eye of his mother.

Frank was a sort of counterpart to Postlethwait, Capt. Richard A. Collins's pet black bear, that shared the fortunes of his battery in Gen. Joe Shelby's splendid command of Missouri Confederates; and to the Militia Pig that campaigned with the Kentucky volunteers during the war of 1812.

He was brought into the Second Regiment by one of the members of Co. B, and long experienced with the men the privations of inclement season, scanty fare and hard marching, and the perils of the field. He went into the engagement at Donelson, was captured with the troops, and spent his six months in prison at Camp Morton: and to all attempts of the Federal guard to coax him away, he returned a silent but very dignified refusal, as much as to say that he preferred to share with his friends the life of a captive and the scraps of the barracks.

When the regiment was marched out from the prison enclosure, on the 26th of August, 1862, Frank was observed to wag his tail joyfully, and he departed somewhat from his ordinarily dignified demeanour, and was gleeful at the prospect of going forth again to "the stern joys of the battle."

In more than one subsequent engagement he was wounded, but that did not deter him in the least from marching out promptly when the "long roll" was sounded next time, and taking his chances. If a soldier fell, Frank looked at him with the eye of a philosopher; and the close observer might have discovered something of pity in his glance, and a half-consciousness that the poor man was dead, or in agony, and that he could not help him. On these, as indeed on almost all occasions, he seemed to partake largely of the spirit of the men. If the conflict was obstinate, Frank was silent and dogged. If the men shouted in the onset, or cheered when the ground was won, he barked in unison.

He took part in the memorable "snow-ball battle" at Dalton, March 22, 1864, and was wounded in the foot, having come in contact, during the *mêlée*, with one of his own species who was serving with an adverse party.

On the march he frequently carried his own rations in a small haversack hung on his neck.

He almost invariably went out, when not "excused by the surgeon," to company, regimental, and brigade drills, sometimes looking on like a reviewing officer, but oftener taking part in the manoeuvres; but he had a sovereign contempt for "dress parade," and generally stayed at his quarters when he found that the men were to go no further than the colour-line.

He was rather choice, too, in his associates; and, though-widely known and friendly to all, he would not allow of much familiarity outside of his own mess. When rations were short, he would visit other messes, and even other companies, and accept the little that his friends could spare; but he did not want them to presume upon his sense of obligation, and indulge in anything like caresses.

In this way he lived the soldier's life. If Co. B had a shelter, Frank had his corner in it. When he was shot, his wounds were dressed, and he had no lack of attention. If the commissariat were well supplied, he fed bountifully, and put on his best looks. If life were eked out on "hard-tack" and a slice of bacon, or of poor beef, Frank had but his share of that, and grew lean and hollow-eyed, like his soldier-friends.

But, in the summer campaign of 1864, he disappeared; and we have to write of Frank, the soldier-dog, as we have done of many a noble soldier boy, "fate unknown." Perhaps some admirer of his species laid felonious hands upon him, and carried him captive away; or, perhaps, a ball from some "vile gun" laid him low while he was taking a lonely stroll in the woods.

CHAPTER 13

The Dalton-Atlanta Campaign, (Continued)

The position of Johnston's army, as noted in preceding chapter, was essentially modified during the night of May 27th. Cheatham's and Walker's divisions, excepting a line of skirmishers, were withdrawn, and the line from Higley's Mill to the left of Walker's skirmish line, left to be defended by the (cavalry) division of Gen. Jackson and by Bate's infantry. Disposition being made to that effect, the latter received, during the afternoon, the following communication from corps headquarters:

Gen. Johnston desires you to develop the enemy and ascertain his strength and position, as it is believed he is not in force.

This was in keeping with the opinion of both Jackson and Bate, and the following order was thereupon issued:

Headquarters Bate's Division, 3 p. m.,
May 28th, 1864.

Gen. Jackson will move his left brigade (Ferguson's) to Van Wort Road, and have it take position in rear of Dallas by 4 p. m., leaving a force in observation on the south and west approaches to said town of Dallas. He will have Ross's brigade to move in flank of Dallas, and be ready, if necessary, to enter said town. Armstrong's brigade will move directly forward, and drive the enemy; and when opposition ceases in his front, he will swing on his right as a pivot. Smith's infantry brigade will advance directly to the front, and execute same movements as Armstrong, when able to do so without exposing his flank. Bullock and Lewis (the latter commanding, in addition to his brigade, the skirmishers on his right), will move at signal agreed upon.

By command of Maj.-Gen. Bate.

C. J. Mastin, A. A. Gen.

After this the major-general had an interview with brigade commanders, and the order was thus qualified verbally:

> Develop him "by this movement, but, if coming in contact with stubborn resistance behind the fences, withdraw without assault, unless satisfied it can be carried.

Gen. Armstrong's brigade charged, and found the enemy in force, and entrenched. He made a gallant charge, entered their entrenchments, and captured a battery; but a brigade's being hurled against him caused his retirement. Gen. Bate then ordered the movement on the right to be stopped, the signal for the advance of infantry not yet being given.

The charge of Armstrong's brigade was made with a yell, which, together with the fire of musketry and the enemy's artillery, caused Gen. Lewis and Col. Bullock, on the right, to believe the entire left was charging; hence they moved forward, and came, amid the thick undergrowth, in close range of the enemy's fire before they were able to see their entrenchments—one or two regiments of the former taking the first line of the breast-works of the enemy, and the latter approaching near the same, both driving everything before them, killing many and capturing some thirty prisoners. Smith, being near the signal station, and therefore better informed, did not advance. The prisoners taken subsequently, said that the enemy conceded a loss of one thousand in the fight.

The enemy was found to be in force and entrenched—Logan's corps, of three divisions, and Dodge with two, under command of McPherson, and Jeff C. Davis, of Palmer's corps, on the left. While the movement accomplished the effect of ascertaining the strength and position of the enemy, and had perhaps some important bearing on his subsequent operations, it was made at an enormous sacrifice to Kentuckians. Col. Bullock received the order to retire before Gen. Lewis got it, and withdrew, and as Smith had not advanced at all, both flanks of the Kentucky Brigade were without support after it had rushed upon the enemy's advanced line, assailed by a literal storm of shot and shell. Cobb's artillery demolished a battery of the enemy, drove it away, and exploded a caisson.

The brigade succeeded as previously stated, in silencing the enemy's batteries in the first line of works, and drove his infantry along its front back into the second line; but the fire was murderous, and to advance further, was certain destruction; yet it held its ground within less than fifty yards of the enemy's line, that swarmed with riflemen, while some artillery in his rear fired upon it as point-blank as possible without endangering the men in the trenches.

When ordered to retire, those who had not been killed or wounded returned and formed in their works. When the signal was given to retreat the Fifth Kentucky had gotten to within twenty yards of the enemy's rifles, and either misunderstood or stubbornly refused to go until Col. Hawkins seized the colours and again ordered it to the rear. It was a desperate charge, and a heroic stand, well illustrating the dashing yet steady and unflinching courage of Kentuckians—the indomitable will that makes them maintain unequal conflict and brave destruction rather than falter or flee. The loss of the brigade in the short period of time was fifty-one *per cent.,* and among those killed outright or mortally wounded were some of our noblest officers and men.

The movement was so futile, however, as compared with results, and so destructive because only partially carried out as planned, as to give rise to much dissatisfaction and complaint at the time; but subsequent inquiry and investigation developed the fact that the major-general had not been either culpably rash or careless. He made the following explanation of it himself, which was accepted by Kentuckians as exonerating him from blame, though they had suffered so terribly:

> The movement was made upon full consultation with brigade commanders, on the receipt and exhibition of Gen. Johnston's order, sent that evening, through Lieut.-Gen. Hardee. We being located several miles distant from the corps as well as army headquarters, and the evening too far spent to await further communications, it was believed that the enemy in our front was not in force; that, as he was several miles from his railroad base, it was merely a force of observation to prevent his right being turned. This belief was partly induced from the fact of our having so easily driven the enemy, at daylight the day before, from the high and advantageous point on my right, where Capt. Donaldson fell, as before shown, which was the key to the left of Gen. Johnston's line, as could be seen by the enemy; and there having been no attempt to regain this point, which, if occupied, would have reversed the left centre of our army line, to

possess which was all important to him, if his object was either to turn our left, or to hold, with tenacity, his right in my front. Those, among other reasons, then discussed, induced the belief with my brigade commanders and the cavalry commander, as well as in my own mind, that the enemy was not in force, nor heavily entrenched in my front; and that he was demonstrating on his right, to draw out and thin Gen. Johnston's line, preparatory to assaulting it at a central point, or to strike his right. Skirmishers advanced in my front, in order to ascertain his strength and state of his position, without being able to develop either, because of the dense and tangled undergrowth, and the heavy timber which intervened between the two opposing lines; and as so many on these advancing skirmish lines had been shot down from ambush, it was concluded to ascertain the strength and position of the enemy before me that evening, as per order of the general, through my corps commander, and especially, as he had written it was of the *utmost importance* to know—we not knowing what other dispositions of the general depended on its execution; hence the order, cited above, for the movement.

It will be seen that the whole advance movement of the infantry depended on the result of Gen. Jackson's cavalry movement on the extreme left of my line, and a signal was to be given for his (Jackson's) movement alone, when he ascertained whether the enemy, on my extreme left, was in force and entrenched; and if so, there was to be no signal given for the advance of the infantry. Jackson advanced Armstrong's brigade promptly at the first signal, which, by a bold, vigorous and direct assault, found him to be in force and entrenched, and reported to me at once. I immediately forbade the signal, upon the giving of which depended the advance of the infantry, and hurried staff officers and couriers to the brigade commanders, ordering them to remain in their works, and not advance; that the enemy in my front was strongly entrenched and in force. Smith's infantry brigade did not advance, as there had been no signal to do so; but two brigades, the Kentucky and Florida, did advance.

Inquiring into the cause, I learned that Gen. Lewis, on my extreme right, not knowing cause of delay, thinking, perhaps, he had failed to hear the signal for his advance, and that the infantry lines were engaged, sent an officer to see how this was. This officer came down the line to the point where Smith's (the left infantry) brigade should have been, and finding his works (the line) vacated, and hearing the charge of Armstrong, took it for granted that Smith was engaged, and that the signal had been given, and under this very natural impression, hurried back and informed Lewis that Smith was engaged, and that they were behind time. Thereupon these two brigades charged.

In point of fact, the signal for infantry to advance had not been given. Smith had not advanced, but had merely vacated his line of works, and formed line of battle under the brow of the hill immediately in his front, so as to move more promptly and in better order should the signal be given. Thus it is seen that the infantry movement depended altogether upon the information from Jackson as to the strength and position of the enemy in his front, (which being received, no signal was given), and that the partial and gallant fight was made under a misapprehension, (and a very natural one under the circumstances).

On the 29th, sharpshooters and skirmishers continued their work all day, and, notwithstanding the defences, Bate's division suffered somewhat. At eleven o'clock that night while Stephenson's brigade was being moved, in accordance with order from Gen. Hardee, from left to right of Gen. Bate's line, and he was extending his line to the left to cover interval thus made, the enemy opened a terrific fire on his right and drove in his skirmishers, but this night assault was promptly repulsed. Artillery and musketry, however, continued at intervals till nearly day to fire furiously upon the position. The lines were properly adjusted during the night, but no reply was made after the charge on the right had been repelled, but the expected assault, which the men quietly awaited, was not made.

On the 30th Gen. Bate was reinforced, and placing his new troops in the trenches, he sent Col. Smith to execute a flank movement, and come down at nightfall on the Federal extreme right.

This was done. Striking the right of their works beyond the point where Armstrong had assaulted, and finding but little resistance, he pushed down to the flank of his line, then occupied only by videttes and skirmishers; the main force having, the night before, been withdrawn from Bate's entire front some miles to his left, where defensive works had been put up at right angles with his main line. Smith reoccupied Dallas, capturing a few prisoners; and he was greeted by the painful spectacle of finding our wounded, some twenty or thirty, who, on the 28th, had penetrated the enemy's lines, and fallen into his hands, lying in hospitals and uncared for, some of them with limbs amputated, and undressed for two days, until, from neglect—the weather being warm—insects had found a lodgement in nearly every wound. There were no attendants, and neither medicine nor provisions left for the wounded prisoners who were found there. Every possible attention was given them, and a detail of surgeons from their respective brigades left with them. The graves in rear of the enemy's line indicated the serious punishment he received on the 28th, corroborating the statement of prisoners.

The campaign from the 7th of May till the 1st of June had been a trying one. There had been much and sometimes serious fighting; the losses, particularly in the Kentucky Brigade, had been great; there had been repeated night marches, during which the division had been rear guard of the army; there had been almost daily labour in the construction of defensive works,—but everything had been encountered cheerfully and executed promptly, and the spirit and zeal of officers and men were unabated.

The enemy gradually extended his entrenched line toward the railroad, while Gen. Johnston kept in his front by extending his own; but his force was rendered proportionately weaker and weaker, as in many instances the men occupied the works not only in single file but even a yard apart. Skirmishing and cannonading were kept up almost without intermission until the army passed over the Chattahoochee River, about the middle of July. On the morning of the 5th of June, the enemy had again succeeded in gaining a position to endanger Gen. Johnston's flank, when he took up a new line, extending from near the railroad, between Acworth and Marietta, to Lost Mountain, on which the left rested. While the main army occupied this line, Bate's division was stationed on Pine Mountain, in advance, and in range of three Federal batteries. Cobb's, Slocomb's, and Mebane's batteries, with also a battery of Parrott guns, were in position on Pine Mountain.

This force remained here until the main line was on the point of being abandoned, engaged in skirmishing, sharpshooting, and cannonading, and enduring almost daily shelling from the various Federal batteries in front.

Gen. Bate speaks as follows of this position and of the notable and distressing casualty which occurred there:

Pine Mountain is an isolated hill rising some two or three hundred feet from the level of the plain, with graceful slopes on either flank studded with timber. The distance from its right to left base across the apex, as I fronted the enemy, was about a mile. Substantial resistive works were rapidly constructed. The enemy appeared on my front the same day, but approached with much caution.

This point was some distance in advance of, and separated from the line occupied by the main army, and hence was found a serious obstruction to his movement, a thorn in his pathway, which he could not well pass without being pierced in the flank, and dared not assault. The enemy hugged its base as near as practicable, and kept up a desultory fire from his skirmish line, while he planted batteries and brought them to bear on my position. An artillery duel, rather furious at intervals, continued several days with but little effect.

On the 14th day of June, Lieut.-Gen. Polk, in company with Generals Johnston, Hardee, and others, visited my lines, and while making observations from the top of Pine Mountain, Lieut.-Gen. Polk was shot through and instantly killed by a rifle cannon shot coming from a battery located in a right-oblique direction from the centre of my line, which was the crown of the mountain. This incident not only threw a gloom over my command, but appalled it with grief.

His gallant bearing, his devoted patriotism and Christian virtues, had endeared him to officer and private to a degree rarely equalled. This lone mountain, rising as a solitary peak from a broad and fertile plain, in full view of hamlet and city, around the base of which constantly sweeps a current of population over a great Southern thoroughfare, is a fit monument to his greatness and goodness, the more so because nature seems to have built it there for the occasion.

On the 19th of June, the Confederate Army was formed with its left on or near the Marietta and Lost Mountain road, the right on the Marietta and Canton road, while the centre, now under Gen. Loring—Gen. Polk having been killed—was stationed at Kenesaw Mountain. Hood was shortly afterward moved from the right to the left of the line, thus leaving Hardee's corps in the centre and somewhat to the left of Kenesaw. The same incessant skirmishing and sharpshooting, with occasional cannonading, were kept up here till the night of the

2nd of July, when Gen. Johnston withdrew, first to Smyrna Church, then to a line of redoubts covering the Chattahoochee bridge, where he remained till the 9th, and then crossed the river, establishing the infantry and artillery south of Peachtree Creek. The enemy, by reason of his greatly superior force, had been able to move constantly, though slowly, on Atlanta, flanking with strong columns, while still leaving an army largely in excess of Gen. Johnston's to confront him.

While at Kenesaw Mountain, the most important action in which the Kentucky Brigade, or any part of it, was engaged, occurred on the 20th of June.

During the day Gist's brigade, prolonging Gen. Bate's line to the right, was covered in front by a strong detachment of skirmishers from the Kentucky Brigade. In the afternoon, the enemy made three unsuccessful assaults upon this outer line, then under command of Capt. Price Newman, Ninth Kentucky, but he was handsomely repulsed. After being reinforced, he made a fourth attempt, which was successful. A new detail was sent out under command of Maj. John Bird Rogers, Fourth Kentucky, who succeeded in retaking part of the line of rifle pits, but chanced himself to mistake for his own, in the dark, an entrenched position from which the enemy had not been driven, and, here, it is believed he was killed, as he was not afterward heard of except through a rumour that a Confederate officer had run up to the entrenchments ordering the men to take or to hold the position. As to what ensued no information could be obtained.

Lieut. Hez. Nuckols, also of the Fourth, was captured near the place where Rogers is said to have struck the works. The men to his left succeeded in driving the Federal occupants of the pits back upon their base, and they held them until about midnight, when they were ordered to withdraw. Gist's brigade withstood a strong line of battle after Newman's repulse, fighting for an hour, taking about fifty prisoners, and driving the main body back; but as he did not man the rifle pits in his front, the enemy had lodged a strong line of skirmishers there before the detail under Maj. Rogers made the effort to retake them.

Except the constant cannonading, infantry skirmishes, and cavalry engagements, nothing of special note transpired till the 18th of July, when Gen. Hood assumed command, Gen. Johnston having been relieved. To the army in general this was a source of surprise and mortification—to many, of the bitterest indignation. And nothing contributed more to the distrust with which the measure was viewed than the fact that Gen. Bragg was known to have visited Gen. Johnston after his passage of the Chattahoochee. The Kentucky troops naturally felt a great pride in Gen. Hood, as a native of their own State, and a dashing officer in battle; but they had the most implicit confidence in Johnston's generalship, which they had not in Hood's, and were adverse to any change. When the order was read to them, they expressed their feelings according to the various dispositions among them.

Gen. Hood soon withdrew his main army into the defensive works around Atlanta, and every effort was made to strengthen them, while the enemy approached, under cover of entrenchments, and gradually extended his lines toward each flank. A slight engagement took place on Peachtree Creek, on the afternoon of July 20th, in which the Kentucky Brigade participated, and suffered some loss, mainly in skirmishers under Col. Conner, who charged those of the enemy and drove them across the creek.

After being up and in motion nearly all night of the 20th, Bate's division was moved from the west of the Burkhead road to the Atlanta and Augusta railroad, on the 21st, then back to the first position.

Hardee's corps had orders to proceed to the vicinity of Decatur, a small town east of Atlanta, for the purpose of attacking the flank of the Federal Army, extended to their left across the Georgia railroad; and about dark Bate moved his command, though much fatigued, through Atlanta, down the McDonough road for some miles, and then to Cobb's Mill on Entrenchment Creek. The march was slow and toilsome, and the point was not reached till 3 o'clock on the morning of the 22nd. Two hours afterward, he moved in the direction of Decatur, and formed line of battle on the extreme right of Hardee's corps. His first orders were to form in two lines, with his right resting at Mrs. Parker's, on the Decatur road, and then to move, at such time as might be designated, in the direction of Renfro's, on the Atlanta and Augusta railroad.

When in motion to assume this position, a staff officer from corps headquarters overtook and directed Gen. Bate, by order of Gen. Hardee, to halt and form in manner directed half a mile before reaching Mrs. Parker's, parallel to the road on which Bate was moving. This he did by placing Lewis' brigade and part of Finley's in the front line, and Tyler's (Col. Smith) and the other regiments of Finley's brigade in rear line. Slocomb's Battery, of Cobb's battalion, being the only artillery with him, was placed between the two lines, and being unable to move through the dense wood and with the line, was directed to take a left-hand road, which turned off in the neighbourhood of Mrs. Parker's, and, as soon as possible, to unite with the lines in the forward movement. Caswell's battalion accompanied as a support.

The major-general had been informed by Gen. Hardee that a brigade from Cheatham's division, would be ordered to him as a reserve force, for which, after getting in line, he made fruitless application. In lieu thereof, a part of a cavalry regiment reported to him for duty, and deployed in his front, with instructions to remain stationary until a line of battle was put in motion, and to keep well advanced until the enemy's locality was ascertained, and then to retire by the right flank and form on Bate's right. In this formation the division remained for an hour or more, waiting for the command on the left to get in position.

This command, as Gen. Bate understood, was to be governed in its alignment by his position; but Gen. Walker informed him that his (Walker's) orders were to form on Cleburne, and all were to dress to the left. This was contrary to original order, and fearing that it might materially affect his movements, he sent a staff officer for definite instructions, who brought an order, after the division was in motion, facing toward the railroad, to dress to the left. Wheeler's cavalry, meanwhile, passed his right, moving in the direction of Decatur, and when it formed facing the enemy, a gap of a mile or more was left between Bate's extreme right and Wheeler's left, and there was no communication between these commanders during the day.

Skirmishers having been deployed, the line was put in motion, and governed in its movements by the command on the left. The undergrowth was dense, and the surface of the country undulating, with a small stream, skirted with broad and miry bottoms along the route. Upon ascending the hill beyond the stream, the lines were so placed as to necessitate an adjustment. While waiting for this, Bate was ordered to move forward at once. He advanced his lines through an old field, beyond which he again corrected the alignment, believing, from information received, that the enemy was but little distance in his front, and probably not aware of the Confederate approach; and receiving another peremptory order to move at once upon the enemy, he advanced before the lines on his left were adjusted.

He had proceeded but a short distance before the enemy opened the artillery in front, across a wooded bottom, filled with an almost impenetrable undergrowth, in which there was an old mill-pond (Widow Perry's), filled with the debris and brushwood peculiar to such. His order was to move right on, regardless of obstacles, resisting every impediment, and, if possible, overrun the enemy. The alignment had been adjusted, but it was impossible to keep it so, in consequence of the thick undergrowth forbidding any scope of vision as well as penetration in line, and the various obstacles preventing regularity of motion. There had been no opportunity for reconnoitring, and he was ignorant of what was in his front; but it was believed the enemy was without defences, and hence the desire to move rapidly, and strike him before he had time to make them after discovering Bate's approach. This was a mistake.

The skirmishers soon began their work. The men moved forward with alacrity and spirit. On the comb of the hill which overlooked this boggy bottom the enemy had a strong force, with breastworks and heavy batteries crowning the eminence. The assailants were under the fire of small arms before this fact was known. The line moved on, though of necessity in fragments, as only stout and athletic men were able to pass the morass in good time, while many were killed and wounded in struggling through its mire. The undergrowth so obstructed the river that the second line closed almost upon the first. The enemy not yet being engaged upon the left of Bate's division, opened his batteries (one of eighteen guns), and his small arms upon that flank, and caused the line, without proper orders, to move by the right flank.

There was also a heavy fire from the front; yet, but for the unfortunate right flank movement, the works would have been carried and held. The men advanced upon them with such spirit as to cause the enemy to evacuate them in places; but finding so few Confederates able to gain them, the retiring Federals rallied, were reinforced, and drove away the gallant spirits who had pressed so far forward. This division now numbering not more than twelve hundred men, was reformed, and skirmishers were thrown out to renew the attack. Its battery was also brought into play on the enemy's lines to divert him from reinforcing other parts of them which were being assaulted with more success.

On the left of Bate the enemy began to advance, but was checked by the skirmishers; but the condition of the division did not justify a renewal of the attack in force. Bate asked for reinforcements with which to do so by moving somewhat to the right, and Maney's brigade, under Gen. Walker, came up shortly afterward; but before anything could be done both this and a brigade of his own (Tyler's) were ordered off by Gen. Hardee for operations in another part of the field, and the remainder of the command merely held the ground and did what it could to bring off the wounded and bury such of the dead as had not fallen in and under the Federal works.

The Kentucky Brigade was peculiarly unfortunate in this affair.

When it came within sight of the enemy it was at once absolutely without cover, at short range, and met by a withering volley, rapidly repeated and unusually destructive; while the artillery played fairly upon both front and reserve lines. In a very brief space of time one hundred and thirty-five men were killed and wounded, and it was noted that more than the wonted number of the most excellent officers and men of the command fell there. An effort was made to advance, but the confusion and destruction rendered it futile. The brigade was withdrawn by order and retired without panic, though subjected to a galling fire while falling back.

The attack on the left of Bate's division had been far more successful, and, altogether, something was achieved, but nothing to compensate for the loss sustained. On the left, the enemy had been driven from his works, and several pieces of artillery, with nearly a thousand prisoners, had been captured.

The corps retired next day into the defences around Atlanta, which was now virtually in a state of siege. The Federal artillery approached so near, that, by the 1st of August, it was throwing shells into the principal streets of the city. Gen. Lewis was sent with his brigade, on the 29th of July, to interrupt a raiding party coming across by way of Fairburn and Fayetteville for the purpose of striking the Macon road at Jonesboro'; but the main body crossed the railroad lower down, and nothing was effected beyond the capture of a few prisoners, after which he returned to Atlanta, and resumed his place in the division.

On the 5th of August, the Kentucky Brigade, and that of Tyler, or, at least, a portion of Tyler's, were ordered to form an extended line, perpendicularly to the main works, and running from near the extreme left of the curve line occupied by the Confederate force.

These troops were placed in single file, a yard apart, extending far out on the Sandtown road, and in the neighbourhood of Utoy Creek. Skirmish pits were immediately constructed in advance, and the main line also fortified. At an early hour next morning (August 6th) the enemy appeared, and lively skirmishing began. About one in the afternoon, the position was charged in gallant style by two Federal brigades. They were allowed to approach very near, having driven in the skirmishers, but were thrown back in great confusion. Three different assaults were made, but with a like result; and they finally retired, with the exception of a portion who were sheltered beyond a kind of abrupt hill, in front of Tyler's brigade, against which, and the Second and Fourth Regiments, the attack had been mainly directed.

These were charged by Col. Tom Smith, commanding Tyler's brigade, and dispersed. About thirty of them were captured. The success was very decided, and the troops were complimented by Lieut.-Gen. Stephen D. Lee, who had succeeded to the command of Polk's old corps, to which Bate's division was now temporarily attached. The following is an extract from Gen. Lee's congratulatory order issued on the next day:

> The lieutenant-general commanding takes pleasure in announcing to the officers and men of this corps the splendid conduct of a portion of Bate's division, particularly Tyler's brigade, and the Second and Fourth Kentucky Regiments, of Lewis' brigade, in sustaining and repulsing, on yesterday afternoon, three assaults of the enemy, in which his loss in killed, wounded, and prisoners, was from eight hundred to a thousand men, with two colours, three or four hundred small arms, and all of his entrenching tools. Our loss was from fifteen to twenty killed and wounded. Soldiers who fight with the coolness and determination that these men did, will always be victorious over any reasonable number.

During the evening, however, a large body of Federal troops succeeded in turning the left of this traverse force, and it was thus compelled to retire into the main defences that night.

About the last of August, when it was known that the enemy was moving to the left and threatening the Macon road, now the only one open into Atlanta, Bate's division was ordered to East Point. The Kentucky Brigade was detached and sent to Jonesboro', where it was joined by an Arkansas brigade, detached from another division. A dispatch from Gen. Armstrong announced the enemy advancing in heavy force, and Gen. Lewis, the ranking officer, in command of the two brigades, ordered them to throw up works hastily, with a view to the protection of the town. This was done on the 29th of August. At an early hour on the 30th, a cavalry commander reported that the Federals would certainly reach Jonesboro' by the close of the day.

Gen. Lewis continued to press forward his preparations to check them and prevent the destruction of the railroad, as the immediate fate of Atlanta depended upon this. Late in the afternoon the cavalry was driven into the town, and skirmishing began from the outworks. The enemy, meeting with a stubborn resistance, and unable to detect the real weakness of the force confronting, encamped for the night, and twenty thousand men were thus held at bay by a few hundred. During the night, Hardee hurried out with the remainder of his own, and with Lee's corps, and reached the place about daylight on the morning of the 31st.

It was now conceived to attack the enemy with these two corps before he could get into position; but the night march had been productive of straggling, and the Confederates were not well in hand until noon of that day, by which time the Federals had gotten into position and fortified. At three o'clock in the afternoon a charge was ordered, but proved wholly unsuccessful, the Confederates were repulsed with loss, and returned to the shelter of their works. The interval over which the charging column had to pass, was, for the most part, an open plain or field terminated by rough, and, in some places, almost impassable ground in the immediate front of the Federal works. Batteries were advantageously posted, so that, in addition to the small arms of the enemy, the air seemed literally swarming with screaming and bursting shells, as the assailants moved across the field toward the Federal position. Lewis' brigade pressed closely upon the works, but, owing to the ground, was unable to preserve formation, and could have reached them only by detached parties, moving on to certain destruction.

The loss of the brigade was severe, and among the killed and those who fell into the hands of the enemy and died in prison, were several gallant and meritorious officers, and privates no less distinguished in their sphere.

It was now evident that Atlanta must be abandoned, and Hood's forces be concentrated as speedily as possible to prevent more dire misfortunes than had yet befallen them. Lee was hurried back with his command to enable the corps yet in Atlanta to withdraw without being cut to pieces in the attempt, thus leaving Hardee alone to hold the works around Jonesboro'.

On the morning of September 1st, the Kentucky Brigade was ordered to the depot to take the cars for some point, but after remaining there till the afternoon, it was moved to the extreme right of the Confederate line, and placed in single file, three feet apart, with orders to dig pits and prepare as speedily as possible to receive an attack. Govan's brigade reported to Gen. Lewis, who was to command the entire force, leaving his own brigade in immediate command of Col. Caldwell. The line to which they were assigned had been designated by some officer of engineers, and when the two brigades were formed, the Kentuckians occupied a space between the Macon road (west or northwest of Jonesboro") and the wagon road leading to Atlanta, their right resting on the railroad.

Govan's brigade prolonged this line to the left, but curving rapidly toward the south, since a prolongation in a direct line with the position occupied by the Kentucky Brigade would have thrown Govan among the Federal troops, who were on that part of the line, much in advance of the force immediately in front of Col. Caldwell. Opposite the point of contact between the Kentucky Brigade and Govan's where the curve began, and almost on a line with the former, was a Federal battery, which, firing at Govan's right, threw its shot in rear of the Kentucky Brigade, having almost a perfect enfilade, while an accident to Govan's line would throw the Kentuckians between the force in their front and another assailing their rear.

After the troops had formed and begun fortifying, Gen. Hardee and staff rode out, and, meeting with Capt. Hewitt, inquired about the position. He had discovered its weakness, and immediately pointed it out, but it was too late to rectify; and in answer to a question as to whether the Kentucky Brigade could hold its position or not, he replied, that though an exceedingly bad one, he thought it could, but that he feared the line on the left was in danger, and that, on the whole, the situation was a perilous one. He advised that a battery be placed across the road at such a point as to enfilade the enemy in case he should occupy the pits of the Kentuckians, or fire upon his right front if Govan should be driven back. Gen. Hardee had two guns placed near the point indicated. The men worked as rapidly as possible with such entrenching tools as they had, but these were few and poor.

One company, which was about as well supplied as any, had an old axe, with a rough bit of sapling for a handle, one old shovel, and their frying-pans (which they used to throw out dirt with after the soil had been broken with the axe and shovel, and the sandy earth was reached). They had scarcely begun this work, when the Federal batteries opened on them, striking front and rear—some shots rolling into the half-made pits while the men were in them at work; and before they could finish even slight defences, the enemy's infantry were upon them. Under cover of the thick undergrowth, the Federals massed a large body of troops and advanced along the whole front of both the brigades under Gen. Lewis.

The first assault was handsomely repulsed, their lines retreating in great confusion; but they again formed, and in greater force; and in the second attempt the half-finished works of Govan were carried. Both the left flank and the rear of the Kentucky Brigade was now exposed, and Col. Caldwell attempted to withdraw, and would have done so, had not an order been transmitted from Gen. Cleburne, that the works should be held, as reinforcements would promptly assist in re-establishing the broken left. But he had scarcely time to order them back into the pits before the Federals were pouring in behind his line. The men fought desperately, and refused to surrender until they knew themselves hopelessly surrounded. The Ninth Regiment, on the left flank, and first reached, behaved with defiant gallantry, till convinced that it was useless to contend longer.

It is not in keeping with the general tenor of our plan, to notice either officers or men individually in the course of the general narratives, as all are accounted for in another department of the work; but we may venture to record, as a mere example of the determination with which the enemy was resisted, that Lieut. Boyd was killed here, refusing to surrender, while another officer, it is said, was pulled out of a pit by the hair of his head, for the same reason, and a strong force was at their backs, as well as having gained the front, before any of them surrendered. About two hundred of the Kentucky Brigade were captured, and most of Govan's brigade. When matters became hopeless, all who could do so escaped, by darting rapidly into the brush in the rear, as the Federals pressed up the line.

Gen. Lewis caused the two guns, placed in position as heretofore described, to open on the enemy now occupying the Confederate works, and the fragments of the regiments were formed back somewhat in the rear of the left of the line which had been occupied by Govan's brigade, and ordered to fire incessantly in the direction of the enemy, who was thus deceived, and failed to advance, though there was nothing in his front to prevent it; and but for the prompt action of Gen. Lewis, and the circumstance of the battery's being in the right place, Hardee's entire corps would have been destroyed.

The casualties of the Kentucky Brigade were few compared with those of the day preceding, but the loss of the captured was sorely felt in a command already so greatly reduced by three years' constant service in the field.

That night, Hardee retreated to Lovejoy's, and erected new works, preparatory to checking the foe till the remainder of the army could arrive from Atlanta. The other corps came out speedily, and the Confederate forces were once more intact. The enemy appeared in front on the morning of the 3rd, but did not seem disposed to offer battle. Bate's division was ordered that evening to proceed to Bear Creek Station, four miles farther down the railroad, for the purpose of checking a cavalry raid, said to be heading in that direction.

The only occurrence at this point, of special importance to any, was the reception of an order by Gen. Lewis, to proceed to Griffin, for the purpose of having his command mounted; and thus the infantry service of the Kentucky Brigade, as also its connection with the Army of Tennessee, terminated here.

Incidents and Anecdotes.

1. Lieut. Geo. Hector Burton and His Sharpshooters.—

I believe that this officer took more pleasure in a fight than any other man I ever knew. He was never wounded, but he exposed himself recklessly. When one of his sharpshooters fell, either killed or disabled, and a new one volunteered to take his place, Burton would take that man and expose him, with himself, to the severest fire from the enemy—generally to artillery firing. If the new man stayed with him without hunting cover, that would be the last time he would put him in danger unless it was absolutely necessary; but if he flinched, he was sent right back to his company.

He had an order never to take his men within less than four hundred yards of the enemy; but he was impetuous, and when the brigade swept by on the charge at Dallas, he said to the sharpshooters, "Boys, let's go; it is too glorious to miss!" They caught his enthusiasm and sprang forward, and one of them was killed within twenty yards of the enemy's breastworks. That night he and those who were not disabled crawled in a pouring rain to those works, feeling around in the dark as they neared them for their fallen comrade and his gun, but they found neither. One gun had previously been lost. Soon after the corps of ten was organised and armed, one man got a bullet fast about midway the barrel of his, and failing to dislodge it otherwise, tried to melt it, and so spoiled the gun. Thus, the lieutenant was left, after the Dallas fight, with but eight.

It was seldom that all these were together, except at night, being divided into twos and fours when on duty. Burton's indifference to danger was conspicuously shown in visiting the little squads. He seemed to know intuitively which was in the hottest place, and there he was sure to go and do what he could to protect, while his presence cheered and encouraged, the men, whose comfort was his chief and ever-present care.

While, as noted above, the young commander would have none but the best, it may not be invidious to mention Taylor McCoy. He seemed to take a stern delight in fighting, and was cool, calculating, deliberate, and daring. He was unquestionably one of the very best.

When the brigade was mounted and Gen. Hardee was to accompany Hood and so lose his Kentuckians, he had Burton and the men who at that time constituted the corps to come to his headquarters, where he addressed them substantially as follows:

> Men, I am sorry to part with you; I hate to give you up. Had every man in our army been as effective as you, had they every one done as much execution as each of you, Sherman would not now have a man left.—JV. Frank Smith, (Second Kentucky).

2. Another Comrade's Account of Burton's Men.—About the 29th of April, 1864, a corps of sharpshooters was organised in the brigade, consisting of two from each of the five regiments. They were armed with English Kerr rifles, a magnificent muzzle-loading gun, and cartridges of English manufacture capable of throwing a ball the distance of a mile with deadly accuracy. Lieut. George Hector Burton was assigned to the command of this corps under the immediate direction of the brigade commander. Its theatre of operations embraced the entire length of the brigade line of battle.

The boys had been chosen because of their superior marksmanship; and their principal duty was to pick off the gunners of such batteries as made themselves troublesome when not in regular battle. Batteries hidden behind their breastworks frequently became very annoying to us, throwing shot and shell among us. Securing, if possible, a position commanding a view of the battery, the boys soon obtained the range, and as the smoke of the gun announced its discharge, they were enabled to pour a volley into the embrasure, which almost surely caught some of the gunners, who, at that moment, ran up to swab and reload the piece. So much execution was done by this kind of fighting that batteries exposed to view seldom took the risk of firing unless some emergency required it.

There was a freedom and hazard in this sort of warfare which made it fascinating to the boys, though no less than seventeen of them were killed or disabled during the march to Atlanta. As fast as they fell others took their places. No part of the army did more effective service during the fearful campaign than did those skilful, fearless sharpshooters. Many a battery did they silence which might otherwise have done us serious injury.

Here I will relate an incident showing the cool gallantry of Lieut. Burton. At the battle of Jonesboro', on the first day of September, lie, with his men, occupied the extreme right of our line; the shadows of night were beginning to fall upon the combatants; the gathering gloom and a dense undergrowth of timber made it difficult to distinguish a friend from a foe. Burton, while striving to rally a mass of fugitives, calling upon them to follow him as he moved forward, ran suddenly against a soldier who ordered him to surrender. Looking quickly around he found himself confronted with a gun in the hands of a grim-looking blue-coat, who repeated his demand. A glance satisfied him that there was no escape, and he promptly yielded himself a prisoner.

His captor conducted him to the line of breastworks we had so recently vacated and directed him to move on back to the Federal lines. He did so, creeping through the bushes, until he reached a point where few were passing, and then turning to the right, and passing between the two lines of battle, the darkness favouring him, he succeeded in getting round our right flank and rejoining us in less than an hour after his capture.

At Lovejoy Station, six miles south of Jonesboro', the last shot of the four-months' campaign was fired, the Federals withdrawing to Atlanta. The brigade was moved on down to Griffin, then to Barnesville, it having been determined to mount it as soon as horses could be procured. The sharpshooters were compelled to exchange their splendid Kerr rifles for common Enfields, but were permitted to retain their organisation intact, and were placed under the command of Lieut. Buchanan, with full permission to roam in any direction where horses might be captured from the enemy. After many miles tramping from Campbellton on the northeast to Newnan on the west and Stone Mountain on the east of Atlanta, the boys returned to the brigade, having had little success in capturing horses, and were respectively assigned to their former companies.—Thomas Owens, (Fourth Kentucky.)

3. *How the Gallant Fellow Lost His Life,*—About noon of June 20th, when the brigade skirmishers were engaged in front of Kenesaw Mountain, Capt. Newman, in command, sent back to the Sixth Regiment for men to take the place of two of its men who had just been killed. Col. Cofer called on Co. H to furnish one of these, when Sergt. Tom Cox, who had been in almost every engagement, great and small, from the beginning, promptly offered to take the place. A comrade reminded him that he himself was next on the list for skirmish duty;

but Cox replied that the comrade had already done more than he, and he wanted to do a full part. He set off with the guide, and soon after taking his place on the perilous line was killed by a sharpshooter.

4. *A Rifleman Up a Tree.*—While the Confederate Army was occupying Pine Mountain in Georgia, a smaller hill a half mile in front of which, if secured by the Federals, would have given them a great advantage, enabling them to enfilade with cannon a part of the Confederate line, was heavily guarded by our skirmishers. These were somewhat annoyed by Federal sharpshooters from the dense woods in front. One day two men of Co. B, Fourth Kentucky, were shot dead within two or three hours, James Chism and John Hennessey. Soon after the death of Chism, who was the last to fall, an orderly came to our rifle pit on the main line, and said another man was wanted from Co. B; whereupon our orderly sergeant, John Brummitt, called out, "Hutchen, get ready for picket."

"There, now," said I, "my time has nearly come. Goodbye, John" —and hastily taking up and putting on my outfit, I was soon at the little hill that had been so fatal a place for my comrades. The line of skirmishers was on the very topmost ridge of the hill and just behind the hill, but a pace or two, and perhaps three feet lower than the ground on which they stood, was a kind of table-land extending the full length of the line. On this table, where there was no sort of danger of the balls from the front, lay the two dead whose names I have given. I looked upon them, sadly, and noticed that each had come to his instant death from a ball in the very centre of the forehead. Noting this, I asked of the skirmishers near me, "Where did these men stand?"

They pointed to a pile of rocks alongside a tree just above me and answered, "There."

"Well," said I, "I will shift the position," and accordingly took a seat several feet to the right of the fatal rock. After a while, not hearing any bullets singing near me, I took a stick upon which I placed my hat, and, crawling to the stones by the trees, elevated the hat to the top of them. In an instant I heard the ping of a ball. On taking down the hat, I found a bullet had made the hat its billet, and three several times the hat was thus stricken by the good marksman in the woods before us. At the last shot I discovered, a long distance off, smoke issuing from a large tree some twenty or thirty feet from the ground, and after the smoke cleared away, plainly saw one of Berdan's pets.

Just then one of our sharpshooters, Taylor McCoy, came up. I tried hard to make him see the Federal sharpshooter, but in vain. Finally, he handed me his long-range gun and said, "Shoot him yourself." I said I would try, and taking careful aim, pulled the trigger, when several saw him fall from the tree. I then went to the pile of rocks and there remained until relieved. It was thought that the stand taken by Co. B's boys was perhaps the only one clearly exposed to the view of the sharpshooters in front.—Virginias Hutchen, (Fourth Kentucky).

5. *"A Roland for An Oliver."*—In 1864, while the Confederate Army occupied the Kenesaw twin mountains, near Marietta, Ga., the Federals let off a shot or shell that exploded a caisson on the top of Little Kenesaw. In a very few minutes afterward the Confederate Battery, on Big Kenesaw, from its lofty perch, sent a missile that exploded a caisson on the Federal line, and before the vast cloud of white smoke had rolled away, both armies gave a shout that made the welkin ring. It was the grandest tit-for-tat perhaps they had ever seen. The "Orphan Brigade" was there.—Virginius Hutchen, (Fourth Kentucky).

6. *They Would Do the Wind-Work.*—When the detail under that splendid soldier, Maj. John Bird Rogers, who lost his life there, was forming to retake the rifle-pits at Kenesaw, on the evening of June 20th, 1864, a man of my company, James F. Jordan, who was one of the detachment, said when he came back, that some of the men who had lost the works bawled out: "Go in Kaintuck! We'll yell!"—Capt. Hugh Henry (Co. H, Fourth Kentucky).

7. *About to Kill His Friend.*—When the order was sent at midnight of June 20th, at Kenesaw, to withdraw the detail from the skirmish pits retaken by them under Maj. Rogers, the men of the Sixth Kentucky did not receive it and were left until their absence was reported at headquarters and Capt. Buchanan went specially to them. These were Lieut. Frank Harned, Wm. S. B. Hill, Milton B. Stotts, and Henry S. Harned. There was a considerable interval between them, Hill on the extreme left and Henry Harned on the extreme right. The latter got warning first and started to creep along the line and notify the others.

As the enemy was known to be near, and even a slight noise or the appearance of a moving object was likely to bring a shot, he was keeping close to the ground and moving cautiously along the front of the line, when Hill, who had heard nothing, perceived what he took to be a Federal picket, at the distance of about twenty yards, creeping towards him. Scanning the object as closely as possible in the darkness, he concluded that the man was trying to surprise and capture or kill a Confederate skirmisher. Bringing his rifle to bear upon him he cocked it. Harned was fortunately by this time near enough to hear the ominous click, and, realising his danger, spoke his name.

Recognising the tones of a messmate and comrade, to whom he was more than ordinarily attached, and realising that but for the timely warning he would have shot him to death, Hill was seized with such a tremor that he dropped his gun and was for a moment dizzy and sick. Having thus narrowly escaped death for the one and distraction for the other, they now made their way back to the main line.

8. *Devoted Brothers.*—John A. Hays and his brother Daniel, of Co. B, Fifth Kentucky, displayed a remarkable brotherly attachment, which was evidently so sincere that their officers respected it and humoured their wish to share every duty and danger in company. They did guard, picket and fatigue duty together, and both fell in the same battle, (July 22nd, 1864), John being killed and Daniel mortally wounded. Their captain expressed the belief that if only one had been shot down, the other would have stayed with him regardless of consequences.

9. *After Entrenchment Creek: If They Had But Known.*—Just after dark on the 22nd of July, 1864, when the men of the brigade who were still on foot had bivouacked in an open wood southeast of the battlefield, the writer was standing near a fire which he and a few messmates had started for the purpose of preparing the scant supper left to them. Capt. Hewitt came by and stopped to relieve the gloom of the so recent disaster with a few cheerful words. "Well," he said among other things, li I passed a group of the Ninth Regiment a moment ago talking about today's affair, and they brought me in. I wasn't hanging around to hear, but it came as I was walking by unperceived. One said, 'I have courage enough to stay and try to do my duty when fighting has to be done, but I do wish I could bear myself like that man Hewitt. He rode down there into the jaws of that hell on the left, to get us out of the tangle, composed and smiling. I like it.'"

And then Hewitt remarked to us: "And I said to myself, 'My friend, if you only knew how badly Hewitt was scared you *wouldn't* like it!'" When it is known that two of the group overheard were Capt. Chris Bosche and Lieut. Henry Buchanan, of Co. H, Ninth Kentucky, the compliment paid their adjutant-general will appear of unusual significance. If Bosche and Buchanan had had Eneas's privilege of visiting Avernus, there would have been short parley with the ill-natured and howling Cerberus, when they got to the gate: they would have told him promptly where they came from and closed in on him for a fight.

10. *A Humane and Heroic Act.*—After the fruitless charge on the enemy's works at Jonesboro', August 31, 1864, across the open field

intervening between the railroad and the Federal position, as hitherto described, and the brigade had retired, the firing from the rifle-pits continued fiercely for a few minutes, and some of the infantry corps were struck while bravely trying to bring off those who had fallen. Above the din could be heard the cries of our wounded men who lay here and there in close range of the enemy's guns, and volunteers were called for to attempt their rescue.

To this there was a quick response by three men whose names deserve to be held in everlasting remembrance. They were John W. Green, Co. B, Ninth Kentucky (sergeant-major of his regiment); John B. Spurrier, Co. B, Sixth Kentucky, and Thomas Young, Co. C, Ninth Kentucky. As they dashed across the space in full view of the Federals, they drew a terrific fire; but when each reached a wounded comrade, lifted him, and turned to bear him off, the enemy suddenly ceased firing and sent up a rousing cheer. The splendid act was too much for honourable foes; ringing applause was substituted for volleys of musketry, and testified to their admiration.

11. *How a Bullet Made a Sans Culotte.*—Wm. M. Robb, of Co. K, Fifth Kentucky, was a thoroughly careless and clownish fellow, who never had his coat buttoned if he could help it, nor his shoes tied, and he scarcely ever had more than one button at a time on his pantaloons. His captain once said that Robb lost more guns and clothing during the war than he could pay for in a lifetime, with wages at $11 per month. At the battle of Jonesboro', August 31st, 1864, he had, as usual, but the one button which secured his pantaloons at the waistband and no suspenders, and this button and waistband were not covered by the cartridge belt.

Presently, having his side towards the Federal lines, his waist was grazed by a bullet which carried away the lone support of the breeches, and down they dropped. He quickly drew them up, and held them with his hand, but there was warm work around him—shot, shell, and rifle balls were fairly sweeping like hail along the lines; and as he had nothing to fasten them with, and was too good a soldier to turn his back upon the foe without orders, he let them go, stepped out of them, and went forth barelegged. He fought it through in that condition, and marched out with flying colours.

12. *Presence of Mind.*—Much was written during the war, and has been since, about the gallant conduct of soldiers who threw shells out of rifle-pits, and from the immediate presence of uncovered lines of battle, before they could explode, and thus saved lives. When the brigade was hurriedly engaged, September 1, 1864, under fire of the Fed-

eral batteries, trying to provide some protection against a charge upon its weak line, William M. Steenbergen, and Mark H. Jewell, Co. E, Sixth Kentucky, each threw a shot out of his pit, under the apprehension that it was a loaded shell. Though all were in deadly peril, Jewell said composedly to a comrade, James O. Wilkinson, as he resumed his work: "Jim, I ought to be promoted to major on the spot for that."

13. *A Hero and a Martyr.*—Father Blemill was a fit counterpart to Chaplain Kavanaugh in his devotion to the men of his command and in his steadfast courage. Comrade Thomas Owens paid him the following just and beautiful tribute in "The Sunny South" some years ago:

> He was of French extraction and a priest of the Catholic Church, and was chaplain of the Fourth Kentucky Regiment. His faithfulness and devotion to the duties of his calling, and to the cause which he had espoused, endeared him to the soldiers of his charge, both Protestant and Catholic. He knew no difference of creed in his preaching to us, or in his ministrations to the sick and wounded. True to a sense of duty, and shrinking from no danger, he always went with his regiment into battle, remaining just in the rear where his services to the wounded would be most needed. And here, while at his post of duty, he was instantly killed by an exploding shell at the bloody battle of Jonesboro', Ga., August 31st, 1864. We carried his body to the rear and reverently buried it in a grave a hundred yards or more southeast from the old stone depot at Jonesboro'.

The manner of his death was peculiar and touching in the extreme. It was after the assaulting column had found it impossible to carry the Federal position, and had been ordered to retire. As Gen. Lewis rode back under the destructive fire of artillery and musketry that was still kept up, observing his broken regiments making their way to shelter, he noticed Father Blemill kneel beside Capt. Gracie, of a South Carolina regiment, and lift his hands to utter a prayer for the dying officer. At that instant a cannon ball from one of the enemy's guns carried away the head of the heroic priest. He had evidently perceived that Gracie was wounded unto death, and halted to supplicate Heaven for the repose of his soul. In the act of making petition his own took its flight, in advance of his for whom he had lifted holy hands. That evening the detail sent to remove our dead found them sleeping together where their life-blood, commingling, had made them a gory bed.

When a branch of the Confederate Memorial Association was

formed at Jonesboro', his remains were removed from where the Kentuckians had buried him to the Pat Cleburne Cemetery and placed between those of Capt. Gracie and a soldier named Ignatius Brooks, who died in hospital there in 1864. About the year 1890 one of the Benedictine Fathers, to whose order Father Blemill belonged, brought his remains to Kentucky, and they now rest in their monastery in Nelson County.

14. A Dreadful Experience.—It is to be lamented that among all who, during the war, held places of power and responsibility, Kentucky developed one Jeffreys, one brutal and blood-thirsty monster, to mar the pages of her history—one whose memory is justly execrated by the honourable men of both armies, and whose monument of infamy is the numerous graves at Frankfort and elsewhere in the State filled by those who were murdered in obedience to his orders.

A member of the Orphan Brigade, Gervais D. Grainger, Co. I, Sixth Regiment, had some experience with Burbridge which may be recited in brief to indicate the treatment to which innocent men and helpless prisoners in his hands were subjected. Grainger was a brave and efficient soldier and an honourable man. From Vicksburg to Jonesboro' he fought with his command in its numerous battles and partook of its hardships as a Kentuckian "leal and true." At Jonesboro', August 31, 1864, he and some comrades were caught within the lines, with the battle-flag in their possession, and when the brigade was driven back, they concealed themselves to escape capture and buried the banner, that it, at least, might not fall into the enemy's hands. They were not discovered, and at night dug up their colours and worked their way around traverses and the pits in front of them, and rejoined their command. The next day, however, he was captured with the rest.

When the Kentuckians were started from Chattanooga, after a week's detention there, towards Nashville, he, with George R. Page, Jack Gavin and others tried to escape from the box car in which they were shut up, but only he succeeded. From La Vergne, Tenn., where he got through the hole which they had cut in the bottom of their box, he made his way, after encountering numerous dangers and difficulties, being once recaptured and again escaping, and suffering with hunger and fatigue, to his father's house in Simpson County. Remaining a few days, he attempted to return to his command, which had now been exchanged; but was recaptured and carried to Scottville, thence to Bowling Green, thence to Louisville, where he was imprisoned with eighteen others.

In less than a month orders came from Burbridge to execute four of them. In the drawing of lots Grainger was not one of the unfortunate ones who were manacled and sent by rail to the place of execution; but next morning the names of eight men were called, of whom he was one; and when they were handcuffed and placed on the east-bound train they supposed they were on the way to be executed, but they were carried to Lexington and placed in prison with about three hundred citizens and soldiers, old men and boys, and their handcuffs removed.

Kept here a month in an almost starving condition, he learned on the night of November 1st, 1864, that he was one of fifteen from whom ten were to be taken and killed. In the drawing which followed he was again fortunate enough to be spared for the time. The full enormity of the proceedings attending the drawing and the preparation of the victims for the slaughter, (apparently ordered in a spirit of fiendish cruelty to prolong the agony of suspense), has been graphically set down by T. O. Chisholm, as related by Grainger himself, and afterward published in the Franklin Favourite. The fifteen men were ordered to a lower floor, where they were surrounded by thirty or forty armed soldiers. Now follows the description of what ensued:

> Two officers stood at a desk nearby, with their backs turned upon us, and a third stood in our midst, holding a hat in his hand. Raising it above his head, he announced that he was ready. One of the officers at the desk came forward, and placing his hand in the hat, he drew therefrom a single slip of paper. This was carried to the officer remaining at the desk, and the name written thereon silently recorded in an open book. Another and another slip was drawn until ten names were registered.
>
> The terrible meaning of this dumb procedure was all too plain. Ten men were to be executed, but which of our names had been inscribed on the death roll was not as yet revealed. We were commanded to go back upstairs, which we did, followed by the soldiers who had been present at the drawing.
>
> The soldiers on duty in the prison were then directed to close up to their right, and the space thus cleared was filled by those who came from below. The walls of the prison were literally lined with loaded guns and bristling bayonets. An officer stepped forward and demanded the attention of the troops. Every prisoner was ordered to lie flat on the floor, and any man who should raise his head unless his name was called was to be

shot without further orders.

Another file of soldiers came up from the fateful room below, the first two bearing an anvil and the others bringing balls, chains and handcuffs. During these preparations a stillness as of death reigned in the room, broken only by the clanking of chains and the solemn tread of those who bore them. Motionless and almost breathless, we lay on the floor and watched the development of the awful program. How our minds flew back to home and loved ones, as we contemplated an approaching fate, in which each of the fifteen expected to share!

The details of preparation perfected, an officer said in tones that were touched with a solemnity befitting the moment, 'Thomas Hunt, come forward.'

He was a young man of twenty years from Maysville, Ky., a magnificent specimen of physical manhood and as brave as a lion. He arose promptly and walked to the officer, holding up both hands as he said calmly and distinctly: 'If it is for my country I die, it is all right.' To this the officer replied: 'You will possibly not be so patriotic before you get through with this.'

Handcuffs were placed upon him, and the click of each cuff as it was pressed together was plainly audible all over the prison. He was then told to sit upon the floor, and shackles, one of which was attached to a long chain and a ball of forty pounds, were put about his ankles. Each foot was placed upon the anvil, and a man, wielding blow after blow with a hammer, riveted the shackles firmly together. This was all. Thomas Hunt's doom was sealed, and he was ready for execution.

Ten minutes had passed since Hunt's name was called until the echo of the hammer's last blow had died away. Who was to come next? The agony of soul which each of the remaining fourteen men suffered baffles the puny insufficiency of language to describe. We were ready if need be to die for the cause we had espoused; but to be executed to avenge a crime we had not committed, and of which we had no knowledge, made the situation tenfold harder to contemplate.

In another moment the suspense of one of us was forever relieved. His name was called, he arose and went forward, and the same process through which the first victim had been carried was repeated. One by one the names were called, and one by one the dooms were sealed, as shackles, chains and cuffs of steel were fastened upon those on whom the lot had fallen.

As the number remaining grew less the suspense waxed more awful. I lay prostrate, with fists clenched, teeth set together and every muscle drawn to its utmost tension. So powerfully was I wrought upon that my finger nails almost pierced the flesh of each palm. Dim oil lamps, few in number, shed a strange, uncertain light upon the solemn scene. Not a word had been spoken, save by him who called the death roll, until the last name was reached, when the same fateful sentence that had been uttered an hour before greeted my ears: 'That's ten.'

This done, the balls and chains were removed from the doomed men. A small space was allotted to them near the stove, and in this they sat grouped together, gazing vacantly into each other's faces. With them the die was cast; and in that despair which sees no gleam of hope they waited for their fate. Some of them procured Bibles and read for hours. The lips of others could be seen moving in prayer. The officers had all gone below, and the lynx-eyed guards that stood along the shadowy walls seems as rows of spectres. The stillness that reigned in the room was oppressive, broken only by an occasional sigh breathed by some of the three hundred prostrate prisoners. The soldiers themselves were deeply impressed with the solemnity of the situation.

I lay in one position on the hard floor the whole of that terrible night, not daring even to move, for fear that my life, grown more precious to me than ever, might pay the penalty. Sleep was of course out of the question, but as I lay and gazed upon the scene about me, the feeling would now and then steal in upon my consciousness that the whole thing was a horrible nightmare. Oh! how I longed for the morning, though it was a longing not unmixed with dread, for I had no assurance that I would not be called upon to meet the doom which had already been assigned to my companions.

Finally the shadows of night gave way to the indistinct light of dawn. A sigh of relief went up from the floor of the prison, saving that space where the ten men sat, quietly awaiting the approach of the end. What storms of agony raged in their bosoms, what keen knife thrusts of despair pierced their hearts, as they thought of the homes where mothers, fathers, brothers, sisters, wives or children were eagerly anticipating their coming back who should never return; what shrinking from the awful fate that was near at hand and what thoughts of the great future upon which they were soon to enter, passed in hurried march through their minds, will never be known until the last great day, though a pitiable index of their feelings was seen upon every face, which wore a cast of inexpressible sadness.

By and by it was fully day. The heavens seemed to be in sympathy with the occasion, as a dismal mist of rain was falling, and the clouds were dark and lowering. Breakfast was announced at six o'clock, and although our appetites had been sharpened by thirty days on quarter rations, I dare say not a morsel was touched by any man in the prison. Soon the scream of a locomotive was heard in the distance, and a moment later it drew up with two or three cars in front of the prison door and stopped. An officer, with some soldiers, ascended the stairs and commanded the condemned men to get ready. Each man rose unfalteringly as his name was called, and with manacled hands clutched the chain fastened to his leg and threw the iron burden over his shoulder. For some reason the names of only eight were called, and it was afterward reported that an indemnity had been offered to secure the release of the other two.

The death procession filed down the stairway, young Hunt leading the way. It was followed by the soldiers who had stood on guard during the night, a fresh detail taking their places. Hunt and his seven comrades were carried to Frankfort, where in the outskirts of the city eight new-made graves were waiting to receive their occupants. The doomed men were assembled in close proximity to the graves, and a minister who chanced to be present asked the privilege to hold a brief religious service, which was granted.

One of the prisoners was an old man of seventy years. His hair was silvery white, and he had tottered along with the rest, scarcely able to bear the heavy iron ball. From long confinement he was much emaciated and very weak. The iron band about his ankle had worn its way into the flesh, and he had torn off a piece of his clothing and slipped it between the shackle and bleeding surface. While prayer was being offered, he managed with the aid of the cloth to slip the shackle from his leg. When the 'Amen' was pronounced he rose with the others, and, quickly whirling about, made a desperate effort to escape. Gun after gun was discharged, but he ran on until he reached a fence.

Just as he was mounting it, the sure aim of a soldier pierced him in a vital part and he fell over the fence dead.

This was witnessed by the other seven, but they seemed unmoved, and were evidently determined to die like brave men. They were ranged in a row and a detachment of fifty soldiers stood in front of them fifteen paces away. One of the prisoners asked for a drink of water before being executed and it is said to have been dipped from one of the graves and handed him. The words 'ready,' 'aim,' 'fire,' were then spoken in quick succession, a volley of bullets was discharged, and seven souls were sent into eternity.

Today there stands in the cemetery at Frankfort a monument erected in memory of these eight men (and of others), and every year flowers are brought and strewn over their graves.

The next day Dick Vance, commander of the post, came into prison. I recognised him, and still fearing that I might be the unlucky victim in another draft, I approached him, told him who I was, and that I desired, if possible, to be released. He had already received a letter from Dr. G. W. Duncan, of Franklin, written in my behalf and had doubtless come in search of me. I was promised a hearing on the morrow, which was had, and which resulted in my being admitted to parole north of the Ohio River.

On the following day myself and four others who had secured hearings when I did, one of them a nephew of John J. Crittenden, were placed in charge of an escort of soldiers. They were part of those who had participated in the slaughter of our comrades at Frankfort, and from them we learned the details of the execution. We were carried across the river to Cincinnati, and were free men once more.

I remained there a month or so, after which, through the instrumentality of Mrs. Francis Ford, of Covington, then Miss Augusta Webb, the Legislature passed an act in my favour, making the corporate line the limit of my parole.

Grainger's experience while in the power of the inhuman wretch was such as to create a vengeful determination to kill him, cost what it might; and in the autumn of 1865, he thought he had found his opportunity. Meeting him in the Metropolitan Hotel, in Cincinnati, in conversation with Garrett Davis, he reminded him of the butchery of his comrades at Frankfort, and drew his pistol to shoot him; but Davis threw himself in the way, and other bystanders interfered, which enabled Burbridge to escape.

The indomitable character of the old Orphan is shown by his conduct since that time, as well as by his record while in the field. For many years he has been almost totally blind, but to all outward seeming has "bated nothing of heart or hope." Engaging in such business as a man in his condition is capable of, he has admirably maintained himself and his family, and is known as an honourable citizen as well as a loyal comrade.

CHAPTER 14

The Brigade, As Mounted Infantry, In Georgia and South Carolina

It had been, for a great while, the earnest wish of the men, and, in most instances, of the officers, that they should be mounted, and thus render it possible for them to accompany some expedition into Kentucky, where they could hope to fill their depleted ranks, as well as enjoy something more of communication with home and friends. They had served long and with exceeding faithfulness, wholly cut off from their native State, and the prospect of returning grew more and more hopeless while they were retained in the infantry service. Various efforts had been made during the past year, but one difficulty after another arose to prevent the Government from taking the action desired. But the change had at last been decided upon, and steps were taken to effect it as speedily as possible.

On the 7th of September, just four months from the time of having marched out from Dalton, the brigade quitted the remainder of the division, and marched to Griffin, thence to Barnesville, where the first instalment of horses was distributed, and life in the "Old Brigade" assumed a new phase.

The four months preceding, however, had told so disastrously upon them that there were few left now for any service. On leaving Dalton, the five thousand, of which the regiments and the battery had originally been composed, had dwindled down to eleven hundred and twenty enlisted men, with the proportionate number of officers. At Barnesville, in September, 1864, there were but two hundred and seventy-eight guns.

The loss during the campaign from Dalton to Jonesboro' had been about nine hundred men, rank and file, and of these only two hundred had been captured. Counting all wounds, as noticed in the quotation from Shaler in Chapter 1, the number was more than fifty *per cent.* greater than that of the men composing the command when the fighting began on Rocky Face Ridge. Many had been struck repeatedly, while very few escaped altogether. Gen. Hardee reports the actual loss of the brigade to have been greater than that of any other in the corps. For four months there had scarcely been a day in which some had not been killed or wounded, sometimes from forty to one hundred and fifty in a single one.

But those who remained entered with great zest into the new project; and for a time there were even accessions to the ranks, as those who had been disabled for infantry service reported as soon as an opportunity to be useful presented itself. Some who were sent on honourable detail service, sought to be relieved, that they might rejoin the ranks and try with their comrades, this (to them) new feature of the service.

At Barnesville, as has been said, more than two hundred horses were distributed among the men; but they were in miserable plight, being, in the main, such as had been abandoned by the raiders who had passed through the State. They were not utterly worthless, however, and the "old web-foots," as the cavalry laughingly called them, got upon them and began their movements, even before saddles were furnished. A detail had been sent to Newnan for the purpose of manufacturing saddles, and these were distributed as fast as they could be turned out; but it was long before those of the command who, first and last, obtained horses at all, were supplied.

Those who had been captured at Jonesboro' were exchanged on the 19th of September, by a special arrangement; and with these and the wounded who had recovered, the aggregate was about nine hundred; but of this number more than two hundred were never mounted, being continually, from that time till the close of the war, moved from place to place, under command, first of Col. Wickliffe, then of Col. Connor, either to guard some threatened point, or assist in collecting abandoned horses designed for their use—sometimes moving in connection with the cavalry troops.

Gen. Lewis left no means untried to have the entire command properly mounted and equipped; but the great scarcity of suitable government horses left him solely dependent upon such as could be gathered up in the track of the raiders; and, though his chief quartermaster, intrusted with the direction of this work, laboured long and earnestly, the object was never wholly accomplished.

The nature of the subsequent service was of so desultory a character that it would be impossible to notice it in detail, even were it necessary or desirable. We may remark, however, as preliminary to the following hasty sketch of this part of their career, that though no important engagements afterward occurred in their department, and but few casualties are recorded, they were nevertheless active until the very last, and lost none of whatever efficiency might be displayed by so small a body of men, in such circumstances as they were afterward placed.

Gen. Lewis, intrusted now with larger discretionary powers, as he was often wholly detached from every other force, exerted himself untiringly, and with excellent judgment, to harass and thwart the enemy, and, when possible, to deal him a blow. In making or receiving an attack, the men always dismounted, as they retained their old weapon, the Enfield rifle, and as their horses were, to say the least, not altogether suitable for a charge, being of that unique kind best adapted to a certain species of ground and lofty tumbling.

From Barnesville, Gen. Lewis went to Forsythe, thence, after a short time, across the Chattahoochee, by way of Newnan, to a point near to Campbellton, for picket duty. After remaining here a few days, he was ordered to Stockbridge, a little post-village on the McDonough road, eighteen miles south of Atlanta. The brigade was now part of the division commanded by Brig.-Gen. Iverson, who established a strong picket-line near Atlanta, on all the roads leading southward, and here the Kentucky Brigade did constant picket and scout duty until the 15th of November, when Sherman began his "march to the sea," and toward the close of the day the pickets were driven in, and Gen. Lewis moved out to skirmish with his advance column. He fell back slowly before the enemy, with the main body, while Col. Hawkins, who had been sent out with a scouting party toward Yellow River, went down parallel with his flank.

When the command reached Griffin, Gen. Wheeler had arrived from the Army of Tennessee, and was collecting such force as he could to oppose the columns of Sherman, or, at least, to prevent the widespread devastation which would result from marauding parties if allowed to operate undisturbed on each flank. He left there with from four to five thousand cavalry and mounted infantry, which, with about eight hundred militia under Gen. Gus Smith, was all the force that was at hand to confront the immense army of Sherman. Successful resistance was, of course, out of the question, and nothing could be accomplished but to prevent small parties from preying upon the people far out of the line of march. Wherever such advance or flanking parties could be found, they were driven back upon the main body, and the Kentucky Brigade, though small, was conspicuous in this service, and in daring scouts, flank and rear.

When Sherman's army reached Savannah, Gen. Hardee, in command there, had one regiment of veteran volunteer infantry, and seven thousand militia, old men and boys, with which to defend the place. The city was well fortified, however, and a few siege guns were in position.

Gen. Wheeler was driven through the works, and crossed the river into South Carolina, with all his force except the command of Gen. Lewis, which was dismounted by order of Hardee, and placed in the works. Their horses were sent over the river, the spurs laid aside, and the long Enfields again made to do execution similar to that which had been wrought upon the enemy's columns between Dalton and Jonesboro'. Heavy skirmishing was kept up from day to day, the enemy showing little disposition to assault, till the 13th of December, when Fort McAllister, on the Ogeechee River, was carried by storm. The enemy's land forces had now established communication with his fleet, and the city was soon so closely invested, that Hardee, being powerless either to attack or prolong resistance, was forced to abandon the place on the night of the 22nd.

At Hardeeville, South Carolina, the Kentuckians again received their horses, and were ordered to the Savannah River for picket duty with Iverson, some distance above Savannah. When Sherman began his march through South Carolina, they were stationed still higher up the river, with a view to checking an anticipated raid on Augusta. At one time it moved over into Georgia, and marched for some days from one point to another, and then returned into South Carolina, by way of Augusta.

Gen. Wheeler, with all the cavalry corps except this division under command of Iverson, moved in front of Sherman, that he might keep the country as clear as possible of marauding bands, as he had done in Georgia.

In February, 1865, Maj.-Gen. P. M. B. Young was placed in command of Iverson's division, and ordered to follow in Sherman's rear. This movement was conducted for some days, but with little progress, on account of the extreme difficulty which attended foraging the horses, since every means of subsistence had been destroyed along the enemy's track. Gen. D. H. Hill, then commanding at Augusta, ordered the division back a few days afterward, and had it stationed at a point on the Savannah river, above Augusta, but within striking distance of that place, as a raid was again expected in that direction. It remained here for several weeks.

About the first of April, Gen. Lewis was ordered to send a regiment to Sumter, South Carolina, for the purpose of protecting rolling stock collected there, and the Ninth Regiment was accordingly dispatched on that duty (see sketch of Col. Caldwell for an account of the operations which took place while his command remained there alone).

When it was definitely known that a strong Federal force was moving up from the coast, in the direction of Sumter, Gen. Lewis was ordered to proceed with the remainder of his mounted men to that point. He marched at once to Columbia, where he learned that the enemy were already near Sumter, and fighting Col. Caldwell, when he marched rapidly to his relief.

Some fortifications had been thrown up eight miles south of Camden, and were now occupied by about three hundred militia. Gen. Lewis proceeded to these works, and found that the enemy was two miles in front, but nothing was known of his strength. He at once dispatched trusty scouts to the Federal rear for information, and, dismounting his men, placed them in the fortifications and proceeded to strengthen them. The scouts returned in a few hours and reported the enemy falling back slowly. He immediately moved forward with the mounted men and two brass held pieces, instructing the militia to follow. Late in the afternoon the Federal rear guard was encountered and driven back on his main force, and a slight skirmish was kept up till dark. Col. Caldwell was now reunited, with his regiment, to the main force. Gen. Young had promised that another brigade should follow directly from Aikin, but it did not arrive for some days.

Next morning, April 15th, pickets reported the enemy's whole command advancing, and skirmishing soon began. Lewis fought them resolutely all day, sometimes with all his little force at a single point, then by detachments, as the nature of the case required, and inflicted considerable loss, though suffering but slightly, and that almost entirely in wounded. He was, however, gradually forced back by the overwhelming infantry force of the enemy, whose superior numbers enabled him to flank successfully any position not readily assailable by front attack

On the night of the 17th of April, Col. Lee was sent with his regiment to check a column of Federal cavalry moving by way of McClernand's ford. Reaching the neighbourhood about midnight, the detachment dismounted and slept till morning, reins in hand. A reconnoissance of the ground at daylight showed that the stream ran through a miry swamp, covered with thick brush, through which it was impossible for the eye to penetrate. The ford seemed to be the only passage near, and that did not cross in a straight line, so that parties on opposite sides could not see each other. Militia had some time before thrown up a slight fortification to cover the ford, and behind this Col. Lee stationed his men, having previously concealed it with branches of trees.

The enemy, on reaching the opposite bank, sent out two or three men to see that the way was clear. They came about half-way across, and, finding everything still as death, returned, and the head of the column was allowed to approach within a few feet, their bridle-reins hanging loosely about the necks of their horses as they leisurely drank from the stream. At a given signal the men in ambush fired, and a scene of the wildest confusion ensued, during which the fire was kept up, until the Federals retreated beyond range. It was afterward ascertained that more than thirty men were killed and wounded, while a number of horses also lay dead in the water.

From the direction in which the enemy was heading, and from information received from scouts, Gen. Lewis became satisfied that his objective point was Camden, as it contained a considerable quantity of government stores, with a number of locomotives and other rolling stock that could not be moved. He accordingly ordered the militia to hasten back to the vicinity of Camden, and begin the erection of fortifications, sending a suitable officer to superintend the work. The Federals continued to press him back in that direction, but so slowly and cautiously that it was three days before he had reached the position occupied by the militia. A heavy skirmish was kept up some time, in front. It was soon evident, however, that the enemy did not intend a direct attack on the fortified line, but, by a flank movement on the left, reach the town without serious fighting.

Unable to prevent this, Gen. Lewis determined to destroy the rolling stock collected there, and whatever other public property that could not be carried away. He accordingly sent a detachment into town for this purpose, which was accomplished before the enemy's advance reached the place; but it was soon occupied by his whole force. They remained only one night, and then set out evidently to retrace their steps to the coast.

Gen. Lewis had hitherto been entrusted with the entire conduct of affairs here, but he was now joined by Gen. Young, the division commander, who was accompanied by the brigade of cavalry which had been expected some days before. They continued to harass the enemy for two days, skirmishing with his rear-guard constantly, but at the end of that time, Young received a dispatch from Gen. Johnston, announcing a truce—the Confederate troops were withdrawn—the Federals pursued their route seaward, and soon Gen. Johnston's surrender was announced. The war had virtually ceased.

Though the last six or seven months had not been prolific of great battles and the usual amount of sacrifice among the Kentucky troops, they had acted well the part assigned them, and many an interesting episode transpired which lent a zest to their experience in the new line of soldiering. Several daring scouts were made during the time by small parties under Capt. Turney, Lieut. Henry Buchanan, Lieut. Kavanaugh, and other officers, the particulars of which would be full of interest were it consistent with our plan, or even possible, to enumerate them.

After it was definitely ascertained that the armies under Lee and Johnston had surrendered, Gen. Lewis proceeded to Washington, Georgia, where he was met by Gen. Wilson's provost marshal, prepared to receive surrender of such troops as should report at that point. The arms were laid by on the afternoon of Saturday, May 6, 1865, paroles were received, the survivors of many trials and many conflicts separated, with a future before them more dark and doubtful than the past had been, and the First Kentucky Brigade as an organisation was no more.

INCIDENTS AND ANECDOTES.

1. Its Effect on a Dead Man.—The relaxation from restraint and repression imposed by four months of daily danger, anxiety, labour,—all the hardships incident to a long and unintermitting campaign,—which came with the order to join the cavalry, speedily brought into play the characteriztic cheerfulness and the exuberant fun of the jolly boys. The latter found expression at one point in rallying the newcomers; and a man had to show proof that he had been absent because he was really a "poor sick soldier," or had been sent to hospital with bullet holes in his hide, if he wished to escape unmerciful guying. On one occasion a lively member of the chosen band that answered to roll-call when the first horses were distributed led a new arrival around and showed him to the different detachments of the brigade as the identical man, he had buried at Shiloh nearly two years and a half before. He had laid him neatly to rest, he said, and patted the dirt down gently but firmly over his head; and yet, here he was, ready to mount a horse and range the woods in search of buttermilk and pine-top whisky.

2. *A Conglomeration of Odds and Ends.*—Dyer, in his Reminiscences of the First Cavalry, presents a pretty hard picture of what the brigade had to encounter in getting itself on a cavalry footing. His intimation that the men made bridles and saddles in their sleep may be set down to a lingering memory of the abuse his regiment got every time it made itself too busy waking up the enemy and getting the Kentucky infantry in trouble. He says:

> It was to be expected that after the long and gallant service of the Orphans, now to be mounted, they would be furnished with the very best of everything. The love of Kentuckians for horses, and their pride in good ones, would naturally, it was supposed, induce at least any effort to give them something good and serviceable.
> Not so, however. All the worn out and disabled horses of the cavalry and artillery were gathered and turned over to the Kentuckians. There were few in the lot able to do duty. Some were worn out with long and hard service, and all were defective in some way. Sore backs, sore shoulders, gun-shot wounds, skinned legs, gravelled hoofs, they had,—in fact almost every ill that horse-flesh is heir to; and all were very poor. It was the greatest aggregation of crow-bait I ever saw, and not good, decent crow-bait at that. A sensible crow would have thought twice before depending on the entire lay-out to furnish him a square meal. And the equipments! If possible, they were worse than the horses. Old dilapidated saddle-trees, innocent of stirrup or leathers, and bridles without bit or head-stall, were the rule; and many had not so much as either bridle or saddle or the semblance thereof.
> But the boys accepted the situation as they found it, and went to work with a will to fix themselves up for business. They concocted all sorts of liniments and lotions, and put in their time bathing, rubbing, and feeding, with such good effect that in three weeks nearly all the horses were ready for duty. The next items were saddles and bridles, which they manufactured in their dreams, at least I suppose they did, as they always procured

them at night. Why they dreamed so many styles of saddles I could never tell. They were of all sorts, shapes and patterns; old men's saddles, young men's saddles, and boys' saddles, but very few of the army pattern.

3. Thought He Knew Cavalry Tactics.—Among the Orphans was a young fellow, hardly grown at the time, who was known as Bill Rhodes. He was rather gawky and somewhat of a butt for his comrades; but he wasn't always asleep, even when his eyes were closed. One Col. Hannen had a small regiment of cavalry that sometimes appeared, for which the brigade had conceived a dislike—presumably because they got most of the buttermilk that was to be had, while the reports never showed that enough of them were killed to compensate for the advantage their good horses gave them. One morning Hannen's cavalry came through the bivouac of the brigade, on a creek between Jonesboro' and Fayetteville, after Stoneman's discarded horses had been turned over to Gen. Lewis, as previously explained.

The Kentuckians were about ready to mount and take the road. Rhodes had no saddle, but he had ingeniously extemporised a pair of stirrups by girding on his blanket with rope in such a way that each end had a loop for the foot and hung down like the stirrup leather of a saddle. As the unpopular cavalrymen were filing by Rhodes was preparing to mount, but he was on the wrong side of his war-horse, with his right foot in the stirrup. This raised a laugh as soon as Hannen's men saw it, and one of them cried out: "Just see that cavalryman! He's mounting on the wrong side! "Rhodes threw himself a-straddle of his barebones, and as he straightened up, he yelled: "You're a d—d fool! We're marching left in front today! "This stopped the laugh, and the merry-makers seemed to wonder whether Kentucky wasn't really better up in cavalry tactics than they were.

4. Kentucky Against Georgia: How Capt. Turney Got the Sheepskin.— After the brigade was partially mounted, Capt. Turney was ordered to take a detail of men and go down below Forsythe, Ga., to gather up mules and horses, as many of the men were still afoot.

One morning as they were saddling up to move, a citizen rode up. He was a stout-looking man, apparently about forty-five years old, and would have done "excellent well" to stop a bullet in the effort which Kentuckians were making to keep Sherman from spreading all over Georgia; but he was evidently one of the stay-at-homes.

There was no inducement for the boys to swap horses with him, as they happened to have as good as he, but he had a splendid black sheepskin for a saddle-seat, and as Turney was new to the use of the rough army saddle, it is at least presumable that there were sore places on him; and besides, he was short of blankets. It was but reasonable that he should covet that sheepskin; it was a good, soft thing, and held out the promise of comfort by day and by night. Badly as he wanted it, however, it wasn't the Kentucky way not to give even a stay-at-home a chance for his life—and his sheepskin; so, he offered to buy it.

The conversation was short, but not at first satisfactory. "Will you sell me that sheepskin?"

"No, I won't sell it."

"But," says Turney, "I'll pay a big price for it."

"Nobody'd be fool enough," said the owner, "to give me what I paid for it."

"How much did you pay?"

"Forty dollars."

"I'll pay eighty dollars."

"But I won't sell at any price."

Turney was about to despair, but he tried a forlorn hope: "Well," said he, "I'll play you a game of seven-up for who shall have it." Fortunately, that struck the old sinner, and he inquired with animation who had the cards.

Turney, of course by mere chance, had a deck himself. The sheepskin was spread in a fence corner; the citizen seated himself; the captain in his eagerness got on his knees, and business began—the latter playing as though his life depended on the game. The Georgian, soon showed why he was so quick to accept the challenge—he knew a thing or two himself; and either his skill or the captain's bad luck was making matters blue; the game presently stood five for Turney and six for his antagonist, and Turney's deal.

Turney stilled his conscience by persuading himself that his struggle for that saddle-seat and night protector from damp ground, was war—and, "everything is fair in war." Success depended now almost wholly upon strategy, so he resorted to that. He shuffled and talked, and talked and shuffled in such a way that he confused his opponent and made him lose his count. "The game now stands five to six, you know—you're five, I'm six."

The citizen studied this assertion a minute and then assented. The next step was to throw the deal on him; so, he went through another process of shuffling, and his talk was wilder than ever; his mind seemed to turn on bushwhackers, and he showed a bloody delight in his ability to kill them.

By this time Georgia was fairly rattled, perceiving which Turney passed him the cards to deal. He studied the situation again, dealt, and turned a club. The crisis had come. Each looked at his hand, anxiously, and Georgia, in great triumph, said, "Here's the ace."

Kentucky asked, with apparent contempt, what good an ace could do a man who only had five while his opponent had six, and held the low; he then showed the deuce.

Having thus lost his sheepskin, Georgia got up and rode away without even saying goodbye. The last audible sound he uttered was: "Here's the ace." It seemed that when Kentucky's deuce beat his ace his tongue was paralyzed; and it is not known to any of that band of Philistines whether he ever recovered. One peculiarity about the game was that in his eagerness to show Turney that other people could play cards as well as Kentuckians, the citizen failed to notice that nothing was staked by the captain, the proposition being simply to play for who should have the hide.

The sorely coveted and cleverly won saddle-seat was used during the remainder of the war; then ridden home; and at last was destroyed by a mule in the barn of Capt. Turney's father.

5. *Jim Price.*—Mr. Lincoln had the misfortune not to know Jim Price, of Co. F, Second Kentucky. A four-year experience with Price would have led him to modify that famous statement of his as to the impossibility of "fooling all the people," etc. Price could elude a camp sentry in broad daylight, cheat a provost guard made up of men from his own brigade, hoodwink his officers, visit his friends inside the enemy's lines, beat his way on railroads, and make himself a welcome guest in Southern homes whenever it struck his fancy to do so. He needed no passes, no tickets, no disguises except such as his face and figure could assume in a twinkling.

A story or two may be recorded now as a sort of monumental tribute to the memory of our jolly comrade, who made a good soldier, fought in many battles, and made a thousand friends, but couldn't take life seriously after he came home. He died a few years ago with little to his credit, except his honourable scars and his fame as the only and unapproachable one of his kind. In moving from place to place by railroad, as it was sometimes possible for troops to do, a man would drop off occasionally, to make friends among the citizens, and better his physical condition by getting something more nourishing than he had in his haversack to eat. Ordinarily, a soldier had to have a little money with which to pay fare when he wanted to take a train for his regiment, but Price did not need money; he could fall off and get on and go on whenever it suited him. How he played conductors will be understood from a single instance.

Taking his place among passengers one day after he had absented himself without leave, and thought it time to be getting back to his command, he awaited the appearance of the conductor. When that individual stopped to collect his fare, Price had metamorphosed himself. Instead of a sensible and soldierly looking body, he was now a staring idiot, with his jaw down, his hair pulled over his forehead, and twiddling his fingers, after the manner of a vacant mind. "Ticket!" said the conductor, holding out his hand.

Jim looked at him with lack-lustre eye and said, as though unable to comprehend his meaning, "Sir?"

"Ticket! ticket!" jerked out the conductor.

Then Jim: "Oh, I'm a co—co—cornscript." (A conscript.)

"You're a damned fool!" rejoined the officer.

"Yes," said Price, "there's lots o' them."

The ticket-gatherer left him in disgust.

Being one day in a store at Albany, Ga., two young ladies, seeing that he was a soldier, asked him where he belonged.

"To the Kentucky Brigade."

"Oh, you're a Kentuckian, and way down here fighting for us?"

"Yes, Miss, that's what we are doing."

"Don't you get awfully homesick, being away so long?"

"A little so, sometimes," he replied; "but nothing like one of your Georgia men I saw up yonder the other day."

"How was that?"

(Price could mimic anything from a crying baby to a hee-hawing donkey, and now he gave the ladies a specimen of his powers.) "Well, I happened to find him out on picket-post, and instead of looking out for the enemy, he had his hands over his face, crying. (Then showing how it was done he put up his hands and boo-hooed and snuffled, while his listeners laughed.) 'They've put me out here by myself, a hundred yards from camp—boo-hoo!' I told him that was nothing— he was in no danger. 'But that ain't all,' he answered (and then Price introduced more mimicry of voice and manner), 'that ain't the worst of it! I've been serving three weeks and haint never drawed a dollar.' I told him that wasn't anything, either; that I'd been out three years and had neither drawn a dollar nor had a furlough. 'Oh,' continued my Georgia friend, 'that ain't the worst yet! every time I shet my eyes I see Betsy and the children (more snuffling)—I can't stand it! I see Betsy and the children every time I shet my eyes!'"

Though the girls could but see that Jim was unmercifully satarising their Georgia soldiers, he won their admiration, and they invited him to stay at their home while in that vicinity.

How quick-witted he was in an emergency is shown by the following: Some time during the war he concluded to visit a family of whose members he had some time before made friends, though it required a trip beyond the enemy's lines. Armed with his usual passport, his cheek, he reached the residence without mishap, and walked in, unexpectedly and unceremoniously, where he found himself in a bad box. Some Federal officers were with the family at dinner. When he realised his danger, he saved himself and relieved his friends by throwing his head up in a silly way, and bawling out: "I come to borry your harrerr!" (sounding the word "harrow" in as clownish a way as he could).

His friend caught on instantly, and spoke up: "Right out there, right out there, go and take it!" Of course, he lost no time in backing out and taking to his heels.

His surviving comrades could add a score of entertaining stories to these—some of them better, perhaps; but these are enough to indicate that Co. F wore the belt in the matter of odd characters.

6. *Dead on His Feet.*—On the morning the enemy occupied Camden, South Carolina, April, 1865, a scout of ten men was sent out in advance of the brigade to ascertain position and movements of Potter's troops. Among them were A. T. Pullen, Co. D, Pius Pulliam, Co. B, and John Miller, Co. I, Second Kentucky. At a turn in the road they unexpectedly ran upon a large detachment of Federals. The scout wheeled, under a furious fire, and narrowly escaped with the loss of one man, John Miller, killed. Pius Pulliam was severely wounded, but escaped capture. Pullen was among the foremost ones, and when he turned to retreat, he had scarcely gotten under way before he discovered Miller standing on the ground beside his horse, and asked him whether he were hurt.

He replied no, but seemed dazed, and Pullen hastily dismounted, lifted him on his horse, gave him the reins, and told him to ride; but glancing back he saw that he had drawn the left rein tightest and was heading toward the enemy. The situation admitted of no attempt to rescue him, and he was seen no more. The story gained currency that he was captured and murdered; but Pullen believed that he received his death-shot at first volley, and was almost unconscious when he replaced him in his saddle. Pullen had thirteen bullet marks in his clothing without a scratch on his body.

7. *My Ole Missis' Skillet.*—On the March to the Sea, the brigade went into bivouac one evening in some woodland skirting the road, and one flank was within about a hundred and fifty yards of a farmhouse by which the road ran. The men of one mess, at least, found themselves short of frying-pans; and a borrower was dispatched to the house to inquire whether "you-uns would lend we-uns" that article. He was furnished a small skillet, which he promised to return; but next morning when the command was preparing to march, it appeared that somebody had a short memory—the property had not gotten home. Seeing the stir, the lady of the house sent a negro woman in haste to demand it.

She came trotting down the road with the inquiry: "Who's got my ole missis' skillet? Some o' you men got dat skillet!" She was abreast of the Second Kentucky (the truly good), when her tongue got loose; but nobody seemed to hear till she grew vociferous. Then a kindly soul desisted from his preparations long enough to walk to the road and inquire earnestly what was wanted. "Whar's my ole missis' skillet? You's de very man, I guess, what's got it!"

"No, I haven't; but I can tell you where it is. Captain Lewis has your skillet. You hunt him up and make him give it to you."

To her eager inquiries as to where "Cap'n Lewis" might be found, he pointed toward where Gen. Lewis and his staff were stationed, down on the other flank, and advised her to call on the "Cap n" immediately and not to be put off. Away she went, demanding to know as she rushed along, "Which one o' dem men is Cap'n Lewis?"—and of course the innocents pointed out the brigadier and encouraged her not to allow him to escape. It is not known to the writer what peculiar phraseology the general used when attacked, or even whether she reached him at all; but it is safe to say that those people died under the impression (if they are dead) that the Cap'n kept that skillet and was a mighty bad man.

8. *New Brains Evolve Old Jokes.*—A writer on "Fact and Fable" has said that most of the striking anecdotes of modern soldiers and eminent public men may be traced to the ancients. This is doubtless true to a great extent; nevertheless, a large proportion of those that relate to

soldiers are as truly their own expressions of wit, humour, and sentiment as though the ancients had never lived. Men of all times fall into similar trains of thought in similar circumstances—certain apposite reflections or ludicrous whims suggest themselves with the occasion, and are as much the offspring of the last brain from which they are coined as though no other head had ever done so. Grimshaw, in his History of the United States, spices a page with a story of an American captain who went with a new hat on into battle with the British and got a bullet through it, which raked his skull with sufficient force to knock him senseless.

When he was removed and had recovered consciousness, some began to condole with him about the severity of his wound, to which he replied: "Ah! Time and the doctors will mend that; but the rascals have spoiled my new hat!" Speeches with the same turn of thought were heard after almost every battle in which the brigade was engaged, from men who had probably never read Grimshaw's story. A soldier detailed for picket duty one day was observed to pull off a new shirt and put on an old and tattered one. "What's that for?" asked an astonished comrade. "Oh!" he answered, "I'm not going to let the Yankees shoot my new shirt!" And another, whose clothes had been badly torn by a piece of shell, settled the question of comparative merits of shell and solid shot by declaring that if a man was hit without being killed the shell was the worse missile because it tore his clothes up so.

9. The Cheerful Brigade.—Comrade Hutchen wrote in an appreciative vein some years ago of what he was pleased to call the "Cheerful Brigade." His evident admiration of the "jolly boys" could but touch a responsive chord in the hearts of all who live to remember under what trying circumstances and what a long succession of them they kept their good humour and drove away dull care, even when hope was waning and there was little to appeal to them except a sense of honour and true manliness. He cites the conduct of certain other troops, with whom the Orphans were sometimes associated as neighbours in camp—how they would mope and moan and repine at their hard fortunes as the star of the Confederacy seemed to pale, and their army was defeated by the overpowering numbers and inexhaustible military resources of their enemies; while their thoughts of peaceful pursuits and their recollections of home life made them fret and fume, and express almost childishly their longing to throw aside the soldier's trappings and return to field and shop and marts of trade.

The condition of the Kentuckians had little of promise in it; as the years went by it had less of hope; and as they gave up their brave and true in every conflict, and reflected that the sacrifice was for a principle which blood and suffering could sanctify but seemed insufficient to save from defeat, it had in it an element of despair. And yet they faltered not, and uttered no curses, complaints or distressful cries. Apparently too much of this has been attributed to the fact that in the main these Kentuckians were young men—unmarried men, upon whom the cares of the world had not yet fallen heavily, and who were not yet bowed down by responsibilities and subdued by suffering.

The exuberant spirits of the young amount to much in giving that elasticity which recovers from repeated blows and rises when borne down by misfortune; but the explanation of the fact that there was a "Cheerful Brigade," even in days of darkness and dire calamity, is found in the simple statement that they were Kentuckians. It is characteriztic of the Kentuckian that he disdains to whine, and he scorns a sniveller. If he assumes a burden or a responsibility, he bears it like a man, and refrains from upbraiding others when he has to meet the consequences of own acts. If he finds himself fairly beaten in a contest, he respects his adversary, and cheerfully pursues his way, instead of sitting down to repine over ill-fortune and invent excuses for being miserable and distressing others with a scowling brow and bitter speech.

They sang their songs—rollicking sometimes, as though they defied fate; had their games and played their pranks; told their stories and read and discussed such favourite authors as they could lay hands upon; knew of uncles and aunts and cousins in strange places and played their officers for leave to slip off and see the dear ones once more—and get something to eat and drink; made life a burden to Joe Brown's militia; scared plantation negroes; made gawkish youth and credulous old men believe that nothing else in earth or atmosphere or sea was like things up in Kentucky; put on the airs of gentlemen and gallants so well, when opportunity for a social evening offered, that mean clothing could not discount the man—in short, were as full of life on the march and in camp as they were full of fight on the bloody field.

10. Our Star-Gazer.—Pat Fitzgerald, of Co. K, 2nd Kentucky, an Irishman, who had cultivated a taste for reading and study, carried a small library in his knapsack and used it with some diligence. His favourite subject was astronomy; and he combined with his reading quite an intelligent observation of the heavens. On one occasion he was corporal of the picket guard, but he had no watch, and declined to provide himself with one by borrowing. So, for a time-keeper he put up at his picket base two sticks, one of which was to cast a shadow from moonlight and the other to indicate the end of the first two hours, when his relief was to be posted.

Frank Mullen, who afterward served awhile in the Confederate Navy, was on post when the sticks were set up; but when at least two hours had passed, as he reckoned it, he began to look for the corporal with a man to relieve him. The weary hours went by, however, and he did not appear till it was almost dawn. It was reported that he found Mullen indulging in an audible soliloquy, the burden of which was profane abuse of a man who in a case of the kind would rely on an extemporised clock. Fitzgerald had miscalculated. While he was watching for the shadow to approach the mark, the moon went down, and he fell into such confusion of mind that he couldn't perceive the difference between two hours and a half-dozen or more.

www.ingramcontent.com/pod-product-compliance
Lightning Source LLC
Chambersburg PA
CBHW021957160426
43197CB00007B/158